W9-AXI-707

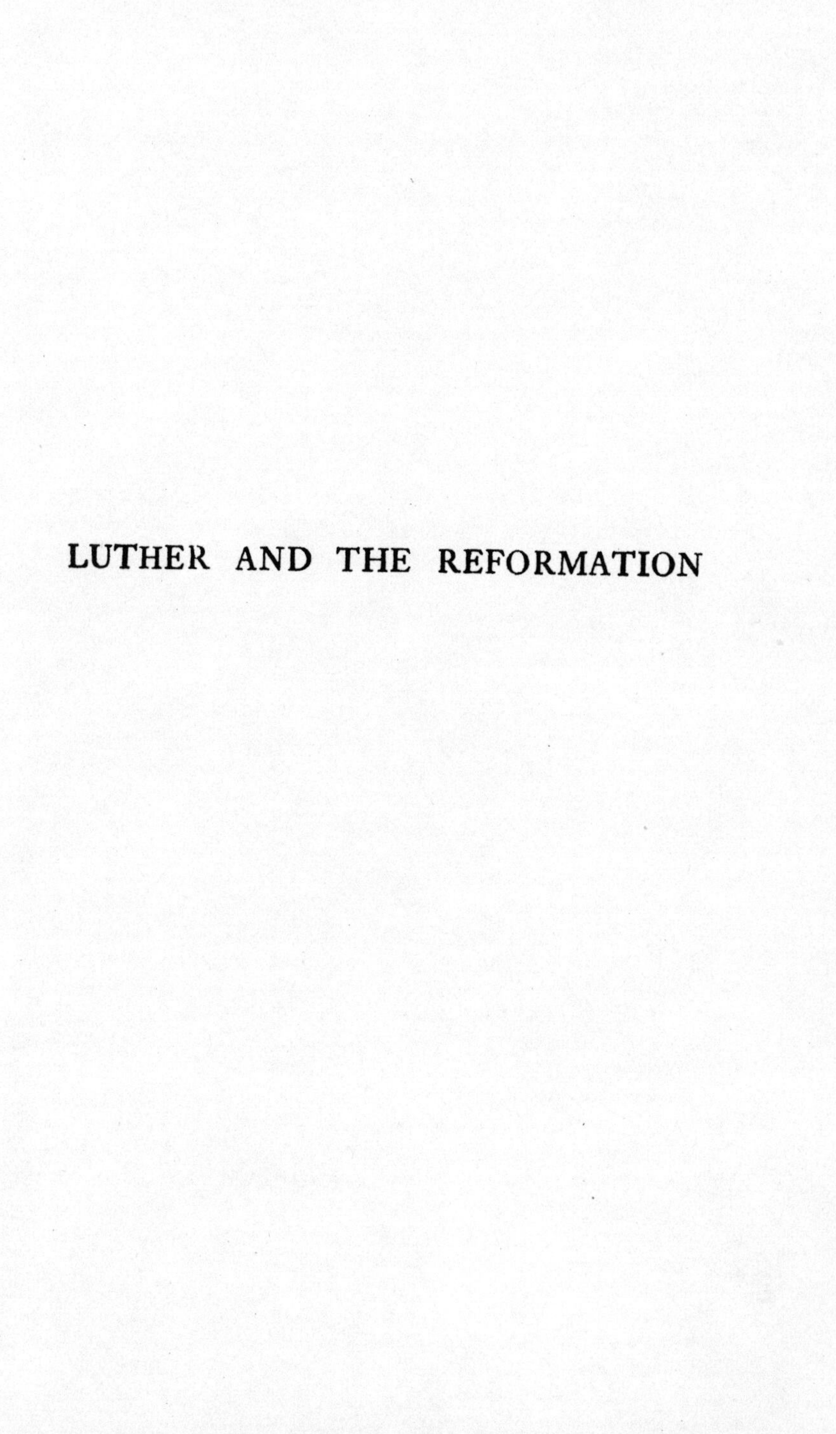

LUTHER AND THE REFORMATION

LUTHER AND THE REFORMATION

BY

JAMES MACKINNON, Ph.D., D.D.
Regius Professor of Ecclesiastical History, University of Edinburgh

VOL. II.

THE BREACH WITH ROME (1517-21)

NEW YORK
RUSSELL & RUSSELL · INC
1962

FIRST PUBLISHED IN 1928
PUBLISHED, 1962, BY RUSSELL & RUSSELL, INC.
L. C. CATALOG CARD NO: 62—10691

PRINTED IN THE UNITED STATES OF AMERICA

PREFACE

THIS volume deals with the development of Luther's views as a Reformer from 1517-21. These four years are of supreme importance for the initiation of the Reformation movement. The history of Luther's life and his religious development to 1517, which formed the subject of the first volume, might be described as the prologue to the Reformation drama. The four succeeding years constitute the first act of this drama, and Kalkoff has justly termed these "the decisive years of the Reformation." They show us the fruition of his earlier religious experience in the sphere of actual life. It was during these years that the monk and the theologian developed into the militant Reformer.

This development took its immediate rise in the Indulgence Controversy of 1517-18, with which the opening chapter of this volume consequently deals in some detail. This controversy led to the intervention of the Pope, and this intervention led in turn to the widening of the controversy and culminated in the breach with Rome, with all the consequences that this breach involved for the Papacy and the mediæval Church. At the outset Luther by no means realised the issue to which the indulgence controversy was to lead him. Superficially viewed, this controversy appeared to be one of those theological disputes in which the scholastic theologians had periodically indulged throughout the Middle Ages. Leo X. himself was disposed at first to regard it as nothing more than a conventional monkish quarrel. The Pope, however, soon learned to know better. For what had seemed, on a superficial view, but a scholastic dispute erelong developed into an attack on the doctrines and institutions of the mediæval Church. The skirmish over indulgences thus became a pitched battle, or rather series of battles, between Luther and his assailants, in the course of which the attack as well as the defence widened its scope until it embraced the whole mediæval doctrinal and ecclesiastical system, and Luther progressively enunciated and maintained his distinctive teaching in ever more aggressive antagonism to this system. In the struggle to assert and vindicate his religious convictions against the forces of tradition as incorporated in the Papacy and the mediæval Church, he was gradually led to question and ultimately to reject the papal absolutism over the Church, to substitute for the papal-hierarchic Church of the Middle Ages the more spiritual and democratic conception of the New Testament, to vindicate the sovereignty and independence of the national State against the papal claim to superiority over the State as well as the Church, to champion the rights of the individual reason and conscience and the principle of religious toleration.

This ever waxing conflict thus led him step by step to the apprehension of certain distinctive principles of far-reaching practical as well as theological import, and to the full consciousness of his mission as a Reformer. His opponents, as he ironically reminds them on occasion, were his best teachers. His is, indeed, a striking case of learning by discussion and controversy. At the same time, he believed that he was being drawn onwards by a divine power which he could not resist or control, and this belief, abetted by his fighting temperament and his original, receptive mind, explains the astoundingly rapid development, both as a theologian and an active Reformer, which it is the object of this volume to delineate.

Whilst the subject-matter is perforce encrusted in theological controversy, not always interesting or edifying to the modern reader, it is of perennial importance in respect both of the principles at issue and their far-reaching effects. Luther became the leader of an emancipation movement of superlative prospective significance in the political and intellectual as well as the religious sphere. At this stage of his career his watchword is Liberty—liberty for the individual, the Church, the State. *Liberi enim sumus ab omnibus* becomes his resounding war cry in spite of his strongly conservative vein. True, it is liberty only as he is able to comprehend it, liberty in the relative sense as against his opponents, who strove to crush him and his cause. His struggle in behalf of liberty is coloured by the temperament and the religious experience of the man, and conditioned by the limitations of his theological standpoint and outlook. We may miss in him the larger and wider spirit of the Renaissance, and fail at times to appreciate the rather one-sided dogmatism of the theologian. Even so, he is undoubtedly during these fateful years the prophet and the apostle of a new age, of a mighty emancipation from inherited and enforced traditions, beliefs, institutions, even if he does not always understand the full implications of this movement. It is this aspect of his heroic struggle, throughout these years of strenuous battling with a host of assailants and ever-threatening danger of the stake, which has particularly interested the writer and which the writer has sought to set in the foreground and convey to the reader. In addition, he has striven to display the personality of the man as it unfolds itself throughout this titanic struggle.

This volume is the fruit of a critical study of the writings in which Luther developed his reforming ideas within this period. Advantage has also been taken of the latest researches on the subject, including in particular the works of the veteran specialist, Paul Kalkoff, to which I have pleasure in acknowledging my indebtedness. Kalkoff's contributions are of solid merit, in spite of the criticisms, in regard to detail, to which they have been subjected and to which reference is occasionally made in the footnotes.

My own studies in this field have been carried on in connection with the Advanced Class or Seminar in Ecclesiastical History of Edinburgh University, and I take this opportunity of dedicating the volume to the former members of this class from many lands beyond the seas as well as Great Britain, and adding the cordial greetings and good wishes of their old professor.

The publication of the book has been encouraged by the Carnegie Universities Trust, which has made a grant in aid of it. My thanks are also due to Mr F. C. Nicholson, M.A., the Librarian of the University Library, who has been unwearying in placing the rich resources of the Library at my disposal and in procuring the additional material required for the purpose of the work. My acknowledgments are also due to the members of the Library Staff.

In view of frequent inquiries as to the extent of the work, I may add that two additional volumes, the manuscript of which is nearly complete, will extend it to the death of Luther in 1546.

THE UNIVERSITY, EDINBURGH,
December 1927.

TABLE OF CONTENTS

LUTHER
AND THE REFORMATION

CHAPTER I

THE INDULGENCE CONTROVERSY

I. Motive and Justification of Luther's Attack

Luther's motive in posting up his ninety-five theses was, on his own testimony, solely to direct the attention of his fellow-theologians to the obscurity of the doctrine and the abuses of the practice of indulgences. Certain Roman Catholic writers, on the other hand, attribute the theses to his doctrine of justification by faith which had led him into antagonism to the Catholic teaching of good works and impelled him to challenge not merely the abuses, but the principle of indulgences in the interest of this doctrine. Janssen, for instance, maintains that "it was not these abuses which impelled Luther to the course he took, but the doctrine of indulgences itself—above all the Church's teaching of good works, which was contrary to his views concerning justification and free will."[1] In this diagnosis of the case he is followed by Pastor, who, however, seems to contradict himself. Whilst, with Janssen, he maintains that "in his secret heart it was not the abuses of the actual system which were at the bottom of Luther's action . . . but his deep-lying antagonism to the Catholic doctrine of good works," he adds on the same page "that he had no object

[1] "History of the German People," iii. 91. Eng. trans., 1910.

beyond attacking the real and supposed abuses attached to the preaching of the indulgence."[2] Luther's doctrine of justification may indirectly have influenced his view of the theory and practice of indulgences, though the theses do not explicitly proclaim this doctrine. But it is not the case that in attacking the system, as practised by Tetzel and his fellow-preachers, his object was covertly to discredit the teaching of the Church on the subject in the interest of this doctrine, and that the attack was, therefore, not really what it professed to be—an attempt to effect a clamant practical reform. Paulus, another Roman Catholic writer, whilst asserting that Luther was already unconsciously estranged from the Church in essential points, has diagnosed his motive more accurately. He scouts the notion that "he only made his opposition to indulgences the pretext stealthily to diffuse his new dogmatic conceptions. When he came out into the open with his sensational theses he had by no means thought out a clear and definite programme for the future. His only object at first was to challenge the abuses of the system."[3]

This is the only conclusion warranted by Luther's own testimony, the veracity of which there is no reason to call in question. He avers again and again during the controversy to which the theses gave rise that his only motive in posting them up was to draw attention to the errors and abuses of the system, to combat and correct these errors and abuses by means of competent criticism and discussion, and thus rouse the ecclesiastical authorities to put a stop to the proceedings of the indulgence preachers in the interest of religion and morality. In the letter to the Archbishop of Maintz accompanying the theses (31st October 1517), he arraigns in scathing terms the conduct of the indulgence preachers in misleading the people by their lavish offers

[2] "History of the Popes," vii. 351-352. Eng. trans.

[3] "Johann Tetzel der Ablassprediger," 168-169 (1899). Bratke, a Protestant writer, is also in error in thinking that Luther's object was not so much to draw attention to the evils of the system, as to attain to a definite idea of the doctrine of salvation, which the problem of indulgences had raised in his mind. "Luther's Ninety-five Theses," 272 f. (1884).

of worthless pardons instead of preaching the gospel. He does not, indeed, claim to speak from personal knowledge of their preaching,[4] for Tetzel and his fellow-vendors were forbidden to carry on the traffic in electoral Saxony.[5] But he has discovered (evidently in the confessional) its evil effects on the people, who believe that by buying an indulgence ticket they are assured of salvation. This false notion is, he adds, also countenanced in the archbishop's "Instruction" to his commissaries, which had come into his hands, and he begs him both to cancel this compromising document and impose on his agents a different form of preaching.[6] The letter clearly shows that in arraigning this nefarious traffic he was actuated not by antagonism to the Church or even to the principle of indulgence in itself, but by a justifiable indignation and anxiety on the score of its evil religious effects. In a letter to Lang shortly afterwards he rebuts the accusation of his opponents that he had posted up his theses at the instigation of the Elector Frederick for the purpose of discrediting the archbishop, and avers on oath that he had done so without the Elector's knowledge.[7] He assures Christopher Scheurl (5th March 1518) that he had neither intended nor desired to excite a public commotion against the practice. He had only drawn up the theses for discussion by those competent to judge in order that, if they failed to gain their approval, they might be rejected, and, if approved, be published.[8] The method of carrying the discussion to the bar of public opinion by translation and publication in the vernacular was by no means to his liking. Not that he did not desire the people to be enlightened on the subject. Only this was not the right way to do it. He had his doubts on some

[4] Enders, "Luther's Briefwechsel," i. 115, non adeo accuso prædicatorum exclamationes quas non audivi.

[5] "T.R.," v. 77.

[6] Enders, i. 117. Eundem libellum penitus tollere et prædicatoribus veniarum imponere aliam prædicandi formam.

[7] *Ibid.*, i. 121-122; *cf.* 156 and 160.

[8] *Ibid.*, i. 166. Non fuit consilium neque votum eas evulgari, sed cum paucis apud et circum nos habitantibus primum super ipsis conferri, ut sic multorum judicio vel damnatæ abolerentur, vel probatæ ederentur.

of the theses, and if he had foreseen the storm which their publication had aroused, he would have expressed himself differently or omitted some of them. He writes in the same strain to his old teacher Trutvetter, whilst emphasising the necessity of exposing the indulgence fraud by which the people are being misled and deceived, and which will inevitably end in disillusion and revolt. The whole indulgence traffic is merely a device of Italian ecclesiastics for making money. They care not a straw for anything else, and he would, therefore, wish the nefarious system abolished throughout the whole Church.[9] Similarly, he informs the Bishop of Brandenburg, in whose diocese Wittenberg was included, that his only object in drawing up the theses was to help by discussion towards a more definite conception of the subject in the face of the prevailing difference of opinion. Whilst the views expressed in them might differ from those of a few of the canonists and some of the scholastic theologians, they did not seem to him to be contrary to the Scriptures, the fathers, and the canons. The discussion was only tentative until the Church should finally decide the question. Meanwhile he declines to accept mere scholastic opinions as articles of faith, and claims the liberty of discussion which the scholastic theologians have exercised without demur for so many centuries even in the most sacred matters. His opponents had straightway treated his theses as dogmatic assertions. Nothing, he energetically protests, is farther from the truth. In some points he is still in doubt, in others he confesses his ignorance. Some of the views attributed to him he denies, and not one of them is he disposed to assert dogmatically. His intention is to dispute, not to dogmatise, and he is ready to submit the whole question to the decision of the Church.[10]

In the letter which he sent to the Pope (30th May 1518), in forwarding his "Resolutions" or amplification of his

[9] Enders, i. 189.

[10] *Ibid.*, i. 148-151. Enders dates the letter 13th Feb. 1518. Kalkoff assigns it to the 22nd May with more probability. "Forschungen zu Luther's Römischen Prozess," 49 (1905); "T.R.," iv. 316-318.

theses, he says that he was impelled by the scandalous preaching of the indulgence agents privately to call the attention of a number of ecclesiastical magnates to this evil which was the talk of every tavern, to the great detriment of the papal authority. His appeal proving ineffective, he determined to challenge the abuse in a public disputation. These theses, he repeats, were not dogmas, but propositions for debate by competent theologians, with a view to the refutation of the errors of the indulgence preachers, and had he foreseen the effects of their publication he would have taken care to make them more intelligible.[11] In the protestation prefaced to the "Resolutions" he is equally explicit. "At the outset, I protest that I desire to advance and hold nothing but what can be established from Scripture, from the ecclesiastical fathers accepted by the Roman Church, and also from the papal canons and decretals."[12] Finally, in his appeal from Cardinal Cajetan to the Pope (22nd October 1518), he adduces anew the uncertainty of the theory and the crass abuse of the practice of indulgences as the sole motive of his action, and professes his readiness to submit the dispute to the judgment of the Church and His Holiness.[13]

Luther's testimony to the gravity of the abuse and the detriment wrought by it to the Church as well as religion is equally incontestable, and amply explains and justifies the challenge which he sounded forth in these theses. Some of the charges against Tetzel's preaching were, indeed, as Paulus has shown,[14] the fruit of popular exaggeration or misunderstanding. He does not, for instance, seem to have asserted that in the case of the living indulgence was valid without contrition, or that it covered future as well as present sins, and therefore carried the right to commit sin with impunity. In ascribing such enormities to the indulgence preacher,[15] Luther allowed himself to be misled

[11] Enders, i. 200-203.

[12] "Werke," i. 529-530.

[13] *Ibid.*, ii. 29-30.

[14] "Tetzel," 56 f.

[15] Luther erroneously includes these in the list of Tetzel's misleading assertions in his later pamphlet, "Wider Hans Worst" (1541). "Werke," li. 539.

by the reports he had heard and uncritically accepted. Tetzel appears to have preached the necessity of contrition for the validity of an indulgence in the case of the living in accordance with the received doctrine of the Church. But it is not so certain that he took pains to impress this doctrine on his ignorant hearers, who were unfitted to understand the theological aspect of the theory, as Luther had found in the confessional. Certain it is that in the case of souls in purgatory he did preach that a mere money payment without contrition on the part of those who made this payment for their dead relatives was sufficient to free the soul from purgatory.[16] Moreover, the motive behind the traffic in this particular instance was the purely mercenary one of raising as much money as possible in order to provide for the financial necessities of the Roman Curia and the Archbishop of Maintz. Luther gauged quite correctly this mercenary motive, though he wrongly assumed that the Pope was personally not responsible for it, except in so far as he had consented to grant a dispensation to the archbishop to acquire the See of Maintz in addition to those of Magdeburg and Halberstadt, which had, of course, to be paid for, and for the payment of which the indulgence was to provide. At worst the Pope, he believed, was merely the unwitting tool of the archbishop's ambition and the greed of his own Medici relatives who were only too eager to share in the spoil.[17] In point of fact, Leo X. was not so innocent of complicity in the odious traffic as Luther imagined,[18] and this complicity only strengthens the case for the indictment which on practical grounds he launched against it in the theses.

Luther was in truth by no means solitary in his denunciation of it. Even those who subsequently took sides against him in the controversy to which this indictment gave rise, deplored and denounced the evil religious and moral effects of the indulgence preaching of Tetzel and

[16] See MacKinnon, "Luther and the Reformation," i. 294.

[17] See Luther's communication to Miltitz in January 1519, in which he explains why he was impelled to attack the indulgence traffic, whilst exculpating the Pope of responsibility for it. Enders, i. 341-342.

[18] See "Luther and the Reformation," i. 290-291.

his fellow-commissaries. Eck, Emser, Murner, Cochlaeus, Duke George of Saxony said some very hard things about it whilst contesting Luther's theological contentions on the subject. Tetzel's fellow-Dominican, Johann Lindner, asserts that his mercenary zeal aroused the indignation and contempt of the people.[19] These criticisms have been repeated by modern Roman Catholic writers who have had the courage to face the facts. "The whole thing," remarks Pastor, in reference to the Indulgence Bull of 1515, "looked at from every point of view, was a disgraceful affair for all concerned. That it, together with other causes, led to the impending catastrophe, appears to us like a judgment from heaven. . . . It is a fact, proved by what took place, that the revolt against the Papacy proceeded from a grave abuse, patent to all beholders, connected with the obnoxious financial transactions of the Roman Curia." [20]

Whilst modern Roman Catholic writers like Pastor and Paulus largely justify Luther's attack on the practice, they rebut his criticism of the doctrine of indulgence and refuse to admit that the current teaching on the subject was either erroneous or obscure. In the theses, Luther accepts the principle of indulgence in itself. But he holds strongly that the principle is liable to misapprehension and error and tends to distort the gospel of God's grace. He treats the subject in a very independent spirit, and is at no pains to conceal his personal convictions on the theory as well as the practice. It is this independent note that repels his Roman Catholic critics, to whom any attempt at independent thought or self-assertion in the face of ecclesiastical authority is necessarily inadmissible. They assume, moreover, that the teaching of the Church on the subject was explicit and incontestable, and they tax Luther with ignorance or presumption in questioning it. The indulgence preachers might err and misrepresent this teaching, but what the Church believed and taught was neither obscure nor doubtful. "The papal Bulls," says Pastor, "all put forth the doctrine of indulgences with dogmatic accuracy, and most theologians of the declining Middle Ages, though

[19] Paulus, "Tetzel," 120. [20] "History of the Popes," iii. 332-333.

they may differ on individual points, agree in essentials, and all unite in explaining indulgences not as being a remission of guilt, but as a remission of temporal punishment. All equally start from the presumption that in order to gain an indulgence the sin must have been already forgiven through contrition and confession."[21] Essentially there was thus nothing to dispute about as far as the doctrine of the Church was concerned.

Whether this teaching was as clear and definite as Luther's critics contend is, however, very debatable. The fact is that there had been throughout the later mediæval centuries a great deal of discussion and difference of opinion on the doctrine itself. The practice had developed out of the old penitential system and the doctrine had been elaborated by the thirteenth-century schoolmen. But it was still open to question whether scholastic theories on such a subject, even if sanctioned by the Pope, were to be received as articles of faith, and in taking objection to this assumption, Luther was only repeating what notable theologians and churchmen of the fifteenth century had said before him. In any case it is certain that he had his own doubts and difficulties on the subject, and profoundly felt the need of a thorough discussion of it, from both the religious and the theological points of view, and a deliberate expression of the mind of the Church on it. His early sermons on indulgences clearly show that, whilst accepting the system, there were many questions on which he was by no means prepared to give a definite answer.[22] In the face of these questionings, the assumption of Hergenröther, Grisar, Paulus, and others that he understood well enough the doctrine of indulgences which he attacked, and that his professed doubts were only a pretext for this attack is unwarranted by the evidence. In support of this assumption they appeal to his sermons on the subject previous to the posting up of his theses as a proof that the ignorance about indulgences of which he later speaks, in reference

21 "History of the Popes," vii. 336; *cf.* Hefele-Hergenröther, "Concilien Geschichte," ix. 42 f. (1890).

22 See "Werke," i. 65 f.; *cf.* 98-99, 141.

to these early years, in his tract, "Wider Hans Worst," was not in accordance with fact, and that his testimony on the subject is, therefore, unreliable. In the passage in this tract, written in 1541, to which they appeal in support of this contention, he, indeed, says that when Tetzel appeared at Juterbog in 1517 and the people flocked from Wittenberg across the Saxon frontier to hear him, "he did not know what the indulgence meant." At first sight this assertion does seem in flat contradiction to the testimony of his early sermons, which certainly show that he knew a great deal about the subject before Tetzel had begun to preach in the neighbourhood of Wittenberg. But, as the context shows, the ignorance of which he speaks refers, not to the scholastic doctrine of indulgences, but rather to the contents of Tetzel's sermons and the archbishop's "Instruction," with which he was not then acquainted.[23] As the early sermons and the theses show, he had been studying this doctrine for at least a couple of years previously. The theses were, in fact, largely the recapitulation of the main idea of these sermons. But this study had only revealed to him the difficulty and obscurity of the subject and aroused serious doubts and misgivings as to the validity of the system from the religious point of view. As the result of these doubts and misgivings the whole theory might well appear to him nebulous and uncertain.

That there was ample ground for his hesitation and uncertainty cannot be reasonably questioned. This was in truth one of these nebulous theological doctrines in which make-believe was too readily accepted as fact, since it rested on the assumption of an inexhaustible supply of merit which the scholastic doctors placed at the disposal of the Pope for the benefit of souls in purgatory as well as those in the flesh. These doctors reasoned on the subject with all the assurance of experts in the knowledge of the world beyond, with which their acquaintance was, to say the least, highly problematic. Objections to the fully-fledged theory were certainly not lacking. The applicability of indulgences to purgatory, for instance, was only a

[23] See the tract, "Wider Hans Worst." "Werke," li. 530 f.

comparatively recent papal innovation and was not above question. Still more dubious, and certainly highly objectionable on moral and religious grounds, was the assumption included in the Bull of 1515 and the relative " Instruction " of the archbishop that the buying of an indulgence ticket without contrition on the part of the purchaser would infallibly benefit the dead. On this point there was a sharp division of opinion both during and before Luther's time.[24] Even the doctrine of the Treasure of Merits, on which the practice was based, was only a theory of the scholastic theologians, though the Pope had recognised the theory as a correct dogmatic basis.[25] Nor was the papal and priestly power to remit sin, which the plenary indulgence assumed, by any means indisputable. In the classical text-book of mediæval theology, which still dominated the schools in Luther's time, Lombard taught that this power was only declaratory and that the actual remission extended only to the abatement of ecclesiastical penalties, penitential works. Though Aquinas and his school attributed the actual power of forgiveness to the priest and this became the accepted ecclesiastical view, later theologians like Duns and his school materially limited it, and Wiclif and Wessel explicitly denied it.[26] On the question whether a Jubilee Indulgence like that of 1515 conveyed full remission of the guilt as well as the penalty of sin, statements were made that, to say the least, were apt to be misleading. Such an indulgence was said to be valid for the full remission of both guilt and penalty, inasmuch as it involved contrition and confession, and thus carried with it spiritual benefits equivalent to those obtainable in the sacrament of penance. It was on this ground that theologians like John von Paltz, for instance—Luther's old teacher in the Erfurt monastery—unhesitatingly asserted that a plenary indulgence availed for the full remission of sin.[27] Only an expert in the scholastic theology could

[24] Paulus, " Tetzel," 157 f.

[25] Bull of Clement VI., 1343, " Documente zum Ablassstreit," 19-20.

[26] See " Luther and the Reformation," i. 88.

[27] Coelifodina, " Documente zum Ablassstreit," 55; and see Paulus, " Tetzel," 94-95.

appreciate the subtle reasoning by which this conclusion was arrived at, and in any case the association of a plenary indulgence in return for a money contribution to an ecclesiastical project like the building of St Peter's, not to mention the mercenary and secret bargain between the Curia and the archbishop underlying it, with the spiritual benefit obtainable in the sacrament of penance was highly objectionable from the religious point of view. It betrays the mercenary and materialist spirit which had invaded the mediæval conception of religion, reflected only too crassly in this sordid traffic in sacred things. In the archbishop's "Instruction" to the subcommissaries, to whom he entrusted this traffic, the grace obtainable by this expedient is extolled as exceeding in magnitude all other spiritual benefits,[28] since it assures to the sinner the perfect remission of all sins (guilt as well as penalty) and complete immunity from the pains of purgatory. This supreme benefit is indeed limited to the contrite and confessed, or to those who have at least the intention of confessing within a given time. But it is not solely to contrition and confession, but to contrition and confession plus a money payment that this inestimable grace is vouchsafed. The attainment of God's justifying grace which it involves is thus made dependent on the purchase of an indulgence, and it was this, among other objectionable features of the transaction, that exercised the mind of Luther, as his indignant protest to the archbishop shows. It is certain that, as Luther learned in the confessional and as he also indignantly represented to the archbishop, the belief in the efficacy of a money payment, apart from contrition and confession, as an insurance against both guilt and penalty, was widespread among the people.[29] Moreover, the acceptance of the lower form of contrition known as attrition (not real repentance, but merely the fear of the consequences of sin), which was recognised by theologians like Paltz, was certainly fitted to make this cheap method of earning forgiveness and

[28] Prima gratia est plenaria remissio omnium peccatorum, qua quidem gratia nihil majus dici potest. "Documente," 110.

[29] "Documente," 144-145.

immunity from punishment here and hereafter appear in a very questionable light, both morally and religiously. No wonder that on this point there was sharp difference of opinion.[30]

From the works of Paltz[31] and others it is evident that the subject bristled with difficulties and gave rise to not a little difference of opinion. On the question of the applicability of indulgences to purgatory, for instance, Paltz tells us that some are wont to doubt whether indulgences apply to purgatory and whether the souls of the dead can be relieved by this expedient.[32] The critics of the system in the fifteenth century included notable churchmen like Gerson and Cusanus,[33] not to mention aggressive antagonists like John of Wesel and Wessel Gansfort, and in his theses Luther was only repeating what critics like the Dominican P. Schwarz had written towards the close of the century, in denunciation of the traffic and its agents, and the detriment accruing thereby to both religion and the authority of the Church.[34] Wessel also anticipated Luther in a remarkable degree in his trenchant criticism of the whole system, and it was not without reason, in respect of his attack on indulgences at least, that Luther later whole-heartedly recognised the affinity of Wessel's teaching with his own.

II. The Counter-Attack

Luther's invitation to his fellow-theologians outside Wittenberg evoked no response, and the proposed disputation

[30] Paulus, " Tetzel," 110 f.

[31] See especially his supplementum to the Coelifodina, in which he replies to the objections of those who contested the system.

[32] Coelifodina, " Documente," 65. Apud nonnullos solet in dubium verti de animabus in purgatorio retentis an via indulgentiarum relevari possent.

[33] On this moderate party see Bratke, " Luther's Ninety-five Theses," 154 f.

[34] See the summary of Schwarz's indictment in Pastor, vii. 341-342.

on the theses was not held.[35] The archbishop did not deign to reply to his letter, and the other bishops [36] to whom he wrote on the subject took no action. His ordinary, the Bishop of Brandenburg, advised him to leave the matter alone. The question involved the authority of the Church, and in attacking it he would only make trouble for himself.[37] "I can well believe," says Luther, "that both he and the archbishop reflected that the Pope would prove much too powerful for a miserable mendicant like me." [38] Some of the other bishops, he tells us, were more favourably disposed; to others his action appeared either ridiculous or infatuated in view of the risk of incurring the papal censure.[39]

Nevertheless, the theses were by no means stillborn. Without his concurrence they were printed and circulated both in the Latin original and in a vernacular translation, and before the end of the year they were being read and discussed all over Germany. They certainly caused a sensation not only among the learned, but among the people who saw in him the man for the hour. "Thus my propositions were posted up against Tetzel's preaching, as may be seen from the printed copies of them. Almost within a fortnight they were known all over Germany,[40] for everybody complained of the indulgence, especially of Tetzel's sermons. And whilst the bishops and doctors kept

[35] Enders, i. 150. Igitur cum in hanc harenam vocarem omnes, veniret vero nullus.

[36] Myconius says that besides the archbishop he wrote to the Bishops of Brandenburg, Zeitz, and Merseburg. "Geschichte der Reformation," ed. by Clemens, 21-22. In his letter to the Pope in May 1518, Luther says that he wrote to several magnates Ecclesiarum, Enders, i. 201-202; in that to the Elector of Saxony, 19th Nov. 1518, he says that he wrote only to the archbishop and the Bishop of Brandenburg.

[37] "T.R.," vi. 238-239.

[38] "Werke," li. 540; *cf.* Myconius, 22. See also his preface to the 1545 ed. of his works, "Documente zu Luther's Entwicklung," 12.

[39] Enders, i. 202.

[40] This is evidently an exaggeration, due to defective memory. Myconius not only repeats this exaggeration, but adds that within a month they were circulated over the whole of Christendom. "Geschichte," 22.

quiet and no one would bell the cat for fear of Tetzel and his fellow-inquisitors of heresy, who threatened all opponents of the traffic with the stake, then it was that Luther became a famous doctor as the one who should come and take a grip of the business. This fame was not to my liking." [41]

Though the archbishop ignored Luther, he could not afford to ignore the sensation caused by the theses. He was keenly interested in the financial side of the traffic, and he had some reason to doubt a scrutiny of his private conduct. For these reasons it was imperative to take prompt measures to silence "the audacious monk of Wittenberg," as he dubbed him, by means of the papal authority. When, therefore, his councillors of the diocese of Magdeburg at Halle, whither Luther had addressed his letter, forwarded it along with others of his writings [42] to Aschaffenburg in the diocese of Maintz, he sent these documents to the Pope, without even waiting for the opinion of the University of Maintz to which he had at first submitted them.[43] Meanwhile, after consultation with his advisers at Aschaffenburg, he directed on the 13th December those at Halle to inhibit "the audacious monk" (*processus inhibitorius*). His Halle council hesitated, however, to adopt this course for fear of the scandal which a refusal of compliance on Luther's part would cause, and advised the archbishop to waive the inhibition.

As clearly appears from the archbishop's letter to them, his main concern was not to probe the evils which Luther had arraigned, but to muzzle the presumptuous monk, who, he says, "was scandalising and misleading the poor

[41] "Werke," li. 540-541.

[42] Brieger concludes that in addition to the theses they sent him his "Disputation on the Scholastic Theology" and his exposition of the penitential psalms. "Zeitschrift für Kirchengeschichte," xi. 115 f.

[43] Kalkoff says that they were already in the hands of the Roman Curia in the beginning of December 1517. "Entscheidungsjahre der Reformation," 24 (1917). Karl Müller, on the other hand, says that they only reached Rome in the beginning of Jan. 1918. "Luther's Römischen Prozess," "Z.K.G.," xxiv. 52. Boehmer thinks that they could scarcely have reached Rome much before Christmas 1517. "Der Junge Luther," 190 (1925). Kalkoff's date seems the more probable.

unintelligent people." [44] There is no sign in the letter of any attempt to face the evils of the system or any sense of the necessity of applying a remedy. It was a fateful dereliction of duty on the part of a high Church dignitary, though we could hardly expect any other attitude in one to whom the indulgence was merely an expedient for paying the debts contracted in the pursuit of his ambition. Such a man was not likely to be impressed by Luther's profession in the preface to the theses that he was actuated solely by the love of truth and zeal for its elucidation. Luther had attacked an institution of the Church, and even if it had become a crying scandal and a source of error, it must be maintained for the benefit of a worldly archbishop and a corrupt Curia. To criticise the system or demand an investigation into its theological presuppositions and its religious aspect was sheer presumption and rebellion. This was also naturally the attitude adopted by Tetzel and his abettors of the Dominican Order, who were already on the warpath against him. Whether the Pope would adopt the same attitude remained to be seen. As the suggestion to proclaim a Jubilee Indulgence as a financial expedient had originated in the Roman Curia and had the papal sanction, the prospect of a radical reform of the system under papal auspices was not very promising. Luther himself seems to have expected that the Pope would espouse his cause and even thank him for his efforts! He was not as yet conscious of any rebellion against the papal authority or any divergence from the true teaching of the Church, far less of any desire to provoke a rupture. "I had hoped that the Pope would protect me. For I had so grounded and armed my disputation with the Scriptures and the papal decrees that I was certain the Pope would condemn Tetzel and bless me." [45] Luther's hope was rather naïve, and he was destined erelong to be disillusioned. But the refusal of the ecclesiastical

[44] "Z.K.G.," xi. 115.

[45] "Werke," li. 543; *cf.* his preface to the 1545 ed. of his works, "Documente," 12. Et in iis certus mihi videbar me habiturum patronum papam. See also "T.R.," v. 76. Tum temporis agnovi Papam dominum meum et putabam me illi rem gratam facturum.

authorities to listen to his challenge was none the less as fateful as it was fatuous. It meant Nemesis not only for this sordid trafficking in sacred things by ecclesiastical hirelings in high places, but for the Church itself, so unworthily represented by its highest dignitaries.

At this stage, however, it seemed a case of Athanasius against the world over again. Would he have the strength of will and conviction to persist in the face of opposition? He had, indeed, struck a popular note in spite of himself, and the diminishing sales of Tetzel's wares erelong attested the practical effect of the theses.[46] "Since the Germans," he wrote long afterwards (1545), "were tired of these plunderings, traffickings, and the infinite imposture of these Roman robbers, they awaited with bated breath the upshot of so great an enterprise which no one before, either bishops or theologians, had dared to tackle. And the popular breeze favoured me, because the arts and ongoings of the Romans with which they filled and exhausted the whole world were hateful to all." [47] Stray notes of encouragement came to him as the expression of the popular feeling. "Go on and carry out your purpose," wrote Dr Fleck from his monastery at Steinlausig, near Bitterfeld, who, on reading the theses exclaimed, "Ho, ho, there he is at last who will do the job." [48] Such encouraging messages were, however, at first exceptional. Luther's friends played the part of Job's counsellors. "Would you write against the Pope?" said the jurist Schurf. "What will you make of it? They will not suffer it." "How," quietly returned Luther, "if they *must* suffer it." [49] His colleagues of the Theological Faculty of the University were equally dubious, and even Carlstadt feared that he was going too far.[50] "You speak the truth, good brother," remarked Albert Krantz on reading the theses, "but you will achieve nothing. Go to your cell and pray God to have mercy on

[46] See Hausrath, "Luther's Leben," i. 179-180.
[47] "Documente," 13.
[48] Walch, "Luther's Sämmtliche Schriften," xv. 489.
[49] "Tischreden," iii. 565.
[50] Walch, xv. 491; *cf.* Enders, i. 155.

you." [51] His fellow-monks were still more alarmed at his daring. The prior and subprior besought him to think of the interest of his Order and not to expose himself and it to the ill will of the Dominicans. "If," replied he, "this business has not been begun in God's name, it will come to nothing. But if God is in it, it will assuredly prevail." [52] To Lang he writes in similar terms, in view of the hostility of the Erfurt theologians, who accused him of rashness and pride. "Who," he asks, "has ever produced anything new without incurring the charges of pride and contention at the hands of those who plume themselves on their own prudence? Why were Christ and the martyrs put to death and doctors have suffered odium? Was it not because they appeared proud and contemptuous of the old and renowned wisdom, or because they dared to produce something new without the counsel of those who think that wisdom consists in clinging to the old? . . . Not by the judgment or purpose of men do I shape my actions, but by the will of God. If this work is of God, who will prevent it? If it is not of God, who will make it prevail?" [53]

These words already foreshadow the great innovator, the master spirit of a religious revolution. Though as yet unconscious of any substantial divergence from the mediæval Church or any defiance of established authority, the independent spirit is already perceptible. It is significant that he signs himself *Martinus Eleutherius*, Martin the Emancipator. He clearly will not discard a conviction merely because it is objectionable to the Erfurt theologians, to whom his theses against the scholastic theology had given offence, which those against indulgences have only aggravated.[54] The conservative attitude of mind which adduced the old as a sufficient argument against the new and decried independent thought as presumption, materially contributed to bring about the Reformation. This conservatism in its reaction on the inquiring mind

[51] Köstlin, "Luther," i. 164 (5th ed., 1903); Boehmer, "Der Junge Luther," 179 (1925).

[52] Hausrath, "Luther," i. 178.

[53] Enders, i. 126.

[54] *Ibid.*, i. 124.

becomes the unwilling nurse of progress. Luther's opponents were in this respect his best teachers. In taking up his challenge Tetzel and his supporters claimed a monopoly of truth in virtue of use and wont. They stood for the papal authority and what they deemed to be the teaching of the Church against individual criticism or conviction. This is the keynote of the series of anti-theses with which Tetzel opened the counter-attack in a disputation held in the presence of a provincial gathering of the Dominican Order, presided over by Dr Rab, prior of the Leipzig monastery, of which Tetzel was a member.

It was natural that Tetzel's Order should rally in his defence. His opponent was an Augustinian and the monastic *esprit de corps* was touched by a challenge emanating from a rival Order. Moreover, the Dominicans were the champions of orthodoxy and the absolute power of the Pope, and saw in the theses a covert attack on both. They had taken the lead in the antagonism to the new learning and were equally quick to scent danger in the new theology of the Wittenberg reformer. The challenging tone of the theses was fitted to excite their active hostility, and in view of their aggressive obscurantism, Luther's idea of discussing the subject solely on its merits was certainly rather naïve. He had not merely challenged a practical abuse; he had raised the question of the principle of indulgence and the papal power in relation to it, and had thus provoked the counter-attack of which he found himself the object. Though he was genuinely astonished at the outcry which his challenge evoked, it was rather naïve to complain if the champions of use and wont in theology and usage hit back. The case of Reuchlin might have warned him that the obscurantists who had waged so bitter a war against the new learning would not be less intransigent in their antagonism to the new theology. Of this uncompromising antagonism Tetzel's counter-theses gave no uncertain intimation. They were indeed couched in the most dogmatic and intolerant terms.

Their real author was, however, not Tetzel, but Konrad Koch, otherwise known as Wimpina, from his native place Wimpfen, Professor of Theology in the University of Frankfurt-on-the Oder, which the Elector of Brandenburg had founded in 1506. Though the theses passed under the name of Tetzel, Luther rightly divined their real author,[55] who seems to have had a personal grudge against the Wittenberg University. Hausrath presumes that in defending the indulgence traffic he was at the same time actuated by the desire to further the interest of the Brandenburg family, the patrons of the Frankfurt University, who were personally interested in the success of Tetzel's mission.[56] At all events he had, it appears, formerly been at feud with Martin Pollich, the first Rector of the University of Wittenberg and a friend of the new learning, whose critical attitude towards the scholastic theology he had resented.[57] He relished still less the anti-scholastic attitude of Luther and his Wittenberg colleagues, and needed no prompting to step into the arena in behalf of Tetzel in 106 theses in refutation of those of Luther.[58] Their Latinity is anything but classic and far from lucid. They bear no trace of original thought and simply reiterate the conventional scholastic teaching on the subject. We miss in them the fertile, inquiring mind which utters itself in Luther's series. Many of them are simply the reproduction of Luther's contentions with the magisterial dictum that so to assert or believe is error, which is qualified on occasion with such epithets as "manifest," "most abominable," "most impious," "pernicious," "insane," "blasphemous." The demonstration of this magisterial dictum is evidently reserved for the disputation itself, for there is little proof adduced in support of the author's assertions. He assumes, in fact, a monopoly of

[55] Enders, i. 170; *cf.* "Werke," i. 532. It was usual enough for a professor to draw up the theses on which a candidate for a degree was to dispute, and Wimpina's authorship is no proof of Tetzel's ignorance of theology, as has been maintained by some Protestant writers.

[56] "Luther," i. 184.

[57] Köstlin, "Luther," i. 81.

[58] The theses were originally not numbered. They are given in this number in vol. i. of "Luther's Opera," ed. 1611, Jena. They are also to be found in Paulus, "Tetzel," 171 f., who reduces them to ninety-five, which he thinks is the correct figure. Also in Köhler, "Luther's Ninety-five Theses" (1903), and "Documente zum Ablassstreit," 128 f. (1902).

knowledge and sapience. Unlike Luther, there is no obscurity or dubiety in either doctrine or practice, nothing really to dispute about, nothing morally or theologically objectionable even in the preaching of the indulgence preachers.

He rejects at the outset Luther's distinction between true repentance and mere penance. He calmly assures us that Christ in calling sinners to repentance instituted the Sacrament of Penance, and did not, as Luther erroneously contends, refer merely to internal repentance involving the lifelong outward mortification of the flesh. Christ thereby, in fact, established confession and satisfaction in the later ecclesiastical, sacramental sense as obligatory practices, and without these internal repentance is of no avail.[59] Satisfaction involves a penalty (*pœna*), or its equivalent, which God accepts as such, and the penalty is imposed by the priest in accordance with his own judgment, or the prescription of canon law, or the divine justice, and is to be rendered in this life or in purgatory. Such satisfaction once made in accordance with priestly imposition, is not as a rule to be repeated or continued throughout life, though the sinner is, theoretically at least, held bound continually to detest the sin from which he has been absolved, and not to be without fear on the score of its forgiveness.[60] Whilst condemning Luther's more spiritual view of repentance as lifelong hatred or sorrow for sin, he is thus fain, in passing, to put in a caveat against the mechanical view of the subject which the indulgence preaching undoubtedly tended to nurture and against which Luther's protest was directed. Luther had admitted the obligation of confession and satisfaction in the Sacrament of Penance, whilst denying the power of Pope or priest to forgive sin and attributing to them only a declaratory power. To this denial Wimpina takes emphatic exception. He categorically asserts the Thomist view of the priestly power to forgive sin, and discards the older view of a merely declaratory power such as Abelard and Lombard had taught long before Luther. Since the sacraments effect

[59] Theses 1-4. [60] *Ibid.*, 5-10.

what they signify and the priest is invested with the power of the keys, the Pope and even the humblest priest can thereby remit the guilt as well as the punishment of sin and not merely declare or warrant its remission.[61]

Moreover, the Pope may by means of indulgences grant remission (*relaxare*) from the punishment of sin after contrition and confession. Whilst the satisfaction in the punitive sense (*pœna vindicativa*) is thus completely remitted, the moral obligation of striving to make satisfaction for sin by good works remains (*pœna curativa*), and the plenary indulgence does not relax this obligation.[62] Whether the indulgence mongers in their eagerness to push the traffic were mindful to emphasise this obligation is a different matter. Luther at all events had discovered in the confessional that the practice of the people did not square with the theory in this respect, and the mere assertion of the theory was not a sufficient answer to his indictment of the questionable moral effects of the traffic.

On the question whether canonical penalties apply to the dead as well as the living, and whether indulgences are valid against the pains of purgatory, Wimpina dogmatises in the most uncompromising style against his opponent. The fact that the Church excommunicates heretics, schismatics, and traitors after their death, and exhumes and burns their remains proves, he avers, beyond question, the applicability of the canon law to the dead.[63] Whilst it certainly proved the barbarous fatuousness of Church practice in this respect, Luther might assuredly be excused for refusing to regard it as conclusive evidence against his proposition to the contrary. In answer to the second question, Wimpina says that those suddenly dying impenitent, or with insufficient penance, are liable to grievous suffering for their sins. Nevertheless, there is no need to despair of them since the least degree of contrition (*minima contritio*) at the point of death suffices for changing the eternal into a temporary punishment. Moreover, since this mutation is quickly attainable by way of a plenary

[61] Theses 19-27. [62] *Ibid.*, 11-15. [63] *Ibid.*, 38-39.

indulgence, how foolishly do they act who dissuade the people from buying an indulgence ticket for use in the case of a sudden death and thus neglect an effective expedient for ensuring against the pains of purgatory and run the risk of being consigned for ever to hell.[64] Against Luther's doubts or denials on the subject [65] he categorically maintains the plenary power of the Pope over purgatory in the remission not merely of penalties imposed by himself, but of all penalties, and the competence of the indulgence preachers to make effective use of it as the Pope's agents.[66] The Pope has not, indeed, the power of the keys in respect of those in purgatory. Nevertheless, he has authority to apply the benefit of a plenary indulgence to them by the method of *suffragium* (*per modum suffragii*). Luther had admitted in his theses that he had this power in the sense of intercession for souls in purgatory. But he had denied that he could make this power effective by way of indulgences. Wimpina, on the contrary, categorically asserts that he can impart this magical effect to a plenary indulgence. Nay, the effect of the purchase of a plenary indulgence on behalf of the dead is instantaneous. It takes effect even before the purchase money clinks in the bottom of the chest, and to call its effect in question, to doubt the instant purification of souls in purgatory by this method is manifest error.[67] Wimpina speaks about purgatory with all the assurance of the man on the spot. So effective is a plenary indulgence that it is not necessary for the purchaser of such an indulgence ticket or "confessional letter" on behalf of friends in this life or souls in purgatory to be in a state of contrition. The mere purchase, apart from the spiritual condition of the purchaser,[68] is sufficient to ensure the desired

[64] Theses 28-37. [65] *Ibid.*, 39 f. [66] *Ibid.*, 45-52.

[67] *Ibid.*, 53-58. Wimpina thus unreservedly adopts the saying attributed to Tetzel. He even heightens the magical effect of buying an indulgence ticket for the dead. Not "as soon as," but even "before" the money clinks at the bottom of the chest the soul flies from purgatory to heaven. That Tetzel actually preached in this sense is certain. See Paulus, "Tetzel," 138 f.

[68] The precautionary expedient of buying a confessional letter conferred the right to absolution for future sins only after confession

spiritual effects! Wimpina even pronounces this questionable assumption to be "a Christian dogma," and magisterially proclaims Luther's denial of it as another of his many errors.

Equally untenable and perverse are Luther's doubts and denials as to the necessity and efficacy of indulgences in the case of the living. In this case confession and contrition are indeed necessary. But every confessed and contrite person who has obtained an indulgence in accordance with the prescribed form is certain of his salvation, and to say that every truly penitent sinner can have plenary and speedy remission from both the guilt and the penalty of sin and participation in all spiritual benefits, without indulgences, is erroneous.[69] Luther had emphasised the moral and religious value of works of charity and mercy compared with mere indulgences. Works of charity, retorts Wimpina, are of more value from the point of view of earning merit. But indulgences are more effective in respect of achieving the speedy satisfaction for sin and the total relaxation of punishment. Whilst giving or lending to the poor may be better from the point of view of augmenting merit, buying an indulgence is preferable from the point of view of satisfaction. It also is a work of mercy and certainly makes a better man if done in a pious spirit. Spiritual alms of this kind are more excellent than material ones, and whoever is in need of this benefit does far better in thinking of his own salvation than in giving to the poor except in a case of extreme necessity.[70] Self first, my neighbour second, is evidently for Wimpina the supreme law in religion.

In regard to the abuses of the system, to say that Leo offers indulgences at a cheaper rate than his predecessors is not a very convincing answer to Luther's charge that the

and contrition, so that ultimately its use was dependent on the spiritual condition of the person later seeking absolution on the strength of the letter. See Paulus, 131 f. But to buy such a letter for future use by oneself or a friend, apart altogether from the religious condition of the person buying it at the time of the transaction, reveals a very gross, matter of fact conception of religion.

[69] Theses 61-67.

[70] *Ibid.*, 71-78.

Pope, albeit unwittingly, is building St Peter's out of the skin and bones of his flock.[71] Nor is it sufficient to say, in reply to the charge that the preaching of the Gospel is sacrificed to the mercenary indulgence preaching, that if on festival days so much time is given to preaching about the saints, it is well to devote an equal or even a larger time to the preaching of indulgences.[72] What Luther has said on the Treasure of the Church (or of merits) is a tissue of error,[73] and his attack on the mercenary spirit of the indulgence preachers is the fruit of malevolence and baseless rumour. The story about violating the mother of God is based on lying hearsay and meant only to excite the hatred of the people against them, though Wimpina gravely assures us, on theological grounds, that an indulgence is capable of absolving even such an enormity. So, too, the repetition in Luther's theses of the popular criticisms of the system is fitted to expose the Pope to contumely, whilst pretending to flatter him, and to foster disturbance among the people.[74]

This, then, is the truth about indulgences which Luther has perverted and which we have deemed it advisable to state in some detail on the principle of hearing the other side. The counter-theses contain indisputable dogma and assume that what the indulgence preachers proclaim on the subject is dogmatically correct. Any attempt to question its correctness is error. Moreover, there is nothing exceptionable in the practice, and Luther, in arraigning it on moral and religious grounds, is guilty of seducing and stirring up the people against the Church. If the didactic professor did not explicitly accuse him of heresy, Tetzel and the preachers made good the omission. They were already denouncing him as a heretic and threatening to burn him within a month.[75] The heresy hunters were, however, somewhat premature. Some of the counter-theses were merely scholastic opinions rigged up as dogmas, and

[71] Thesis 83.
[72] *Ibid.*, 88.
[73] *Ibid.*, 90-94.
[74] *Ibid.*, 97 f.
[75] Enders, i. 155, in omnibus conscionibus me hæreticum clamant; *cf.* i. 169, me promittunt populo certissime comburendum.

such dogmas had many critics among orthodox churchmen. Theologians like Cardinal Cajetan, himself a Dominican, had doubts about the vaunted efficacy of indulgences for souls in purgatory, and expressed themselves strongly on the conduct of the indulgence preachers in passing off their own notions as the teaching of the Church. The theologians of the Sorbonne were very dubious, and in May 1518 denounced the assumption that one could redeem a soul from purgatory by merely purchasing an indulgence ticket as "a false and scandalous proposition." Even the Pope is said by Miltitz to have condemned the ranting of Tetzel on the subject in no measured terms.[76]

III. Luther's Defence

With the Elector's permission Luther had invited Tetzel to come to Wittenberg to discuss the subject with him.[77] Tetzel deemed it advisable not to risk an encounter with the Wittenberg theologian and preferred to defend himself at Frankfurt with the aid of Wimpina. He sent instead a consignment of the counter-theses towards the middle of March 1518. Without Luther's knowledge the students took the opportunity of indulging their frolicsome zeal and at the same time putting a stop to the sale by making a bonfire of the obnoxious prints in the market-place. Luther deplored this youthful escapade, for which he disclaimed all responsibility and which, as he wrote to Lang, would only make the situation more dangerous for him.[78] He adopted the more legitimate expedient of preaching a sermon on the subject in which he criticised the counter-theses and the heads of which he published under the title of "A Sermon on Indulgence and Grace." [79] By this time he

[76] Enders, i. 327; Paulus, "Tetzel," 163-165.

[77] See "Werke," i. 392; Kalkoff, "Entscheidungsjahre," 27.

[78] Enders, i. 170; *cf.* "Werke," i. 277.

[79] "Werke," i. 237 f. Köstlin, in the 3rd edition of his "Life of Luther" (1883), assumed that the sermon was composed at the time he posted up his theses and that he published it in Feb. 1518. "Luther," i. 174, 182. Knaake adopted this conclusion in his preface to the

had reached the conclusion that indulgences were "a mere fooling of souls and of no use to anyone except the sluggards and dullards in the way of Christ." [80] In the sermon he discards the more technical and scholastic method of the ninety-five theses and confines himself to the religious aspect of the question. Whilst he doubts at the outset whether the Sacrament of Penance has any scriptural warrant, he accepts it as an ecclesiastical institution. He is concerned chiefly with Wimpina's argument in favour of indulgence as a means of securing the remission of penitential satisfactions which consist in prayer, fasting, and works of charity. If, he asks, indulgence assures the remission of these things, what remains for the penitent to do in pursuit of the Christian life? That it can take away in addition the punishment of sin demanded by the divine justice, he denies point blank. It can at most only remit the penalties imposed by the priest. For the forgiveness of sin God requires nothing but true repentance, which will rather seek to bear the Cross of Christ and give proof of its sincerity in good works, not strive to evade the moral discipline to which God by this means subjects the soul. This discipline is in God's hands and no one has any power to dispense from it. The distinction between punitive and curative satisfactions is a mere scholastic invention in order to find room for a system which is incompatible with the divine discipline of the soul and only leads to the neglect of this discipline. It is, moreover, fundamentally wrong to strive to make satisfaction for sin. God forgives freely out of His immeasurable grace and requires nothing in return for this grace except a life of well-doing. It is only the lazy and indifferent Christian that seeks indulgence which makes no one better, but leaves him in his imperfect condition. Money spent on such an object is money misspent. The whole principle of the system

sermon in Luther's "Werke," i. Brieger has, however, shown that the sermon was written after the publication of Wimpina's counter-theses. It contains evident references to these and is undoubtedly a reply to them. "Z.K.G.," xi. 112 f.

[80] Enders, i. 155.

is bad from the religious point of view. Its motive is mercenary and selfish. There are other and better ways of spending money for religious objects, such as the care of the poor and the legitimate schemes of the Church, without thereby seeking to purchase spiritual benefits for oneself which money can in no sense secure. An indulgence is one of the usages which are not obligatory, and though he would not prevent anyone from making use of this ecclesiastical expedient, he would exhort all Christians rather to exercise themselves in good works and freely submit to the discipline of suffering. Further, all this dogmatising about purgatory rests on mere scholastic opinion in which he has no faith and which the Church has not decided. The only way to benefit the dead is to pray for them. In conclusion he is not much moved by the bluster of the indulgence preachers whose money chests have felt the ill effects of his teaching and who accordingly denounce him as a heretic. These "dark heads" have no real knowledge of the Scriptures or the best Christian teachers and do not understand even their own teachers. Otherwise they would have learned not to calumniate an opponent unheard and unrefuted.

Tetzel himself took up the attack in a "Vorlegung" against the "audacious" sermon (April 1518). Luther's twenty heads are so many errors. His teaching is contrary to the Council of Constance and is in part a repetition of the heresies of Wiclif and Hess. Against these errors he sets forth the High Church view of the papal power in the matter of indulgences and accuses Luther of an artful design to undermine the papal authority and that of the Roman Church, which cannot err in matters of faith. He expands the contentions of Wimpina and defends the scholastic doctors against his aspersions. The sermon is full of poison and he augurs the worst of this poisonous teaching. "For many will be led to despise the supremacy and power of the Pope and the Holy Roman See. Works of sacramental satisfaction will be neglected. Preachers and doctors will no longer be believed. Every one will interpret the Holy Scripture according to his good pleasure. The whole of Christendom will necessarily be greatly endangered, for each one will come to believe just what he pleases." [81]

Luther resented the cry of heresy on a question of this kind, with which Tetzel sought to intimidate him and thus silence an inconvenient adversary. Criticism of an ecclesiastical usage which had become a glaring abuse was not necessarily heresy and he was determined to maintain the right of criticism. He gave his reasons for exercising this freedom in a tract entitled "Eine Freiheit des Sermons" (Freedom of Preaching) which he published in June 1518. He betrays his irritation in the invective in which he trounces his opponent. The master of the popular diatribe is already in evidence. The style cannot certainly be called academic. Unlike the theses, the tract was meant for the people and it shows that Luther could play the part of the popular publicist as well as the profound theologian. In this effusion we have a foretaste of the rough sarcasm in dealing with opponents which was to prove far more potent in effecting a reformation than the academic tilting by way of thesis and counter-thesis. Tetzel has denounced him as a heretic and threatened to burn him. Luther tells him that he might do better to make use of his fire to roast his geese with. On the question at issue he confronts his opponent with the testimony of Scripture and reason which Tetzel has handled as the sow does a bag of oats. The Scriptures are the grand test of faith and usages, and he pours out his scorn on the method of reading into them what is not there and twisting them into warranting one's own crude notions. By this method they cook a mess the sight of which fills one with disgust. No one has a right to distort Christ's teaching in this arbitrary fashion. Tetzel only shows his crass ignorance in discovering in this teaching the Sacrament of Penance and the indulgence system. The Pope does not possess the power, which he ascribes to him, of playing fast and loose by such an expedient with Christ's command to repent. Nor have his opponents the right to proclaim

[81] Article 19. The "Vorlegung" is given by Löscher, "Reformationsakta," i. 484 f. (1720). In contracted form by Köhler, "Documente," 146 f.; Hergenröther, "Concilien Geschichte," ix. 33 f.

mere scholastic opinions as Scripture truth, since it belongs only to a General Council to interpret Scripture. They only mislead the people with their chatter about the papal power of forgiveness and indulgences in order the better to empty their pockets. He is ready to recognise the usages of the Church, but these usages are not to be confused with the abuses of them. That the Pope allows such abuses is not surprising, since even worse evils are suffered to exist at and out of Rome. To denounce this abuse is not heresy which has to do only with what it is essential to believe, and belief in the indulgence system is not obligatory. All this bluster about heresy and apostasy is merely the braying of a big ass. Whilst emphasising the supreme authority of Scripture as the test of right belief, he is so far unconscious of any divergence from ecclesiastical orthodoxy. All this outcry about danger to the faith is mere bluff. "Tetzel complains," he ironically concludes, "that my sermon will cause great scandal and lead to contempt of the Roman See, the faith, the sacraments, the teachers of Scripture, etc. I cannot otherwise understand all this than that the heavens will immediately fall down and to-morrow not a single pot will remain whole." [82]

Before the publication of this counterblast to the "Vorlegung," Tetzel had returned to the charge in a series of fifty theses in barbarous Latin drawn up by himself about the end of April or the beginning of May 1518,[83] which he proclaimed his intention of defending in the University of Frankfurt. In these he deals with the indulgence

[82] "Werke," i. 393. In a letter to Link, 10th July 1518, Luther tells him about the publication of this tract, which he describes as a trifle and says that he had followed the exhortations of his friends rather than his own inclination in publishing it. Enders, i. 211.

[83] Paulus, "Tetzel," 54. It does not appear that the disputation on these theses took place. Paulus adds that in the course of this year he obtained the degree of doctor of theology either from the University of Frankfurt or from the General of his Order. *Ibid.*, 55. Kalkoff has, however, made it clear that he obtained the degree at the General Chapter of his Order in the summer of 1518 as a reward for his polemic against Luther, "Z.K.G." (1925), 222. The theses are given in Luther's "Omnia Opera," i. 7-9 (1611), and Hergenröther, "Concilien Geschichte," ix. 47 f.

controversy only incidentally and transfers his polemic to the larger question of the papal power. The controversy was, in fact, henceforth overshadowed by this far more fundamental issue, and its importance lies mainly in the fact that it erelong forced Luther to face this issue in further conflict with his opponents. In this respect Wimpina, Tetzel, Eck and others did him an unwitting service. They compelled him to criticise and revise his own conception of the Church and the papal power in the light of Scripture, history, and his own religious experience, with results little dreamt of either by him or them. At this stage, however, he had little fault to find with Tetzel's contentions on these points, except in so far as they contained a renewal of the threats against himself as a heretic and did not spare even the Elector of Saxony as the protector of his heresy. He contented himself, in fact, with a sarcastic allusion to them at the conclusion of his "Freiheit des Sermons," whilst professing his willingness to admit the greater part of them as truth [84] and renewing his invitation to Tetzel to come to Wittenberg under the Elector's safe conduct, with free lodging and board, to discuss the question.

The admission is all the more surprising inasmuch as Tetzel sets forth the papal power without qualification. This power is supreme in the Church and cannot be restricted or amplified by any single individual or by the whole world, but by God alone. The Pope's jurisdiction extends over all in things pertaining to the Christian religion and the Apostolic See. He wields supreme authority over Church and General Council and all are bound to obey his decrees in so far as consonant with divine and natural right. He alone determines the faith. He alone interprets Scripture and approves or condemns the opinions and acts of others. He cannot err in the least degree. In his official capacity he is infallible and every one who questions his authority is guilty of treason and heresy, is excluded from the hope of heaven and merits the penalty of death. The keys of the Church were not given to the Church universal, but to Peter and to the Popes as his successors. The Church possesses the

[84] "Werke," i. 392-393, halt ich das mehrer Theil vor Warheit.

truth without falsity, and its doctrines are to be believed by all even if they are not expressly contained in Scripture or the ancient doctors. All observances decreed by the Apostolic See are also to be esteemed as Catholic truth even if the warrant of Scripture is lacking. Whatever the doctors approved by the Church have taught is similarly to be accepted without such warrant. All who deliberately doubt the faith thus accredited or interpret the Scriptures otherwise, or set forth new and false opinions of their own, or attempt to detract from the privileges of the Roman Church are heretics. To maintain any proposition that tends to produce schism by undermining the authority of prelates, princes, or the papal bulls is to be guilty of sedition. Even to question what the preachers proclaim as Catholic truth is inadmissible, and to refuse to amend error against the counter-assertions, say, of a Tetzel, is heretical contumacy. In other words, if a Luther challenges the teaching and conduct of the indulgence preachers and declines to yield to their superior wisdom, he is to be esteemed *ipso facto* a heretic. Nay, those who protect him (a thrust at the Elector of Saxony) and intervene to prevent his punishment are to be excommunicated, and if they do not make amends within a year, are to be esteemed infamous and subjected to the most severe penalties. He concludes the series with still more ominous threats against Luther himself. "The beast that toucheth the mount shall surely be stoned" (Exodus xix. 13).

Luther did not deem it worth while to continue the controversy with Tetzel, who henceforth recedes into the background. He denounces the theses in a single sarcastic sentence. Tetzel, borrowing from Luther, had prefaced each of his contentions with the clause, "Christians are to be taught." This, retorted Luther, should rather read: "The indulgence mongers (*quæstores*) and the inquisitors of heresy are to be taught." [85]

By this time a more redoubtable antagonist had appeared in Dr John Maier, otherwise known as Dr Eck, the name of his Suabian birthplace, Professor of Theology at Ingolstadt.

[85] "Werke," i. 393.

Eck was a theologian of rising reputation, who had taken his master's degree at Tübingen in 1501 at the age of fifteen. He had continued the study of theology, begun at Tübingen, at Köln and Freiburg, and in his twenty-fourth year attained the theological doctorate (1510). In the same year he was appointed through Pfeffinger's influence to a chair of theology at Ingolstadt and became canon of Eichstädt. He was ambitious as well as able and his resource and ability, coupled with an inordinate self-assurance, had gained him considerable notoriety in academic debate at Bologna and Vienna. He professed humanist sympathies and courted the friendship of Peutinger, Scheurl, and other champions of the new culture. Through Scheurl he had early in 1517 sought that of Luther, and this introduction resulted in a friendly correspondence which led Luther to regard him as a kindred spirit and to speak appreciatively in his letters to Scheurl of his learning and ability.[86] He was, therefore, justifiably surprised on learning in March 1518 that he had without warning attacked his theses in a communication to the Bishop of Eickstädt which, though not printed, was circulated in MS. under the title of "Obelisks."[87] "I should marvel," wrote Luther to Egranus, "did I not know the machinations of Satan, at the fury with which Eck has dissolved a very recent and agreeable friendship without a word of warning or farewell. In these 'Obelisks' he called me a virulent Hussite, a heretic, a seditious, insolent, and rash fellow, and, to omit the lesser contumelies, a despiser

[86] Enders, i. 110. Eccio nostro, eruditissimo et ingeniosissimo viro; *cf. ibid.*, i. 92, 97, 112, 166. For his early life see Wiedemann, "Dr Johann Eck" (1865) and the article "Eck" in Herzog-Hauck, "Encyclopädie für Protestantische Theologie," 3rd ed. See also the interesting introduction by Virnich to "Eck's Disputation" at Vienna (1517) and other pieces, "Corpus Catholicorum," vi. 13 f. (1923).

[87] Enders, i. 172-173. Literally "little daggers"—the signs to denote questionable statements in ancient writings, used for this purpose by Origen. A copy was sent to Luther by Link. "Werke," i. 281; *cf.* Enders, v. 2. Eck himself entitled his notes on the theses "Adnotationes." But in the text he describes them as "Obelisks," and this was the title under which Luther referred to them. See Greving, "Johannes Eck, Defensio Contra Carolstatini Invectiones," "Corpus Catholicorum," i. 8 (1919).

of the supreme pontiff. Briefly, they contain nothing else than the most offensive calumnies against me and my theses and only reveal the spite and malice of an infuriated mind. I wish, nevertheless, to swallow this stuff worthy of a Cerberus with patience. But my friends have compelled me to reply, though I have done so only privately. . . . The more these zealots rage against me, the more I make headway." [88] Eck in a letter to Carlstadt sought to excuse himself by saying that he had only penned these animadversions "privately" at the request of his bishop and had no idea that they would be circulated. He disclaimed all responsibility for their circulation and declared that he had no intention of hurting Luther.[89] There seems to be no substantial reason for doubting the sincerity of these professions and ascribing his antagonism merely to the craving for notoriety, self-advertisement,[90] which appears to have played a not inconsiderable part in his public activity. In his "Defensio" against Carlstadt he tells us that he had occasion to visit the bishop on some other business, and had taken advantage of the opportunity to discuss the theses at great length and express his dissent from them. At the end of the discussion, the bishop, who apparently did not share his unfavourable impression of them, asked him to submit his animadversions in writing. Hence these notes, or "Obelisks," which were a private communication,[91] but a copy of which was, it seems, sent to Link by the bishop's nephew, Bernhard von Adelmann, Canon of Augsburg, who was Eck's personal enemy.[92] Though a professed humanist, he was at bottom a votary of the scholastic theology, and in attacking the theses he

[88] Enders, i. 172-173.

[89] *Ibid.*, i. 174; Barge, "Karlstadt," i. 125 (1905).

[90] Knaake ("Werke," i. 278) suspects him of insincerity in these professions and thinks that he himself circulated these notes in his desire for notoriety. See also Hausrath, "Luther's Leben," i. 196. Greving has, however, made out a strong case in favour of his honesty in this matter, "Corpus Catholicorum," i. 9-10. See, however, Kalkoff's criticism in "Z.K.G." (1925), 220-222.

[91] "Corpus Catholicorum," i. 36-37.

[92] Greving, "Corpus Catholicorum," i. 10.

seems to have been giving expression to the conservative, reactionary tendency which accorded with his real theological standpoint. At all events, Luther was convinced, as he wrote to Staupitz, that he had incurred the hostility of Eck and other blind followers of the schoolmen simply because he preferred the Bible and the Fathers to the scholastic theologians and followed the apostolic injunction to prove all things.[93]

Eck's critical notes were hastily written and repeat for the most part the objections and accusations with which we are already familiar. He views the subject from the traditional standpoint and draws his arguments from the scholastic theology. Luther, on the other hand, he contends, has drunk at the poisonous fountain of Bohemian heresy, has undermined the Sacrament of Penance and the papal power, and his teaching will tend to beget tumult, sedition, and schism in the Church.[94] The blunt and acrid style in which those criticisms were couched and the offensive epithets liberally interspersed amply bear out Luther's description of the virulent character of the attack in his letter to Egranus. His reply took the form of a detailed commentary which he entitled "Asterisks" (signs also used by Origen to denote explanatory passages). He emphatically rebuts the imputation of Hussite heresy. He reminds Eck that it had been falsely said by the enemies of Christ that He was possessed by a demon, and accuses him of downright mendacity. If to dispute on matters of opinion is poisonous heresy, then Eck, with his predilection for disputation, has been infecting a number of the universities with this kind of poison and is, on this assumption, the

[93] Enders, i. 176, iidem de scholasticis doctoribus mihi conflant odium, quia enim illis præfero ecclesiasticos et Bibliam, pæne insaniunt præ fervore zeli sui. Ego scholasticos cum judicio, non clausis oculis (illorum more) lego. Sic præcepit Apostolus omnia probate.

[94] Luther's "Werke," i. 303; *cf.* 285, 296, 305. They are also given in "Opera Latina Var," i. 410. The "Asterisks," along with the "Obelisks," were first published in the 1545 edition of Luther's Latin works. For a critical examination of the text by Pietsch see "Werke," ix. 770 f.; *cf.* Greving, "Corpus Catholicorum," i. 8-9.

most pestilential heretic in the Church.[95] He belongs to that class of people who raise the cry of sedition and schism whenever one arraigns the abuses in the Church and thereby menaces their tyranny over the Christian people. Are not the papal decrees and the books of the schoolmen full of denunciations of all sorts of abuses? If these have not caused seditions and schisms, is it a fair criticism to say that his arraignment of only one abuse will produce these tragedies? [96] Eck regards the denial of the priestly power of remitting sin as derogatory to the Sacrament of Penance, since the sacraments effect what they signify. Luther meets this by insisting that personal faith is essential to the efficacy of the sacraments, since it is not the sacrament, but the faith of the sacrament that justifies, brings the remission of sin. Paul and all the Fathers teach this, and to teach otherwise is to render the sacramental system entirely inefficacious.[97] Not he, but Eck and other flatterers of the Pope, who ascribe to him their own falsehoods, are subverters of the papal authority. The Pope, who is but a man, may be deceived by their specious chatter. But God is the truth and cannot be deceived. For his part he will not be browbeaten by such adulation of the Pope or mere appeals to the schoolmen. If Eck wishes to convince and conquer, let him adduce solid reasons from the Scriptures and the Fathers. "If Christ and His Word are with me, I will not fear what the whole world may do to me." [98]

He evidently writes in a state of extreme irritation and pays Eck back in his own coin in the matter of opprobrious epithets. In his eyes he has proved a treacherous friend, who in spite of his specious association with the party of enlightenment, has joined in the hue and cry of the obscurantist heresy hunters and has adopted towards him the same tactics as the obscurantists had done in the case of Reuchlin.[99] To be called a Hussite was in those days the last word in theological calumny. This was very

[95] "Werke," i. 303.
[96] *Ibid.*, i. 297.
[97] *Ibid.*, i. 286.
[98] *Ibid.*, i. 306.
[99] *Ibid.*, i. 302. Per omnia mihi facit Eckius secut Johanni Reuchlin fecit ille suus Satan.

provoking, and in his irritation Luther overwhelms him with contempt as well as sarcasm. He calls him a sophist, a heretic, an ignoramus, etc., though in his non-controversial mood he had a high opinion of his learning and his ability.[100] As we learn from a letter to Spalatin in February 1518, he tried to moderate his vehemence in dealing with his opponents, though he found it difficult in the heat of controversy to practise due self-restraint.[1] Apart from these unfortunate personalities into which his irritation and his impulsive temperament betrayed him, the "Asterisks" give a foretaste of the depth of conviction and the stubborn intrepidity which were erelong to manifest and maintain themselves in a far wider area than that of the scholastic tournament.

This encounter did not go farther in the meantime, since neither the "Obelisks" nor the "Asterisks" got the length of the printing press, and Luther was not anxious for its continuance. Carlstadt, who took up the cudgels in his behalf, during his absence at the meeting of his Order at Heidelberg, in a formidable series of theses, did so without his knowledge and against his inclination.[2] In a letter to Eck, 17th May 1518, Luther intimated his readiness to close the controversy, and contented himself with sending the "Asterisks" in MS. to him through Link.[3]

[100] Enders, i. 209.

[1] *Ibid.*, i. 155. Ego multo amplius laboro quomodo me ipsum cohibeam ne illos contemnam, et sic peccem in Christum quam quomodo eos triumphem.

[2] *Ibid.*, i. 209. They were 406 in number. Eck's "Defensio" in reply to them is given by Greving in "Corpus Catholicorum," i.

[3] *Ibid.*, v. 2.

CHAPTER II

THE DEVELOPING SITUATION

I. Roman Intervention

Luther's opponents were not content to urge a paper warfare against him. As we have noted, the Archbishop of Maintz had betimes brought his theses and other writings to the notice of the Pope. In consequence of this communication, Leo, in December 1517, submitted these documents for examination to the General of the Dominican Order, Thomas de Vio, titularly known, from his birthplace Gaeta, as Cardinal Cajetan. Cajetan was a staunch curialist and had distinguished himself in the fifth Lateran Council as the uncompromising champion of the papal power.[1] He was the most capable exponent of the Thomist theology at the papal court,[2] and his theological learning consequently fitted him to give an expert opinion on the question at issue. He responded with a reasoned statement (dated 8th December 1517) of the doctrine of indulgences markedly different in tone from the effusions of Wimpina, Tetzel, and Eck. He contented himself with merely referring to the divergent views on the papal power of indulgence of certain professors of theology [3] without mentioning Luther's name, and refrained from explicitly condemning his teaching. As his statement shows, the subject bristled with objections and he was too conscious of the evil effects of the compromis-

[1] See article "Cajetan" in Herzog-Hauck, "Realencyclopädie," and Lauchert, "Corpus Catholicorum," x. 9 f.

[2] Pastor, viii. 252.

[3] "Opuscula Omnia," i. 129 (1582). De quanam vi quum varias pontificii juris theologiæ professorum opiniones esse animadverterem. Lauchert thinks that Cajetan's tract did not refer to Luther's theses. "Corpus Catholicorum," x. 9 (1925). He does not give any reason for this conclusion.

ing propaganda of the indulgence preachers to raise forthwith the cry of heresy on a question of this kind.[4] The theses evidently furnished, in Cajetan's opinion, no substantial ground for a charge of heresy, and as the result of his report the Pope appears to have taken no immediate action against Luther. Leo was, in fact, not disposed to take the matter very seriously. "A drunken German has written this stuff," he is reported to have remarked. "He will think differently when he is sober." [5]

The incentive to such action came from the German Dominicans who, under the leadership of Dr Rab, the prior of the Leipzig monastery, to which Tetzel belonged, forwarded in January 1518 to Rome a number of charges against the Wittenberg professor. They found a powerful abettor at Rome in their fellow-countryman Nicolas von Schönberg, a member of the Order and secretary of Giulio di Medici, cousin of the Pope and papal vice-chancellor.[6] At his instigation the Pope, on the 3rd February 1518, directed Gabriel della Volta, whom he had designated the successor of Cardinal Aegidius de Viterbo as General of the Augustinian Order,[7] to restrain Luther, either by letter or through suitable intermediaries, from farther propagating his new doctrines.[8] The case, urged the Pope, demanded prompt handling. The fire once kindled might easily become a conflagration if not quickly extinguished. The evil increases daily and hesitation or delay is dangerous. By this time Cajetan had also come to take a more serious

[4] See, for instance, his condemnation of the indulgence preachers in another tract on the subject, 20th Nov. 1519. "Opuscula Omnia," i. 150. Prædicatores ecclesiæ personam agunt dum prædicant Christi et ecclesiæ doctrinam. Dum autem ex proprio sensu aut cupiditate dicunt ea quæ nesciunt non agunt ecclesiæ personam; et ideo non est mirum sit in istiusmodi verbis errant.

[5] "Tischreden," ii. 567.

[6] Kalkoff, "Entscheidungsjahre," 25.

[7] See the letter in which Leo informs him of his decision that he should succeed Aegidius in Walch, xv. 518-521 (23rd Jan. 1518).

[8] Bembi, "Epistolæ Leonis X.," xvi. 18; Kalkoff, "Forschungen," 44. A German trans. of the letter is given in Walch, xv. 521-523. The original has been lost and the version in Bembi's collection has been recast. See Pastor, vii. 362, and viii., Appendix, 22.

view of the case. Among the documents remitted by the Archbishop of Maintz to the Pope were probably the two Disputations on Grace and the Scholastic Theology of 1516 and 1517, in which Luther had boldly controverted the scholastic teaching on these subjects.[9] He had not only criticised the indulgence system. He had attacked the Thomist theology and appealed from Aristotle and the schoolmen to the Bible in support of his teaching on free will, grace, good works, and justification by faith. To Cajetan, the most distinguished exponent of this theology in the sacred college, this attack raised a more vital issue than the polemic against the indulgence system. Here in truth was a fundamental divergence from the teaching of the Church which demanded energetic intervention, and in the actual missive sent by Volta to Staupitz it was apparently mainly on the question of his divergence from the traditional theology that he challenged the Wittenberg professor. That this was the real issue we can discern from the letter which Luther, on the 31st March, wrote in reply to that of Staupitz in forwarding to him Volta's injunction to refrain from farther agitation. From this letter it appears that the missive contained a threefold accusation. He had condemned in his sermons and writings the endless repetition of prayers and psalms (Rosaries, etc.) which to the Dominicans constituted the essence of meritorious devotion, but which he regarded as mere mechanical "works," detrimental to spiritual religion as represented by Tauler and Staupitz himself in his recently published book "On the Love of God." He had farther taught that men should not confide in anything but Jesus Christ alone, not in their own merits and works, since in the words of Paul (Rom. ix. 16) "salvation is not of him that runneth, but of God that hath mercy." From these words they suck the venom which they disseminate against him. He had, in the third place, incurred their fury and their hatred by his preference for the Bible and the Fathers over the scholastic theologians.[10] On these grounds he had acquired an evil reputation in the

[9] See "Luther and the Reformation," i. 274 f.
[10] Enders, i. 175-176.

Dominican Order at least,[11] and nothing less than the renunciation of these detestable opinions will satisfy them and the Pope. With this demand Luther will in no wise comply. He will maintain at all hazards his convictions and defend his right of free discussion. It has happened to him as to St Paul at the hands of those who calumniated the Apostle's teaching. "I have not begun this work, nor will I desert from it because of fame or infamy. I read the scholastic theologians with discrimination and not with closed eyes, as is their habit. Has not the Apostle commanded to prove all things and hold fast to that which is good? I do not reject all these opinions, but neither do I approve all. As is their wont, these clamourers make of the part the whole; out of a spark they make a conflagration, out of a midge an elephant. For these spectres I, as long as God is propitious, care nothing. Words they are and words they will remain. If it has been permissible for Scotus and Biel to dissent from St Thomas, and again for the Thomists to contradict the whole world, so that there are among the scholastic theologians almost as many sects as there are heads, yea as many hairs of each head, why will they not permit to me the same right of free discussion against them as they arrogate against each other? If God is in this enterprise no one will prevent it. If He is quiescent no one will set it in motion. Farewell, and pray for me and the truth of God whatever it may be." [12]

[11] Enders i. 175. Valde credo nomen meum apud multos fœtere.

[12] *Ibid.*, i. 175-176. Kalkoff ("Forschungen," 45 f.; and "Entscheidungsjahre," 29 f.) interprets Luther's letter as a reply to one written to him by Staupitz, who in turn had received a communication from Volta directing him to call his subordinate to account. This interpretation does not rest on any extant letters, but only on the inference of their existence. Boehmer ("Der Junge Luther," 190) pronounces this to be "a mere supposition," whilst not denying the possibility of its correctness. Stracke ("Luther's Grosses Selbstzeugnis, 1545," 30-31 (1926)) comes to the same conclusion and states it more positively, with reasons given. There is, indeed, in Luther's letter to Staupitz no direct mention of these inferred communications. But it is very probable that Volta did carry out the papal instruction and communicated with Staupitz, and equally probable that Staupitz brought this communication to Luther's notice. At the same time, it is only

At the same time, he was prepared to waive farther controversy in deference to the request of his ordinary, the Bishop of Brandenburg, who had also received instructions from Rome to use his authority to prohibit farther discussion.[13] The bishop wisely avoided the peremptory tone of Volta's missive to Staupitz, and his tactful intervention evoked from Luther a very different response. Luther had previously notified him of his intention to publish in self-defence an amplification of his theses (" Resolutions ") which he had prepared for the press,[14] and at the bishop's request, courteously conveyed to him through the Abbot of Lehnin, at once agreed to defer publication. As he wrote to Spalatin, he did so solely in recognition of his considerate treatment at the hands of the bishop who, in asking him to defer farther controversy, expressed himself very freely on the indulgence system.[15]

In thus refusing to surrender his convictions in deference to the behest of his Dominican opponents, Luther was doubtless encouraged by the knowledge that the Elector was resolved to stand between him and his enemies. In case of his refusal to comply with Volta's demand, Staupitz seems to have been directed to bring the matter before the forthcoming chapter of the German Augustinian Order at Heidelberg, which should exact his submission and in case of non-compliance send him to Rome for trial. The indulgence preachers were prophesying that he would be burned within a month and he was warned not to risk the journey to Heidelberg in view of the danger of being

right to say that the interpretation given in the text, following Kalkoff, is based only on this inference. The inference does, however, seem to fit the actual situation. It is most unlikely that Volta paid no heed to the urgent papal instruction of 3rd Feb. 1518. Luther does, in the beginning of his letter to Staupitz, apparently refer to a communication from him (Primum valde credo nomen meum apud multos fœtere). This is not necessarily limited to Germany, as Stracke maintains, but is quite general. The tone of the whole letter shows that he is face to face with the menace of very serious consequences, which he is prepared to brave to the uttermost.

[13] Kalkoff, " Entscheidungsjahre," 32.

[14] Enders, i. 166.

[15] *Ibid.*, i. 178.

arrested on the way thither.[16] Nor were these threats and warnings unfounded. He now knew that, if the Dominican Order had its way, a heretic's doom awaited him if he persisted in maintaining his convictions. But he also knew that he could rely on the Elector to prevent his seizure and deliverance to the tender mercies of the Roman Inquisition. In a letter to Lang (21st March 1518) he announced his determination to undertake the journey which his obedience as a monk required of him. "I shall, notwithstanding, fulfil my duty and proceed on foot. . . . Our prince with a wonderful goodwill and inclination to the solid study of theology has, unasked, energetically taken me and Carlstadt into his protection and will in no way suffer me to be given up to Rome." [17] Frederick the Wise refused to be bribed into compliance by the grant of certain privileges for the castle church at Wittenberg and confessional "faculties" for Spalatin, his chaplain.[18]

The Elector not only gave him a safe conduct and made known his express wish that no attempt should be made to delay or prevent his return. He commended him to the protection of his fellow-Elector of the Palatinate, Ludwig V., with whom he maintained a close friendship, and to his brother the Count Wolfgang, who had recently been a student at Wittenberg.[19] He gave him, besides, letters to several notables, including the Bishop of Würzburg, in order the better to ensure his safety on the way to Heidelberg.[20]

II. The Heidelberg Debate

Thus safeguarded, he set out on the 9th April [21] and continued his journey in a confident and sanguine mood, which is reflected in the letters in which he recorded his experience to Spalatin, the Elector's chaplain and secretary and the influential intermediary between him and his

[16] Enders, i. 169. [17] *Ibid.*, i. 169-170.
[18] *Ibid.*, i. 179-180. [19] *Ibid.*, i. 192. [20] *Ibid.*, i. 186.
[21] Enders, i. 171, supposes that he left Wittenberg on the 11th, Knaake on the 9th April. "Werke," i. 350.

powerful patron. His only complaint is about the fatigue of the journey, which he made on foot as far as Würzburg, and the lack of passing empty waggons. He was accompanied by a young member of his Order, probably Leonhard Beier, with whom, as respondent, he was to dispute a series of theses at the Heidelberg Chapter. The Bishop of Würzburg, Lorenz von Bibra, an enlightened and cultured prelate, gave him a cordial reception and added his safe conduct to that of the Elector. From here he travelled in a waggon with his friend Lang and other members of his Order and sent back the courier, whom the Elector had directed to accompany him, with the request that Spalatin should see that he was suitably rewarded for his faithful service. " For I am poor and ought to be and have little to give him." In the early stage of his journey he had travelled as much as possible incognito in view of the danger in which the accusation of heresy might involve him. At Coburg he was recognised by the local priest, an old Wittenberg student, and treated to a festive meal. His friendly reception at Würzburg and at Heidelberg, which he reached on the 21st April, proved that the Dominican clamour about heresy had so far completely missed fire. At Heidelberg his Vicar-General Staupitz and Link, his former colleague in the Wittenberg monastery, received him as an old friend and refused to gratify the Dominican rivals of the Augustinian Order by treating him as suspect of heresy. The large majority of his brethren adopted the same attitude, whilst Count Wolfgang, as an old Wittenberg student, showed him special honour by inviting him, along with Staupitz and Lang, to a banquet in the magnificent electoral castle overlooking the town and showing him its treasures and its wonderful armoury. He was evidently greatly impressed by the castle and its splendours, and his monastic devotion did not scorn the pleasures of the table. He was already learning to appreciate the human side of life. " We spent a happy time in delightful and joyous conversation, eating and drinking the while." [22] Rather an unpromising prelude to the inquisition with

[22] Enders, i. 192.

which his Dominican opponents had threatened him, and which was to secure either his retraction or his surrender to Rome. There was no inquisition and Luther was called on merely to discuss his characteristic teaching which his Dominican accusers had arraigned in the missive to Staupitz. The question of indulgences was entirely ignored. The discussion only gave him an opportunity of making known his distinctive theology to the members of his Order and others, including members of the Dominican monastery who were present and took part in the debate, and the professors of the Heidelberg Theological Faculty.

It was as the exponent and propagandist of this theology, not as an accused heretic, that he submitted and defended forty theses which he had prepared for discussion. The first twenty-eight deal with purely theological questions; the last dozen with points of the scholastic philosophy as dominated by Aristotle. The debate seems, however, to have been confined to the first series, and in the preface to these he appeals to the authority of "the divine Paul, the most choice instrument and organ of Christ," and to "St Augustine, his most faithful interpreter," as the standard of theological truth. They compress the teaching of his Commentaries on Romans, Galatians, and Hebrews in axiomatic form and assert the doctrine of the nullity of man's works for salvation and the impotence of the will to the good in the most uncompromising terms.[23] His teaching is in this respect ultra-Augustinian. The attempt to fulfil the law, he contends, cannot make a man righteous, for the law only produces the sense of sin. Much less can he attain righteousness by his own natural powers. Thus it follows that his works, however specious and good they outwardly appear in his own eyes, are only sins and cannot become good unless they spring from a right inward disposi-

[23] After finishing the course on Romans he had lectured on Galatians during the winter of 1516-17 (Schubert, "Luther's Vorlesung über den Galaterbrief, 1516-17"; "Einleitung," vi. (1918)), and on Hebrews from Easter 1517 to Easter 1518 (Ficker, "Luther, 1517," 36 (1918). As Ficker has shown, the course on Hebrews shows a certain advance in definiteness in his ideas on grace, faith, the certainty of salvation, etc. *Ibid.*, 14 f., and relative notes containing extracts from this course.

tion which begins in self-distrust, humility, and fear. In other words, his works cannot possibly be good unless he discards human presumption, acknowledges that his every act is worthy of damnation by a just God, and realises his utter dependence on Him for the good. It farther follows that in virtue of this sinful state he possesses free will only in name.[24] The will is free only to do evil. It is indeed possible to conceive of the will as capable of the good.[25] But in the sinful state induced by the fall it cannot but do the evil because it has become the captive and slave of sin. Therefore, when a man does what in him lies he cannot but sin. Nay, in striving to merit God's grace by doing what he can, he only adds sin upon sin and becomes doubly guilty. Even in the state of innocence he was not endowed with the power of active goodness in virtue solely of free will.[26]

Half of the first series of theses thus enforced the pessimistic religious psychology which he had drawn from the Scriptures, the mystics, Augustine, and his own spiritual experience. This psychology was certainly fitted to challenge dissent on rational and ethical grounds and might well lead to fatalist despair or indifference. In the second half he provides the antidote to this pessimism. Here the optimist displaces the pessimist. The Gospel takes the place of the law. "You ask, What then? Shall we give place to ease, because we can do nothing but sin? I answer, By no means. But prostrate yourselves and pray for grace and transfer your hope to Christ in whom is our salvation, our life, our resurrection. For we thus teach and the law so makes sin to be known in order that, having discovered our sin, grace may be sought and obtained."[27] This conviction of sin, of the absolute futility and nullity of human works is the first condition of salvation, which begins in self-despair and the humble and zealous quest of the grace of Christ. In thus humbly seeking does man

[24] Liberum arbitrium post peccatum res est de solo titulo.
[25] In bonum potentia subjectiva.
[26] Theses 1-16.
[27] Demonstration of the sixteenth thesis.

become fitted to find this grace, and thus to preach sin is to preach life, not despair.[28] The sick man only desires medicine when he perceives the existence of his disease, and to tell him of the existence of his disease is only to incite in him the desire to be cured. We must seek and know God not in our own wisdom and good works, but in sufferings, in the Cross (*per passiones et crucem*). In Christ crucified is the true theology and knowledge of God.[29] The scholastic theologians have distorted this knowledge by their exaltation of works and human wisdom above the suffering and foolishness of the Cross. They have ignored the wisdom of God hidden in this foolishness, and have mistaken by this preference the evil for the good and the good for the evil. They are those whom the Apostle calls the enemies of the Cross.[30] This true wisdom we learn from the law which judges and condemns whatever is not in Christ and leads to a true understanding of the theology of the Cross, without which we can only make the worst use of the best things. The wisdom of the law is indeed in itself not evil, nor to be shunned. But it consists not in the self-glory of works, but in destroying our confidence in works and leading us to confide in God, who works in us. It thus kills us in order to make us alive. To be born again we must first die in order to rise to new life in Christ. Righteousness is not acquired by the accumulation of righteous acts, as Aristotle teaches, but is infused by grace and faith. Not that the righteous man does no works. Only his works do not make him righteous in God's sight, but faith infused by God first makes him righteous and produces in him its own works. Justifying righteousness is, therefore, the work of God in us, not our own. It is operated solely through faith in Christ who works in us. The law says, Do this, and nothing is achieved. Grace says, Believe in Him, and all is accomplished. Through faith Christ enters into us, who has fulfilled the law for us and in whom we are also enabled to fulfil it by His inspiration and the

[28] Theses 17-18.
[29] Ergo in Christo crucifixo est vera theologia et cognitio dei.
[30] Theses 19-22.

imitation of His example. With this teaching, he insists in conclusion, the philosophy and ethics of Aristotle are altogether at variance, and in the last dozen theses he adds some arguments in proof of his contention that it is dangerous for anyone to make use of his philosophy unless he has first become a fool in Christ, and declares his preference for Plato and even Parmenides and Anaxagoras.[31]

To Luther these theses are not mere theological propositions, but truths of his own religious experience. They bespeak profound personal conviction and are expressed in very dogmatic language. In his preface he nevertheless proferred them for discussion in a diffident spirit and quoted the text, " Trust not in thine own understanding." According to Bucer, who was present, he spoke with admirable suavity in answering objections and showed the utmost patience in listening to counter-arguments as well as remarkable acuteness, promptness, and knowledge of Scripture.[32] The testimony of Count Wolfgang in a letter to the Elector Frederick is equally emphatic. " He showed himself so skilful a debater that he has gained for your university no little praise and many learned men have complimented him in high terms." [33] The disputation in the hall of the Augustinian monastery seems to have been conducted with good feeling on both sides, and in his report to Spalatin, Luther speaks in very appreciative terms of the self-restraint and courtesy with which the professors of the Heidelberg Theological Faculty, with one exception, parried his arguments. " Although this theology appeared strange to them, they nevertheless skirmished against it

[31] The theses are given in " Werke," i. 330 f.; Stange, " Die Aeltesten Ethischen Disputationen Luthers," 49 f. (1904). Bauer has given a detailed exposition in " Z.K.G.," xxi., " Die Heidelberger Disputation Luther's " (1901)—a careful examination which has, however, been superseded by the publication of Luther's Commentary on Romans and by later Luther research. Köstlin has criticised Bauer's exposition of Luther's teaching on free will in " Z.K.G.," xxi. 577 f. For a criticism of Kalkoff's version of the proceedings at Heidelberg see Stracke, " Luther's Grosses Selbstzeugnis, 1545," 131 f. (1926). See also Hirsch, " Die Heidelberg Disputation," " Z.K.G."

[32] Letter to Beatus Rhenanus in Luther's " Werke," ix. 162.

[33] Walch, xv. 519.

both acutely and finely." [34] The discordant note was struck by the youngest of their colleagues. "If," he burst out, "the peasants were to hear such things, they would certainly pelt you with stones and kill you." This appeal to the peasants as referees on such abstruse reasonings convulsed the whole assembly with laughter. There was, however, an opposition party led by his old teacher, Usingen, who stoutly resisted all his efforts to persuade him to a better opinion both during the disputation and in private intercourse. Luther was equally staunch in resisting counter-arguments in defence of the old theology. "However much," notes Bucer, "the champions of the old theology might ply him with their sophistic arguments, they were unable to move him a finger's breadth from his position." [35] Another old teacher, Trutvetter, though not present, sent him a letter bitterly condemning his views and telling him that he was ignorant of dialectic, not to speak of theology.[36] It appears, farther, that the charges against him contained in Volta's missive to Staupitz were submitted to the assembly, coupled with the demand for his retraction.[37] The majority of the members were, however, too much impressed by his forcible exposition of his evangelical views to play into the hands of his Dominican enemies either by demanding a retraction or by venturing, in the face of the Elector's explicit wish, to deliver him to Rome as suspect of heresy. They seem to have contented themselves with a promise to send to Rome an explanation of his position, which he erelong implemented in the submission of the "Resolutions" on his ninety-five theses against indulgences to the Pope.[38] The tone of his letter to Staupitz clearly shows that if he had failed to gain the assent of the older theologians, he had won the sympathy of the younger members of his Order as well as others who attended the debate. He made, in Bucer, one of these enthusiastic young converts, whose name was to become famous as one of the leading

[34] Enders, i. 192.

[35] "Werke," ix. 162.

[36] Enders, i. 192.

[37] *Ibid.*, i. 212. Literas quas in capitulo coram audiebas.

[38] Kalkoff, "Z.K.G.," xxvii. 322-323.

reformers of Southern Germany. Though a member of the Dominican monastery at Heidelberg, Bucer was already veering, by way of the humanist approach, towards the militant reform party. To Luther he owed the impulse that carried him farther on the way thither. Arrested by the arguments of the brilliant debater, he sought an interview with him and was captivated by the magnet of his personality and genius during the meal which he invited the eager young Dominican to share with him. "Whatever problem I raised," wrote he to Beatus Rhenanus, "he explained most abundantly. He is altogether of one mind with Erasmus, except that in this one thing he excels him, viz., that what Erasmus merely enunciates, he teaches openly and freely. Would that I had time to write you more about him. He has brought to pass that at Wittenberg these trivial authors (the scholastics) are banished to a man and Greek letters, Jerome, Augustine, Paul are publicly expounded."[39] Several other reformers of the future, including Brenz and Billican, who were also present, carried away impressions that were to bear fruit in due season. Luther himself already counted on the support of the young generation. "Though those that have grown old in their bad ways of thinking are difficult to move, the minds of the younger generation are turning away from the narrow ways of the elders and I have every reason to hope that, as Christ, when rejected by the Jews, migrated to the Gentiles, now likewise the youth will transfer itself to the true theology which these old men reject."[40]

There was, indeed, some reason for the hesitation of the votaries of the old ideas to go all the way with him in his reaction towards Paul and Augustine. His evangelical teaching was really incompatible with the teaching and institutions of the Church as well as with the theology of the schools. Trutvetter, with whom he sought an interview at Erfurt on his return journey, evidently perceived the revolutionary drift of the new theology, and turned a deaf ear to his arguments.[41] Luther, in fact, made no secret of his determination to bring about a radical revolution of

[39] "Werke," ix. 162. [40] Enders, i. 193. [41] *Ibid.*, i. 193.

the scholastic theology. "I simply believe," he told him, "that it is impossible to reform the Church unless the canons, decretals, the scholastic theology, philosophy, and logic, as they are now taught, are eradicated and other studies instituted. Clinging to this opinion, I daily pray the Lord that it may forthwith be brought about that we may be recalled to the study of the Bible and the Fathers pure and simple. To you I appear to be no logician. Perhaps neither I am. But this I know, that I fear the logic of no one in defending this opinion."[42] He adds that he had first learned from Trutvetter himself that faith is owed to the canonical books of Scripture only, and to exercise his judgment in regard to all others, as Augustine, Paul, and John teach. "Permit me, therefore, to use the same liberty towards the scholastic theologians as has been permitted to you and all others hitherto. I wish to follow this example if I shall be taught better things through the Scriptures and the Fathers of the Church, whilst following the scholastic theologians as far as they are founded on their teaching. From this conviction I shall not be debarred by your authority, which with me is certainly very weighty, far less by that of others."[43] The old schoolman insisted on relying on the dictates of natural reason as well as the traditional interpretation of Scripture, and Luther carried away the impression that he could neither prove his own doctrine nor confute his. At the same time, his own teaching on the absolute impotence of the will, for instance, was by no means so self-evident as he assumed, nor free from objections from the moral and even the scriptural point of view. Moreover, his exegesis in support of this and other contentions is not always impeccable. He quotes Paul with effect in demonstration of his doctrine of grace, works, and justification. But to the modern reader at least his striving to make the prophets and the other Old Testament writers as well as the Gospels speak in terms of the Pauline-Lutheran theology is not convincing.

The Heidelberg visit evidently inspired him with new courage to face the attacks of his Dominican opponents.

[42] Enders, i. 188. [43] *Ibid.*, i. 190.

The tone of the letters to Spalatin in which he describes the debate is that of one who was learning to have faith in himself and his mission as a reformer. The journey, he tells him, has been of great benefit to him physically. The food and drink had agreed so well with him that he has become stouter and better conditioned.[44] For nearly six months he had kept silent, with the exception of his sermon on "Indulgence and Grace," in spite of the embittered clamour of his Dominican enemies. Once back in Wittenberg he boldly challenged them in a public protest in defence of his right of disputation on the question that had aroused the outcry of heresy against him. Neither the University of Wittenberg nor the civil and ecclesiastical authorities had, he tells them, condemned him for making use of this right—a contention amply justified by the friendly attitude of the Elector and his university colleagues and by the kindly reception accorded him by Staupitz and his brethren at Heidelberg. In his letter to Trutvetter he assures him that the whole university, the Elector, the Bishop of Brandenburg, many other prelates, and ever so many enlightened people are on his side.[45] He, therefore, publicly protests against the gratuitous and ignorant clamour of those who have denounced him as an evildoer and a heretic and begs them either to show him a better way, or subordinate their judgment to that of God and the Church. "I am not," he sharply concludes, "so wickedly infatuated as to set up my own judgment above that of all others, nor so presumptuous as to make God's Word subservient to human fables." [46]

His opponents had threatened him with excommunication or worse. He knew that they were exerting themselves at Rome to put their threat in execution [47] and he determined

[44] Enders, i. 192. [45] *Ibid.*, i. 188.

[46] The protestation was originally written in German and subsequently translated into Latin. The Latin version is given in "Werke," ii. 620, and the editor dates it 1519. Clemen, who gives the original German version, has shown that it belongs to 1518 ("Z.K.G.," xxvi. 246 f.), and Kalkoff demonstrates that it was drawn up immediately after Luther's return from Heidelberg in May 1518 ("Z.K.G.," xxvii., 320 f.).

[47] Enders, i. 199.

to try to counteract their machinations by an appeal to public opinion. Hence the sermon on the validity of excommunication,[48] which he delivered on the 16th May. The communion of the faithful, he contended, is of a twofold character—spiritual and external. The first consists in oneness of faith, hope, charity, the second in participation in the sacraments and usages of the Church. God alone can give or take away this spiritual communion and no creature can deprive another of it. Only through one's sin can one lose it and only God can restore it by reconciling the sinner to Himself. The excommunication of the Church comprehends only the deprivation of external communion by means of the refusal of the sacraments, etc. It does not extend to spiritual communion which remains intact as long as faith, hope, and charity remain in the heart of the believer. In the case of a just excommunication, *i.e.*, of any one in mortal sin, it only signifies that the sinner has by reason of his sin already deprived himself of this spiritual communion and given himself to the devil. Exclusion from the Church does not bring this about, but only presupposes and declares it. Moreover, it is to be applied only for the purpose of correction, salvation, not of perdition.[49] In the case of an unjust excommunication the sentence of the Church has no validity from the spiritual point of view. An excommunication imposed for no real sin, or for what may really be a just action, does not deprive the soul of spiritual communion. To incur such an excommunication is, in fact, the highest merit in the sight of God.[50] Such excommunication is all too common. As practised at the present time, in connection with the indulgence traffic in particular, the system has become a detestable tyranny over the people and whilst inflicting ecclesiastical censure for trifling causes, allows the most horrible and scandalous crimes to go unpunished. Nevertheless, even an unjust excommunication is to be borne patiently, since Christ gave this power to the Church, and we must submit to the abuse, as well as the use of this power, out of reverence

[48] Sermo de virtute excommunicationis.

[49] "Werke," i. 640.

[50] *Ibid.*, i. 642.

for Mother Church. In this we must follow Christ's example, who submitted to the injustice of Caiaphas and Pilate. Nay, we must not seek to evade such suffering, but gladly endure it as part of God's discipline. At the same time, we may not, on account of this suffering or the fear of it, prove untrue to the righteous cause for which we have incurred it, even if it exposes us to death itself.[51] If we are refused the Eucharist, yea if our bones are exhumed and cast into the ditch because of an unjust excommunication, we shall gain the eternal crown as the reward of endurance in a righteous cause. Luther, it is evident, already foresees the papal ban and is prepared to face the ordeal in the firm conviction that if the Pope may kill the body, he cannot kill the spirit or deprive it of its indefeasible right of the crown of life in virtue of its spiritual union with Him, from whom neither Pope nor priest can sever it.[52]

III. Appeal to the Pope

Luther farther attempted to counter the tactics of his opponents at Rome, and at the same time fulfil the undertaking given to the brethren at Heidelberg, by a direct appeal to the Pope. During the winter months he had been working at an elaborate exposition and defence of his ninety-five theses against indulgences. This disquisition he now quickly completed, and on the 30th May he dispatched it in MS. to Staupitz with the request to forward it, along with a letter, to the Pope.[53] In the letter to Staupitz he reminds him of their intercourse years ago in the Wittenberg monastery and speaks of the help he had derived from his fatherly counsel in his spiritual conflict as a young monk. To him he owed the dawn of the insight into the meaning of repentance as a change of heart and mind and

[51] "Werke," i. 643.

[52] The sermon is given in "Werke," i. 634 f. Though preached on the 16th May, it was only printed in Aug. 1518, in consequence of the outcry evoked by an inaccurate version of it circulated in MS. in the form of theses by his enemies. He tells us that he only gives the sense of it as far as he could remember, not the actual words (*sensa non verba*).

[53] Enders, i. 198.

the difference between it and penance or penitential works. This new insight which the study of the Scripture had fully unfolded to him,[54] had ultimately led him to challenge the pernicious teaching of the indulgence preachers and the evils of the indulgence system. As a consequence he has been charged with subverting the papal power, and therefore he has been co npelled to vindicate himself, though he would fain remain in his own obscure corner. Hence this " inept effusion," which he begs him to transmit to the Pope in the hope that it may serve in the place of an advocate against the ceaseless machinations of his enemies. Not that he desires him to share his danger. He has taken this step solely at his own risk. Christ, he is assured, will see whether he has set forth His will or his own, for the mouth of the Pope, like the heart of the king, is in His hands. Wherefore he awaits the Pope's decision speaking as judge from the Roman Seat. " To these threatening friends of mine," as he ironically calls them in conclusion, " I have nothing to respond, except in the words of Reuchlin, ' He who is poor fears nothing, has nothing to lose.' I have nothing and desire nothing. If I have had fame and honour, let him who so wills deprive me of them. One thing remains to me, a weak body overmuch plagued by ceaseless toils. If they deprive me of these by force or cunning, they will perchance make me poorer by the loss of one or two hours of life. Sufficient for me is my sweet Redeemer and Propitiator, my Lord Jesus Christ, to whom I will sing as long as I live. If anyone will not sing with me, what matters it ? Let him howl if he likes by himself." [55]

He begins his letter to the Pope himself with an ironic reference to " certain friends " who have done their best to give a very evil odour to his name in the Curia. They have denounced him as a subverter of the papal authority and the power of the keys, as a heretic, apostate, traitor, and hundreds of other ignominious names. Against this clamour he finds a sure protection in his innocence and in a quiet conscience. There is nothing new in these charges. " These most honour-

[54] See " Luther and the Reformation," i. 125-129.
[55] Enders, i. 196-199.

able and veracious gentlemen" have already distinguished him in his own country with these insignia in order to screen their own evil deeds by vilifying him. With this spirited exordium he proceeds to arraign the indulgence commissaries, the official instructions under which they carry on their mission, and their mercenary and offensive methods in despite of the papal decretals against the indulgence traffic. They have thereby brought the greatest scandal and derision on the ecclesiastical authority, whilst striving to silence those who have opposed their scandalous utterances with threats of fire and the terror of the papal name. They have thus done their best to excite schism and sedition among the people by their tyranny, to the detriment of the priestly authority in the whole of Germany. For this result the blame does not lie with him. He had refrained from appealing to the people against this evil and had, in the first place, brought it to the notice of the ecclesiastical authorities. Failing to secure their intervention, he had resorted to the expedient of a public discussion as the best available method of counteracting their questionable dogmas. This right of discussion he claims on the ground of the papal authority, which entitles him as a doctor of theology to dispute not merely on indulgences, but on incomparably more important theological questions. This expedient he has been impelled to make use of by his opponents, who mix up the fancies of Aristotle with the verities of theology. Hence this conflagration by which they have sought to set the world on fire and which it was far from his intention to instigate. Nay, if he had foreseen this agitation he would have striven to couch his theses in more intelligible language. "What now shall I do? Revoke I cannot." He has, therefore, yielding to the desire of many, determined to send forth these trifles in explication of his theses under the protection of the Pope, so that all who will may perceive how sincerely he cherishes and reverences the ecclesiastical power and the keys and, at the same time, how wickedly and falsely his adversaries have tainted his name with so many opprobrious epithets. In conclusion, he significantly reminds the Pope that he can confidently reckon on the protection of others besides his

Holiness. Had he been such an evildoer as his adversaries seek to make out, it would not have been possible for the illustrious Elector of Saxony, distinguished among all for his love of Catholic and apostolic truth, to suffer such a pest in his university, nor would he have been tolerated by his quick-witted and zealous colleagues. " Wherefore, most blessed Father, I prostrate myself at your feet with all that I am and possess. Make alive, kill, call, recall, approve, condemn, I will acknowledge thy voice as the voice of Christ, presiding and speaking in thee. If I have merited death, I shall not refuse to die. The earth is the Lord's and the fullness thereof." [56]

He had already a week earlier written in a similar strain to the Bishop of Brandenburg, to whom, as his bishop, he was also accountable.[57] In spite of the humble tone of the conclusion of the epistles to the Pope and the bishop, he is not content to stand on the defensive. He carries the war into the camp of his enemies, boldly retorts the charges of sedition and heresy against his opponents. He claims and vindicates in uncompromising fashion the liberty of discussion and teaching which belongs to his office as professor of theology and will not renounce it at the bidding of obscurantist monks. He pits against the heresy hunters the ardent support of his liberal-minded colleagues and makes use of the growing reputation of his university as a centre of light and leading in an age of enlightenment. He reminds the Pope that he can count on the goodwill and protection of a powerful prince of the empire. He reminds him, too, of the scandalous abuses which cast discredit on his régime and have begotten a widespread revulsion from the Church and the Papacy. The dedication to the Pope is at the same time an indictment of these evils and a plain intimation that the moral sense of Christendom, as represented by this intrepid monk, is at last demanding a reckoning.

[56] Enders, i. 200-203. The draft of a letter to the Pope in a milder form has been preserved, and is printed in "Werke," ix. 133-135. Luther appears to have discarded it for the more vigorous statement of his case actually sent.

[57] *Ibid.*, i. 148-151.

This is also the note of the work itself. The " Resolutions " expound and accentuate the characteristic ideas of the ninety-five theses. They mark an advance on the standpoint of the theses in respect particularly of their conception of the priestly power of absolution and the papal authority, and they explicitly enunciate the evangelical doctrine of justification by faith as a fundamental criterion of belief and practice. They thus reveal the growing influence of his personal experience of sin and saving faith, as well as of the controversy with his opponents, in moulding his attitude towards the dogmas and institutions of the Church. Accordingly, whilst recognising the priestly power of absolution, as in the theses, he materially limits it and ascribes the forgiveness of sin to God alone. God, he contends with an evident reference to his own religious experience, first humiliates the sinner, begets in him the consciousness of sin and the fear of the Lord before justifying, forgiving him. Salvation begins in fear, humility, and misery of conscience.[58] This is an indispensable condition of forgiveness. It is here that the priestly function comes in. It is the office of the priest, in view of the humility and contrition of the repentant sinner, to absolve him and thereby impart peace of conscience.[59] It is so far indispensable inasmuch as Christ has invested him with the power of absolution in the declaratory sense, and his function is thus part of the divine ordinance. Luther cannot yet dispense with the priest as the divinely authenticated medium of certifying salvation. Nevertheless, forgiveness does not essentially depend on the priestly power of absolution. It is the function of God alone to forgive. The remission of sin takes place before the remission of the priest.[60] It is the work of God alone and is the result of faith, trust in the Word of Christ. It is not essentially in the power of the priest, but dependent on personal faith in Christ's word of promise given to the

[58] " Werke," i. 540.

[59] *Ibid.*, i. 540.

[60] *Ibid.*, i. 541. Remissio culpæ fiat per infusionem gratiæ ante remissionem sacerdotis.

Church.[61] "You will only have peace of conscience in as far as you believe the word of promise. For Christ is our peace, but only in faith. Because if one does not believe in His Word, one will never have this peace even though absolved a thousand times by the Pope himself and confessing to the whole world." [62] "Peter did not absolve before Christ. He only declared and showed His absolution, and it is only in virtue of the confidence of his faith in the word of promise that the sinner obtains peace and remission with God." [63] "You have peace of conscience not because the Pope gives it, but because you have received it in faith. You only have it in as far as you believe on account of Christ's promise." [64] The whole system of work righteousness founded on the Sacrament of Penance is fundamentally misleading. Salvation is not dependent on penitential satisfactions which only give rise to misery and despair on the score of these works, but on the gratuitous remission due to the mercy of Christ, and begetting trust and joy of heart. The Gospel, the theology of the Cross, in contrast to the scholastic theology, is not a gospel of works, but of the grace of a merciful God in Christ through whom the law has been fulfilled and is to be fulfilled by us, not by working, but by believing, not in offering anything to God, but in receiving all from Christ and participating in His fullness.[65]

Nor does Luther hesitate materially to circumscribe the papal power. He, indeed, cherishes and expresses a deep reverence for the papal authority. Like the temporal authority, it is divinely ordained and we must submit to its exercise even when it is unjust and oppressive, as the history of the Church, past and present, has found by experience of the infinite burdens which it imposes. The Pope possesses the power of the keys and we are not actively to resist the abuse of this power, though we are not bound to approve it.[66] But this does not involve acquiescence

[61] "Werke," i. 541. Non propter ipsum prælatum aut potestatem ejus ullo modo, sed propter verbum Christi qui mentiri non potest dicendo, quodcunque Salveris super terram.

[62] *Ibid.*, i. 541. [63] *Ibid.*, i. 542. [64] *Ibid.*, i. 543.

[65] *Ibid.*, i. 616-617. [66] *Ibid.*, i. 618-619; *cf.* 621.

in the nefarious doings and teachings of the papal agents against which it is the duty of all good Christians to protest and oppose.[67] He sees in Leo X. the best of popes, whose culture and integrity are the admiration of all good men. He seems to have been sincere in his appreciation of the Pope's good qualities, though the expression of his sense of his worth may also have been actuated by the diplomatic motive. But he does not hesitate to tell him in the plainest terms what he thinks of the papal power as represented by a Julius II. and an Alexander VI., or of that veritable Babylon, the Rome of this generation, which is governed by such popes.[68] Nor does he hesitate to circumscribe the power of the keys. He asserts the supremacy of a General Council in the examination of matters of faith and denies to the Pope the right to establish new articles of faith which belongs to it alone.[69] "The Pope is but a man who may err in faith and morals, and the faith of the whole Church would assuredly be involved in danger if whatever seems good to him is to be necessarily believed as truth." [70] Even if the Pope, supported by a great part of the Church, should decide in favour of any view, it is not sin or heresy to hold the contrary, especially in a matter not necessary to salvation, until a General Council has either approved or condemned it.[71] The Pope claims to dispense the superfluous merits of the saints as part of the Treasure of the Church. The saints, as sinful men, boldly retorts Luther, can have no superfluous merits, and to assert that they have is heresy.[72] He questions the assumption that the Pope possesses the power of the two swords—temporal as well as spiritual—and wonders who first invented this figment. He protests emphatically against this assumption of the flatterers of the Pope's power and condemns the monstrous use of force in the suppression of heresy. He does not approve of heretics like the Picards, but he would overcome

[67] "Werke," i. 621. [68] *Ibid.*, i. 573.

[69] *Ibid.*, i. 582-583. Solius papæ non sit novos fidei statuere articulos, sed secundum statutos judicare et rescindere quæstiones fidei. Hic autem erit articulus novus; ideo ad universale concilium pertinebit ejus determinatio.

[70] *Ibid.*, i. 583. [71] *Ibid.*, i. 583. [72] *Ibid.*, i. 606.

them by love, not by force.[73] The Pope is the servant and minister of the keys to Christians (*servus et minister*) and does not possess those terrible powers with which his flatterers seek to terrorise over them.[74] He demands a reformation of the Church, which it is not the office of the Pope and the cardinals alone, but of the whole of Christendom, yea of God only, to effect. How futile any mere ecclesiastical attempt to remedy incontestable abuses has proved, the example of the recent Lateran Council has amply shown.[75] Though the very stones cry aloud for reformation, the efforts of good and learned men here and there are wholly impotent to effect it. It remains only to pray for the Church and tolerate these manifest evils as marks of God's wrath in the hope that He will in his own time send the remedy.[76]

The note of antagonism throughout the "Resolutions" to traditional doctrine and usage is thus very striking. The work is an indictment as well as an apology. Its author has certainly made free use of the right to criticise and dispute which he claims as an accredited teacher of the Church. It bespeaks supreme courage to dedicate such a document to its head, who laid such store on his absolute power as the supreme lord of Christendom.[77] If Leo took the trouble to read it, he would certainly not be disposed to accept the audacious Wittenberg monk's version of what constituted heresy or ecclesiastical allegiance. Luther, however, was not conscious of either heresy or disloyalty. He protested at the outset that he intended neither to assert nor to hold anything that was not in agreement with the Scriptures and the Fathers received by the Roman Church, and hitherto preserved in the papal canons and decrees. He was, moreover, prepared to submit, in the case of any controversial point left undecided by the Scriptures and the Fathers, to the judgment of his ecclesiastical superiors, whilst claiming, in the name of Christian liberty, the right to accept or reject what was merely a scholastic

[73] "Werke," 624-625. [74] *Ibid.*, i. 596. [75] *Ibid.*, i. 627.
[76] *Ibid.*, i. 627-628; *cf.* 573.
[77] Kalkoff, "Entscheidungsjahre," 27.

opinion, even if supported by the authority of Aquinas. Of one thing he is convinced. He was liable to err, but he will not be thought a heretic, however much his opponents decry him as such.[78] What if the ecclesiastical authorities to whom he professed submission judged differently? Would he recognise the validity of their judgment and submit? So far it is Luther *versus* the scholastic theologians and the indulgence preachers, from whom he appeals to the Scriptures and the Fathers. Not he, but they are the real heretics who foist their dogmas on the Scriptures and the Fathers. He forgot that the Church had gone a long way in doctrine and usage beyond his supreme authorities, and he was already discovering that his antagonism to the scholastics had, at the same time, involved him in antagonism to the Pope and the priesthood, though he had not yet clearly apprehended the fact.

[78] "Werke," i. 530. Errare quidem potero, sed hæreticus non ero, quantunlibet premant et tabescant ii qui aliter sentiunt vel cupiunt.

CHAPTER III

THE PAPAL PROSECUTION OF LUTHER

I. The Citation to Rome

MEANWHILE his Dominican opponents had been busy fomenting his prosecution at Rome, and on the failure of the attempt to effect his submission through Staupitz and his brethren in Germany, they succeeded in inducing the Pope formally to institute proceedings against him in the middle of June 1518. To this end they denounced him to the Procurator-fiscal Perusco, whose office it was to take cognisance of such an accusation.[1] At his instance Leo commissioned Hieronymus Ghinucci, Bishop of Ascole and Auditor of the Apostolic Chamber, and Silvestro Mazzolini, named from his birthplace, Prierias, Master of the Sacred Palace, to cite Luther to appear personally at Rome for examination as suspect of heresy and a subverter of the papal power, under certain penalties for refusal.[2]

As Master of the Sacred Palace, Prierias exercised the office of censor of books, and to him was assigned the task of examining Luther's ninety-five theses against indulgences and drawing up a statement in justification of the citation. As a member of the Dominican Order and a staunch adherent of the Thomist theology, his judgment was a foregone conclusion. He was, in fact, an obscurantist of

[1] Ad importunam eorum instantiam, says Luther. "Werke," ii. 30. The procurator had jurisdiction only over the members of the Curia and could only take cognisance of such a case as Luther's by special commission from the Pope. See K. Müller, "Luther's Römischen Prozess," "Z.K.G.," xxiv. 51. The main source of information regarding the initiation at Rome of the process against him are his two appellations and the papal brief to Cajetan in "Werke," ii.

[2] "Werke," ii. 30-31; *cf.* 38 and 23. This procedure was in accordance with canon law. See K. Müller, "Z.K.G.," xxiv. 64-68.

the first water who had distinguished himself by his antagonism to Reuchlin.[3] A hurried examination of the theses which, as he afterwards boasted, he completed in three days, sufficed to convince him that the charges of Luther's opponents were justified and that he was guilty of propagating heretical or false teaching. This examination, to which he gave the title of "A Dialogue against the Presumptuous Conclusions of Martin Luther,"[4] was certainly not couched in a judicial spirit. For Prierias the standard of theological truth is the teaching of Aquinas, and he begs the question by proclaiming, in accordance with the teaching of his master, as a fundamental axiom the absolute and infallible power of the Pope, as incorporating that of the Roman Church, in matters of faith and morals, and, consequently, in respect of the theory and practice of indulgences. In virtue of this absolute power of the Roman Church he has the right to compel by the secular arm all those holding heretical views of the faith and is not bound to persuade the heretic of his errors,[5] or give reasons for his decisions.

[3] Kolde, "Martin Luther," i. 161.

[4] "Dialogus in præsumptuosas M. Lutheri Conclusiones." Prierias published it with a dedication to the Pope immediately after. There is no reason to doubt the identity of the "Dialogue" with the statement drawn up by Prierias in justification of the citation. Köstlin, "Luther," i. 189-191; Kolde, "Luther," i. 161-162; Enders, i. 164-165, assume that it was written earlier (Feb. 1518) and that Prierias had thus already taken sides against Luther and was therefore unfitted to act as judge. This assumption is erroneous. The "Dialogue" was written in June by command of the Pope. The unfitness of Prierias to act as judge does not consist in the fact that he had already taken sides against Luther, but in the manifest partisanship of the document which he composed. Extracts from it are given in Köhler, "Luther's Ninety-five Theses," and in Luther's reply, "Werke," i. It is given *in extenso* in the Erlangen ed. of Luther's works, "Opera Latina Var.," i. 341 f.

[5] Ecclesia Romana quæ in Romano pontifice virtualiter inclusa est, temporalis et spiritualis potestatis apicem in papa tenet et sæculari bracchio (prout jura decernunt) potest eos qui fide primo suscepta deinde male sentiunt, compescere, nec tenetur rationibus certare ad vincendos protervientes. Köhler, "Luther's Ninety-five Theses," 209; *cf.* 205. Unde tibi pro regula observandum est quod ecclesia Romana sicut in dicto, ita et in facto suo non fallitur in fide aut moribus, alioqui a via salutis aberras.

Moreover, he mingled with his reasonings on behalf of this *a priori* dogma gross personal abuse and threats most unbefitting the function of a judicial investigator. As Luther in his reply humorously reminded him, he assumed the right to baptize him with a plethora of opprobrious names.[6] He repeatedly denounces him as a heretic. He describes him as " a leper and a loathsome fellow," " a false libeller and calumniator," and not content with calling him a fool, ends by telling him that he is " a dog and the son of a dog, born to bite and snap at the sky with his doggish mouth."

On the ground of this partisan and atrociously ill-mannered document, Luther was accordingly cited to appear at Rome within sixty days after the receipt of the citation as a heretic and a rebel against the ecclesiastical power, under penalty of excommunication and the consequences therein implied.[7]

The citation, with the "Dialogue," was dispatched to Cardinal Cajetan, then on his way to Germany as papal legate to the Diet of Augsburg, where he arrived on the 7th July. From Augsburg the legate forwarded the documents to Wittenberg,[8] and on the 1st of August they were in Luther's hands.[9] He had been expecting the ultimatum ; had in fact been warned by Count Albert of Mansfeld not to leave Wittenberg, and rumour had it that his enemies were scheming to seize him and " baptize him with death."[10] He had become, he wrote to Link, " like Jeremiah, a man of strife and contention to the whole earth." But his courage only rose with the increasing danger. " The more they threaten, the greater becomes my confidence."[11] " My wife and children," he adds sardonically, " are provided for, my lands and goods are disposed of, my fame and good name are already gone. One thing only remains, a weak and worn body which, if they destroy, they will only make me poorer by an hour or two of life. The soul they cannot deprive me of. With Reuchlin I will sing, ' He

[6] " Werke," i. 685.

[7] The citation is not extant, but it has been reconstructed by K. Müller, " Z.K.G.," xxiv. 59-60.

[8] Kalkoff, " Forschungen zu Luther's Römischen Prozess," 52.

[9] Enders, i. 214. [10] *Ibid.*, i. 211. [11] *Ibid.*, i. 211.

who is poor fears nothing because he has nothing to lose.' I know that, from the beginning, the Word of Christ has been of that character that he who would proclaim it on earth must, like the Apostles, leave and renounce all and hourly expect death. Unless this were so, it would not be the Word of Christ. It is gained by death; it is proclaimed and preserved by dyings, and it will ever be renewed and repaid by death. Pray, therefore, for me that the Lord Jesus may increase and preserve this spirit of his most devoted sinner." [12]

These words were not mere arm-chair rhetoric. For Luther knew that to obey the citation to Rome was to take the road to the stake. At the same time, he was determined not to surrender his cause and his life at the bidding of a vulgar obscurantist like Prierias. He would try at least to make sure of a fair trial at the bar of a less prejudiced tribunal than that of his Dominican enemies. On the day after receiving the citation he addressed a letter to the Elector requesting him to obtain from the Pope the remission of his case to a German tribunal.[13] He wrote at the same time to Spalatin, who was with the Elector at Augsburg, to use his influence with him and his councillors to this end. He immediately set to work on a reply to Prierias,[14] which he finished in two days.[15] In spite of its outrageous style, he put restraint on his pen out of respect for his opponent's age and on the principle of not returning evil for evil.[16] But if studiously courteous, considering the gross insults of his Italian opponent, it is certainly not lacking in spirit and incisive refutation. His courage is all the more remarkable inasmuch as he was faced in the "Dialogue" with an official challenge on the

[12] Enders, i. 211-212.

[13] *Ibid.*, i. 214. Pastor says that he wrote also to the Emperor, vii. 367. But this does not appear from his letter to Spalatin, in which he says that he wrote to the Elector to use his influence with the Emperor.

[14] Ad Dialogum Silvestri Prieratis de potestate Papæ Responsio, "Werke," i. 647 f.

[15] "Werke," i. 686.

[16] *Ibid.*, i. 686; *cf.* 683.

part of the highest ecclesiastical authority, not with a mere academic disputation. None the less he declines to own himself a heretic or accept the deliverance of a high papal dignitary, writing by commission of the Pope, as to what constitutes heresy. If this dignitary swears by Aquinas, Luther does not hesitate to pit against that paragon of orthodoxy the superior authority of Paul and Augustine. He claims anew the right of Christian liberty in discussing and judging not merely the doctrine of indulgences, but the Thomist conception of the Church and the papal power. In the name of this liberty he boldly refuses to accept the opinions of Aquinas, with which his opponent bombards him, without proof based on Scripture, the Fathers, the canons, and reason.[17] He is not a heretic if he merely holds certain opinions provisionally until a General Council shall decide.[18] He objects to have the opinions of Aquinas thrust on him as articles of faith, especially as the Thomists do not agree among themselves and a proposition which is approved in Germany is damned in Italy.[19] For the Thomists a heretic is simply one who differs from them,[20] and therefore Prierias, when argument fails him, has recourse in his fury to the cry of heretic.[21] He is no believer in the blind acceptance of the high doctrines of Aquinas and his disciple, and champions the appeal to reason as well as the Scriptures and the Fathers. Such blind belief is highly detrimental to the Church. To the theology of the schoolmen he opposes the true theology derived from the Scriptures and the Fathers—Paul and Augustine—which under the influence of Aristotle they have corrupted.[22] "The authority of Augustine is greater in the Church than that of Thomas, and Paul especially is my main foundation."[23] He rejects as a Thomist figment the conception of the Church as virtually embodied in the Roman Church and the Pope. Christ alone embodies the universal Church and of this Church a General Council is

[17] "Werke," i. 647. Ideoque meo jure, id est Christiana libertate, te et illum (Aquinas) rejicio et nego.

[18] *Ibid.*, i. 655, 658, 665.

[19] *Ibid.*, i. 658, 674.

[20] *Ibid.*, i. 662.

[21] *Ibid.*, i. 672.

[22] *Ibid.*, i. 677.

[23] *Ibid.*, i. 662.

the sole representative.[24] If the popes alone embody the Church, what crimes must be ascribed to it under popes like Julius II. and Boniface VIII., for instance. Must it not, then, bear the responsibility and the odium of the bloodshed perpetrated by the bellicose Julius and the tyranny of Boniface, of whom it was said that "he entered the Church as a wolf, governed it as a lion, and died like a dog." [25] The Pope as well as a General Council may err, though he professes reverence for both, and in matters of faith is ready to abide by the decision of a Council.[26] Prierias calls the Roman Church the rule of faith. The faith, retorts Luther, derived from the Scriptures, supported by the authority of the Fathers, is the rule of the Roman Church and all Churches, not vice versa, as the flatterers of Rome assert, though he holds that the Roman Church has always maintained the faith and that the faith of all ought to conform to it.[27] He refuses to attribute to the Church and its priesthood powers which belong only to God, such as the forgiveness of sin. the changing of attrition into contrition, etc.[28] In thus exalting the ecclesiastical power, the Thomists have in view not the common good of the Church as a ministry of all, but merely the domination of the few and the servitude of the many.[29] This "imperial" power which the flatterers of the Pope thus confer on him has resulted in the oppression and extortion of Christendom. He excepts Leo personally, of whom he has a high opinion, from this charge. Leo is as a Daniel in Babylon.[30] But he will not be terrified by potfuls of threats and the menacing clash of Prierias's words, "If I am put to death, Christ, my Lord, lives." [31] "You threaten me with maledictions, invectives, censures. What and whereto? Spare your threats, my Father. Christ lives. He not only lives; He also reigns, not only in heaven, but even at Rome, however

[24] "Werke," i. 656. Ergo ecclesiam virtualiter non scio nisi in Christo; representative in Concilio.

[25] *Ibid.*, i. 656-657.

[26] *Ibid.*, i. 656. Nec satis ibi esse credo etiam factum ecclesiæ quia tam papa quam Concilium potest errare.

[27] *Ibid.*, i. 662. [28] *Ibid.*, i. 658-659. [29] *Ibid.*, i. 658.

[30] *Ibid.*, i. 679. [31] *Ibid.*, i. 686.

much she may rage. If I am cursed for the truth, I shall bless the Lord. The censures of the Church will not separate me from the Church if the truth joins me to the Church. I would rather be cursed and excommunicated by you and your like than blessed with you. I have nothing to lose. I am the Lord's. If I perish, I perish to the Lord, that is I am found by Him. Seek, therefore, somebody else whom you may terrify." [32] Finally, he tells him that if he wishes to return to the charge, he had better bring Thomas better armed into the arena lest he should not be received with that restraint which he had exercised towards him in this encounter.

Luther's hope of the intervention of the Emperor to prevent his extradition to Rome was all too sanguine. His Dominican opponents transferred their activity from Rome to Augsburg, where the Diet of the empire had assembled to consider the Pope's demand for a subsidy in prosecution of a war against the Turks. They found in his sermon on "Excommunication" an aggravation of his attack on the papal authority and the pretext for a new accusation of heresy. Luther, it seems, had intended to hold a disputation on the subject, but had waived his intention at the instance of the Bishop of Brandenburg and in deference to the advice of his colleagues.[33] He had, however, expressed himself rather freely on the subject at a supper in the house of Dr Emser, the secretary of Duke George of Saxony, on the occasion of a visit, along with Lang, to Dresden towards the end of July. A Dominican monk played the part of eavesdropper behind the door of the supper room. In the heat of the discussion over Aristotle and Aquinas, indulgences and excommunication, Luther had indis-

[32] "Werke," i. 680. The "Responsio" was printed and published at the end of August. Enders, i. 221. It was forwarded to Prierias who, to his credit, sent in due course a missive couched in an explanatory and even a friendly tone, and dealing only with Luther's personal references to himself. He promised a fuller reply later. This missive Luther sent to the printer in Jan. 1519 with a sarcastic preface (Replica Prieratis Ad Mart. Luther, "Werke," ii. 50 f.), and this finished the controversy beween them as far as Luther was concerned.

[33] Enders, i. 212.

creetly declared that he cared nothing for the papal ban and was prepared to die quietly under this disability.[34] These utterances were duly reported by the eavesdropper to the Dominican heresy hunters who had, it seems, fabricated a series of theses out of the reports of his sermon on "Excommunication," which they passed off as Luther's, to which they added a biting diatribe against the avarice of the Curia, and which they presented to Cajetan as an additional proof of the aggressive audacity of the heretic.[35] This unworthy artifice proved a master stroke in tactics. These bogus theses created a sensation at Augsburg and contributed to discredit Luther in the eyes of many of the members of the Diet, including the Emperor Maximilian. "I cannot express," wrote Spalatin to Luther, "how much harm these theses against excommunication have done you, how much ill will they have kindled against you."[36] They have, he adds, been denounced to Cajetan and his fellow-legate Cardinal Lang, Archbishop of Salzburg, who, he fears, have transmitted them to Rome to his infinite detriment. He therefore (evidently assuming their genuineness) begs him to be more careful of his words in future and not rashly irritate these hornets against him.

Spalatin's estimate of the mischief wrought by this unworthy artifice was no exaggeration. It certainly contributed to dash Luther's hope of the imperial intervention in his favour. At this juncture Maximilian's main preoccupation was to secure the papal support of his project of getting his grandson, Charles of Spain, elected as his successor to the imperial crown, which the Elector of Saxony staunchly opposed. In view of this opposition he was not disposed to join the Elector in any intervention

[34] Enders, i. 224-225, note 8; Kawerau, "Hieronymus Emser," 28 f. (1898); Hausrath, "Luther," i. 220; Herzog-Hauck, "Encyclopädie," art. Emser; Thurnhofer, "Corpus Catholicorum," iv. 11-12.

[35] Enders, i. 224, Luther's letter to Staupitz, 1st Sept. 1518; *cf.* Spalatin's letter to Luther, 5th Sept. *Ibid.*, i. 232-233.

[36] *Ibid.*, i. 232-233. The result of the fabricated theses was that Luther published his sermon on "Excommunication" in self-defence before receiving a request from the Elector, through Spalatin, not to publish. *Ibid.*, i. 220.

on behalf of his protégé and was all the readier to become the tool of Cajetan in his efforts to effect his extradition to Rome. Hence the imperial letter of the 5th of August to the Pope, which was evidently drafted by Cajetan.[37] In this missive the Emperor emphasises Luther's "damnable and heretical notions" on indulgences and excommunication, as exposed by Prierias, and (with a side thrust at the obnoxious Elector) deplores the fact that he pertinaciously adheres to them under the patronage of powerful protectors. The Pope alone can deal effectively with this contentious and sophistical innovator who maintains his pestilential opinions against the teaching of the recognised doctors of the Church. His beatitude is, therefore, requested to enforce the old papal decree against the license of teaching which presumes to pit its own hallucinations and opinionated fancies against the orthodox doctors. Thereafter follows a significant reference to the case of Reuchlin, which, it is implied, is connected with this most dangerous and pernicious discussion on indulgences and the validity of the papal censures. Unless the Pope and the cardinals make use of their authority to repress this licentious spirit, it will not only reduce the unthinking multitude, but will gain the ear and the favour of its rulers (another thrust at the Elector and his councillors). The result will erelong be that every one will prefer his own fancies to the teachings of the best and holiest doctors, with the direst consequences to the papal and ecclesiastical authority. His reverence for this authority has compelled the Emperor to bring this dangerous and captious contention to the Pope's notice, and in conclusion he offers to compel obedience throughout the empire to what he decrees for the praise and honour of God and the salvation of the faithful.[38]

The imperial voice is plainly that of Luther's Dominican opponents, which Cajetan has attuned in befitting official form. The situation thus astutely engineered was now a menacing one. Hitherto the Elector had been the only

[37] Ulmann, "Kaiser Maximilian I.," ii. 728 (1891); Kalkoff, "Z.K.G.," xxv. 278-279.

[38] Luther's "Opera Latina Var.," ii. 349-350 (ed. by Schmidt, 1865). German version in Walch, xv. 534-536.

bulwark of Luther against the machinations of the heresy hunters, who had now enlisted on their side a greater than the Elector in order to deprive him of this bulwark. Thereby Luther's case assumes a new aspect. It is no longer a purely theological or ecclesiastical question. This interminable and scholastic disputation has become a question of state, Luther a pawn in the game of high policy which at the moment centres in the question of the election of a successor to the imperial crown. In this question the Emperor, the Elector, the Pope, and other potentates are deeply concerned, and Luther's fate is indirectly involved in it. In it the Emperor and the Elector are in dire disagreement and this disagreement materially influences the imperial attitude towards the Elector's protégé. Had Frederick been prepared to support the election of the Emperor's grandson, it is a fair conclusion that the imperial missive to the Pope would have been worded very differently. Even so, it was very doubtful whether the imperial profession of zeal for the papal authority expressed the real feeling of the Diet which, in its statement of grievances against the papal régime, gave vent to its resentment in no complimentary terms at the oppressive and corrupt expedients by which the Curia drained the material wealth of Germany Romewards.[39] It was not very likely that its members would be disposed to accept the Pope's henchmen of the Dominican Order, who defended this mercenary régime, as the infallible exponents of theological truth. Moreover, the Elector's political astuteness was more than a match for that of the knightly Emperor, and his sense of justice might be trusted not to abandon Luther to the tender mercies of his enemies without the guarantee of a fair trial. Even in this menacing emergency Luther could, therefore, afford to trust in God in defence of the truth. He had heard through Spalatin of the efforts of Cajetan to prejudice the Emperor and the Elector against him.[40] He is not dismayed by this new

[39] See the statement of grievances in Walch, xv. 530 f.; Pastor, vii. 246 f.

[40] Enders, i. 218. Audivi antem Rev. Card. Cajetanum id potissimum habere mandati a Summo Pontifice ut omni studio mihi Cæsaris et Principum animos faciat adversos. Letter to Spalatin, 21st Aug.

menace. "I am not afraid in the midst of all this," he wrote to Spalatin (21st August). "Even if by their arts and power they succeed in making me odious to all, there is left to me the consciousness that all which I have and of which they seek to deprive me, I assuredly have from God, to whom I willingly and freely offer it. If He takes it away, let it be taken away; if He preserves it, let it be preserved and His holy name be blessed for ever."[41]

At the same time, the ingenuity of his legal colleagues and friends has, he informs him, suggested an expedient for countering the machinations of his enemies. They have advised him to demand a safe conduct from the Elector through his lands before undertaking the journey to Rome, and that the Elector should refuse his request and thus afford him a substantial excuse for declining the citation to Rome. He was all the readier to adopt this clever suggestion inasmuch as he knew beforehand that his request would not be granted.[42]

II. Cajetan and Luther

Meanwhile the imperial missive had produced a deep impression at Rome. It left no room for doubt as to the seriousness of the situation in Germany and the notoriety of Luther's heresy. Moreover, the offer of the imperial co-operation in stamping out the movement encouraged the Curia to take energetic measures to reduce him to submission, or failing this, to execute summary judgment on him as an incorrigible heretic. Hence the resolution to discard the citation for examination to Rome on the ground that he has meanwhile abused the papal goodness and aggravated his previous offence by publishing additional heretical writings.[43] In view of the notoriety of his heresy, thus established,[44] Cajetan is commanded, in a brief dated

[41] Enders, i. 218-219.

[42] *Ibid.*, i. 219. Scio mihi negaturum.

[43] Papal brief to Cajetan in Luther's "Werke," ii. 23.

[44] Quoniam res apud nos tum ex fama tum et facti permanentia notoria et inexcusabilis est.

the 23rd August, without further delay to summon Luther to appear before him, to invoke the aid of the secular arm to compel him to appear, and to retain him in confinement pending further instructions. If Luther comes of his own accord and submits with true penitence for his offence, the legate is empowered to receive him into Holy Mother Church. If he refuses, he is to excommunicate him and his adherents and cut them off from the communion of the faithful by public edict. All ecclesiastics, princes, and other magnates, and all communities and corporations are bound to seize and surrender him and his followers under penalty of excommunication (the Emperor only excepted). If any prince or public body should presume to render him aid or favour, publicly or privately, directly or indirectly, they should incur the penalty of interdict, whilst to all who obeyed the papal mandate a substantial reward was held out at the legate's discretion.[45]

In a letter of the same date to the Elector, the Pope fulminated against Luther, "that son of iniquity who, as if fortified by his protection, obtrudes himself on the Church of God and fears no authority or reproof." Whilst professing to disbelieve in the Elector's complicity, he reminds him that his attitude in this matter is fitted to excite suspicion and misunderstanding. He therefore exhorts him to do his utmost to deliver Luther to Rome for judgment. In so doing he will render an honourable service to the Catholic faith and guard himself from the danger of incurring the guilt of fomenting a most pernicious heresy in the Church of God. With this ill-veiled threat was mingled the problematic assurance that, if Luther shall establish his innocence, he may rely on the papal grace, although he had already declared him to be a wicked and incorrigible heretic.[46] The

[45] "Werke," ii. 22-25; "Opera Latina Var.," ii. 354-358. The authenticity of the papal brief to Cajetan has been called in question by Ranke and others on the ground of its incompatibility with the citation to appear within sixty days at Rome, and Luther himself adopted this attitude. Ulmann ("Deutsche Zeitschrift für Geschichts Wissenschaft," x. 1 f., 1893) and Müller ("Z.K.G.," xxiv. 62 f.) have adduced proofs of its authenticity.

[46] "Opera Latina Var.," ii. 353-354.

Elector certainly had some justification for scepticism on the score of the papal assurance. Still more rabid was the missive, of date the 25th August, addressed by direction of the Pope by the General of the Augustinian Order to Gerhard Hicker, the provincial head of the Order in Saxony. Hicker is enjoined to arrest and detain Luther, chained hand and foot, in custody under penalty of excommunication and interdict against all acting to the contrary and with the offer of ample reward for obedience.[47]

These fulminations are based on " the notoriety " of Luther's heresy as evidenced by certain writings which have recently come under the notice of the Pope.[48] On this ground the Pope has decided to abandon the original plan of citing Luther to Rome for examination and judgment and to institute a new and summary procedure against him. This procedure took no account of the sixty days after receipt of the citation allowed him to appear at Rome and defend himself against the original charge of heresy. As a notorious heretic he was now, in the middle of the interval of sixty days, presented with the ultimatum, usual in case of notoriety, of peremptory submission, with ecclesiastical outlawry as the consequence of refusal to surrender. As K. Müller has shown, this change of procedure was legally justifiable. In a case of notorious heresy the Curia was entitled to cite the delinquent before a tribunal for judgment without the necessity of leading proof of his heresy, though it might hear what he had to say.[49] Even so, this legal right of summary procedure does not appear in accordance with what we should regard as a fair trial. Notoriety might be based on mere rumour or falsified evidence, and in Luther's case it was certainly, in part at least, based on a fabricated series of theses which he justly disowned and which he was denied the right of proving to be false. From the standpoint of strict justice such a summary procedure

[47] This missive was discovered by Kolde at Münich and published in the " Z.K.G.," ii. 472 f. (1878).

[48] " Werke," ii. 23. Nonnullas alias conclusiones ac famosos libellos similiter publicavit. Libelli famosi is the legal phrase for actionable calumny.

[49] " Z.K.G.," xxiv. 63 f.

was a grossly arbitrary and high-handed exercise of absolute power which was concerned not with the question of establishing fact or considering the truth of Luther's views, but with the expediency of seizing and silencing him at all hazards. Notorious heresy was *ipso facto* a crime, just as the confession of Christianity in ancient times was in itself a sufficient reason for proscription and death at the hands of the Roman State.[50] Moreover, this procedure was in the circumstances precipitate and ill-advised. The Pope and his advisers, misled by the imperial missive, wholly misconceived the situation in Germany. The age of the Renaissance was not the age of a Hildebrand. Pope Leo could ill afford to indite such a fulmination breathing the spirit of the absolute lawgiver in matters of conscience and belief, and bristling with threats not only against the heretic, but against all, from the highest to the lowest in the empire, who, if they did not share his views, at least desiderated for him a full and fair hearing before condemnation. The prestige of the Papacy in Germany was not so indefeasible as to risk a recourse to an expedient which might easily exacerbate the widespread resentment against it on national and economic grounds. As an institution, it was doubtless still a force in Christendom. But its influence had been seriously undermined by the demoralisation, the corruption and oppression which had loosened the bond of allegiance between it and the German nation and intensified the critical and even the sceptical spirit, which was by no means confined to the redoubtable monk of Wittenberg. Luther, in fact, was only expressing in his theological and academic fashion what was seething in the minds of many serious-minded people in Germany, as the pamphlet literature of the time abundantly proves.[51] Further, the Emperor, in

[50] K. Müller is concerned merely to establish the legal aspect of the prosecution, and while he exonerates the Curia on the ground of law, he does not give due weight to the objections that the accused person might urge against it on the ground of justice.

[51] For instance, the "Exhortatio" of the Würzburg canon Friedrich Fischer, which circulated in the popular form of a letter from Rome and is mentioned in Luther's letter to Spalatin, 2nd Sept. Enders, i. 227. See also the grievances presented by the clergy of the diocese of Liege

proferring the temporal co-operation in the execution of the papal fiat, was reckoning beyond his capacity. He was but the figurehead of a confederation in which the real power inhered in the territorial princes. Without the co-operation of the princes and the Diet his executive power was practically nil, and as long as one of these princes—and he the most capable and powerful of them—refused to implement the imperial policy, the papal fulmination was so much wasted breath.

The papal missive to the Elector led him to approach Cajetan for the purpose of countering the summary procedure against his protégé. To this end he strove to secure the free and fair hearing which, on receipt of the citation to Rome, Luther had suggested and which he repeated in his subsequent letters to Spalatin.[52] In that of the 2nd September, in reference to the difficulties in which the efforts to protect him had involved the Elector, Luther disclaimed any desire to compromise him as a patron of his views. He only asked that in defending them he might be guaranteed against the violence of his enemies, *i.e.*, summary arrest and condemnation.[53] The Elector found the legate less intransigent than Luther had been led to believe. Cajetan, it seems, was not disposed to give ear indiscriminately to the Tetzel faction,[54] and as the result of the Elector's diplomatic intervention, Spalatin was able to report on the 5th September that there was a good prospect of receiving a fair hearing of Luther's case. "Cardinal Cajetan, unless he deceives the prince and me, is not so prejudiced against you as to endeavour to do you only harm with the Pope and the Diet. For as the result of a lengthy and friendly interview with our most illustrious prince, I have conceived the hope of a much more lenient and tolerable consideration of your case than I had feared would be possible. I have no doubt that with the help of God the prince will succeed in pulling you through

to the Diet at Augsburg. Walch, xv. 566 f. It was wrongly ascribed to the Bishop of Liege; *cf.* Pastor, vii. 247-248.

[52] 21st Aug. and 2nd Sept. Enders, i. 219 and 226.

[53] Enders, i. 226.

[54] "Tetzeliastri," Enders, i. 232.

this crisis. In my judgment you have obtained that your case will be legally examined and adjudicated in a safe place by impartial judges." [55] Accompanying the letter of Spalatin was one from the Elector himself to the same effect.[56]

Spalatin's forecast of a hearing before an impartial tribunal in Germany was too optimistic. The legate, it appears, forthwith rejected this proposal and suggested instead that Luther should appear before him at Augsburg, at the same time expressing his readiness to accord him "a fatherly" hearing with a view to a peaceful settlement of the case.[57] Though the exact understanding was subsequently the subject of dispute, the Elector certainly understood that, while rejecting Luther's proposal of an impartial German tribunal, the legate would grant him a friendly hearing and refrain from attempting to constrain him to abjure his opinions.[58]

Cajetan's conciliatory attitude was not the result merely of the Elector's diplomatic skill or of a revulsion on principle in favour of Luther. It was largely actuated by political considerations connected with the Emperor's plan of securing the election of his grandson as his successor. On the 27th August, Maximilian had succeeded in gaining the support of five of the seven Electors for his project. The two dissentients were the Electors of Saxony and Trier, and the former in particular had stoutly withstood the proposed agreement, whilst supporting on principle the papal demand for a subsidy for the war against the Turks. The imperial policy was by no means agreeable to the Pope, who for political reasons was strongly opposed to the aggrandisement of the young King of Spain, who was also King of Naples and whose election might upset the balance of power to the disadvantage of the secular interest of the

[55] Enders, i. 232.

[56] *Ibid.*, i. 237.

[57] This appears from the Elector's own statement, subsequently made (Kalkoff, "Forschungen zu Luther's Römischen Prozess," 153) and from a letter of Luther to Spalatin on 14th Oct. (Enders, i. 246); *cf.* Luther's statement in the preface to the 1545 ed. of his works, "Documente zu Luther's Entwicklung," 13, and "Opera Latina Var.," i. 17.

[58] Kalkoff, "Forschungen," 154.

Papacy in Italy. Hence the accommodating attitude of the legate in the negotiation with the Elector in behalf of Luther which Spalatin had reported in too optimistic a strain to Wittenberg on the 5th September. He accordingly dispatched a missive to Rome in behalf of this conciliatory policy, along with a report on the Emperor's successful diplomacy in securing the promise of the election of his grandson and the Elector's uncompromising opposition to it.

The report produced a marked effect on the attitude of the Curia towards the Elector and his protégé. The Pope in a consistory on the 3rd September had already resolved to send the Elector the Golden Rose and a grant of indulgence for his church at Wittenberg in the hope of thereby cajoling him into abandoning Luther. He purposed, in fact, to commission the Saxon nobleman, Miltitz, a relative of Schönberg and titular gentleman of the papal chamber, as the bearer of these marks of his special favour.[59] At this juncture the receipt of the communication from Cajetan, relative to the political question, led him to postpone the mission of Miltitz and seek to conciliate the Elector's goodwill by adopting a less drastic attitude towards Luther. He accordingly, on the 11th September, empowered the legate to summon Luther (through the Elector) to appear before him at Augsburg and, having heard and examined his case, to absolve or condemn him as he should deem right, without, however, allowing himself to be drawn into a disputation. Should he find that Luther had fallen into error and was prepared publicly to confess and abjure his errors, he was empowered, after imposing salutary penance, to absolve and rehabilitate him in his reputation and dignities.[60] The brief does not say that, in case of refusal, Luther is to be arrested. To have done so would have nullified Cajetan's assurance of a fatherly hearing which the Elector understood as implying the absence of all constraint. At the same time the brief of 23rd August is assumed to be still in force and is only modified in the meantime in order to enable

[59] Kalkoff, "Forschungen," 56; "Z.K.G.," xxv. 279-281.
[60] Papal brief in Kalkoff, "Forschungen," 57-58.

the legate to give Luther a hearing in accordance with the Elector's request.[61]

On this understanding the Elector directed Luther to appear at Augsburg, and Cajetan, after the close of the Diet on the 23rd September, devoted himself to a study of the controversial questions at issue between him and his opponents in preparation for the forthcoming interview.[62] The Elector, nevertheless, took steps to procure an imperial safe conduct for his protégé.[63] He granted a safe conduct through his own dominions [64] and a letter of recommendation to Cajetan.[65] He sent him twenty gold florins for his journey [66] and directed the University of Wittenberg to write strong testimonies in his behalf to the Pope and to Miltitz.[67] He commissioned his councillors Feilitzsch and Rühel to act as his assessors at Augsburg and instructed him not to venture into the presence of Cajetan before receiving the imperial safe conduct, and in case of necessity to appeal from the cardinal to the Pope.[68] He did not, however, think fit to communicate to him the secret assurance of the cardinal to allow him freely to depart in case even of a refusal to abjure, and Luther set out on his journey to Augsburg, on the 26th September, along with Leonhard Beyer, his companion on the Heidelberg visit,[69] in ignorance of the conditions which the Elector's secret diplomacy had extorted in his behalf. He was, it appears, under the impression that he had been summoned to Augsburg in fulfilment of the papal citation which had reached him on the 7th August. What he had requested and what Spalatin had led him to expect was a hearing before an impartial German tribunal, with full freedom to discuss the questions at issue. What he now received was a

[61] Papal brief in Kalkoff, "Forschungen," 58-59.
[62] *Ibid.*, 59-60.
[63] Enders, i. 269.
[64] "Tischreden," ii. 595.
[65] Enders, i. 269; "Werke," ii. 7.
[66] "Tischreden," ii. 596.
[67] Letters in "Opera Latina Var.," ii. 361 f., 25th Sept. Luther, according to Kalkoff ("Forschungen," 60), took these letters to Augsburg along with other documents which were forwarded by Cajetan to Rome.
[68] "Tischreden," ii. 596; Enders, i. 267.
[69] Enders, i. 241.

summons through the Elector to appear before the legate at Augsburg without being informed of the exact nature of the interview as arranged by his princely patron. At Weimar where, on the 29th September, he preached before the Elector and received the electoral safe conduct and other documents,[70] he does not seem to have been accorded a personal interview with the man who was striving his utmost to protect him and who, in spite of his interest in his famous professor, maintained a studiously aloof attitude towards him personally.

It is not surprising, therefore, that his journey to Augsburg, despite the Elector's patronage, was clouded by forebodings of coming doom which were shared by his brethren. "On the road," he tells us in the "Table Talk," "the thought again and again gripped me, 'Now you must die.' I saw before my eyes the funeral pile and I said often to myself, 'Oh what a disgrace shall I bring on my parents.' And thus the flesh shrank before the ordeal." [71] He reproached himself that he had ventured on the journey before receiving the imperial safe conduct.[72] He was certain that he had not three months to live. His friends on the route strove to dissuade him, and he must at times have been tempted to retrace his steps or seek the problematic refuge which Staupitz had offered him at Salzburg.[73] At Weimar the prior of the Augustinian monastery, where he spent the night, implored him to beware of the trap into which he was walking. "Dear doctor, these Italians are a cunning lot and I fear you will not be able to maintain your case before them. They will burn you at Augsburg." [74] The same experience at Nürnberg. "I have found many here who are faint-hearted in my cause and try to tempt me not to go to Augsburg." [75] The journey was a continuous wrestling with his own fears

[70] Kalkoff, "Forschungen," 64.
[71] "Tischreden," ii. 595.
[72] *Ibid.*, ii. 596.
[73] Enders, i. 234-235.
[74] Myconius, "Geschichte," 28.
[75] Enders, i. 238. Letter to his Wittenberg colleagues, 3rd or 4th Oct.

or those of his friends. But the sense of duty, the conviction that his cause was God's cause steeled him in his resolution to go on even in the face of the martyr's doom. "But yet I stood fast," he wrote, anticipating the famous saying at Worms: "Let the Lord's will be done. Even at Augsburg, yea in the midst of His enemies Jesus Christ rules. Let Christ live, let Martin die and every sinner, as it is written, God will be exalted to my salvation. It is needful that we be rejected either by men or by God. God is true though every man be a liar." [76] "They will begin with the nettles; they will hardly at once resort to the fire," was his reply to the prior at Weimar. "Pray for me, brother, that God whose cause it is, will be gracious to it. If He takes it up it is already won, if not I can do nothing to win it, and the disgrace will be His, not mine." [77] It was in this intrepid spirit that he entered Augsburg on the 7th October, tired and ill though he was as the result of his long and anxious journey on foot.[78]

On the same day he sent Link to announce his arrival to the cardinal, but on the advice of friends refrained from seeking an interview until he had received the imperial safe conduct.[79] Cajetan resented this precaution as a slur on his good faith, and though he did not oppose the application to the imperial officials which the cautious Elector had made in his behalf, he subsequently reproached him with this lack of confidence in his pledged word. The reproach was, however, unmerited, since the precaution was directed not against the cardinal, but against the Emperor, of whose attitude towards Luther the Elector was by no means certain in view of his letter to the Pope of the 5th August.[80] Luther, at all events, was only acting in accordance with the Elector's instructions and the advice of his friends in awaiting this guarantee of his personal safety,

[76] Enders, i. 238. In the "Table Talk" he speaks of the doubts which assailed him as he neared Augsburg, v. 78. Nam dæmon multis cogitationibus et acerrimis me vexabat.

[77] Myconius, "Geschichte," 28-29.

[78] Enders, i. 239.

[79] *Ibid.*, i. 239-240. "Tischreden," v. 79.

[80] See Kalkoff, "Forschungen," 155-156.

which was handed to him on the 11th October. These Augsburg friends warned him, in fact, not to presume too much on the cardinal's clemency, and assured him that he cherished a very bitter spirit against him, however much he might outwardly profess a friendly attitude.[81] They were so doubtful of the issue that they expressed their astonishment at his temerity in venturing to enter Augsburg before first obtaining the safe conduct and merely on the Elector's assurance of the cardinal's goodwill.[82] The interval was, indeed, an anxious one, fear alternating with hope. On the one hand, the absence of the Emperor and Cardinal Lang appeared to some a favourable circumstance. He found a staunch supporter in Conrad Peutinger, the Augsburg patrician and patron of the humanists, who asked him to supper, as well as in other members of the senate of the free imperial city.[83] He was, too, encouraged by the ardent sympathy of the citizens. The poor monk, who had tramped the long, tragic road to what seemed a martyr's doom, suddenly discovered that he had become a popular hero, the cynosure of all eyes. "The city," he wrote to Melanchthon, "is full of the reputation of my name, and all desire to see the man, the Herostratus who has lighted such a conflagration."[84] On the other hand, he divined from a conversation with the Italian Serralonga, whom the cardinal sent to sound him, that he would be denied the right of discussion and would be met with the demand for a revocation in unconditional obedience to the papal will.[85] The Italian tried hard during several visits to induce him beforehand to yield to the demand. "You have only to pronounce the six letters 'Revoco' and the business is finished. The cardinal is very well disposed to you." Luther had been warned against this slippery gentleman and would not be talked over. He replied that he was ready to be taught and if convinced of error would be the first to pronounce judgment on himself. "You will argue the point, then?" queried the Italian cynically, adding that it was quite permissible for the indulgence

[81] Enders, i. 240. [82] *Ibid.*, i. 285. [83] *Ibid.*, i. 240.
[84] *Ibid.*, i. 244. [85] *Ibid.*, i. 240-241; "Tischreden," v. 79.

preachers to make lying statements if it brought good money into the chest.[86] "Think you," he asked during a final visit, "that the Elector of Saxony will take up arms on your behalf?" "I by no means desire this," was the reply. "Where, then, will you find a refuge?" "Under the wide heavens," returned Luther. "If you had the Pope and the cardinals in your power, what would you do?" "Show them all respect and reverence," was the reply.[87] "Thus I hover between hope and fear,"[88] he wrote to Spalatin, and the fear at times overmastered the hope. "For you and the youth whom you teach I stride towards the victim's doom," he wrote to Melanchthon. Nevertheless he was determined not to recant. "I prefer to perish rather than revoke what I have long spoken and become the instrument of destroying this best of works."[89]

It was in this resolute mood that on the 12th October he prostrated himself at the cardinal's feet in accordance with the customary ceremonial.[90] He excused himself for the delay in appearing on account of the safe conduct by saying that he had been warned not to venture out of Wittenberg for fear of the plots of his enemies against his life and had acted in keeping with the instructions of the Elector and the advice of friends. He humbly begged the legate to pardon him if he had said or done anything rashly and expressed his readiness to be taught and guided to a sounder way of thinking.[91] He had come to hear from him and profess the acknowledged truth. So the cardinal subsequently informed the Elector.[92]

His reception was more gracious than he had been led to expect. In accordance with his promise to the Elector, Cajetan adopted a kindly and fatherly tone in the hope of thereby bringing him to acknowledge his errors.[93] He warmly commended his humility and readiness to receive

[86] Enders, i. 240-241.

[87] "Tischreden," ii. 596-597; v. 79. See also Luther's preface to the 1545 ed. of his Latin works, and Stracke's critical examination of the passage. "Luther's grosses Selbstzeugnis," 56 f.

[88] Enders, i. 241. [89] *Ibid.*, i. 245. [90] "Tischreden," v. 79.

[91] Enders, i. 285. [92] *Ibid.*, i. 269.

[93] *Ibid.*, i. 246; *cf.* i. 289; and "Tischreden," v. 79.

instruction.[94] In his eagerness to be conciliatory, he even appeared to be "almost deferential," and Luther was struck by the suavity and friendliness which contrasted so strikingly with the violent spirit of the heresy hunters of his Order, who had pursued him so fiercely.[95] His impression was so far accurate, inasmuch as the cardinal was evidently sincere in his striving to wean him into retraction by gentleness and thus effect a pacific conclusion of the case. He had no desire to make a martyr of him and was genuinely anxious to compose the matter in virtue of the papal authority with which he had been invested.[96] But he could only do so if, in accordance with the papal brief of 11th September, Luther retracted unconditionally. For him instruction meant submission to the papal will without discussion, whereas for Luther it meant conviction as the result of adequate proof of error from Scripture and reason. His opening move was, therefore, perforce of the nature of an ultimatum. He required Luther at the outset (*ante omnia*), in terms of the papal mandate, to take to heart and revoke his errors and to promise to abstain from propagating them in future or disturbing the peace of the Church in any respect.[97] No discussion, he added, was permissible.[98] In reply Luther asked for a copy of the papal mandate—a request with which the cardinal was unable to comply.[99] He next asked that he might be shown wherein he had erred, as he was not conscious of any error.[100] With this request the cardinal complied so far as to point out, still in a fatherly tone, that his views on the Treasure of the Church and the Sacrament of Penance, as expressed in the fifty-eighth and the seventh theses on "Indulgences" and the "Resolutions," were contrary to the received teaching of the Church. The

[94] Enders, i. 285.

[95] Acta Augustana, "Werke," ii. 7.

[96] Enders, i. 269. Omnia componerem sanctissimi Domini nostri Papae Leonis X., autoritate; *cf.* "Acta Augustana," ii. 7.

[97] Acta Augustana, "Werke," ii. 7; *cf.* Enders, i. 285-286 and 269.

[98] Acta Augustana, "Werke," ii. 7; *cf.* Enders, i. 246.

[99] Enders, i. 286.

[100] Acta Aug., "Werke," ii. 7; *cf.* Enders, i. 286.

former was plainly incompatible with the Bull Unigenitus of Clement VI. (1343) which he incorrectly presumed Luther had not consulted. The Bull, he pointed out, explicitly affirmed that Christ by His suffering had acquired for the Church an infinite treasure, to which the Virgin and the saints had added their quota, and which Christ committed to Peter and his successors as keepers of the keys of heaven to be dispensed by them for the benefit of the faithful.[1] He characterised as "a new and erroneous doctrine," Luther's assertion in the explication of his seventh thesis that faith is absolutely necessary to the efficacy of the absolution of sin in the Sacrament of Penance. Such an assumption was contrary to Scripture and the true doctrine of the Church which taught that the grace of the sacrament was independent of the faith of the recipient. To teach otherwise would be to render its efficacy doubtful, since no one could be certain of obtaining grace in virtue of individual faith. He spoke in the confident tone of one to whom this is a self-evident truth and his bland assurance was accentuated by his Italian attendants, who smiled and laughed their approval, thus giving expression in this tactless fashion to their assumption that Luther was utterly vanquished.[2] On these grounds he must, therefore, revoke his views on indulgences and justification by faith without demur.[3] The oracle had spoken and could not be gainsaid.

The cardinal and his Italian claque speedily learned that self-evident truth was not necessarily for Luther synonymous with papal and ecclesiastical belief. For the brother with the deep eyes and wistful gaze, who stood there and asked so humbly to be instructed, had learned by long years of wrestling with the problems of the spirit to probe to the heart of things. For him the search for truth had been the search for a gracious God through an abyss of doubt and fear and despair, not the mere study of old parchments and the acceptance of scholastic dogmas authoritatively interpreted by Popes or papal representatives. Out of this abyss he had painfully emerged with convictions of his own,

[1] See the Bull, known also as the "Extravagans," in Köhler, "Documente zum Ablass-streit," 19.

[2] Enders, i. 286.

[3] Acta Aug., "Werke," ii. 7.

a message and a mission, born of soul-searching religious experience as well as long and toilsome reflection. Though no specialist in the Thomist theology like the cardinal, he had learned from this experience and reflection far more than the scholastic doctors wot of and had fairly earned the right to his convictions. Such a man had assuredly not undertaken the tragic journey to Augsburg merely to be told that he must recant in obedience to the papal fiat, as conveyed by the papal representative. He could, he afterwards wrote in his account of the proceedings, have learned that at Wittenberg without exposing himself to the danger and suffering which the journey had entailed.[4] Nor had he come there to learn the contents of the Bull of Clement VI. with which he was as well acquainted as Cajetan.[5] Above all, he had not come to surrender his doctrine of justification by faith in deference to the cardinal's exposition of the ecclesiastical conception of the inherent efficacy of sacramental grace apart from faith. In singling out this doctrine Cajetan had struck at the core of Luther's religious convictions, and in so doing he had unwittingly defeated his purpose of evading a disputation. For Luther this was a life and death issue. It was no mere speculative opinion or dogmatic generalisation, such as the theory of the Treasure of Merits. It was the great fact of his religious experience, in comparison with which such a theory was of subordinate importance, except in so far as it bore on this superlative issue. This issue Luther could not possibly allow to go by default, and on this issue, in particular, he drew the cardinal in spite of himself into a long debate.

Cajetan was, in fact, too keen a theologian and dialectician and temperamentally too fiery in the face of contradiction to resist the challenge he had himself unwittingly provoked. Despite repeated protestations and demands for revocation, he was drawn ever farther into a wordy and warm dispute with his humble interlocutor. On the question of the Treasure of Merits he contended that the words of the Bull were clear and conclusive.[6] Granting the scholastic assumption on which the theory was based, they certainly were

[4] Acta Aug., "Werke," ii. 7.
[5] *Ibid.*, "Werke," ii. 7.
[6] Enders, i. 269.

precise enough, and Luther's attempt to make out that the Bull could be interpreted in a sense favourable to his view was really without much force.[7] He was more convincing when, eschewing this rather sophistic reasoning, he had recourse to the argument that the doctrine of the Bull, viewed from the scriptural standpoint and not from that of the Thomist theology, was neither clear nor conclusive, and tended rather to distort the sense of Scripture. It was, therefore, for him lacking in authority.[8] The charge of distortion, he sarcastically adds, " mightily distorted " the cardinal,[9] who warmly replied by insisting on the absolute and inerrant power of the Pope, who is superior to a General Council and even to Scripture, and supported his arguments by adducing the repudiation and abrogation of the Council of Basle by the fifth Lateran Council under the present Pope. Even Gerson and his followers, who championed the superiority of a General Council over the Pope in that of Constance, deserved to be included in the condemnation.[10] Luther in reply stoutly denied the absolute supremacy of the Pope and instanced the recent appellation of the University of Paris against this dogma.[11]

On the second point, which was to Luther the crucial one, Cajetan adduced the Thomist view of the inherent efficacy of sacramental grace and maintained that this was also the scriptural view.[12] On this point Luther was adamant. He quoted passage after passage of Scripture in support of his doctrine of justification by faith and challenged his Thomist opponent to disprove them from the same source. Only on this condition would he give up his conviction of the absolute necessity of individual faith. To do so without this warrant would be to deny Christ. He might give way on the question of indulgences. But he would die rather than revoke this fundamental verity.[13]

[7] Acta Aug., " Werke," ii. 12-13; Enders, i. 254-256.
[8] Acta Aug., " Werke," ii. 8; Enders, i. 287.
[9] Enders, i. 287
[10] Acta Aug., " Werke," ii. 8; *cf.* Enders, i. 287-288 and 290.
[11] Acta Aug., " Werke," ii. 8; Enders, i. 290.
[12] Enders, i. 286. [13] *Ibid.*, i. 287.

The long discussion thus ended in a complete impasse, argument being met by each in turn by counter-argument, the cardinal punctuating his with the papal mandate to revoke, until Luther at length put an end to the altercation by asking time to deliberate before giving a final reply.[14]

On the following day (13th October) he was accompanied by Staupitz whom he had summoned to Augsburg, a notary, and four imperial councillors.[15] As the result of a consultation with his advisers he protested in writing that he accepted the teaching of the Holy Roman Church and declared his readiness to renounce anything in his writings contrary to this teaching. At the same time, he had only sought in what he had written to establish the truth and he could not abandon this search, much less make an enforced revocation unheard and unconvinced. He was still unconscious of having affirmed anything contrary to the Scriptures, the Fathers, the papal decrees, or right reason, and believed that his convictions were sound, true, and Catholic. Nevertheless, since as a man he was liable to error, he was ready to submit to the judgment and legitimate determination of Holy Church and all who held a better opinion. He therefore offered wholeheartedly to vindicate on the spot or elsewhere in public discussion his views, with reasons given. If this were denied him, he was prepared to respond in writing to the cardinal's objections to his teaching and to refer this written statement to the judgment and opinion of the Universities of Basle, Freiburg, Louvain, or in the last resort to the University of Paris, the mother and the most authoritative of all learned bodies.[16] This was in effect what he had professed and proposed all along, viz., the arbitration of an impartial tribunal.

Such a proposal the cardinal could not, in view of his instructions, entertain even if he had been disposed to do so. He, therefore, repeated in the kindly tone with which he had opened the interview on the previous day the demand for a retractation and exhorted him to give up this insane

[14] Acta Aug., "Werke," ii. 8.

[15] Enders, i. 291.

[16] Acta Aug., "Werke," ii. 8-9.

plan and not vainly to kick against the pricks.[17] Luther thereupon asked to be allowed to hand in a written statement, adding that they had had enough of mere battling in words on the previous day. At this the cardinal, who could not afford to admit anything of the nature of a disputation, fired up at once. The term " battling " seemed the height of audacity.[18] " My son," he remonstrated, " I have neither crossed words with you nor do I wish to do so. I am prepared in deference to the suggestion of the Elector to hear you paternally and kindly, not disputatiously, to admonish and teach you on behalf of the truth, and even reconcile you with the Pope and the Church." [19] As Luther remained silent, Staupitz intervened to support his request to allow him to submit a written statement, which the cardinal, who was loth to give up the hope of securing a retraction, reluctantly but benevolently conceded.[20]

Accordingly, on the 14th Luther, accompanied on this occasion by Feilitzsch and Rühel, as representatives of the Elector, presented a detailed exposition of the two main questions in dispute.[21] It was certainly not lacking in insistent and plain speaking advocacy of his side of the case. In the plainest terms the high dignitary, who was invested with all the prestige of the papal majesty, was told that Popes might err and had erred, that their decrees were only to be received as far as they were consonant with Scripture, that the Fathers of Basle were right in their contention that a General Council is superior to the Pope, nay, that the opinion of even the individual Christian is to be preferred to a papal decretal if it is supported by adequate authority and reason, that justification by faith in the Lutheran sense is an infallible scriptural verity, as shown by numerous quotations, and that without individual faith the Sacrament of Penance can only involve the recipient in damnation. Moreover, in matters of belief

[17] Enders, i. 270.

[18] *Ibid.*, i. 270, ego audaciam hominis miratus.

[19] *Ibid.*, i. 270; *cf.* 291.

[20] *Ibid.*, i. 292. Luther acknowledges the cardinal's considerate treatment of him.

[21] Enders, i. 246; " Opera Latina Var.," ii. 365-366.

the testimony of the individual conscience as the voice of God is supreme. "In the face of this supreme authority I cannot do otherwise than obey God rather than man. Let therefore your Fatherhood be pleased to intercede for me with our lord, Leo X., that he may not with such inclement rigour be moved against me, and not plunge into darkness a soul seeking only the light of truth and most ready to give up, to change, to revoke all if it can be led to think differently. For I am not so arrogant and desirous of vain glory that I may be ashamed to revoke what I may have erroneously said, yea it will be my greatest joy that truth should be the victor. Only let me not be forced to do violence to my conscience. For without any hesitation I firmly believe this to be enjoined by the Scriptures." [22]

This deliberate statement evoked a heated altercation. According to Luther, the cardinal treated the document with contempt, saying that he would forward it to Rome, repeating the Thomist doctrine on the points at issue, demanding anew his revocation, and threatening him with the penalties of the Church. Again and again Luther vainly attempted to interrupt the objurgatory outburst. At length he too lost his temper and began to shout his counter-arguments until the cardinal terminated the stormy scene by ordering him to leave his presence. "Begone," cried he, "either revoke or come not again into my presence." [23] Luther retired in the conviction that further overtures were hopeless.[24] On reflection, however, Cajetan resolved to make one more effort indirectly to move him to submission. He sent for Staupitz and begged him to persuade him to recant, promising that he should suffer no humiliation in so doing.[25] To this end he prescribed a

[22] Acta Aug., "Werke," ii. 16; Enders, i. 261.

[23] Acta Aug., "Werke," ii. 16; Enders, i. 247, 292; "Tischreden," v. 79-80. In his version of what took place in his letter to the Elector, Cajetan is careful to point out that he agreed to the request to be allowed to present this statement as an act of kindness, not in his judicial capacity, and affirms that he continued to treat Luther in a fatherly fashion, Enders, i. 270. The tone of the letter reflects, however, the irritation of which he says nothing in his account to the Elector.

[24] Acta Aug., "Werke," ii. 16; Enders, i. 292.

[25] Enders, i. 292. Sine ulla nota.

form of revocation, which Staupitz, with whom Link associated himself, presented only to be told that Luther could not revoke against his conscience without express scriptural warrant, which his Vicar-General was unable to adduce.[26] He was, in fact, preparing an appeal from the cardinal to the Pope.[27] Ultimately, in deference to the entreaties of Staupitz and Link, he consented to write a humble and reverential letter (17th October) in which he admitted that in the heat of disputation he had spoken indiscreetly, bitterly, and irreverently of the Pope. For this he begged forgiveness and undertook not to treat further of the subject of indulgences if his opponents were enjoined to do likewise. He would, moreover, revoke at the command and advice of his Vicar-General in as far as conscience would permit, though he could not do so merely on the ground of arguments based on the views of Aquinas, which seemed to him not to rest on a sufficiently firm foundation. He, therefore, begged the cardinal to refer the case to the Pope in order that doubtful points might be determined by the Church, which he was only too eager to hear and to follow.[28] To this communication, which was in effect merely a repetition in very humble terms of what he had said already, he awaited a reply for a couple of days without result. This silence seemed to bode a sinister ending of the case in view of the cardinal's threat to excommunicate him and the rumour that he was meditating the arrest of both Staupitz and himself.[29] Staupitz, in fact, had become very nervous. He had striven to play the part of mediator on Luther's behalf and had brought him as far as it was possible to go towards submission. The situation had become not only compromising, but dangerous for him as well as for Luther. He ran the risk of having at the cardinal's command to compel Luther, in virtue of his vow of obedience, to retract on pain of excommunication. To obviate this contingency he formally absolved him from his vow and along with Link hurriedly set out for Nürnberg without informing the cardinal (16th October).

[26] Enders, i. 293. [27] *Ibid.*, i. 248. [28] *Ibid.*, i. 263-265.
[29] Acta Aug., "Werke," ii. 19; Enders, i. 293.

Thus left alone, Luther on the 18th made a last attempt to conjure an answer to his humble appeal in a letter in which he intimated his intention of doing likewise and of appealing from the Pope ill-informed to the Pope better informed.[30] He waited in vain another couple of days and then on the night of the 20th-21st October slipped out of Augsburg through a postern in the city wall, and rode away with a trusty attendant towards Nürnberg on a horse placed at his disposal by his friend Langenmantel, canon of the cathedral.[31]

III. Significance of the Hearing

He left behind him the Appellation to be handed to the cardinal by his fellow-monk Beyer,[32] who, instead of carrying out this risky commission, begged the notary to affix it to the door of the Augsburg cathedral (22nd October).[33] In this document he justified his attack on the indulgence traffic, objected to the unjust charge of heresy on the ground of the prejudices of his accusers against him, adduced reasons for not appearing at Rome, protested against the oppressive and minatory conduct of the cardinal in refusing him a fair hearing, professed anew his desire for instruction and his readiness submissively to receive it from the Pope, who is assumed to be well disposed towards him, and appealed accordingly.[34] He questions the cardinal's impartiality on the ground that like Tetzel, Prierias, and others, he belonged to the Dominican Order. Cajetan had, however, acted as the commissioned representative of the Pope, whose instructions he was bound to observe, and the charge of bias is from this point of view legally weak. In virtue of this commission he was not at liberty to treat the matter as an open question, whilst he had done his best to implement his promise to the Elector to give him a fatherly hearing, though he had not succeeded in maintaining

[30] Enders, i. 266-268.
[31] "Tischreden," v. 80, 102.
[32] Enders, i. 273.
[33] *Ibid.*, i. 277-278.
[34] See the Appellation in "Werke," ii. 28 f.

his equanimity in the heat of the discussion into which he had allowed himself to be drawn.

In a letter to the Elector (25th October), Cajetan gave vent to his indignation at what he deemed the deception and treachery of Luther and his associates in thus frustrating by their flight his efforts to reach a settlement. The fear of violence at his hands seems, indeed, to have been unfounded. He had promised the Elector to hear and treat Luther in a fatherly fashion and allow him to depart in safety. There is no reason to believe that he contemplated his seizure, even if he persisted in his refusal to recant, though the papal chancellor had empowered him in a missive of the 7th October to take what measures he deemed expedient.[35] Not only had he to reckon with his promise to the Elector. Any attempt to arrest one under the protection of the imperial safe conduct, as well as that of the Elector, merely for attacking what was incontestably an intolerable abuse would, in the state of public opinion, have been the height of rashness. Moreover, in view of the political situation, it was imperative to respect the wishes of the Elector who was determined that Luther should have a fair and unconstrained hearing before being condemned. Such a hearing the cardinal professed that he had conceded. He had in truth done his best to implement his promise, and Luther's fear of violence at his hands at anyrate, though natural, was unfounded. But his insistence on revocation in virtue of his instructions, and his rigid Thomist orthodoxy, made it difficult, if not impossible, for him to understand or appreciate a standpoint so radically different from his own, whilst his choleric temperament, which bore contradiction hardly, and led him at last to threaten pains and penalties, tended to frustrate his purpose of bringing about an amicable settlement.

At the best this hope was exceedingly problematic in the case of a man of Luther's calibre. The humble monk who stood there in the character of an accused heretic was the prophet of a new age in religion. What he stood for was nothing less than the indefeasible right of individual

[35] Kalkoff, "Forschungen," 61.

liberty of thought and conscience against the mediæval principle of unquestioning obedience to established, corporate authority. He did not, it is true, realise all that this right involved and still professed his willingness to submit to the judgment and determination of the Church, as distinct from the Roman Church, *i.e.*, the Roman Curia,[36] or accept the arbitration of an impartial tribunal. His plea is for freedom to investigate the truth untrammelled by traditional theological opinion, to follow the light of Scripture and reason in the search for truth, and to hold fast to his convictions as a sacred obligation which he owes to God and his conscience. What he really stood for was the divine right of the individual reason and conscience against external authority, whether ecclesiastical or academic. Subject to this indispensable condition, he was willing to yield to what he called a better opinion. But while admitting the possibility of a better opinion, it is evident that, in regard to his fundamental doctrine of justification by faith, he was not prepared to give way to any conclusion that militated against his conviction that the just shall live by faith and faith alone. This conviction was to him the very ark of the covenant of his religious experience, the *sine quâ non* of his salvation The question of indulgences might be debatable, though he holds strong opinions on the subject.[37] On the question of faith there could be no yielding. " Although on this point I deferred to the judgment of the Pope, you may not nevertheless conclude that I did so because I had any doubt concerning the thing itself, or that I shall ever change my conviction. Divine truth is the lord even of the Pope.[38] I await not the judg-

[36] Acta Aug., " Werke," ii. 17. Nec tamen hanc violentiam ejus ægre tuli, sciens eam facultatem interpretandi ex longa Romanæ Curiæ consuetudine et scholasticorum distinctorum usu sibi præsumptam. Creditum est enim jam diu quod quicquid Romana Ecclesia dixerit, damnarit, voluerit, id mox omnibus dicendum, damnandum, volendum esse, nec aliam reddi rationem oportere quam quia sic sedes apostolica et Romana Ecclesia sentit.

[37] Hausrath entirely misses the point when he says that to Luther the main thing was the question of indulgences. " Luther," i. 265.

[38] Veritas divina est etiam domina papæ. Acta Aug., " Werke," ii. 18.

ment of men when I have already recognised the judgment of God. . . . On this point depends the whole *summa* of salvation. You are not a bad Christian whether you acknowledge or ignore the Bull Unigenitus. But you are indeed a heretic if you refuse faith in the word of Christ." [39]

Cajetan quite correctly pointed out to the Elector that though Luther professed that he had only set forth in his theses his views as matters for disputation, he had in his subsequent writings again and again asserted these views as indisputable and irrevocable truths.[40] These assertions were, he held, partly against the doctrine of the Apostolic See, partly open to condemnation (from the ecclesiastical point of view). Here also he spoke truly. And for him, as the representative of the papal authority and the champion of ecclesiastical orthodoxy, the only alternative was to denounce him to the Pope as a traitor and deceiver and to demand that the Elector should send him to Rome for judgment, or banish him from his dominions and not further incur the slur of protecting a rebel against the Roman Church and thus stain the ancient glory of his house.[41]

Luther's attempt, in his refutation [42] of the cardinal's letter to the Elector, to invalidate this contention is by no means convincing. He had, he said, been cited only on the ground of his theses, which he had undoubtedly intended as the subject of a disputation, not of his other writings. He either did not know or ignored the fact that these writings had been submitted to the papal commission and that the Pope had taken cognisance of them in his brief to Cajetan on the 23rd August. In these he had undoubtedly advanced his views not merely in a disputatious, but in an assertive style, and had questioned the papal authority in no very deferential tone. The fact was that behind the mere question of indulgences was the all-compelling power of religious conviction which no argument could shake. In this, and not in mere disputatious stubbornness, lay the real secret of the refusal to recant. It was this that constituted the

[39] Acta Aug., "Werke," ii. 17-18.
[40] Enders, i. 271.
[41] *Ibid.*, i. 271-272.
[42] *Ibid.*, i. 293 f.

real strength of his position. But just herein lay its essential weakness in the eyes of his opponent. The Papacy embodied the principle of absolute authority over mind and conscience against the claims of the individual, on which Luther took his stand as the very rock on which to build his salvation. These claims the Papacy could not afford to admit without the surrender of itself, and this was the sacrifice which Luther in the name of Scripture, conscience, and reason demanded that it should make. Here at last was the ominous challenge which a long series of Reformers, from Marsiglio of Padua and William of Occam onwards had made, and which the Papacy had hitherto succeeded in frustrating or evading. Here, too, was the equally ominous revival of the old contention championed by the Fathers of Constance and Basle, whom Luther quotes, and surviving to his own time, on behalf of the errancy of the Popes and the superiority of a General Council. "Even Peter erred, yea after receiving the Holy Spirit, and even a cardinal can err, however learned."[43] The challenge and the claim were now voiced by this brave and bold monk who, in the strength of an adamant faith, refused to utter the six letters *Revoco*[44] at the bidding of the cardinal as the representative of absolute authority. Herein lies the significance of the encounter at Augsburg between this representative and his indomitable interlocutor.

It was a case of moral force and religious conviction incorporated in an inflexible soul, defying an absolutism that has become a byword for scandalous corruption and nevertheless claims to be the unerring arbiter of religion and morality. At last the man enters the arena with the strength of will and conviction to challenge this system in the name of individual liberty and in allegiance to what he deems the truth. "I see," wrote he to Langenmantel in reference to the cardinal's letter to the Elector, "that the Romanists persist in their purpose of damning me. But I have steeled myself in my purpose not to yield. And thus I await their condemnation. The Lord will be to me a counsellor and a helper."[45] "For long they have molested

[43] Enders, i. 297. [44] *Ibid.*, i. 296. [45] *Ibid.*, i. 306.

John Reuchlin, and me they now molest for the new and resounding crime of having wished to be taught, of having sought the truth. And this in the Church, the kingdom of truth, in which it behoves to render a reason to all who demand it." [46]

[46] "Werke," ii. 6.

CHAPTER IV

THE SEQUEL OF THE AUGSBURG HEARING

I. Appeal to a General Council and the Papal Declaration on Indulgences

At Nürnberg Luther received through Spalatin a copy of the papal brief of the 23rd August.[1] He found it difficult to believe that such a mandate could have emanated from Leo X. and concluded that it was the fabrication of his enemies in Germany. He incorrectly treated it as such in a postscript to his account of the proceedings at Augsburg, though he included it in this document as an example of Romanist perfidy and tyranny.[2] It seems, however, to have shaken his belief in the Pope's impartiality,[3] and on his return to Wittenberg on the 31st October he set about the preparation of an appeal from the Pope to a General Council.[4] He was confirmed in his purpose by the belief that the Curia, as the result of Cajetan's report, was preparing to launch the censure of the Church against him.[5] Hence the determination to parry the expected stroke by an appeal to the Church itself, which he made on the 28th November in the presence of a notary and two witnesses and which he sent to the press.[6] He has been compelled to make use of this expedient by the action of the cardinal in instigating

[1] Enders, i. 273-274.

[2] "Werke," ii. 22 f.

[3] Enders, i. 274. Nam incredibile est tale quid monstri a summo Pontifice egredi . . . aut si vere etiam a curia emanavit, docebo eos suas impudentissimas temeritates et iniquissimam ignorantiam.

[4] *Ibid.*, i. 273. Parabo appellationem ad futurum concilium.

[5] *Ibid.*, i. 304. Cæterum expecto maladictiones ex urbe Roma quotidie; *cf.* i. 306, 316.

[6] "Werke," ii. 36; *cf.* Enders, i. 314. Appellavi ad futurum concilium.

the Pope to take further measures to secure his condemnation, in spite of his appeal to his Holiness and his readiness to receive instruction. The Pope, he boldly affirms, being a man, is liable to err, and in as far as he errs, is not to be obeyed, nay, is to be resisted. In view of his unjust and oppressive treatment at the cardinal's hands and the evident intention of Leo X. to abet this injustice and oppression, he now appeals from the Pope not rightly advised (*non recte consulto*) to a future Council, convened in a safe place, before which he may freely plead his cause.[7]

The challenge was certainly a daring one, though Luther in sending it to the press did not intend to publish it forthwith, but only to have it in readiness in case the Curia should proceed to extremes against him. It is not, therefore, surprising that the Elector attempted to prevent its publication, which, as Luther explained in a letter to Spalatin, had taken place against his express injunction to the printer who, for the sake of gain, had distributed copies without his knowledge.[8] Its publication was, in fact, fitted to hamper his patron in his efforts to secure for him more considerate treatment. It was thus, in the circumstances, highly impolitic and was besides futile from the legal point of view. In a case of notorious heresy such as the Pope had, in the brief of 23rd August, declared Luther to be guilty of, an appeal was invalid by canon law.[9] Moreover, an appeal to a General Council had been, since the time of Pius II., accounted *ipso facto* heresy and punishable as such.[10] Luther could only justify his contention by going back to the principle of the old conciliar party of Constance and Basle that a General Council is superior to the Pope, which, however, it had ultimately failed to establish. At the same time, such an appeal was by no means a dead letter. It had recently found corporate expression in a Council convened by Louis XII. and a section of the cardinals

[7] "Werke," ii. 36-40.
[8] Enders, i. 323-324. Letter to Spalatin, 20th Dec.; *cf.* i. 316.
[9] K. Müller, "Z.K.G.," xxiv. 74.
[10] Bull Execrabilis, Jan. 1460; and Creighton, "History of the Papacy," iii. 239-240; K. Müller, "Z.K.G.," 73.

at Pisa (1511-1512),[11] and in the University of Paris, whose example Luther professedly followed, and the conviction was widely held that in matters of doctrine the ultimate and supreme authority lay with a General Council.

In the meantime, Cajetan had come to the conclusion that there was some force in Luther's demand for a clear and definite declaration on the question of indulgences and that such a declaration was an indispensable basis of further procedure against him. The Pope himself, if Miltitz may be trusted, had declared in no measured terms his indignation at the report of the ongoings of the indulgence preachers, and had sarcastically remarked, in reference to Prierias's boast that he had confuted Luther's theses in three days, that his work would have been more convincing if he had spent as many months on it.[12]

As the result of his intensive study of the question and his discussions with Luther, Cajetan drew up and forwarded to Rome [13] (25th October), along with a report on the case, the draft of an official declaration on the subject of indulgences.[14] This draft was transformed into a papal decretal bearing the date 9th November, and was entrusted, along with other documents relative to the case, to Miltitz to be conveyed to the cardinal. It categorically asserts, in opposition to the views of "certain religious in Germany," that the Pope as Peter's successor is invested with the power of the keys. This power includes that of the remission not only of the guilt of sin in the Sacrament of Penance, but of the temporal punishment for actual sins to which the sinner is still liable in accordance with the divine justice. The remission of the temporal punishment is attained by means of indulgences in virtue of the superabundant merits of Christ and the saints. On this Treasure of Merits the Pope can draw for the benefit of the dead as well as the living, and the remission thereby obtained is valid as far

[11] Creighton, "Hist. of the Papacy," v. 150 f.

[12] Enders, i. 327.

[13] Kalkoff, "Forschungen," 66.

[14] His preliminary studies of the subject are in his "Opuscula," i. 153 f.

as the specific indulgence extends. It may, in other words, be partial or plenary as the case may be, and evidently depends in part at least on the price paid for it as well as the spiritual condition of the purchaser, though this is implied rather than explicitly stated.[15] This doctrine all are bound to hold and teach under pain of excommunication *latæ sententiæ* (*i.e.*, without special judgment) from which only the Pope can absolve. And in order that no one may henceforth be able to allege ignorance of the true doctrine thus officially decreed, the cardinal is empowered to require the ecclesiastical authorities in Germany to make known this decretal in their churches within a given time under penalty of suspension for disobedience, and they and all their clergy are to accept and teach and not to attempt to gainsay it under the aforesaid penalty of excommunication.[16]

This document Cajetan, on the 13th December, duly received at Linz, whither he had removed from Augsburg.[17] Though Luther's name is not mentioned, everybody knew who was specifically referred to in the phrase "certain religious in Germany." He was now instructed in unmistakable terms by the Vicar of Christ himself that his interpretation of the Bull Unigenitus was erroneous and that his contentions on the subject were inadmissible in the eyes of the supreme head of the Church, speaking *ex cathedra*. He was, therefore, *ipso facto* excommunicated if he persisted in maintaining either. Along with this document Cajetan seems, in fact, to have received a Bull of excommunication against Luther personally, though he refrained in the

[15] "Opera Latina Var.," ii. 431. Ac propterea omnes tam vivos quam defunctos qui veraciter omnes indulgentias hujusmodi consecuti fuerint a tanta temporali pœna secundum divinam justitiam pro peccatis suis actualibus debita liberari, quanta concessæ et acquisitæ indulgentiæ æquivalet. The spiritual condition of the purchaser is referred to in the previous words: "qui caritate jungente membra sunt Christi." *Ibid.*, ii. 430.

[16] *Ibid.*, ii. 429-432. The decretal bears the title "Cum Postquam."

[17] *Ibid.*, ii. 428, 432-433. It was shortly after printed and published at Vienna along with a German translation, for the benefit of the unlearned. Kalkoff, "Entscheidungsjahre," 88-89.

meantime from publishing it.[18] Luther had professed his readiness to receive instruction from the Pope, and here was the thing he had asked for. On the other hand, he had also told the Pope in his prefatory letter to the "Resolutions" that he could not revoke, and the Pope takes no account of his specific objections and contentions about the power to remit sin and to grant indulgence even in the case of the dead. The decretal assumes the absolute validity of the Thomist-Dominican version of the theory of indulgences and the papal power in this matter. It takes no account of the appeal for scriptural reasons, nor does it enter into any discussion of the points at issue. It is purely assertive and relies entirely on the principle of an unerring external authority, which to Luther was no longer the certain norm of truth, whilst recognising the principle of a money payment which had rendered the indulgence traffic a crying scandal, without a single word in condemnation of this scandal. Cajetan had simply stated the conventional Thomist doctrine and hushed up the scandal of its abuse in deference to the fanatics of his Order and the corrupt officials of the Curia. This was certainly not good enough for Luther or for his high patron as a final decision of the conflict.

The situation now looked very threatening. The Curia, it was reported, was determined to root out the tares of the Lutheran heresy. "Rome fears you," wrote Scheurl to Luther.[19] It was felt at Rome that not for 100 years, *i.e.*, since the days of Hus, had there been so anxious a situation for the Papacy, and the Pope and his advisers were resolved to brook no further evasion. Luther might have a bishopric if he would recant and anyone who could prevail on him to do so was sure of a cardinal's hat! [20]

[18] This may be inferred from a letter of Scheurl (20th Dec.) to Luther, in which he says, in reference to the documents which Miltitz had brought from Rome: "ne opus sit fulminibus quæ ille (Miltitz) *immania* habet." Enders, i. 329.

[19] Enders, i. 328. Formidat te Roma.

[20] This was according to Miltitz the prevailing mood at Rome when he left the city in the middle of Nov. as the bearer of the papal decretal, etc., to Cajetan. After his arrival in Germany he thus pictured to Scheurl

Luther was not the man to be won by such a bribe. He had been expecting the papal condemnation when he made his appeal to a Council on the 28th November, and he was resolved to brave exile and even death if it came to the worst. He would leave Wittenberg, seek a refuge in a foreign country, and offer his life to Christ.[21] He was, in fact, beginning to ask himself whether the real Antichrist, spoken of by Paul, was not reigning in the Roman Curia, whose régime was worse than that of the Turk.[22] Reports reached him from Nürnberg that Miltitz had arrived there bearing a number of papal briefs directed against him,[23] and the rumour had reached Spalatin that he had actually preached a farewell sermon to the people of Wittenberg. The rumour was unfounded. He had, he wrote, only announced the possibility of his doing so.[24] He thought of going to France and putting himself under the protection of the French king and the University of Paris. But the money for the journey could not be found. He mentions, too, the alternative plan, suggested by the Elector's advisers, of surrendering himself to the Elector, who should keep him captive in a safe place until he could have a fair trial. Nothing came of this proposed anticipation of his later captivity in the Wartburg, though he mentions the plan to Spalatin and is content in the meantime to trust himself to the providence of God and the discretion of his friends.[25]

In this emergency much depended on the Elector's attitude. It was a critical situation for him as well as for his protégé. On the one hand, the Pope was attempting to bribe him into the surrender or banishment of Luther by the offer of the Golden Rose and indulgence privileges

the prevailing mood at Rome, which Scheurl communicated to Luther on the 20th and 22nd Dec. Enders, i. 327 and 335. The phrase 10 years in Scheurl's letter should probably be 100. Miltitz's report is confirmed by the letters of the Pope and the Vice-Chancellor, Giulio de Medici, to Pfeffinger, 24th and 11th Oct., of which Miltitz was also the bearer. "Opera Latina Var.," ii. 446-448, where they are wrongly dated Jan. 1519.

[21] Enders, i. 308; *cf.* 299, 304, 314.

[22] *Ibid.*, i. 316; 18th, not 11th Dec., as it is dated by Enders.

[23] *Ibid*, i. 314, 316.

[24] *Ibid.*, i. 314-315.

[25] *Ibid.*, i. 308.

for his church at Wittenberg, of which Miltitz was the bearer, but which were only to be conferred on condition of his compliance with this demand. On the other, Cajetan in his letter of the 25th October relative to the Augsburg interview, which he only received on the 19th November,[26] had virtually threatened him with the consequences of a refusal. He was faced with the alternative of abandoning Luther or defying the Pope. It was a harassing problem, and throughout November and December there was anxious consultation between him and his advisers and between Luther and Spalatin in the attempt to solve it. Luther declared his readiness to leave Saxony and commit his fate to a higher hand than any earthly protector. He would on no account compromise the Elector in his cause or involve him or anyone else in danger on his account,[27] whilst begging him to petition the Pope for a fair trial of his case.[28] He had, in fact, made up his mind to dare and suffer for the truth and was not too amenable to the restraint of the diplomacy of his far-sighted and wary protector, who was chagrined by the precipitate publication of his appeal to a Council and the Acta Augustana, as fitted to frustrate his diplomatic efforts on his behalf. It is, indeed, difficult for the prophet to accommodate himself to the arts of the politician in such matters. In spite of such provocation, however, the Elector was resolved not to abandon him to his enemies, and there seems to be no ground for the assumption that he sent him an order to remove from Wittenberg without delay.[29] The idea of leaving Wittenberg had originated with

[26] Enders, i. 310.

[27] *Ibid.*, i. 299. Letter to the Elector, 19th Nov.; *cf.* letter to Spalatin, 2nd Dec., i. 308.

[28] *Ibid.*, i. 282.

[29] The report which is circumstantially related by Bavarus seems to have no real foundation. Bavarus relates the report on the 12th Aug. 1536, *i.e.*, eighteen years later. Extract in Enders, i. 309; German trans. in Walch, xv. 831. Did he have it from Luther himself? If so, Luther's memory must have been at fault. There is nothing in his correspondence at the time to indicate such a mandate on the part of the Elector. The expression in his letter to Spalatin, 2nd Dec., "Nisi venissent heri literæ tuæ jam parabam recessum, sed et adhuc sum in utramvis partem paratus," does not necessarily indicate such a mandate.

Staupitz and Luther himself, not with the Elector, and the latter at most only weighed the advisability, in case of necessity, of such a step, to which Luther himself was a consenting party.[30] He intervened, in fact, through Spalatin to prevent him from too hastily carrying out his intention and warned him against the rash idea of seeking a refuge in France.[31] He seems also to have considered the expedient of making a show of arresting him (naturally with his own consent) and concealing him in some safe place pending further developments.[32] He endeavoured to influence the Emperor in favour of the reference of his case to an impartial German tribunal.[33] At all events he was determined to stand between him and his enemies and to exhaust all the ingenuity of a resourceful diplomacy to this end.

His letter to Cajetan on the 8th December[34] affords convincing evidence of this determination. The letter is a reply to that in which the cardinal on the 25th October gave an account of the Augsburg interview and which the Elector had submitted for Luther's criticism. He not only enclosed this criticism[35] in his reply; he firmly declined the cardinal's demand for his surrender or banishment. In support of his refusal he adduced the fact that the University of Wittenberg supported Luther's demand that, before being condemned, his errors should be refuted with sufficient reasons, and had begged him to shield him from the malignity of his enemies.[36] If it were proved by adequate reasons that he was guilty of heresy, he would need no exhortation and admonition to proceed against him. He was desirous

[30] Enders, i. 317. Princeps prius fuerit contentus me non in loco (Wittenberg), postea voluit omnino ut manerem; *cf.* i. 319. On this subject see Kalkoff, "Forschungen," 163.

[31] *Ibid.*, i. 319.

[32] *Ibid.*, i. 308.

[33] The Elector's letter to Pfeffinger, his minister at the imperial court. Walch, xv. 807-809.

[34] It was only forwarded on the 18th Dec.

[35] Luther's letter of the 19th Nov. to him. Enders, i. 284 f.

[36] He is referring particularly to the letter, which the University at his request directed to him, 23rd Nov. "Opera Latina Var.," ii. 426-428; *cf.* Enders, i. 304.

to act in this matter as became a Christian prince in accordance with his honour and his conscience, but he would not be moved by threats to send Luther to Rome or expel him from his dominions as long as he was not fairly convicted of the crime of heresy. To expel him would be detrimental to the university which was both Christian and contained many good and learned men. He enclosed Luther's response as evidence on the other side, and supported his demand that his case might be submitted to the judgment of certain universities by which he was willing to be guided, or that at least his errors should be shown to him in writing. He begged, in conclusion, that he might be favoured with the reasons for adjudging as a heretic a man who had not yet been convicted of heresy and assured the cardinal that he would not willingly be allured to error, nor be found disobedient to the Holy See.[37] Luther had ample reason for the joy with which he read and re-read[38] this spirited epistle and for the heartfelt gratitude which he asked Spalatin to convey to his protector. He will now assuredly remain at Wittenberg and await the upshot of Roman devices against him.[39]

II. The Mission of Miltitz

He had not long to wait. On the 28th December Miltitz arrived at the Elector's court at Altenburg. Along with his commission as bearer of the Golden Rose and the indulgence Bulls, he had received the faculty, usually bestowed on a papal emissary of this kind, to confer various privileges. This faculty vouchsafed the right to confer certain offices, such as that of notary, to grant a number of academic and other titles, to legitimate forbidden marriages and a number of bastards, and thus earn the fees payable for such concessions. In particular, he was empowered to legitimate two persons born out of wedlock

[37] Enders, i. 310-312.
[38] Quam cum gaudio eas (literas) legi et relegi.
[39] Enders, i. 324, 333.

and thereby entitle them to high ecclesiastical preferment.[40] This significant concession was evidently intended for the benefit of two illegitimate sons of the Elector; was, in fact, to be used as an additional bribe for the surrender of Luther. In the document and in the papal instructions relative to his mission, Miltitz was given the title of Nuntius. But he was enjoined to act in strict subordination to the legate and was bound under pain of excommunication to adhere to his instructions in this subordinate capacity. In particular the Golden Rose and the indulgence privileges were to be handed, not to the Elector, but to the cardinal to be made use of by him as expediency might decide.[41]

The enterprising commissary was, however, not content to confine himself to this subordinate rôle. He was eager to earn the substantial reward which awaited anyone who should secure Luther's surrender or submission, and gave himself and his mission an importance which was not warranted by his commission. He was certainly not empowered to enter into any independent negotiation for the settlement of the Lutheran heresy, but at most to explore the situation, report to the Curia and the legate, and abet the demand for its suppression contained in the papal letters to the Elector and his advisers, of which he was the bearer.[42]

In these letters the Pope left no room for dubiety as to the fate of Luther. He denounced him as "a son of perdition" and exhorted them to take summary measures for the suppression of his detestable heresy.[43] Miltitz speedily discovered that he had come on a vain errand, as far as this part of his mission was concerned. The Elector was resolved

[40] See the document conferring this faculty in Kalkoff, "Forschungen," 180 f.

[41] Papal instruction to Miltitz, Walch, xv. 811-812. Miltitz was not a fully commissioned diplomatist (nuntius et orator), but only a subordinate agent (nuntius et commissarius). See Kalkoff, "Z.K.G." (1925), 215.

[42] See the Pope's letter to the Elector, Walch, xv. 814; K. Müller, "Z.K.G.," xxiv. 76-77; Kalkoff, *ibid.*, xxv.

[43] The letters to the Elector, Pfeffinger, Spalatin, and the Town Council of Wittenberg in "Opera Latina Var.," ii. 446 f.; Walch, xv. 812 f.

not to send Luther to Rome, and parried the demand for his banishment by pointing out that he could only seek a refuge in Bohemia and that his presence there would only increase the danger to the Church. Whereupon Miltitz, in his eagerness to start a negotiation on his own account, begged him not to allow him to depart and to summon him to Altenburg to discuss with himself the terms of a settlement of the case.[44] Such a proposal was clearly in contravention of his commission. But he seems so far to have impressed the Elector by his self-importance, and Luther accordingly appeared at Altenburg on the 4th or 5th January 1519. The shallow, voluble, and self-seeking commissary was ill-fitted to treat with the impassioned seeker after God and truth. He was totally ignorant of the problems at issue. He was a mere wirepuller with an eye to his own advantage—an adept in make-believe and dissimulation—and his pretension to authority had no real justification in his commission, though the Curia might be ready enough to take advantage of any success he might achieve. Such an intermediary was not likely to make much impression on a man of Luther's calibre, and Luther seems to have quickly taken his measure, whilst treating him with outward respect as the papal representative and sincerely desirous to reach a feasible understanding. He responded to his amicable professions and discussed his proposals in a friendly tone.[45] But he was not deceived by "the Judas kiss" and "the crocodile tears" of his interviewer.[46]

He had been informed by Scheurl in general terms of the tenor of the documents of which he was the bearer, and rightly assumed that his professions of goodwill were merely assumed for his own purposes. Miltitz had learned on the way that Luther was so popular a figure that the policy of violence had no chance of success.[47] Of every five men

[44] The Elector's declaration on the subject in Walch, xv. 854 f.; Kalkoff, "Entscheidungsjahre," 99; "Forschungen," 168-169.

[45] Enders, i. 348-349. Cum Carolo amicissime conveni.

[46] *Ibid.*, i. 408; *cf.* 431.

[47] *Ibid.*, i. 408. Sed per viam a Domino prostratus, id est multitudine mihi faventium territus, juxta quod curiosissime ubique de mei opinione exploraverat.

he had spoken to on the subject scarcely two or three favoured the Roman side of the case.[48] He found the people so fervent in their support of the new teaching that, as he told Luther, if he had 25,000 Swiss soldiers he would despair of bringing them through Germany to Rome.[49] He adapted his tactics accordingly in the hope of achieving by dissimulation and blandishment what violence could not effect.[50]

In the course of the interview, which took place in Spalatin's dwelling and lasted two days, Luther, under the prompting of Feilitzsch and Spalatin, went a considerable length towards accommodation. On the first day Miltitz proposed at the outset that he should recant.[51] To this Luther responded with the old demand that he might be shown wherein he had erred,[52] and Miltitz was fain to drop the imperious vituperation of Cajetan and adopt a more diplomatic method of attaining his object. He proposed that Luther should refrain from further controversy, should write a humble letter of submission and apology to the Pope, should publish a statement of his views for the purpose of counteracting the misrepresentation of his writings, to the detriment of the Roman Church, among the people, and should submit his case to the judgment of a German bishop.[53] In the course of the discussion Luther justified his attack on the indulgence system, which had given rise to the proceedings against him, on the ground of the shameful deception and extortion practised on the people by Tetzel and the indulgence preachers. For this, not Tetzel, not the Archbishop of Maintz, but the Pope himself, whom he believed to be the mere tool of his greedy relatives and

[48] Enders, i. 430. According to Luther's later version of what Miltitz told him about his discovery, the ratio was three for Luther to one for the Pope. Preface to the 1545 ed. of his works, "Documente zu Luther's Entwicklung," 16.

[49] "Tischreden," i. 74; *cf.* iii. 308.

[50] Enders, i. 408. Mutavit violentiam in benevolentiam fallacissime simulatam.

[51] *Ibid.*, i. 408. Agens mecum multis sane verbis ut pro honore ecclesiæ Romanæ revocarem mea dicta; *cf. ibid.*, i. 431 and 443.

[52] *Ibid.*, i. 408, 431.

[53] Luther's report of the first day's interview to the Elector. Walch, xv. 840-842; "Werke," 53, 5-7 (Erlangen ed.).

courtiers, was in the first instance responsible, since by his compliance in allowing the archbishop to hold several Sees he had caused him to have recourse to this mercenary traffic to pay for the price of them. It was this swindle, by which the people were deceived and fleeced, that had compelled him to denounce the indulgence system and had not only involved him in controversy, but alienated the people from the Roman Church.[54] If his opponents had not raised such a hue and cry over his writings this storm would not have arisen, and in order to forestall worse consequences he was prepared to refrain from further agitation if his opponents would undertake to do likewise. He was ready to submit himself humbly to the Pope and to acknowledge that he had been too hasty and sharp in the heat of controversy. At the same time, he had no intention of attacking the Roman Church, but only, as a true son of this Church, of vindicating it from the contempt and discredit which the scandalous preaching of the indulgence agents had brought upon it in the eyes of the people. On this understanding he was willing to make amends to the Pope and, farther, to issue an explanatory statement to the people that what he had written was not to be understood as derogatory to the Roman Church or subversive of the obedience and reverence which they owed it. Finally, he agreed to the suggestion made by Spalatin at the instigation of Feilitzsch, that the case should be submitted to the decision of the Archbishop of Salzburg, acting in consort with unsuspected men of learning, on condition that if he was not satisfied with this decision, he was to be at liberty to adhere to his Appellation. His difficulty was that the Pope would not accept such a tribunal, and in that case he could not accept the papal judgment. The Pope would merely write the text-book to which he would supply the comments and this would only spell failure.

Miltitz was of opinion that the concessions thus made by Luther would not prove acceptable, though he did not insist on revocation, and the decision on these four points was accordingly postponed till the morrow. In reporting

[54] Enders, i. 341-343.

the discussion to the Elector, Luther, while assuring him of his earnest desire to do his utmost to reach a settlement, made it clear that revocation was for him out of the question.[55]

Pending its renewal on the following day he drafted a letter of submission to the Pope in accordance with his promise. In this draft he expresses his sorrow that what he had intended for the vindication of the Roman Church has brought upon him the charge of irreverence towards its head and aroused the gravest suspicion in the mind of the Pope. Miltitz has urged the revocation of his writings, and if it had been possible he would without delay have complied. But this was now impossible in view of the fact that, beyond his expectation and wish, they had attained so wide a circulation. Moreover, he adds, with an evident touch of irony, there are so many men of learning and intelligence in Germany nowadays that if he wished to honour the Roman Church, the very thing that he ought not to do was to revoke. For this would only tend to make this Church more hideous in the sight of men and give occasion to them to cry out the more against it. Not he, but his opponents have inflicted injury on the Church and brought it into evil repute among the Germans by their utterly absurd declarations in the name of the Pope. These men have been concerned only to satisfy their most disgraceful avarice and have thus contaminated the Church with "the abominable reproach of Egypt" (*opprobrio Ægypti*). And, as if these evils were not sufficient, they have inculpated him at Rome, who has opposed their monstrous doings, as the author of their own audacity! Nevertheless, he testifies in the presence of God and all men that it never was, and is not now his intention to attack in any way the power of the Roman Church and its head or craftily diminish it. "Yea, I acknowledge most fully the power of this Church over all and that nothing is to be esteemed above it in heaven or earth beyond Jesus Christ, the Lord of all. Therefore let not your Beatitude give credence to their

[55] Aus der Revocation wirt nichts, Walch, xv. 842; "Werke," 53, 7 (Erl. ed.). See also von Schubert, "Die Vorgeschichte der Berufung Luther's auf dem Reichstag zu Worms" (1912).

evil devices who concoct calumnies concerning Martin." He will maintain silence if these calumniators are also enjoined to repress their vain bombast, and he will undertake to instruct and admonish the people sincerely to reverence the Church and not impute to it the audacious conduct of his adversaries, nor imitate the excessive acrimony against it into which he has been betrayed in his conflict with these babblers, in the hope that by God's grace and his earnest efforts the discord may be lulled to sleep. One thing only he has sought, and that is, that the Mother Church of Rome may not be polluted by the abomination of alien avarice, nor the people seduced to error or be taught to esteem love less than indulgences. All else he accounts of far less importance. If, however, he can possibly do more he will assuredly be most ready to comply.[56]

Fearlessly and truly spoken. A few expressions of humility, but not a word of regret for attacking the evils which indubitably disgraced the Church and against which he protests in the strongest terms in the name of religion and morality. The document was in fact a scathing indictment of the corruption of the Roman Curia and a vindication of himself rather than an apology. The denunciation of the curial régime was in truth more pointed than in the prefatory letter to the "Resolutions." Miltitz felt that it was useless to serve his purpose of mollifying the Pope and his advisers. It contains, indeed, a far-reaching acknowledgment of the papal-Roman primacy, and in this respect is hardly consistent with the limitation of the papal power and the assertion of the superiority of a General Council contained in the Appellation and the Acta Augustana. Nor does it seem to accord with the belief expressed in the letter to Link in the previous month that Antichrist was ruling in the Roman Curia. Luther's dicta in such matters are dependent on the situation, and it is not surprising that one who was called on to face a series of crises should have halted at times between two opinions. It must be remembered that he was still feeling his way towards the logical conclusions

[56] Enders, i. 443-444.

of some of his premises and that it was not the Roman Church or the Pope as ideally conceived that he had been engaged in controverting, but the Roman Church and the papal power as embodied in the actual Curia. To this ideal Church, as he conceived it, he is still ready to subscribe in all sincerity. There need be no doubt of the sincerity of his assurance that he did not desire to attack the Church thus ideally conceived or dispute the rights which he still believed it might justly claim.[57] His assumption from the beginning was that his opponents misrepresented and abased this ideal for their own mercenary purposes. And in the draft he certainly does not hide this assumption. He lets the Pope clearly understand on what terms he may expect him to acknowledge the superiority of the Roman Church. Only on condition that he disowns the other side and the abominations with which he charges it may he count on his submission.

This condition was, however, what the Pope could not afford to concede. At the interview on the second day Miltitz seems, therefore, to have dropped the suggested letter of apology as impracticable and along with it the explanatory statement which would likely enough have been couched in equally inacceptable terms, and to have limited the agreement to the conditional undertaking to observe silence and to refer the case to the arbitration of a German bishop.[58] The draft of the letter was neither put into final shape by Luther, nor forwarded to Rome by Miltitz, who himself undertook to write to the Pope an account of the proceedings.[59]

[57] Pastor, Grisar, and other Roman Catholic writers question his sincerity. Pastor, "History of the Popes," vii. 383-384; Grisar, "Luther," i. 366.

[58] See Luther's report of the final agreement on the second day to the Elector. Walch, xv. 842; De Wette, "Luther's Briefe," i. 207; Brieger, Lutherstudien, "Z.K.G.," xv. 204 f.

[59] Walch, xv. 842. Zum anderen will er, Carol, dem heiligsten Vater Pabst kürzlich Schreiben aller sachen wie er erfunden gelegenheit. The date of Luther's letter to the Pope is given by Enders, Walch, Knaake, and others, as 3rd March 1519. But this is inaccurate, and the inaccuracy rests on a later addition to the letter, Ex Alden burgo, 3 Martii 1519. Luther was not at Altenburg on the 3rd March, and as

In this letter he gave his own version of the concessions which he had extracted from Luther, and led the Pope to believe that Luther had not only professed sorrow for his errors and his violence in asserting them, but was prepared to retract them and refrain from farther propagating them. He would even have made this retraction to Cajetan had not the legate adopted a partial attitude in favour of Tetzel.[60] The Pope, it seems, was now only too willing for political reasons to settle the case on these terms. With the death of the Emperor Maximilian on the 11th January the question of the election of a successor had entered on a new phase. The Emperor's agreement with five of the Electors for the election of his grandson now lapsed, and the diplomatic campaign began afresh. The Pope was anxious to prevent the election of either Charles of Spain, who was also King of Naples, or Francis I., who was master of Lombardy, though of the two he preferred Francis to Charles. To aggrandise the power of either was to jeopardise the temporal power of the Papacy in Italy. In the interest of this power it was thus imperative to secure the election of a neutral candidate. For this reason the Pope favoured the choice of the Elector of Saxony, and to secure the Elector's support of his policy, he was ready to temporise on the question of the Lutheran heresy for the time being. Pending the final decision of this absorbing issue, which did not take place till the end of June, the Lutheran heresy was of subordinate importance. The Pope was thus fain, in response to Miltitz's optimistic missive, to cultivate the Elector by welcoming back to the papal fold the repentant

Brieger has shown, the draft was written during the visit to Altenburg in the beginning of January, in the interval between the first and the second day's interview with Miltitz who, finding it unsuitable for his purpose, dropped the proposal and did not forward the letter to Rome. In all the older historians the version of what was actually and finally resolved on at Altenburg is thus inaccurate, and Brieger rendered a great service to Luther research in bringing out clearly the facts of the case.

[60] Miltitz's letter, which, he informed the Elector on the 5th Feb. (Walch, xv. 865), he had written to the Pope, is not extant. But its tenor is contained in the brief which the Pope wrote to Luther as the result of Miltitz's communication, and which is given by Enders, i. 492-493.

"son of perdition," whom he now addressed as his beloved son, though he certainly took a considerable time to arrive at this resolution. In his brief of the 29th March he gives thanks to God that He has deigned to enlighten him and has thus prevented the spread of his pernicious errors among the people who might have been misled by his teaching, and, not willing the death of a sinner, accepts with paternal affection his excuses. He invites him to appear and retract in his own presence and assures him that he may freely and safely undertake the journey to Rome for this purpose, in the hope that he will prove an obedient son and will experience the joy of finding in him a gracious and clement father.[61]

The letter, which never came into Luther's hands, was based on a complete misunderstanding, due to Miltitz's irresponsible and unreliable optimism, of his real position. The summary retraction which it presupposed, he had consistently refused to both Cajetan and Miltitz, and even to the Pope, and he was no nearer this concession at the end of March than at the beginning of January. During this interval, in fact, it had become evident that even the stipulation of observing silence was impracticable. Miltitz had, indeed, in passing through Leipzig towards the end of January, administered a harsh reprimand to Tetzel as the cause of this contention and reported very unfavourably to the Pope on his private life and his conduct as indulgence agent.[62] The unfortunate indulgence preacher, as Luther pointed out, was treated as a convenient scapegoat for the sins of his superiors and fell into complete discredit. He dared not, he had written in reply to Miltitz's summons to appear before him at Altenburg in the beginning of January, venture out of the monastery at Leipzig for fear of his life or show himself in the pulpit of the monastery church without exciting the angry looks of the people.[63] It was left to Luther to say a kind word of his discredited

[61] Enders, i. 492-493. Burkhardt ("Luther's Briefwechsel," 23, 1866) wrongly dates the papal brief Nov. 1519. There is no reason to doubt the authenticity of the document.

[62] His letter to the Elector, 22nd Jan. Walch, xv. 862-863.

[63] Letter in Walch, xv. 860-862.

opponent [64] and to show his magnanimity by writing him a consolatory letter in the midst of the mental misery (*ægritudine animi*) to which he succumbed a few months later. "He should not," he wrote, "worry himself about the matter, since he had not really set the ball a-rolling. This child had quite another father." [65] He died on the 4th July, the day on which Luther began the debate with Eck at Leipzig.[66]

Miltitz might objurgate the wretched Tetzel. But he could not prevent the pugnative and fame-loving Eck from challenging the Wittenberg professor to an academic duel on the question at issue between them. The challenge was, indeed, directed to Luther's colleague, Carlstadt. But one of the theses which he proposed to debate was manifestly directed against Luther, and Luther was not the man to observe silence in the face of this provocation of the author of the "Obelisks." He might ignore the "Replica" of Prierias [67] and contented himself with a written reply to Dungersheim, who exchanged letters with him in defence of the papal power,[68] but he was irritated by what he regarded as Eck's underhand attack, and early in February determined, though reluctantly, to enter the arena against him.[69] In vain, therefore, that the Bishop of Brandenburg, who paid him a visit at Wittenberg, intervened at the instigation of the Pope to prevent any further contention. The bishop expostulated with him to no purpose on the rashness and the risk of disturbing the peace of the Church, and charged him with pride in setting himself up against ecclesiastical authority. Luther felt, if he did not say, that in attacking what were grave abuses he was only doing what it was the duty of the bishops to have done and what, to their shame, they had neglected.[70]

[64] Enders, i. 413.
[65] So Emser wrote in 1521. Paulus, "Tetzel," 81.
[66] Paulus, "Tetzel," 81-82.
[67] Enders, i. 348; *cf.* 345 and 353.
[68] *Ibid.*, i. 366-367, 438-441.
[69] *Ibid.*, i. 408-409.; *cf.* 410, 411, 412, 413.
[70] *Ibid.*, i. 413. Fui cum Rev. Dom. Episcopo Brandenburgensi Wittenbergæ, et multis mecum, familiariter tamen, expostularit quod tanta auderem. Intelligo episcopos nunc tandem sapere, sui fuisse

Meanwhile, pending the arrangement of the place and date of the debate, he sent forth a popular statement of his views for the purpose of counteracting the misrepresentation of them by which his opponents were seeking to mislead the people. This "Instruction to the People" was issued at the end of February at the instigation of the Elector and his chaplain and had nothing to do with the discarded suggestion of Miltitz at the Altenburg interview.[71] Its purpose was, in fact, to vindicate himself from the aspersions of his opponents, and in doing so he says very plainly what he thinks of the Roman Church and its institutions, whilst instructing the people in the sense in which they are to be held in reverence. In this respect he himself virtually departs from the agreement to let sleeping dogs lie and seems to have regarded the challenge of Eck as justifying its non-observance by him. His opponents, he begins, have sought to mislead the people and render him suspect in regard to his teaching on the intercession of the saints, purgatory, good works, the power of the Roman Church, etc. He will shut the evil mouths of these detractors so that the people may cease to believe them and learn the facts from himself. He believes in prayer to the saints, but protests against the tendency to have recourse to their intercession for material rather than for spiritual benefits, and the superstition which invests them with powers that belong only to God. He believes also in purgatory and in the duty of seeking by prayer, fasting, and almsgiving to relieve those suffering in this intermediate state. But we know nothing definite on the subject and he does not believe we may or can arbitrarily influence God's jurisdiction over souls in purgatory by such an artificial expedient as the purchase of an indulgence on their behalf. An indulgence is merely the remission of ecclesiastical satisfactions. It is

scilicet officii, quod in me vident præsertim, ideoque non nihil pudere. Superbum me vocant et audacem, quorum autem neutrum negavi; sed non sunt ejusmodi homines qui sciant quid vel Deus vel ipsi simus.

[71] Unterricht auff etlich Artickell die im von seinin abgonnern auffgelegt. "Werke," ii. 69 f.; Enders, i. 446. Brieger has adduced strong arguments for holding that the document had no connection with Miltitz's proposal, "Z.K.G.," xv. 212 f.

optional and much inferior to good works which are obligatory on all, and to buy an indulgence ticket and neglect almsgiving is to deceive God and oneself. The rest can be left to the learned to dispute about. The ordinances of the Church are to be observed, but not so as if they were equal to the commands of God and as if to eat flesh on Friday was as great a sin as cursing and swearing, or neglecting to help one's poor neighbour. The formal observance of ecclesiastical regulations on which the priesthood lays such stress, without real goodness, is a travesty of religion, and for teaching this true religion he has been denounced as an enemy of the Pope and the canon law and worse than a pagan. One should observe both God's commands and the Church's ordinances, but at the same time learn to discriminate between true piety and the mere formalism which makes an outward show, but is not concerned about the inward disposition. So in regard to good works, which are of no avail for salvation unless they spring from God's grace operating in the heart of man. They are, therefore, the fruit of a truly religious spirit which consists in humility, self-condemnation, and dependence on God. Where this spirit is absent all so-called good works are only bad works. But so to teach is certainly not to dissuade from good works, as his adversaries proclaim, but rather to ensure the doing of what is acceptable and essential in God's sight. The Roman Church is undoubtedly to be honoured above all as the Church of Peter and Paul, a long succession of Popes, and so many thousands of martyrs. Despite the evils rampant at Rome, it is thus not permissible to separate from this Church. Separation will not make things better. The theologians may dispute about the extent of the papal power and supremacy, but on these things the salvation of the soul does not depend at all. They are mere externals, and Christ has founded His Church not on these externals but on true humility and unity of spirit. As an external ordinance the Pope's jurisdiction is to be obeyed just as obedience is to be rendered to the temporal power, even that of the Turk.[72] He will not deprive the Roman Church of

[72] "Werke," ii. 73; *cf.* Enders, i. 446, 447.

this obedience, but the recognition of this right does not oblige him to accept all the exaggerations of his "dear friends" who, in attacking him, have raised the cry of the Papacy in danger, and he will not be intimidated by the bubbles of these hypocrites. It is none the less evident that though he regards the papal power as an essential of the visible Church, he has by this time ceased to see in it an essential of religion. Even in regard to the external power of the Pope the doubt whether the Pope is not Antichrist or his apostle is becoming an obsession as the result of his intensive study of the papal decretals in preparation for the debate with Eck. "I am looking through the papal decretals for my disputation at Leipzig," he writes to Spalatin on the 13th March, "and (I whisper it in your ear) I am in doubt whether the Pope is Antichrist or his apostle, so miserably is Christ (that is the truth) corrupted and crucified by him in these decretals. I am terribly tormented by the thought that Christ's people is so fooled under this specious form of law in the name of Christianity. I shall make a copy of my notes on the decretals in order that you may see what sort of laws they have ordained in defiance of Scripture in their striving to establish their bombastic tyranny, not to speak of the other similar works of Antichrist which the Roman Curia pours forth." [73]

[73] Enders, i. 450.

CHAPTER V

THE LEIPZIG DISPUTATION

I. Before the Encounter

During Luther's visit to Augsburg in October 1518, Eck had, in a personal interview, expressed a desire for a public disputation with his colleague Carlstadt, who in the previous May had directed against him a long series of theses in response to his " Obelisks " against Luther. In these Carlstadt had asserted the Lutheran view of penitence, the supreme authority of Scripture, in and above the Church, the impotence of the will in the religious sense, the futility of works apart from grace, etc.[1] Eck, of course, retorted with a counter-series, and in conclusion challenged his opponent to a public disputation.[2] It was in prosecution of this challenge that he asked Luther to mediate a meeting between them. Luther suggested Wittenberg, in place of Rome or Cologne, which Eck proposed, and finally Eck was left to choose between Leipzig and Erfurt. To this preliminary arrangement Carlstadt assented,[3] and ultimately Eck decided for Leipzig, and in the beginning of December 1518 applied to Duke George of Saxony and the university authorities for the necessary permission to hold the debate. Without waiting for this permission he published on the 29th December a series of theses dealing with penance, purgatory, indulgences, the papal authority to remit sin, which he proposed to debate with Carlstadt at Leipzig.[4] For the specific issue between him and his opponent—the

[1] Barge, " Karlstadt," i. 118 f.

[2] See " Corpus Catholicorum," i. 81-82.

[3] Enders, i. 268, 280-281 ; " Werke," ix. 208.

[4] Eck's theses in their original form are given in Luther's " Werke," ix. 208-209.

problem of free will and grace—he substituted one on the superiority of the Roman Church over other Churches and the supreme power which the Pope as the successor of Peter and the Vicar of Christ had always possessed. " We deny the contention that the Roman Church was not superior to other Churches before the time of Sylvester (beginning of the fourth century), and, on the contrary, we recognise that he who possessed the seat and the faith of St Peter was always (*semper*) the successor and the Vicar-General of Christ." This thesis was evidently aimed against Luther's contentions on the subject in his " Resolutions "[5] and in the Acta Augustana. The whole series, in fact, which dealt with the many points raised during the indulgence controversy might be regarded as an attack on Luther's teaching as championed by Carlstadt. There could, at all events, be no doubt that the twelfth thesis on the papal supremacy was deliberately intended to draw Luther into the debate and thus earn for Eck the glory of combating the great innovator on behalf of the Pope and the Roman Church. On receiving the theses Luther at once saw that they were meant for him rather than for his less distinguished colleague.

Whilst resenting Eck's underhand method of involving him in a controversy in which he had acted only as mediator for the purpose of bringing about an amicable discussion between the parties, Luther decided to accept the challenge and range himself by the side of his colleague. A public discussion of these questions was what he had contemplated from the outset and had repeatedly asked the ecclesiastical authorities to sanction. On this ground alone he was ready to meet the Ingolstadt professor and defend his views in the presence of an academic assembly. In an open letter to Carlstadt early in February 1519 he publicly announced his determination and roundly denounced Eck as a vain-glorious, presumptuous, and double-dealing sophist.[6] In the same drastic style he made known his intention in a letter to Eck himself, reminding him of his considerate

[5] In a passage of the " Resolutions," Luther had denied that the Roman Church in the time of Gregory I. was superior over other Churches. " Werke," i. 571.

[6] Enders, i. 402-405.

treatment of him in refraining from publishing his "Asterisks" against him and reproaching him for this insidious return for his conciliatory efforts as mediator.[7] Before receiving this letter Eck announced that he had obtained the permission of Duke George and the university to hold the proposed disputation and had fixed the 27th June for the meeting. He excused himself for virtually challenging Luther by saying that as he was the principal and Carlstadt only the seconder in the dissemination of these false and erroneous doctrines in Germany, it was only fitting that he should be present to defend them or to disprove his counter-theses, to which he had meanwhile added one on free will and grace with special reference to his controversy with Carlstadt. He confessed, in fact, that his theses were drawn up not so much against Carlstadt as against Luther's perverse teaching,[8] and condescendingly expressed the hope that he would render obedience to the Pope and surrender to the truth as taught by the doctors of the Church.

In pursuance of his determination Luther had drafted a dozen theses to which, following Eck's example, he subsequently added one on free will and grace, and which he published along with those of Eck and the open letter to Carlstadt.[9] In the first twelve he maintains his characteristic views on penitence, the papal and priestly remission of sin, and indulgences. The last of the series, the thirteenth, on the papal supremacy contains the crucial issue on which the debate was to turn. It reflects the deliberate conclusion to which the long controversy with his opponents, the interview with Cajetan, the measures of the Curia against him, and his intensive study of ancient Church history had driven him. "That the Roman Church is superior to all other Churches is, indeed, proved by the far-fetched decrees promulgated by the Roman pontiffs within the last 400 years. But this ecclesiastical dogma is contrary to the

[7] Enders, v. 6-7, 18th Feb. 1519.

[8] *Ibid.*, i. 429.

[9] Early in Feb. 1519, under the title "Disputatio et Excusatio F. Martini Luther adversus Criminationes Joh. Eecii." "Werke," ii. 153 f.

approved histories of the previous 1100 years, the plain teaching of divine Scripture, and the decree of the Council of Nicæa, the most sacred of all the Councils."[10] In an extraordinarily daring preface he gave expression to his defiance not only of Eck, but of all such sophists and sycophants who, in their exaltation of the papal monarchy, raise an altar to Baal. He is content to believe that the Apostolic See neither desires nor is able to do anything to the detriment of Christ. But he refused to accept the fictitious claims clamorously adduced for it by its flatterers, and in this matter he fears neither the Pope nor those who invoke his name, far less these scarecrows and puppets of Rome. "Let them seek to terrify others with their flatteries and their deifications (*per adulationes et consecrationes suas*). Martin Luther holds these priests and deifiers of the Roman cult in contempt."[11]

It is not surprising that this daring declaration aroused the misgivings of his friends as well as exasperated his enemies. Carlstadt found his thirteenth thesis too sweeping and irritated his great colleague by his apprehensions.[12] Luther even suggested that he was afraid to lose his prebend! Spalatin urged him to be cautious,[13] but Luther, in his appeal to ancient history, was on surer ground than his nervous friends divined. His early religious experience had led him to the Bible as the supreme guide to a gracious God. The indulgence controversy, which eventuated in the summary demand for a revocation, led him to question the right of the Pope to enforce this demand in virtue of mere external authority, and compelled him to make an intensive study of the constitution of the ancient Church as well as the decrees of the mediæval Popes. In so doing he applied the critical spirit and method of the humanists to the study of institutions as well as doctrines. In this respect he had become a follower of Erasmus, whose friendship, at the instigation of Capito, he now sought in a letter full of appreciation of his learning and his merits as a reformer. He proclaims

[10] "Werke," ii. 161.
[11] *Ibid.*, ii. 160.
[12] Enders, ii. 4, 10; Barge, i. 141-142.
[13] Enders, ii. 4.

himself his disciple and his humble admirer. "Many a time I talk with you and you with me, O Erasmus, our glory and our hope. . . . For who is there whose inmost soul Erasmus does not utterly possess, whom Erasmus does not teach, in whom Erasmus does not reign? I speak of those who love literature uprightly. For I greatly rejoice that, among other gifts of Christ, this one is numbered, that you displease many. By this test I am wont to distinguish the gifts of a gracious God from the gifts of an angry one." [14] He has learned through Capito that his name and his works are not unknown to him and begs him to recognise a little brother in Christ as his most devoted admirer, though by reason of his lack of culture and his obscurity he does not merit his notice. Erasmus answered in a friendly though non-committal vein. The commotion caused by Luther's writings has made itself felt far and wide, has been most falsely traced by the insensate theologians to himself as its inspirer, and has given them a handle to attack him. With characteristic caution he tells him that he is entirely ignorant of his works, which he has not read, with the exception of his Commentary on the Psalms, which he hopes will prove of great service. He assures him that he has friends in England and the Netherlands who favour his cause, whilst warning him against the danger of aggressive agitation and theological controversy and clearly giving him to understand that he is not minded to become a theological partisan. The tone is on the whole kindly and sympathetic up to a point, but reserved and cautious.[15] On the other hand, Luther found warm admirers in Capito and especially in Melanchthon, the brilliant young humanist whose services he had enlisted as Professor of Greek at Wittenberg and whose classical knowledge proved of sterling service to him in his study of ancient sources. Of these sources the Scripture is the touchstone of truth which the papal decrees and the sophists of the schools have corrupted. "The matter," he wrote to Pirkheimer, on the 20th February, in sending him the open letter to Carlstadt and the theses on both sides, "veers against their sacred canons,

[14] Enders, i. 489. [15] *Ibid.*, ii. 66-68, 30th May 1519.

that is, the profane corruptions of the Holy Scripture, which I have long desired, but have not willingly dared to force on their attention. . . . Not that, trusting in my own strength, I boast of fame before victory, but that I confide in the mercy of God who is showing His wrath against human traditions. I will preserve and confess the power of the supreme pontiff. But I will not suffer the corruption of Holy Scripture." [16] The early Fathers stand next in authority to the Scriptures and it was the study of their writings as well as the Scriptures that revealed to him the striking contrast between the constitution of the ancient Church and that of the mediæval Church as reflected in the papal decretals. It was this contrast that suggested the doubt whether the Pope was not the very Antichrist.[17]

Nor did he shrink from the implications which this study was forcing upon him. What gave him strength to stand firm amid his shrinking colleagues and friends was the conviction that God Himself was begetting in his mind these strange and startling thoughts and was leading him in a way not of his choosing. "I know not whence come these thoughts to me. The thing itself is but at its beginning in my judgment." [18] "The Lord draws me and not unwilling I follow." [19] "You know," he wrote in another epistle to the fearful Spalatin, "that unless Christ had wrought through me and my works from the beginning, I would have been utterly lost, especially during my visit to Augsburg. For who did not either fear this one man (Cajetan) or did not hope that he would bring destruction upon me? . . . The truth of Scripture and the Church cannot be handled, but these hearts must needs be offended. You will, therefore, not hope for peace or safety for me unless you wish me to give up theology entirely. Permit, therefore, my friends to think me mad. This enterprise will not finish (if it be of God) except, as the disciples did in the case of Christ,

[16] Enders, i. 435-436; *cf.* 349 and his dedication of the Commentary on the Psalms to the Elector, i. 480 f.

[17] *Ibid.*, i. 450; *cf.* 316.

[18] *Ibid.*, i. 316. Nescio unde veniant istæ meditationes; res ista necdum habet initium suum meo judicio. Letter to Link, 11th Dec. 1518.

[19] *Ibid.*, i. 436. Letter to Pirkheimer, 20th Feb. 1519.

all my friends forsake me and the truth is left alone, which saves itself by its own right arm, not by mine, or yours, or that of any man. This hour I have beheld from the beginning. . . . In a word, if I perish, the whole world will not go under. The Wittenbergers by the grace of God have made such progress that they will not feel the lack of me. What do you want? I, miserable man, only fear that perhaps I am not worthy to suffer and die for such a cause." [20]

In this spirit he set himself to prepare for the great encounter, which was exciting a keen interest not only in Germany, but in Italy, France, Spain, England, and the Netherlands, where his theses were being eagerly read and were finding not a few supporters.[21] So Frobenius wrote to him from Basle in April. He studied the passages in the New Testament adduced in support of the papal claims, as well as others which are plainly incompatible with these claims, for the purpose of establishing their historic sense. For the same end he reviewed the relative passages in the writings of Cyprian, Jerome, Augustine, Gregory the Great, and other ancient Fathers, and the decrees of the early Councils, especially the Council of Nicæa. He then examined the canon law in its bearing on the later development of the papal power, especially from the beginning of the twelfth century onwards, and tested this evidence in the light of Scripture, the Fathers, the ancient ecclesiastical constitution. From this evidence he marshalled a formidable array of arguments against the contentions of the Popes, canonists, and schoolmen of the last 400 years in favour of the divine right of the Papacy. The results of this intensive study he embodied in a work on the papal power which he sent to the press in the beginning of June, with a view to publication in case he should be debarred from taking part in the Leipzig debate.[22] Though pugnative in tone, it is comparatively free from the invective against his opponents which characterises his correspondence during these harassing months of preparation for the debate, and for which he

[20] Enders, ii. 1-2.

[21] *Ibid.*, ii. 12.

[22] *Ibid.*, ii. 70. The work was entitled "Resolutio Lutheriana Super Propositione XIII. de Potestate Papæ." "Werke," ii. 183 f. Republished in an enlarged form after the Leipzig disputation.

excuses himself in the preface on the ground of Eck's carping and malevolent misinterpretation of his views.[23] He claims the right of free historic inquiry even on the subject of the papal power.[24] He is ready to recognise the actual Papacy just as he is ready to acknowledge the temporal power as *de facto* established in accordance with the divine order. But actual (*de facto*) power does not necessarily involve power by divine right (*de jure divino*). Nor does the mere assumption of divine right prove the validity of the claim made by the later Popes and their scholastic champions, or debar him from discussing and criticising this claim in the light of Scripture and history.[25] He is ready to submit to the papal decrees, but not slavishly as if they were on a par with God's Word, and certainly not if they are not in accordance with the Word and can only be defended by wresting and distorting it in order to establish the divine right of the mediæval Popes. To say that the Popes have not erred and that they alone truly interpret Scripture is to fly in the face of history and is nothing but perverse adulation and sophistic make believe.[26] His opponents call him a heretic, an innovator, and other opprobrious names. Well, then, go back to Scripture and ancient history and see whether they do not bear out his contention that he is not an innovator, but a renovator, and that not he but they are worthy of the name of heretic.

As a piece of research, apart from its controversial aspect, the work is a remarkable example of the application of the critical historic method in the attempt to appraise the value of dogma and assumption in the light of history. His critical insight might at times be lacking in penetration; his historic scholarship not altogether adequate from the standpoint of later criticism. But he was undoubtedly on the right lines in striving to view the past in its own light and not through the haze of the later middle age, and thus to impart the true perspective to the picture he delineates. He certainly had no little justification for his claim to speak

[23] "Werke," ii. 183-184.
[24] *Ibid.*, ii. 185. Hujus rei veritatem libere inquirere et disputare.
[25] *Ibid.*, ii. 200-201; *cf.* 186-187.
[26] *Ibid.*, ii. 199, 201.

with expert knowledge on a problem which is not so much a theological as a historic one, even though he holds from the outset a brief on his own side of it. It was, in truth, a fallacious and futile method, from the historic point of view, to find the developed mediæval Papacy in the New Testament, the Fathers, and the records of the ancient Church, as the ultra-papal party in the schools and their champion, Eck, professed to do. Very risky, too, the attempt to do this against an antagonist who had taken such pains to study the sources [27] and could bring to bear on the discussion the weight of knowledge, a powerful and nimble intellect, and a resourceful dialectic.

II. The Theological Battle of Leipzig

The disputation had been fixed to begin on the 27th June.[28] But Luther had not been included in the formal concession granted by Duke George of Saxony and the University of Leipzig to Carlstadt and Eck, and in spite of repeated requests the Duke declined to extend to him this concession. He excused himself by saying that it had been made only in favour of Carlstadt and Eck and could not be extended unless Luther could come to a preliminary arrangement with Eck to this end.[29] To Luther's letter requesting his compliance [30] Eck paid no attention, and as the Duke persisted in his stipulation, Luther remained in uncertainty before his arrival at Leipzig at the end of June whether he would be allowed to take part in the encounter. It was only as Carlstadt's supporter that, along with Melanchthon, Amsdorf and others of his col-

[27] "Werke," ii. 227. Ex his indiciis volui nasuto lectori satisfactum ut me non sine causa sic posuisse cognosceret nec ignorantia, sed de industria sic locutum fuisse, simul, ut insidiosæ et adulatoriæ propositioni Eccii per omnia par referrem.

[28] Enders, i. 429.

[29] See the Duke's replies to Luther's letters, Gess, "Akten und Briefe zur Kirchenpolitik Herzog Georgs von Sachsen," i. 73 f. (1905); Enders, i. 445-446; ii. 27, 59.

[30] Enders, v. 7-8, 5th April 1519.

leagues, Duke Barnim of Pomerania, Rector of the University, and a guard of 200 students, he entered Leipzig on the 24th of June.

On the day of their arrival the Bishop of Merseburg attempted to bring about a deadlock by affixing to the door of the churches a mandate inhibiting the disputation in virtue of the papal declaration of the 9th November 1518.[31] To his credit the Duke vindicated against the bishop the right of free discussion [32] and the Town Council imprisoned the bishop's emissary.[33] Though a confirmed votary of use and wont in religion, he was not indifferent to its practical evils, more especially to the devices of the Curia for filching the money of his subjects to Rome. He could deal very drastically with clerical opposition to his will and had browbeaten the Theological Faculty into compliance with the proposed disputation, which the Faculty at first opposed and which he hoped would raise the prestige of the university. He was not by any means predisposed in favour of Luther, to whom the stigma of heresy was attached, and he was ultimately to become his uncompromising antagonist. But he treated him with considerate courtesy, inviting him three times to his table, discussing with him his recent exposition of the Lord's Prayer in the vernacular,[34] and reminding him of the danger of the Bohemian heresy.[35] Luther divined in this reminder the influence of his secretary Emser, who, in contrast to Spalatin, in the case of his cousin the Elector, was playing, he suspected, the part of his detractor, whilst wearing the mask of friendship. "I was not so stupid," wrote Luther in reference to this interview, "that I did not distinguish between the flute and him that played it." [36] Emser himself, however, seems to have made no secret of his dubiety about Luther's views, and in an interview besought him for God's sake to beware of casting a stumbling-block among the people. "This matter," retorted Luther, with a thrust at Eck's motive in drawing him into the debate,

[31] Gess, "Akten und Briefe," i. 88-90; Enders, ii. 81.
[32] Walch, xv. 1432 f.
[33] Enders, ii. 81.
[34] "Werke," ii. 80 f.
[35] Enders, ii. 85.
[36] *Ibid.*, ii. 85.

"has not been started for God's sake and will not be interrupted for this reason." [37] In spite of this adverse influence behind the scenes, Luther warmly acknowledged the Duke's hospitality and his evident striving to vindicate liberty of discussion in the pursuit of truth.[38] He praises, too, the impartiality of the civic authorities and the more notable citizens. Even within the university he found sympathisers in Mosellanus, the Professor of Greek, Auerbach, Professor of Medicine, and the jurist Pistorius.[39] The Leipzig theologians, on the other hand, reserved their hospitality and their generosity for Eck, whom they feasted and lionised as the champion of the scholastic theology,[40] and who understood how to create an atmosphere in his favour and multiply his partisans.

The theological tournament had attracted a large gathering from far and near which filled the hall of the ducal castle to overflowing on the afternoon of the 27th June when Eck and Carlstadt led off on the subject of free will and grace. Mosellanus had closed the opening religious ceremonies in the forenoon by a long harangue on the art of disputing in matters theological.[41] More interesting to the modern reader are the word pictures of the three disputants, which he delineated in a letter to Justin von Pflug. Luther, he tells him, is of medium height and emaciated by care and hard study. One can almost count the bones through the skin. Nevertheless, he makes a manly and vigorous impression and his voice is clear and loud. He is a dungeon of learning and his knowledge of the Scriptures is so extraordinary that he can quote them with the utmost readiness. He knows Greek and Hebrew sufficiently to test the interpretation of any passage. He has a marvellous gift of expression as well as a wealth of matter. In manner he is courteous and friendly and there is nothing of the misanthrope or the Stoic about him. He

[37] Enders, "Luther and Emser," ii. 5; *cf.* 12, 32 (1890). See also Thurnhofer, "Corpus Catholicorum," iv. 13-14.

[38] *Ibid.*, ii. 105-106. [39] *Ibid.*, ii. 85, 105. [40] *Ibid.*, ii. 85.

[41] De ratione disputandi, præsertim in re theologica. Wiedemann, "Dr Johann Eck," 98-99. The original Latin in Löscher, iii. 567 f. German trans. in Walch, xv. 999 f.

can adapt himself to circumstances. In company he is agreeable, jocose, vivacious, always joyous, and bright and confident, however much his adversary may press him, so that one can hardly believe that he does not undertake such high matters without the divine assistance. He has only one fault, which nearly all disapprove. He is apt to be more aggressive and biting in discussion than becomes one who has started something new in theology, or the character of a theologian. Melanchthon's estimate of Luther on this occasion was equally favourable. "I admire the vivacious genius, the learning, and eloquence of Martin, known to me from a lengthy familiar intercourse, and whose pious and sincere Christian mind I cannot overestimate." [42]

Mosellanus attributes to Carlstadt Luther's qualities in a lesser degree. Only he is of smaller stature. His face is dark brown and sunburnt, his voice weak and disagreeable, his memory less tenacious, and his temper choleric. On Mosellanus, who is frankly pro-Lutheran and by his account of the disputation contributed to win for him the goodwill of his fellow-humanists, Eck, on the other hand, made an unfavourable impression. In contrast to his two opponents he is of large stature, big limbed, broad chested, with a voice like a town crier, harsh rather than distinct. His face, eyes, and features are those of a butcher or a mercenary soldier rather than a theologian. His memory is prodigious, and if his intellect were equally remarkable Nature would have created in him a masterpiece. Unfortunately, he is lacking in acuteness and penetration of judgment. He can heap up a mass of arguments and quotations from the Scriptures and other writings, but without order or point or relevancy, and knows how to impress with this imposing show those who cannot judge for themselves. He is dexterous in evading embarrassing arguments by changing the subject or adopting his opponent's position, or trickily attributing to him the very opposite of what he has asserted.[43] As a humanist, Mosellanus was perhaps prejudiced against Eck as the representative of the old scholastic culture,

[42] "Opera Corpus Ref.," i. 96. [43] Walch, xv. 1422-1424.

for which he had forsaken his earlier humanist learning. He repelled by his overbearing, blustering manner, his provoking self-assurance, his vainglorious hankering after notoriety, his artful dialectic which was more concerned with scoring points against an adversary than establishing the truth.[44] He hardly does justice to his ability and his learning, which included the ancient languages and the Fathers as well as the mediæval philosophy and theology, though he conveys the impression that in a contest for victory rather than for truth he was a resourceful antagonist. In spite of his self-seeking, he appears, too, to have been genuinely in earnest in defending the traditional standpoint against his opponent. His moral character seems to have been rather vulnerable, to judge from a remark in one of his letters, in which he relates his experience at Leipzig.[45]

The first four days' debate with Carlstadt on free will and grace gave him a chance of displaying his characteristic gifts in debate. The Wittenberg theologian had fortified himself at the outset with a pile of books and papers from which he laboriously supported his contentions on the impotence of the will and its absolute dependence on grace. This might appear to Luther as well as Mosellanus the surest method of demonstrating the truth.[46] But it was hardly fitted to interest or enthuse the audience and, from this point of view, Eck decidedly shone by the ease with which he could quote his authorities from memory and the volubility with which he could overwhelm his embarrassed antagonist and hold the attention of his hearers. On the second day he prevailed in his demand that Carlstadt should be debarred the assistance of his books and papers and should respond directly to his arguments. Bereft of this support, his lack of memory and readiness in retort exposed him to the sarcasms of his opponent, and the efforts of his friends to prompt him certainly did not increase

[44] That he has on the whole correctly estimated Eck in these respects appears from the overbearing, self-assertive tone of Eck in his communications relative to the disputation. This impression was also that of Luther himself. See Stracke, "Luther's Grosses Selbstzeugnis," 83-84.

[45] Walch, xv. 1461.

[46] Enders, ii. 82-83; *cf.* ii. 107.

his prestige with his audience. "Truly an unequal pair," remarks Mosellanus. Despite his hesitations and his diffidence, he succeeded, however, in improving his position in the course of the second two days (1st and 3rd July). Though Eck appeared the more skilful debater, the question at issue bristled with difficulties and the difficulties were not all on one side. Whilst Carlstadt maintained the complete impotence of the will to the good, even in the extreme sense that apart from grace good works are only sins, Eck contended that it possesses by nature a certain power to work the good. From the rational point of view the contention was certainly the more forcible, and he could adduce strong arguments from Scripture as well as common sense in its support. At the same time, he was hard put to it to maintain his thesis from the religious and theological point of view and was fain to change his ground under Carlstadt's searching cross-examination. He admitted that whilst the will is king of the soul in comparison with its lower powers, it is, in comparison with grace and God, only a slave and a servant.[47] Carlstadt at last seized his opportunity. He claimed this concession as an admission of the truth of his main position and forced Eck to have recourse to subtle word-splitting in order to reconcile the contradiction. He quibbled over the distinction between *totum* and *totaliter*, for instance.[48] In Melanchthon's judgment this scholastic word-splitting was sheer sophistry, and on the whole he was disposed to agree with Luther that Carlstadt had made good his thesis against this kind of quibbling, which he regarded as largely a waste of time and of precious little practical value.[49]

Far more fateful was the encounter with Luther, which began on the 4th July and lasted till the 14th. With

[47] "Der authentische text der Leipziger Disputation," 25, ed. by Seitz (1903).

[48] Seitz, 36 f.

[49] "Opera," i. 92; Walch, xv. 1446-1447. Strohl awards far too emphatically the victory to Eck: Eck avait incontestablement l'avantage. "Epanouissement de la Pensée Religieuse de Luther," 276 (1924). Hausrath is equally one-sided, i. 155 f. Barge is more discriminating. "Karlstadt," i. 297-298.

Luther's appearance on the rostrum the discussion was lifted out of the purely metaphysical and scholastic sphere into the more concrete one of ecclesiastical government and authority. Eck had the advantage of championing established beliefs and institutions against one whose teaching was startlingly revolutionary and who, in challenging the existing ecclesiastical system, had set out on what seemed a forlorn hope, though he was not fully conscious of the extent of his divergence from this system. On a question like free will and grace the scholastic theologians might dispute without much risk of incurring the charge of heresy or of collision with ecclesiastical authority as long as they professed unquestioning obedience to this authority. It was far more daring and dangerous to challenge the principle of authority itself as embodied in the Papacy and the mediæval Church. To question this principle was equivalent to setting oneself against the divine order, proclaiming oneself an apostate from the Catholic faith. In so doing Luther seemed to be taking his life and his salvation in his hands, judged by the standard of current belief. Thus to stand up to the ecclesiastical convention of centuries might well seem a desperate enterprise to his auditors as well as to his self-assured antagonist, who had besides the force of established order and belief behind him.

Eck began by asserting the divine right and institution of the papal monarchy on the ground that the Church constitutes one body under one head.[50] Luther quietly replied that the argument did not concern him. He, too, believed in a universal head of the Church.[51] Eck then claimed that the headship of this monarchy was invested by Christ in the Pope as the successor of Peter in proof of the divine right of the Papacy, and quoted Cyprian and Jerome in support of his contention.[52] The head of the Church on earth, retorted Luther, is not man, but Christ. Witness numerous passages of the New Testament[53] which

[50] "Werke," ii. 255; Seitz, 56-57.
[51] "Werke," ii. 256; Seitz, 57.
[52] "Werke," ii. 256; Seitz, 58.
[53] "Werke," ii. 257; Seitz, 58-59.

plainly disprove the assumption of his antagonist, whose quotations from Cyprian and Jerome, which he misinterprets, are not to the point. Both regard all bishops as successors of the Apostles and, as Jerome points out, there is no distinction in the New Testament between bishop and presbyter. Each community was governed by its presbyters or bishops in common. The mother of all Churches may be said to have been Jerusalem, not Rome, and to it the Council of Nicæa accorded a primacy, whilst recognising the equality of the Bishops of Alexandria and Antioch with the Bishop of Rome. At most Rome was regarded by the Western Fathers as the principal Church of the West and as such was honoured by them. But in the early centuries there was no such thing as a primacy by divine right vested in the Roman bishop, or a universal bishop, as is evident from the decrees of the Council of Nicæa and the African Council of 397, as well as the letters of Cyprian, which clearly prove the equality of bishops in the ancient Church. The Greeks have never recognised the Roman primacy to this day.[54]

Eck appealed to St Bernard in support of the necessity of an earthly head of the Church and controverted Luther's interpretation of the passages from Scripture, Cyprian, and Jerome in favour of his view of the Roman primacy by divine right.[55] The Roman Church, being founded on the rock against which the gates of hell shall not prevail, as they have prevailed in the case of those of Jerusalem, Antioch, Alexandria, which were contaminated by heresy, has preserved the truth uncorrupted.[56] As Christ is the head of the Church triumphant, so the Pope, as His vicar and the successor of Peter, is the head of the Church militant. In virtue of this fact the Papacy exists by divine, not by human right. It is vain, therefore, to adduce the case of the Greek Church as a proof of the contrary. In departing from the Roman Church the Greeks have made themselves exiles from the Christian faith.[57] Moreover,

[54] "Werke," ii. 258-259; *cf.* 285; Seitz, 60-61; *cf.* 95.
[55] "Werke," ii. 260; Seitz, 63.
[56] "Werke," ii. 262; Seitz, 65.
[57] "Werke," ii. 262; Seitz, 65.

though the ancient Church rejected the title of universal bishop, this does not preclude the fact that the Pope was recognised as bishop of the universal Church.[58]

Against arguments in support of the divine right of the Papacy derived from St Bernard or even the Fathers, Luther adduced the supreme authority of Scripture. "The word of God is above all words of man. . . . I venerate St Bernard and do not condemn his opinion. But in this discussion the genuine and specific sense of Scripture is to be accepted and to decide the issue." [59] From the Scripture it is evident that the Apostles were all equal and that Peter had no power over the others. He was, indeed, the first in the ranks of the Apostles, and to him, therefore, is owing a prerogative of honour, though not of power. This prerogative he is willing to grant to the Roman pontiff, always reserving the equal power of each.[60] But, contended Eck, does not Scripture explicitly teach that Christ founded His Church on Peter as the rock (Matt. xvi. 18)? The brunt of the battle then centred on the interpretation of this crucial passage. According to Eck, Christ in this passage constituted Peter monarch of the Church by divine right and conferred this power on his successors. The Roman primacy thus divinely constituted is essential to the unity of the Church and was instituted to this end.[61] In support of this interpretation he adduced the opinions of Jerome, Ambrose, Augustine against his antagonist, who suggested that the rock meant Christ Himself, or the common faith which Peter confessed, and maintained that in any case, whatever

[58] "Werke," ii. 263; Seitz, 65.

[59] "Werke," ii. 263-264; Seitz, 67. Sed in contentione accipiendus est sensus genuinus et proprius scripturæ, qui stare in acie possit.

[60] "Werke," ii. 265; Seitz, 69. Hoc sane fateor apostolum Petrum fuisse primum in numero apostolorum et ei deberi honoris prærogativam, sed non potestatis. Equaliter electi sunt et æqualem potestatem acceperant. Ita et de Romano pontifice sentio quod honoris prærogativa ceteris debeat anteferri, salva cuiusque æquali potestate.

[61] "Werke," ii. 274; Seitz, 80. Venio ad principale, quod petit, probaturus primatum ecclesiæ Romanæ esse de jure et constitutione Christi ita quod Petrus fuerit monarcha ecclesiæ a Christo institutus cum suis successoribus . . . probo per illa verba Christi (Matt. xvi.) Tu es Petrus, etc.

the interpretation of the word "rock," the word "Church" did not refer to the Roman Church, but to the Church generally.[62] In reply Luther claimed the bulk of patristic exegesis in support of his view. It did not occur to him to ask whether in view of the absence of the words, "On this rock I will build my Church," from the other synoptic Gospels, it was not a later interpolation on behalf of a Petrine supremacy in the early Church. This would have been too daring an anticipation of modern criticism. He was on surer ground when, leaving aside the various interpretations of the Fathers, he claimed that Eck's exegesis was incompatible with the characteristic testimony of the New Testament that Christ is both the foundation and the head of the Church. Even if Augustine or any other late Father interpreted the text in certain passages in the Eckian sense, their authority is inferior to that of Paul and Peter himself, who explicitly taught that Christ is the foundation on which the Church is built (1 Cor. iii. 11; 1 Peter ii. 4 f.).[63] Moreover, it is historically certain that the Eastern Church did not recognise the papal primacy, that it existed before that of Rome was founded, and that its bishops down to the present day have not accepted confirmation from Rome. Are then the Greeks, who for 1400 years have produced so many saints and martyrs, to be regarded as outside the Church? Was Gregory of Nazianzus, for instance, a heretic, a schismatic, a Bohemian?[64]

This was indeed a poser? Eck, who had at first roundly pronounced the Greek Church to be heretical and schismatic,[65] was fain to admit that it had produced many saints and martyrs in spite of heresy and schism.[66] From this slippery ground he adroitly sought to remove himself and at the same time embarrass and discredit his antagonist by shifting the debate to the Hussite heresy. In denying the papal primacy by divine right Luther, he contended, was defend-

[62] "Werke," ii. 272; Seitz, 78.
[63] "Werke," ii. 277-278; Seitz, 85.
[64] "Werke," ii. 276; Seitz, 83.
[65] "Werke," ii. 269; Seitz, 74.
[66] "Werke," ii. 280; Seitz, 89.

ing the damnable and pestiferous errors of Marsiglio of Padua, Wiclif, Hus, which had been condemned by the Church. He was, therefore, a patron of the Bohemians who were reported to be jubilant over their new champion.[67] It was an artful move, for the University of Leipzig owed its foundation to the racial and religious conflict between Czech and German, which had eventuated on the secession of the German teachers and students from Prague to Leipzig in 1409. The anti-Hussite spirit was particularly keen in ducal Saxony, and Eck's insinuation was an evident appeal to the prejudice of his audience. It was besides entirely irrelevant to the question of the Greek Church which Eck failed to face squarely in his desire to score a debating point against his opponent. Luther at once disclaimed any sympathy with the Bohemian or any other schism.[68] He strove to hold Eck to the question of the Greek Church, and at the end of the sitting begged that he would refrain from further imputing to him the contumely of favouring the Hussites.[69]

On resuming the discussion in the afternoon, however (5th July), he himself reverted to the subject and boldly asserted that among the articles of Hus, which have been unjustly condemned by the Pope's flatterers, were many which were most Christian and evangelical. The admission fell like a thunderbolt among the audience. According to Fröschel, who was present, Duke George swore audibly. "The plague take the fellow." [70] Luther nevertheless persisted in substantiating his contention. "For instance, the article that it is not necessary to salvation to believe that the Roman Church is superior to other Churches. I care not whether this is asserted by Wiclif or Hus. I know that Basil the Great, Gregory Nazianzus, Epiphanius of Cyprus, and innumerable other Greek bishops have been saved and nevertheless did not hold this article. It is not in the power of the Roman pontiff or the Inquisitor of heresy to establish new articles of faith, but only to judge

67 "Werke," ii. 275; Seitz, 81-82.
68 "Werke," ii. 275; Seitz, 82.
69 "Werke," ii. 278; Seitz, 86.
70 Walch, xv. 1430. Das walt die sucht.

according to those established. Nor can any believing Christian be compelled to believe whatever is beyond Scripture, which alone is of divine authority, unless there may have supervened a new and proved revelation. Yea, we are debarred by divine authority from believing anything unless it is proved either by Scripture or a manifest revelation, as Gerson more recently asserted in many passages, and Augustine anciently laid down as a specific canon. . . . Even the canonists declare that the opinion of a single private person is more valid than that of Pope or Council if it is supported by a better authority or reason." [71] He was prepared to acknowledge the Roman supremacy from a feeling of reverence and for the sake of avoiding schism. But he was not prepared on the pretext of divine right to condemn the holy men who had disputed it.[72]

In reply Eck charged him with defending the perfidy of the heretics under the guise of the sanctity of some of the Greek Fathers,[73] and persisted, in spite of Luther's repeated protests against the wilful misrepresentation of his views, in calling him a patron of the Hussites. Still worse, he has had the effrontery to champion certain of the tenets of Wiclif and Hus against the holy and praiseworthy Council of Constance, convened by the consent of the whole of Christendom.[74] In so doing he had not only championed the Hussites; he had given them reason for saying that, if the Council had erred in regard to the articles in question, it could err in regard to others, and, therefore, its authority would necessarily become suspect even within the Church. Eck will not waste words over the question as to what a Christian may be compelled or permitted to believe. But it is an axiomatic truth that an opinion, on which a Council or the Pope has authoritatively pronounced, cannot be defended without suspicion of heresy which might otherwise be defended without injury to the faith.[75] In response Luther reproached his antagonist with a breach of the preliminary agreement by which both had bound themselves

[71] "Werke," ii. 279; Seitz, 87.
[72] "Werke," ii. 280; Seitz, 88.
[73] "Werke," ii. 280; Seitz, 89.
[74] "Werke," ii. 283; Seitz, 92.
[75] "Werke," ii. 284; Seitz, 93.

to refrain from using such contumelious terms as "heretic" and to refer the question of heresy to authoritative judges at the conclusion of the disputation. He, therefore, called the attention of Duke George to the fact that his opponent had violated the public faith and demanded that he should specify the pestilential articles of Hus that he had called most Christian or retract his accusation. He proceeded to adduce a number of tenets attributed to Hus which were held not only by him, but by Augustine and Lombardus, and even by Eck himself. The charge of Bohemian heresy was, therefore, equally applicable to his opponent. Out of reverence for the Council of Constance, he would rather believe that the condemnation of these and similar articles had been interpolated into its records by some impostor. Moreover, the Council had declared only some of the articles to be heretical. Others it had merely pronounced to be erroneous, or rash, or offensive to pious ears. Such charges had been made against Christ Himself. The accusations against himself are, therefore, baseless and merely show Eck's rashness and presumption. In support of his contention that if error is ascribed to a Council its authority is endangered, Eck had quoted Augustine. But, retorted Luther, Augustine was referring to the Scripture, which is infallible, not to a Council which is but the creature of the word, and in applying this reasoning to the case of a Council he has done an injury to the Scriptures, since it is admitted even by the canonists that a Council may err. Pope and Council are men and are, therefore, not exempt from the apostolic command to prove all things and hold fast to that which is good.[76] Here again Luther was treading on dangerous ground, and at the beginning of the following sitting Duke George's chancellor, Pflug, intervened with a caveat not only against mutual recrimination, but against the rash handling of such themes as the Church and its Councils.[77] Eck was,

[76] "Werke," ii. 287-289; Seitz, 98-100. Solutionem meam confirmo auctoritate Pauli ad Thess. (v. 21), omnia probate, quod bonum est tenete. Rom. Pontifex et concilia sunt homines, ergo probandi sunt et sic tenendi; nec eximendi ab hac regula apostolica.

[77] Seitz, 102.

however, not minded to forego his advantage in luring Luther into this dangerous byway. He maintained as an infallible dogma that whatever a Council, legitimately convened, determines and defines in matters of faith is to be received as absolutely certain. It was rankly abominable to say that because a Council is composed of men it is liable to err, since, if legitimately convened, it is ruled not by men, but by the divine spirit.[78]

He was proceeding at the following sitting (7th July) to enlarge on the subject of the Council and the pestilential Hussite heresy for the purpose of discrediting his opponent in the eyes of his hearers, who did not understand Latin and were being misled by all kinds of sinister rumours to Luther's detriment. In order to counteract the rising prejudice against him thus artfully fostered, Luther interrupted to ask leave to explain his position in German. He had, he said, heard more than enough of this odious insinuation of complicity with the heretical views of the Hussites, in spite of his repeated disclaimers. He had no desire to impugn the existing Roman primacy or dissuade from obedience to the Roman Church. What he maintained was that this primacy was not by divine right. But this did not imply any lack of allegiance on his part to the *de facto* Papacy. The imperial power in Germany was likewise without divine warrant. Nevertheless obedience to this power was not to be infringed because it was not founded in Scripture, and for the same reason he implicitly recognised the duty of obedience to the Papacy.[79] He so far receded as to agree that the decrees of a Council are generally to be received, but with this reservation, that a Council has sometimes erred and is liable to err, especially in matters not of faith. He again categorically denied that it has authority to establish new dogmas. Otherwise there would be as many articles of faith as there are human opinions.[80] This conviction he will continue to hold until Eck has proved that a Council cannot err or has not erred. To do this he would require to ascribe divine right to a

[78] "Werke," ii. 296; Seitz, 109-110.
[79] "Werke," ii. 298-299; Seitz, 113.
[80] "Werke," ii. 303; Seitz, 119.

Council which by its very nature it cannot possess. No opinion can be heretical which is not against divine right.

It was now Eck's turn to be driven into a tight corner. All he could do was to give himself an air of infallible sapience, and to evade Luther's demand with a mere dogmatic generalisation. "The reverend father asks me to prove that a Council cannot err. I know not what he means by this demand unless he desires to cast suspicion on the laudable and glorious Council of Constance. But this I say to you, that, if you believe that a Council lawfully assembled has erred or errs, you are to me a heathen and a publican." [81]

From the 9th to the 14th July the disputants discussed purgatory, indulgences, penance, absolution.[82] Luther professed belief in purgatory, but contended that it could not be proved from Scripture and refused to allow the evidence of the Second Book of Maccabees, which Eck cited and which was not included in the canon.[83] On the subject of indulgences Eck was much more accommodating. He was not concerned to defend the indulgence preachers or the abuse of the traffic. Nor did he regard indulgences as necessary or obligatory, though he accepted the institution as an ecclesiastical ordinance, defended the papal power of remission in virtue of true contrition, and contended that it was not limited merely to the remission of penitential works.[84] He went a long way, in fact, towards justifying Luther's attack on the system and his contention that indulgences are good if one does not confide in them for salvation. "On the subject of indulgences," wrote Luther to Spalatin, "we were almost in agreement. If this doctrine had been preached by the indulgence sellers, the name of Martin would to-day have been unknown and the indulgence commissaries would have died of hunger if the people had been taught not to rely on this wretched system." [85] There was again sharp difference of opinion on the interpretation

81 "Werke," ii. 311; Seitz, 129.
82 "Werke," ii. 322 f. ; Seitz, 143 f.
83 "Werke," ii. 323; Seitz, 144.
84 "Werke," ii. 349 f.; Seitz, 177; *cf.* 182.
85 Enders, ii. 111.

of Scripture texts bearing on penance and absolution, and Luther at last, on the 14th July, gave vent to his impatience of what he deemed the quibbling exegesis of his opponent in a parting characteristic outburst. "The learned doctor, I grieve to say, penetrates the Scriptures as profoundly as a water spider does the water, yea he flees from the face of them as the devil flees from the Cross. With all reverence for the Fathers, I prefer the authority of the Scriptures and commend them to the future judges of this debate." [86] "The impatient monk," retorted Eck as a parting shot, "is more scurrilous than becomes the gravity of a theologian. He prefers the authority of Scripture to the Fathers and sets himself up as a second Delphic oracle who alone has an understanding of the Scriptures superior to that of any Father." [87]

Carlstadt and he thereafter began a final bout on free will and grace which ended on the following day, the 15th July.

Both disputants had displayed no little erudition and debating power. Eck had, perhaps, a more intimate knowledge of canon law and could cite the ancient Fathers and the scholastic theologians with the greatest ease. Luther himself acknowledged his culture and erudition, whilst disputing his claim to a sound knowledge of the Scriptures.[88] Luther's knowledge of the Fathers was at least equal to his, and his method of interpreting them was more in accordance with historic fact. He was superior in his profound knowledge of the Scriptures, and Eck, whilst depreciating the debating power of Carlstadt, was fain to pay a tribute to that of his greater colleague.[89] The debate suffered, in fact, from the excess of learning shown on both sides and the wearisome repetition of arguments

[86] "Werke," ii. 382; Seitz, 217.

[87] "Werke," ii. 382; Seitz, 217.

[88] Enders, ii. 107. Nam etsi in literis humanis et opinionibus scholasticis varie et copiose eruditus, tamen sacrarum literarum ego inanem inveni disputatorem; *cf.* Melanchthon, "Opera," i. 96; Cæterum apud nos magnæ admirationi plerisque fuit Ekius ob varias et insignes ingenii dotes.

[89] Qui vegetior sit memoria, ingenii acumine et eruditione, quoted by Wiedemann, "Eck," 134.

and counter-arguments based on the endless citation of passages from the Scripture and the Fathers. Little wonder that the Leipzig theologians went to sleep over this prolonged iteration of citations and arguments, and had to be wakened up at meal times. "They listened so intently," sarcastically remarks Fröschel, "and the debate tasted so sweetly that they had to be roused out of their sleep at the conclusion of each sitting in order not to miss their dinner." [90] The excitement and keenness of the opening days were continued mainly in the lively discussions in the taverns of the city. The popular interest was kept alive by the sermon in which Luther expounded his characteristic religious views to a large audience at the instigation of Duke Barnim of Pomerania, the Wittenberg Rector, and the counter-sermons in which Eck carried the contentions of the rostrum to the pulpit. [91]

Whilst Eck claimed the victory, Luther was by no means satisfied with the course of the debate. Eck had irrelevantly, if cleverly, managed to bring in side issues (Hussitism and the Council of Constance) which Luther rightly resented as beside the point and meant merely to increase his own reputation and discredit him with the audience, rather than to establish the truth on its merits. Moreover, Luther felt that he was struggling against convention in an atmosphere of suspicion and prejudice in his effort to vindicate the new truths to which his personal religious experience and his study of the Scriptures and the Fathers in the light of this experience had led him. *Male disputatum est,* he wrote to Spalatin. [92] "No wonder," he added, "that it began badly and finished worse." [93] Nevertheless, though he had felt the strain and the difficulty of breasting the fortification of the mediæval Papacy in which his antagonist entrenched himself, he was unshaken in his conviction that on the main issue the weight of Scripture and early Church history was on his side. He left to Eck and his

[90] Walch, xv. 1430.

[91] Enders, ii. 85-86.

[92] *Ibid.*, ii. 85; *cf.* 117. Hac disputatione magis tempus est perditum quam veritas quæsita.

[93] *Ibid.*, ii. 86.

patrons the temporary satisfaction of glorying in victory.[94] From the standpoint of actual institutions and beliefs he might seem an opinionated visionary, who stood alone and single-handed against the divine order in its mediæval form with nothing but the Bible and the testimony of a remote past to appeal to. In the course of the debate he had startled his hearers by denying the divine right of the Papacy, ascribing to the Scriptures the supreme authority in the sphere of religion, questioning the condemnation of Hus, and refusing to acknowledge the inerrancy of a General Council. The debate under the artful manipulation of his opponent had carried him further on the way of both affirmation and negation than he had reckoned on going. The glory of the defence might seem greater than that of the attack. But the attack had this advantage, that it had contributed to make clear the way to a fuller understanding of his own position. In this respect it was to prove a fatal blow to the mediæval Papacy. Eck's boastful assumption of victory was certainly premature. Though clever and resourceful in debate, he only scored by means of the dogmatic interpretation of Scripture and history. Luther followed the more scientific method of interpreting both in the light of their own evidence and not of mere dogma, though he also had his dogmatic prepossessions and did not at times hit on the correct historical interpretation. At the same time, he justly contended that the books of the New Testament, if rightly used, are the really normative sources for the constitution and doctrines of the early Church. Merely as an appeal to the sources, his insistence on the supreme authority of Scripture as the arbiter of early Christian faith and institutions was indefeasible. Equally convincing was his contention that there was nothing like the mediæval Roman Papacy in the New Testament Church or for hundreds of years afterwards. Similarly he was not only perfectly honest in his repudiation of the Hussite heresy, though he might be nearer it than he suspected. He was nearer the truth than his opponent

[94] Enders, ii. 85. Interim tamen ille placet, triumphat, et regnat, sed donec ediderimus nos nostra.

in his contention that a number of the articles objected against Hus contained no heresy in the theological sense of the term, but were either part and parcel of orthodox belief or were capable of a less objectionable description. Eck certainly did not err on the side of modesty in constituting himself the supreme arbiter of either heresy or history. Moreover, even on the question whether a Council was capable of error, Luther's appeal to history was far more effective and his demand for proof far more rational than his opponent's denial of fact on merely dogmatic grounds.

CHAPTER VI

THE SEQUEL OF THE LEIPZIG DISPUTATION

I. Aftermath of the Disputation

Both disputants had at the outset agreed to refer the official report of the debate to the judgment of the Universities of Erfurt and Paris, instead of to the Pope, as Eck at first suggested.[1] Luther expressly reserved his appellation to a Council and urged that all the Faculties of the respective universities should be entitled to give judgment. The case of Reuchlin had shown what the truth had to expect from the scholastic theologians, in whose hands it would fare no better than the sheep among the wolves.[2] To this proposal Eck would not agree, and Duke George, to whom the question was referred, decided in favour of the theologians. Eck further stipulated that the Augustinian members of the Erfurt Faculty should be excluded, and Luther consented on condition that the exclusion should apply to the Dominicans.[3] Both likewise agreed that the official report should not be published until judgment had been given.

Eck expected an easy victory as the result of this arrangement; was, in fact, already boasting of his triumph over his adversary. As a former Erfurt student and lecturer, Luther perhaps counted on a decision in his favour from the Erfurt Faculty. Though Trutvetter had bitterly resented his attack on the scholastic theology, he was not a member of the theological faculty, and the Occamist tradition of the university might predispose it in favour of his view of the papal power. Luther was, in fact, only repeating in his own

[1] Gess, "Akten und Briefe," i. 91 f.; Enders, ii. 73; *cf.* 82.
[2] Letter to the Elector, 18th Aug. Walch, xv. 1550.
[3] Enders, ii. 72-73; Wiedemann, "Eck," 130-131.

fashion what the great schoolman had maintained a couple of centuries before him and what the conciliar party of the previous century had actively championed. Moreover, he had in his friend Lang, the prior of the Erfurt monastery, an active if indirect champion. For the same reason he had no little ground for believing that his arguments against the divine right of the Papacy would appeal to the Sorbonne theologians who actively represented the old conciliar standpoint. These hopes proved, however, illusory. It was not merely a question of passing judgment on a theory of the papal power, but of espousing the cause of one who had practically been condemned as a heretic and a pertinacious rebel against the Holy See. To decide for Luther against Eck was to risk the charge of defending heresy and rebellion, and as the weeks passed without a decision, Luther began to suspect that the Erfurt Faculty on grounds of prudence was not disposed to compromise itself in his favour.[4] A report in the middle of October that Erfurt had decided for Eck proved indeed unfounded.[5] But the Faculty, which was at first divided on the question, ultimately, in December, declined to give a decision and the Sorbonne likewise evaded the issue in spite of Eck's efforts, through Hoogstraten, to influence it in his favour.[6]

Meanwhile neither side was disposed to waive further controversy pending the judicial decision, which was supposed to settle the issue on its own merits. Instead of a truce the disputation continued for nearly a year longer in the form of an epistolary and pamphlet warfare. As Luther humorously wrote to Lang, "Whilst professing to await judgment, we mutually pass judgment on each other, both learned and unlearned mingling in the fray." [7] Eck and his partisans had their fair share of the responsibility for this long and bitter aftermath of argument and recrimination. They clamorously claimed the victory and the glory of having routed the heretics, whilst upbraiding them with a breach of the truce. The boasting was, to say the least, both unseemly and provocative and the

[4] Enders, ii. 139.
[5] *Ibid.*, ii. 203.
[6] Eck's letter to Hoogstraten, 24th July. Wiedemann, "Eck," 131.
[7] Enders, ii. 139.

charge of breaking the truce highly questionable. The parties had only agreed not to publish a copy of the official report until the arbiters had given judgment.[8] The agreement did not preclude them from sending reports of the proceedings to their friends, as Luther, Melanchthon, Mosellanus, and others did, and Luther quite correctly maintained their right to do so if they pleased. Nor did it apply to reports which any of those present might have made and circulated.[9] Moreover, Eck, within a week after the conclusion of the debate, set a glaring example of this truce breaking in a letter to the Elector of Saxony on the 22nd July denouncing Luther's views as subversive of the faith and the Church and suggesting that his books should be burned.[10] He likewise wrote to the Pope a vainglorious epistle giving a minute account of the disputation, urging instant action against the heretics, and claiming a substantial recognition of his merits.[11] On the 25th July he indited a philippic against Melanchthon, who had written a dispassionate account of the disputation to Oecolampadius, preacher at Augsburg and the future reformer of Basle.[12] Melanchthon had no great relish for such wordy tournaments as a means of ascertaining the truth. Whilst he recognised that the conflict of wits had been waged on both sides with no little learning and logical display, he was of opinion that it did not contribute much to true piety, whilst emphasising that Luther, as compared with Eck, was actuated by a sincere passion for the truth.[13] In reply he pilloried Eck's scholastic sophistry and his unscientific method of interpreting the Scriptures and the works of the Fathers, of which he justly claimed to have a sounder and more critical knowledge than his detractor. The Scriptures, he reiterated with Luther, are the supreme standard of Christian truth and are to be interpreted in their own light, not in the absurd fashion of the schoolmen who distort them by reading into them a fourfold or even a

[8] Enders, ii. 72.
[9] *Ibid.*, ii. 118; *cf.* Melanchthon, "Opera," i. 111.
[10] *Ibid.*, ii. 91-95.
[11] *Ibid.*, ii. 194-195; *cf.* Crotus Rubianus to Luther, *ibid.*, ii. 212.
[12] Melanchthon, "Opera," i. 97 f.
[13] "Opera," i. 96.

sixfold sense.[14] Even the Fathers, whom Eck misinterprets while professing to vindicate, are not above criticism and may only be used with reserve and judgment, in view of their discordant and often erroneous exegesis of the supreme source of Christian truth.[15]

The loud-voiced, vainglorious, and self-assuming scholastic theologian fared very badly at the hands of the highly cultured and scholarly young humanist, the admiration of Erasmus as well as Luther. Equally so at the hands of Luther himself, to whom the Elector sent his letter of the 24th July. Far from admitting his defeat, he reiterated his views in a spirited and cogent statement for the Elector's enlightenment. He not only claimed the right of free discussion. In the matter of heresy he paid Eck back in his own coin. To suggest the burning of an opponent's books before he had read them was doubtless the stamp of an honourable theologian. Equally significant of his bankruptcy in argument the silly story circulated by him and his partisans that Luther had brought the devil himself in his bag to Leipzig! It would better become him to remember the Latin proverb about a pig trying to teach Minerva.[16]

This preliminary exchange of blows was the prelude to a lengthy pamphlet mêlée between the principals and their respective partisans, in which Emser, Dungersheim, Rubeus, Hoogstraten, the theologians of Cologne and Louvain, Alveld, Prierias, the Bishops of Brandenburg and Meissen intervened on the side of Eck; Oecolampadius, Spengler, Bernhard Adelmann, canon of Augsburg, Pirkheimer, Pellican, Bucer, Capito, Montanus, Museus, Crotus Rubianus, and Ulrich von Hutten on the side of Luther. Luther himself contributed his full share to this controversial literature. A lengthy account of the disputation to Spalatin (15th August) forms the introduction to an amplification of the main positions which he had defended at Leipzig and which issued from the press towards the end of August.[17]

14 "Opera," i. 115.

15 *Ibid.*, i. 115.

16 Walch, xv. 1538 f.

17 Resolutiones Lutherianæ super propositionibus suis Leipsiæ disputatis. "Werke," ii. 391 f.

Some weeks later he fired another broadside against Eck, who had been asked by the Bishop of Brandenburg to annotate some articles drawn up by the Franciscans of Jüterbog against Luther's old pupil, Francis Günther. Günther had been preacher at Jüterbog and had introduced his master's teaching into his sermons. Luther himself became involved in the quarrel in defence of his old pupil, and Eck was only too ready to seize the opportunity to arraign him as a heretic. Luther retorted with a reasoned defence in which he discovered as many as twenty-four heresies in the contentions of the Franciscans and the comments of their champion.[18]

Eck had meanwhile been exercising his critical faculty at Luther's expense in dissecting the epistle in which he had recounted to Spalatin the course of the Leipzig debate.[19] To this Luther retorted in the beginning of November with an " Epistola " in which he tells him freely what he thinks of his veracity and congratulates him on the glory of misrepresenting the truth.[20] Eck's vexation at length found vent in a proposal to burn Luther's books at Ingolstadt, and he was only dissuaded from carrying out his purpose by Reuchlin, who had taken refuge at Ingolstadt from the pestilence, and prevailed on the authorities to refrain from making fools of themselves and exposing the university to the ridicule of the world.[21] Baulked in his purpose, he determined (January 1520) to prosecute the campaign against his adversary at Rome itself, taking with him a Latin translation of Luther's vernacular writings and the MS. of his own *Opus magnum* on the papal Primacy,[22] based on the writings of the pseudo Dionysius, the forged decretals of Isidore, the interpolated canon of the Council of Nicæa, and other equally fallacious sources which he gravely accepted as authentic. This crude, uncritical

[18] " Werke," ii. 625 f. Contra malignum Joh. Eccii Judicium super aliquot articulos, Sept. 1519.

[19] Expurgatio Joh. Eckii adversus criminationes Mart. Lutheri, Sept. 1519.

[20] Epistola super Expurgatione Ecciana. " Werke," ii. 700 f.

[21] Enders, ii. 319.

[22] De Primatu Petri adversus Ludderum.

fabrication he presented to the Pope who, according to his own account, bestowed high encomiums on his genius as a historian and a theologian and promised to gratify his quest for additional benefices.[23]

Meanwhile all Germans who could read Latin were exploding in laughter over the coarse but clever satire, "Eccius Dedolatus" (Eck planed down), in which some witty humanist, long supposed to have been Pirkheimer,[24] mercilessly ridiculed and doubtless exaggerated the foibles of the hero of Leipzig. Though this coarse burlesque repels the taste of a more refined age and Luther to his credit expressed disapproval of this method of controversy, it suited the rather indelicate palate of the sixteenth century and succeeded as effectively in discrediting the anti-Lutheran leader as the "Epistolæ Obscurorum Virorum" had done in the case of Reuchlin's opponents.

Much more to Luther's taste was the telling defence of his cause in the form of a vindication of the brothers Adelmann of Augsburg, to whom Eck had contemptuously referred in a missive to the Bishop of Meissen as "the unlearned" propagators of Luther's errors.[25] This pamphlet is on a level with Melanchthon's "Defensio" and amply deserved Luther's cordial appreciation. It shows how strongly his scriptural teaching and reforming zeal appealed to the serious minds of the age, and the satire of his blustering, self-seeking opponent, which it mingles with this appreciation, made Eck wince more than even the "Eccius Dedolatus."[26]

From the attack on Eck himself he occasionally swerved to castigate his partisans. Of these the slippery Emser fared worst. Emser had indited an open letter to John

[23] See Eck's letter to Fabri with Luther's comments, "Opera Latina Var.," iv. 256 f.; Walch, xv. 1658 f.

[24] The authorship of Pirkheimer has recently been contested. Metzler, "Corpus Catholicorum," ii. 92 (1921), says that Pirkheimer was "undoubtedly" the author, without, however, adducing his reasons for this emphatic conclusion. Merker ascribes it to Nicolas Gerbelius. "Der Verfasser des Eccius Dedolatus" (1923).

[25] Canonicorum Indoctorum Lutheranorum ad Joh. Eccium Responsio. "Opera Latina Var.," iv. 61 f. German trans. in Walch, xv. 1513 f.

[26] Enders, ii. 341.

Zack, administrator of the archbishopric of Prague, in which, while professedly vindicating Luther from the suspicion of Bohemian heresy, he deftly sought to convey this impression to the minds of his readers.[27] So at least Luther interpreted his object, and the fact that he magnified Eck as the prince of theologians did not tend to lessen his indignation.[28] Emser had the vanity to parade his noble descent, which was not above suspicion, by stamping his arms (a goat with shield and helmet) on his writings. Hence Luther's onslaught on the Emser goat, in which he gave free rein to his indignation at the double dealing of his would-be friend, whom he described as a second Joab.[29] Some excuse for the virulence of this philippic may be found in the fact that his opponents were circulating silly stories of his Bohemian descent, and so seriously were these fables taken that he found it necessary to write to Spalatin a detailed account of his Thuringian parentage and birth.[30] He expected, he jocularly remarked, to hear soon that he had a wife and children in Bohemia.[31] Emser gave vent to his not unnatural indignation in a counterblast,[32] in which Luther found "nothing to the point," [33] and learned to his amusement that his hostility to the Papacy was due to his resentment that he and his Order had been denied any share in the indulgence traffic.

Towards Dungersheim, the long-winded and pedantic Leipzig professor, who had for some time pestered him with letters on the Papacy, he showed more patience and restraint till he at last told him to spare him this infliction.

[27] De Disputatione Lipsensi Epistola Hier. Emseri. "Opera Latina Var.," iv. 3 f. (Aug. 1519); "Corpus Catholicorum," iv. 29 f.

[28] Emser stoutly denied that he had written the letter to Zack with an unfriendly purpose. Enders, "Luther und Emser," ii. 6. Thurnhofer accepts his disclaimer as sincere and also believes that he had the right to the crest which he paraded so ostentatiously. "Corpus Catholicorum," iv. 9 f.

[29] Ad Aegocerotem Emserianum Mart. Lutheri Additio, Sept. 1519. "Werke," ii. 658 f.; "Opera Latina Var.," iv. 13 f.

[30] Enders, ii. 293-294.

[31] *Ibid.*, ii. 291.

[32] A Venatione Aegocerotis Assertio, Nov. 1519. "Corpus Catholicorum," iv. 45 f.

[33] Enders, ii. 262; *cf.* ii. 264.

"You have nothing on your lips but Church, Church, heretics, heretics, and you pay no attention to our repeated demand to prove all things. The Church is for you only one man, the Pope, to whom you attribute everything, and yet you do not prove by a single word that he is infallible. But we have discovered in the papal decretals more heresies than in any heretic. You ought to prove your contention, but instead of doing so you are continually begging the question by the most vicious kind of reasoning. You ought to prove that the Church of God is among you and nowhere else in the world. We desire the Scriptures as judge. You, on the other hand, desire to be judges of the Scripture. Please leave off fatiguing me with such stuff, or, as you threaten, publish your notions. . . . You always misinterpret what I say like that ass Rubeus in your midst at Leipzig. This is the habit of you Leipzig critics. You read the works of others without due attention. You judge rashly. You are too dull to understand these writings." But let him not presume too much on the patience with which for a whole year he has borne his scribbling. "I am but human as you are. Whilst you sit at ease and secretly nag at me, I am overwhelmed with work and every one shows his teeth at me. I alone am expected to show humility whilst being attacked by ravening wolves. The weight of the globe oppresses me, and if at length I hit back, God knows how I am pilloried, whereas you, if I only nod, cannot bear it. This I write that you may understand that I desire rather peace and concord. But if it cannot be, let God's will be done." [34]

In reply Dungersheim sent the inevitable epistle announcing that he was about to go to the press with a dialogue against him.[35] Luther had no time to waste on the dreary and persistent pedant and left both letter and dialogue without an answer.

Rubeus, whom Montanus, the Rector of the Wittenberg school, answered, he contemptuously dismissed as "an ass," whose braying was beneath his notice.[36] He bestowed the same title on Hoogstraten, the Inquisitor-General, with the

[34] Enders, ii. 163-165. [35] *Ibid.*, ii. 166-167. [36] *Ibid.*, ii. 203.

qualification that for sheer ignorance, in spite of his vaunted dialectic, he had never met a more complete one in his life.[37] Another victim of his slashing style was no less a personage than the Bishop of Meissen, who took exception to the Hussite heresy which Duke George and he sniffed in a sermon on the "Sacrament of the Body of Christ," printed for the benefit of the Duchess of Brunswick-Luneburg in December 1519.[38] The Duke and the bishop seem to have given credit to the story of his Bohemian birth,[39] and whilst the Duke wrote to the Elector a warning on the subject, the bishop issued a mandate prohibiting the circulation of the sermon in his diocese and containing a misrepresentation of Luther's views.[40] Hence the outspoken trouncing to which he subjected the official of the diocese and indirectly the bishop himself in February 1520. The official, we read, must have lost his senses in wine when he penned such a lying, drunken, blockhead effusion. The grim humour and drastic language with which he belabours the unlucky culprit in the Saxon dialect was too much for the gravity of Miltitz, who tells us that he was having a drink with the bishop and his official at Stolpen when the unconscionable piece was handed to his reverence. As the bishop read it aloud, the official swore, and the more he swore the louder Miltitz laughed. From the same source we learn that even Duke George on reading it "laughed outrageously."[41] In deference to the representations of Spalatin, Luther published a less offensive reply in Latin.[42]

In the same month appeared a diatribe of the Universities of Louvain and Köln, in which a number of his writings were sentenced to be burned and he himself to be compelled to retract his damnable heresies.[43] The Louvain theologians,

[37] Enders, ii. 386-387.

[38] *Ibid.*, ii. 266; "Werke," ii. 742 f. Sermon von der hochwürdigen Sacrament der heiligen wahren Leichnam Christi.

[39] "Werke," vi. 81.

[40] The episcopal mandate, 24th Jan. 1520, is given in "Werke," vi. 151-153.

[41] "Werke," vi. 135 f. Doctor Martinus Luther's Antwort auff die Tzedel so unter des Officiel's zu Stolpen Sigel ist ausgangen.

[42] *Ibid.*, vi. 144 f. Ad Schedulam Inhibitionis, etc.

[43] *Ibid.*, vi. 174 f,

who were inclined to favour the conciliar party, as represented by the University of Paris, ignored his attack on the papal power. Those of Cologne, who were staunch defenders of the papal absolutism, included in their condemnation his views on this subject.[44] To the delight of Erasmus and the humanists, who had suffered at the hands of these obscurantist theologians and bore them a grudge for their treatment of Reuchlin, Luther let himself go once more [45] against " the asses of Louvain and Cologne," as he dubbed them in a letter to Spalatin on the 19th March 1520. He excepted some of the members of the Louvain Faculty (Dorpius, for instance, had refused to agree [46]) from the folly of having composed this farrago of words without any proofs of their delirious reasonings, worthy of the besotted habitués of a brothel or a tavern. God preserve us from these scolding old wives, whom in His anger and for our sins He has set in the seats of the learned. But what can we expect from the persecutors of Reuchlin, who have not the sense to reflect that the condemned heresy of yesterday has often become the received belief of to-day, as has happened in the case of the great Occam, of Valla, Pico Mirandola, Wessel, Lefèbre, Erasmus, whose so-called heresies have prevailed in spite of the hysterics of the obscurantists.

The Leipzig Franciscan, Alveld, next entered the lists with a defence of the divine right of the Papacy on grounds of reason, Scripture, the opinions of the schoolmen, and sundry other considerations.[47] The embittered spirit of the monkish author exploded in objurgatory and contemptuous epithets. Luther did not take this mediocre production seriously, Alveld being for him but another " ass." But as the vernacular version was fitted to mislead the people, he took the trouble to discuss for their benefit

[44] " Werke," vi. 180. Sedem apostolicam irreverenter palam et scandalose taxet, autoritatem summi pontificis impudenter attenuet.

[45] *Ibid.*, vi. 181 f. Responsio Lutheriana ad condemnationem doctrinalem per magistros nostros Lov. et Col. factam.

[46] *Ibid.*, vi. 182 ; *cf.* Enders, ii. 367.

[47] Super apostolica sede, April 1520, and a popular pamphlet in German on the same theme, May 1520.

the twofold question whether the Papacy derives its power by divine or human right, and whether the Greek, Russian, Hussite, and other Churches, who hold the latter view, are to be regarded as heretics and apostates, though they share the common Christian faith and observe the sacraments. In discussing this question he concerns himself more with the subject matter than with the author and develops his characteristic conception of the Church.[48] He does so with force and prefers not to retaliate in the abusive language of his adversary. "The calumny and vituperation with which my person is attacked so lavishly, I shall leave unanswered and make a present of this to my dear Romanists. These do not worry me. I have resolved never to avenge myself on those who vituperate my person, work, and character. I know too well that I am not worthy of commendation. But that I am sharper and bitter when it boots the defence of the Scripture, let no one reproach me in this age. I will not take this lightly. Scold, vituperate my life and my person as much as you will. I can easily forgive this. But let no one expect from me reverence or patience who ventures to make a liar of my Lord Jesus preached by me, and the Holy Ghost speaking in Scripture. My person is nothing. Only I will answer for Christ's Word with joyful heart and blithe courage without respect of persons. For this God has given me a joyous, fearless spirit, which they cannot take from me." [49]

In a final reply to Prierias—couched in very violent terms—he limited his remarks to a preface and a conclusion to the author's "Epitome," which he interpolated with short, critical footnotes. He ascribes the ultra-High Church conception of the Papacy contained therein to the inspiration of Satan and concludes that, if this conception really represents the current view at Rome, the Pope is indeed the Antichrist of Scripture and the Roman Curia the synagogue of Satan, which he invites the emperor, kings, and princes to destroy. It is a declaration of war to the

[48] Von dem Bapstum zu Rom wieder den hoch berumpten Romanisten zu Leiptzick, June 1520. "Werke," vi. 285 f.

[49] "Werke," vi. 323.

finish against the antichristian power that reigns in the modern Babylon.[50]

Such controversies were common enough in the mediæval schools in which the art of disputation, whilst sharpening wits, tended to nurture the pugnative spirit and resulted in frequent academic and monastic quarrels. From this point of view there was nothing extraordinary in this aftermath of the Leipzig debate, in which both sides repeated *ad nauseam* the old arguments and gave themselves the satisfaction of indulging in personal invective. As a mere scholastic quarrel the controversy between Eck and Luther and their respective partisans is not particularly engrossing. What redeems it and imparts to it a particular interest is the fact that it forms an important phase of an epoch-making movement. The personality of Luther would alone lift it out of the ordinary academic rut. Here we have a man of undoubted genius asserting and revealing himself in his conflict with a set of mediocrities, who represent the conventional religious system against one who represents himself and pits himself against the dominant system and its representatives of the merely ordinary type. Luther is certainly no ordinary scholastic disputant of the dry-as-dust type. He has something new and startling to say and he says it in a style all his own. Whether he writes in Latin or the Saxon dialect he expresses himself in singularly distinctive fashion. There is a personality behind the style, a genius, originality, force which are lacking in his mediocre opponents. In conflict with these opponents he is opinionated, headstrong, intolerant. He is oftener than not unable or unwilling to look objectively at the opponent's point of view, too prone to see " an ass " in an antagonist. He does not suffer fools gladly, or hesitate to call a man a fool because he cannot or will not see eye to eye with him. The tendency to objurgate the opposition is there, and if the tendency becomes a habit, as it is likely enough to do, in a man of his temperament, it may well lead him to mistake obstinacy for conviction. At this stage, however, it is a virtue rather than a vice. For Luther is engaged in

[50] Epitoma Responsionis ad Martinum Luther, June 1520.

a desperate struggle to maintain his individual convictions against a power that has no place for individual conviction and only one way of dealing with it—the dungeon and the stake. In these circumstances Luther has need of all the intolerance and the opinionated assurance with which Nature has endowed him if he is to maintain himself against the dominant religious and ecclesiastical order. The bull-dog spirit against the enemy is the only possible one, if he is not to go under.

But this in itself would not explain this aggressive and persistent polemic. Behind it is also the strength of religious conviction, the irrefragable belief that his cause is the cause of God, that he is called on to vindicate the Word of God, the Gospel against its perverters even in the highest seat of authority, and that the time has come to make an end of this perversion and the corruption and tyranny for which it is responsible. The conviction that he stands for the truth and seeks the truth and nothing but the truth is the sheet anchor of this polemic as far as he is concerned in it. *Veritas vincet.* Truth will conquer, he assures Spalatin, in spite of the loud shout of victory that resounds from the camp of his enemies.[51] Whatever the universities decide, he further tells him, he will not retract a single syllable. The Lord's will be done.[52] There is undoubtedly character in this contention. In this respect he is far superior to his chief antagonist, as the champions whom he rallies to his side clearly realise and do not hesitate to express. Eck, Prierias, Dungersheim, Alveld were convinced enough of the strength of their case. But though they were convinced that they were defending the established divine order, their case was both historically and morally far weaker than they realised. It was bound up with an appalling travesty of religion and morality. Even Eck was fain to admit in his letters from Rome the crying degeneration of the Curia.[53] But, unlike Luther, the orthodox Eck was a braggard with an eye to his own reputation and advancement, and Dungersheim and the others,

[51] Enders, ii. 139. [52] *Ibid.*, ii. 203.

[53] "Opera Latina Var.," iv. 257. De Roma multo peiora audivi quam sentiam.

while respectable, did not rise above the ecclesiastical level of their time, to which the dominant system, whatever its shortcomings, was indefeasible. Luther, on the other hand, in this daring enterprise was treading the dangerous path that had hitherto led to the stake, breasting Bible in hand misrepresentation, defamation, threats, death itself for the sake of what he deemed to be the truth. With the ceaseless strain of self-defence, the stigma of heresy, the contingency of martyrdom to exacerbate his spirit, in addition to the exacting labours of his office as professor and preacher, it is hardly to be wondered that his overstrained, overworked condition found vent at times in fierce invective, one-sided judgment, and lack of self-restraint.

The long-drawn out pamphlet warfare is further important, inasmuch as it materially contributed to develop his views on the questions at issue. From this point of view it would have paid the Curia to muzzle his opponents and devote itself instead to the clamant task of radically reforming the evils which lent such force to Luther's indictment of the Papacy and the Church. It was surely a most unpropitious time to parade the extravagant claims and pretensions of Rome when Germany was seething with indignations and impatience over papal exactions and Rome was synonymous for all that was corrupt and oppressive. Nevertheless this was the situation in which an alien Italian prelate like Prierias chose to flaunt the papal absolution in its crudest form before a people ripe for revolt against what it was being told was an intolerable usurpation and tyranny.

This foolish exaltation of the papal power not only tended to intensify the reaction against it. It drove Luther to turn the searchlight of historic criticism more intently on this provocative theory, only to find increasingly cogent reasons for his counter-theory that the Pope was the very Antichrist of Daniel and the Apocalypse. Moreover, the charge of Hussitism which was intended to ensure his discredit in Germany led him to study the works of Hus, only to discover that he had been a Hussite all along without knowing it. The development of his thought under the pin pricking of his opponents, the relative rapidity with which he reaches a clear apprehension of the issue is, indeed, an astonishing feature of this year of stressful battling. His controversial and his didactic writings alike show the progress he has made in what his critics call his apostasy, but what he himself regarded as his emancipation. At the end of this year of attack and counter-attack he has come to the parting of the ways. He has already formed the resolution that unless the Pope disowns his opponents and their baneful contentions, he will utterly renounce him and the Roman Curia. The fateful breach with Rome is already discernible. Its champions have certainly done their best to bring it about.

II. Progress of Luther's Reforming Views

In the " Resolutiones Lutherianæ " he renews in a more defiant and uncompromising spirit the battle of Leipzig all along the line. He takes the place of Carlstadt in defending his characteristic views on sin, free will, grace, works, justification by faith, and shows himself a far more effective disputant. He controverts and rejects the doctrines of the schoolmen on these themes as a perversion of Paul's teaching and roundly denounces their teaching as Pelagian error.[54] He has, he says, had to unlearn all that he learned in the schools. " I know and confess that I learned nothing else from the scholastic theology than ignorance of sin, righteousness, baptism, and the whole Christian life, nor was I taught therein truly to understand the power, work, grace, and righteousness of God, nor what faith, hope, and charity really mean. Briefly, not only have I learned nothing, but I have learned only in unlearning what was altogether contrary to the divine writings. I wonder whether others have learned more to the purpose in this study. If there are any I frankly congratulate them. I for my part lost Christ in this labyrinth, and now I have found Him in Paul." [55] The teaching of Paul is, therefore,

[54] Resolutiones Lutherianæ super propositionibus suis Lipsiæ disputatis. "Werke," ii. 411 f.

[55] *Ibid.*, ii. 414.

for him the supreme test of the true theology, and the personal faith of the believer, as taught by Paul, is of more validity than all the subtle reasonings of the schoolmen.

In spite of his emphasis on Scripture as the supreme standard of truth, he begins to apply the critical method even to this standard and anticipates in tentative fashion the modern view of the relative value and authority of its component parts. He discovers that the Epistle of James is inferior to the Epistles of Paul. Its style is far below the majesty of apostolic diction and is not in any way to be compared with that of Paul.[56] He distinguishes between a living faith and mere opinion.[57] The schoolmen are crassly ignorant of the true sense of Scripture. On the question of the authority of Scripture in relation to that of the Church he roundly affirms that to understand the saying of Augustine that he would not have believed the Gospel unless the authority of the Church had induced him to do so, in the sense of placing the Church and the Pope above the Gospel, as his opponents do, is a doctrine worthy of Lucifer, who sought to be equal with God.[58] He reverences the authority of the Church, but he distinguishes between it and the Roman Church, and equates it with the whole body of believers throughout the world in which the spirit of Christ rules. It does not consist merely of the Pope and the cardinals—the Church of papal notaries, penitentiaries, and Masters of the Sacred Palace like Prierias.[59] Nor does it consist even in a General Council, which, he agrees, is superior to the Pope, but which, he contends even more explicitly than at Leipzig, is liable to err. Did not the African Council convened by Cyprian err on the question of the rebaptism of heretics? The Councils of Constance and Basle decreed that the Pope is inferior to a Council. The recent Lateran Council at Rome, on the other hand, decided for the papal supremacy over a Council. Both cannot be true. Which of them erred?[60]

[56] "Werke," ii. 425. Stilus epistolæ illius longe est infra apostolicam majestatem, nec cum Paulino ullo modo comparandus, deinde de fide viva loquitur Paulus.

[57] *Ibid.*, ii. 425.

[58] *Ibid.*, ii. 429-430.

[59] *Ibid.*, ii. 427-429.

[60] *Ibid.*, ii. 405.

Nor can he find a divine warrant for certain ecclesiastical practices or ordinances which his opponents regard as essentials of religion. He denies, for instance, the monastic distinction between the precepts and the counsels of the Gospel, and maintains that there is only a common standard of the religious life for all Christians, who are bound to strive after the highest perfection.[61] Auricular confession is not taught in Scripture, but brotherly confession to one another. Though he will not condemn it outright, he denounces it as a source of needless torture of conscience to sensitive souls and a priestly tyranny. There is no institution of the Church which stands so much in need of reformation.[62] The whole system of laws and regulations developed by the Roman Curia is noxious to the liberty of the Church, let alone the mercenary spirit which it nurtures.[63] Eck had said something about the Pope's power to canonise the saints. Luther asks where in all Scripture the power of canonisation is ascribed to the Pope, and puts sundry other queries about the necessity and the utility of the practice. Let every one canonise as much as he likes for all that he cares.[64] He is beginning to question the current belief in purgatory, to treat it as an open question. It is not an article of faith and he is certain that it is not heretical to deny its existence.[65] He doubts, too, whether there are more than three sacraments—Baptism, the Lord's Supper, and Penance. What the theologians have fabled about the other four is very problematic.[66] The first three he explains in the vernacular sermons dedicated to the

[61] Contra malignum J. Eccii Judicium. "Werke," ii. 644.

[62] *Ibid.*, ii. 645-646. Non est in ecclesia negotium quod æque ut istud confessionis et pœnitentiæ indigeat reformatione. Nam hic omnes leges, quæstus, vis, tyrannis, error, pericula et infinita mala omnium animarum et totius ecclesiæ grassantur pleno impetu.

[63] *Ibid.*, ii. 646.

[64] *Ibid.*, ii. 652.

[65] Enders, ii. 225. Hoc certum est neminem esse hæreticum qui non credit esse purgatorium, nec est articalus fidei.

[66] Enders, ii. 278-279. De aliis sacramentis non est quod tu vel ullus hominum ex me speret aut expectet ullum sermonem donec docear ex quo loco queam illa probare. . . . Quæ autem de sacramentis illis septem fabulati illi sunt, alio tempore audies.

Duchess of Brunswick-Lüneburg, in which he already adumbrates the distinctive ideas later developed in "The Babylonish Captivity of the Church." In these sacraments the great requisite is faith which alone makes effective what they signify.[67] In the Sacrament of Penance the forgiveness of sins is given to no one because of the merit of his repentance, or any satisfaction made for sin, but solely because of his faith in God's promise in Matt. xvi. 19, although repentance and good works are not to be neglected, but are to be sedulously practised for the honour of God and the good of our neighbour.[68] It follows, therefore, that forgiveness does not depend on Pope, bishop, or priest, or any man's power, but on the Word of Christ and faith alone. For Christ willed not to make our salvation dependent on man's word or deed, but on His own. Pope, bishop, and priest can only be the servants of God's Word, and forgiveness is entirely a matter of His mercy in Christ accepted by faith. "For this depends not on the priest or on your own works, but solely on your faith. As much as you believe, so much you have." [69]

Etymologically and in primitive practice, baptism involves both the immersion and the raising of the baptized person out of the water, and in accordance with the original significance and the primitive practice, immersion, not sprinkling, should be observed.[70] For baptism symbolises spiritual death to sin and resurrection or rebirth by God's grace. But the spiritual death and regeneration which are thus symbolised are not completed in the ceremonial act. This act is but the beginning of a lifelong process of conflict with sin, the old man, which only ends with life itself. It is a mistaken notion that baptism magically takes away sin, as if the evil in human nature were thereby eradicated and the necessity of continuous dying to sin no longer existed, and as if the baptized person may therefore evade or grow slack in the struggle with the flesh. In baptism God enters into a covenant or bond with the baptized

[67] "Werke," ii. 715. Und an dem glauben ligt es als miteynander der allein macht dass die sacrament wircken was sie bedeuten und alles war wirt was der priester sagt, dan wie du glaubst so geschicht dir.

[68] *Ibid.*, ii. 716. [69] *Ibid.*, ii. 719. [70] *Ibid.*, ii. 727 f.

person, who is under the obligation to carry out throughout his whole life, in conflict with the passions, the process of dying to sin and regeneration by God's grace. This is only possible in as far as God does not impute to him the sin which inheres in all his actions, in spite of baptism, and necessitates the continuous exercise of God's mercy and grace in the non-imputation of sin. As Augustine says, "Sin is wholly forgiven in baptism, not so that it is no longer there, but that it is not imputed." We are, therefore, conscious of sin to the end of life. At the same time, he is able to place against the sense of sin and condemnation the fact of God's forgiving mercy and grace which have become operative in baptism and whose sway and regenerating power continue to operate till death brings the final deliverance from the sinful state. Here again faith is the essential thing, for faith alone can give the assurance of the forgiveness of sin and the regeneration of our nature. This is due not to our own satisfaction, our works, which are necessarily tainted with sin, but to God's mercy in Christ, of which we lay hold by faith.[71] Luther thus envisages baptism from a new angle, that of his personal religious experience and his doctrine of justification by faith, which have led him to modify the current doctrine in accordance with the teaching of Paul.

In the sermon on the Sacrament of the Altar[72] he would fain restore communion in both kinds by means of a General Council, whilst not condemning the practice of limiting the cup to the priest who partakes of the wine on behalf of the people. Communion in one kind is not in accordance with the original institution or with the fundamental idea of this sacrament, which signifies the union or communion of all Christians with one another and with Christ. The sermon gives a beautiful picture of the Christian ideal of mutual service and suffering for the common benefit

[71] "Werke," ii. 732. Dieser Glaub ist der aller nötigst, denn er der grund ist alles trostis; wer den nit hatt der muss vorzweyffelnn in sunden, dass die sund die nach der Tauff bleybt macht das alle gute werck nit reyn seyn vor Gott. Derhalben muss man gar keck und frei an die tauff sich halten und sie halten gegen alle sund und erschrecken des gewissen.

[72] *Ibid.*, ii. 742 f.

in accordance with Christ's example. Whilst sharing the current belief in transubstantiation he has no taste for the subtleties with which the scholastic theologians strove to explain the mystery.[73] He is content to accept without attempting to rationalise it or questioning the current conception which a more historic view of the institution would have led him to do. In this respect he allows his dogmatic prepossession to get the better of his historic sense and still implicitly believes in the transformation of the bread and wine into the very body and blood of Christ. But here again he emphasises faith as the indispensable condition of the efficacy of the sacrament. It has not in itself a magic efficacy (*opus operatum*) apart from the faith of the recipient (*opus operantis*). The mere saying of Mass brings no spiritual benefit. This is a mischievous fable, for without personal faith, spiritual participation, the Sacrament of the Altar is of no avail in the sight of God.[74] It is also significant that he says nothing about the Mass as an offering or sacrifice, whilst he vigorously denounces the brotherhoods who make the sacrament the occasion of gluttony and carousing (*fressen und saufen*) instead of devoting the contributions of the members to good works.[75]

The sermon on the Sacrament of the Altar is a masterpiece of Luther's gift of popular exposition. But the suggestion that a General Council should be convened to restore communion in both kinds aroused the bitter ire of his opponents. Was this not rank Bohemian heresy? Did the sermon not prove beyond question the truth of Eck's insinuation at Leipzig that he was a patron of Hus? Was it not an incontestable evidence of his Bohemian birth and education? The audacity and the scandal of such a challenge fairly took away the breath of Duke George, the Bishop of Meissen, and other horrified anti-Hussites, who saw in this proposal not only the worst of heresies, but the presage in Germany of a Hussite revolution and civil war. Even the Elector and Spalatin were troubled, though the Elector refused to respond to his cousin's request for active intervention against the heretic. He limited

[73] "Werke," ii. 749-750. [74] *Ibid.*, ii. 751-753. [75] *Ibid.*, ii. 754 f.

himself to an expression, through Spalatin, of his anxiety at this new storm.[76] Luther responded with an explanation of his sermon in which he contended that the Roman Church had never declared communion in both kinds to be heresy, had in fact consented to recognise such communion in the case of the Bohemians (Ultraquists). To refuse to do so would be to condemn the institution of Christ Himself. Christ had, however, not expressly enjoined both, and the Hussites have erred in causing schism over this question. He had no sympathy with the extremists among them who deny transubstantiation and whom he regards as heretics. But the moderate party of the Ultraquists are at most schismatics and of the schismatic spirit there is more than enough in the Church itself, which overflows with quarrelsome, heresy-hunting zealots who would be better employed in striving to bring back the Hussites by gentleness and persuasion instead of scolding and cursing them as heretics.[77] He has, moreover, not condemned communion in one kind which he regards as sufficient, but merely suggested the advisability of referring the question of communion in both kinds to the decision of a General Council.[78] To reassure the Elector he wrote letters, at the request of Spalatin, to the Archbishop of Maintz and the Bishop of Merseburg protesting that his only object in treating of this and other questions was to advance the cause of evangelical truth among the people.[79] At the same time, while ready to moderate his tone and write irenic epistles to powerful churchmen, in deference to the Elector's wishes, he was not prepared to surrender his convictions merely to evade the new danger which the controversy over his sermon had evoked. "Be it so," he writes to Spalatin on the 12th February 1520, "I foresee a new and great conflagration. Who can resist the purpose of God? Who knows whether these insensate men are not predestined by Him as the means of the revelation of the truth? Allow the thing, I pray you, to go by its own motion. God alone is in this business. We are carried away by Him. We

[76] Enders, ii. 293 f. 14th June 1520.
[77] "Werke," vi. 78 f. [78] *Ibid.*, vi. 138.
[79] Enders, ii. 308 f.; *cf.* 315.

are led rather than lead." [80] "I have already written to you," he tells him in another letter, "not to presume that this affair has been begun or carried on by your judgment, or mine, or that of any man. If it be of God it will be completed far against, above, beyond your comprehension and mine." He has not written merely to please men, and if he has seemed overfoolish, let him remember that God has chosen the foolish things of this world that He might confound them that are wise. The mandate of the Bishop of Meissen is directed not against him, but against the Word of God. His faith in his divine vocation is unshakable, and if his steadfastness in the cause brings him banishment or worse suffering, Spalatin knows how little he is troubled by such a prospect. "I beseech you, if you rightly understand the Gospel, do not imagine that this enterprise can be carried out without tumult, scandal, sedition. You will not make a feather out of a sword, nor peace out of war. The Word of God is a sword, war, ruin, offence, perdition, poison, and as Hosea says, a bear in the path and a lioness in the wood." [81] God has laid hold of him and He has foreseen what He will accomplish through him. Certain it is that he has not sought these things of himself, but all he has done has been forced upon him by a frenzy outside his control.[82] Faith, he reminds him, is the proof (*argumentum*) of things not seen. Why, then, judge according to the appearance of things? He seeks not his own glory. There is One that seeketh and judgeth, and whether the cause stands or falls, he gains nothing and loses nothing. He is, indeed, prone to vehemence. But it is difficult to moderate style and temper under this continual strain. Was Christ Himself always placid? Did He not denounce the Jews as a race of vipers and hypocrites? Was Paul always patient, who denounced the false prophet as a son of the devil and an enemy of the truth? He who is conscious of the truth cannot be patient against its inveterate and unconvincible enemies.[83]

[80] Enders, ii. 323. Rapimur, ut video, et agimur potius quam agamus.

[81] *Ibid.*, ii. 328.

[82] *Ibid.*, ii. 329. Omnia alieno furore mihi extorqueri.

[83] *Ibid.*, ii. 329-330.

To his amazement he had by this time discovered that he had been a Hussite all along. Immediately after the Leipzig disputation two Hussite pastors,[84] who had read some of his works, wrote him letters congratulating him on his defence of the Gospel and encouraging him to persevere in his struggle for the truth against the Roman Antichrist. He had, they assured him, many friends in Bohemia who regarded him as the Hus of Saxony and prayed for him day and night. At the same time one of them sent him a copy of Hus's work on the Church.[85] Luther only received these letters in the beginning of October 1519.[86] In return he sent them a number of his writings, and he and his Wittenberg associates joined in a reply which Melanchthon put into classic Latin, for both correspondents were disciples of Erasmus.[87] Hus's work on the Church, which he had not previously read, profoundly impressed him. He realised that he had been anticipated by the Bohemian reformer in some, at least, of his contentions, and he unreservedly claimed him as his forerunner in the common cause. "Without knowing it," wrote he to Spalatin, "I have hitherto been teaching all that John Hus taught and so has Staupitz. In short, we are all Hussites, though hitherto unconscious of the fact. Yea, Paul and Augustine themselves were really Hussites. See the marvellous pass to which we have come without a leader and teacher from Bohemia! I know not for very stupor what to think, in the face of these terrible judgments of God among men, of the fact that the clearest evangelical truth, publicly consumed more than 100 years ago, is still regarded as damnable error and is not allowed to be confessed. Woe to the earth!" [88]

His insight was certainly at fault in making this sweeping generalisation. He was far more original than at such moments he believed. He was no mere reproduction of Hus. He saw in the work of Hus more than was there, for the martyr of Constance was only in a limited degree

[84] Johann Poduska, Ultraquist pastor at Prague, and Wenzel Rozdalowsky, Provost of Kaiser Karl College in the same city.

[85] Enders, ii. 79.

[86] *Ibid.*, ii. 183.

[87] *Ibid.*, ii. 201.

[88] *Ibid.*, ii. 345.

his counterpart as an evangelical reformer. His vision was narrower and he had not attained to Luther's basic principle of justification by faith. But he had, at least, like Wiclif, from whom he borrowed, anticipated his views on indulgences, the papal power, the Church, his plea for liberty of conscience, and to this extent his generous judgment was well merited.

Another work which came into his hands in February 1520 made a still more overwhelming impression on his receptive mind. This was Valla's exposure of the so-called Donation of the Emperor Constantine, which Hutten had recently republished with a prefatory letter to Leo X.[89] In this forged document Constantine is represented to have recognised the primacy of the Roman Bishop over the whole Church and to have conferred on him sovereign jurisdiction over the West. The exposure of this fabrication fairly took away Luther's breath. It was for him the last nail in the coffin of the vaunted divine right of the Papacy. The discovery of this barefaced fabrication of history for the purpose of bolstering up the claims of the mediæval popes filled him with horror and excited anew the thought of the Roman Antichrist. "Good God," he wrote to Spalatin, "how great the darkness and the villany of these Romanists! How we must wonder at the judgment of God that these have not only endured, but have prevailed throughout so many centuries, and that such impure, gross, and impudent lies have been included among the Decretals, nay, that nothing may be wanting to these monstrosities, have wickedly acquired the force of an article of faith. I am so horrified that I have almost no doubt that the Pope is that very Antichrist which the world expects and of whose advent we read in the current vernacular literature, so closely does the Pope resemble him in all his life, deeds, words, and laws." [90]

The influence of Hus is discernible in the conception of the Church which he developed with remarkable argu-

[89] "Hutteni Opera," I., 155 f.; ed. Böcking; Enders, ii. 332, 24th Feb. 1520. Habeo in manibus, officio Dom. Schleupner, Donationem Constantini a Laurentio Vallensi per Huttenum editam.

[90] Enders, ii. 332.

mentative power against the Leipzig Franciscan Alveld. Alveld had maintained that, on the analogy of the State, the Church must have an earthly head and that this head is, by divine right, the Pope. Luther replies that the analogy does not apply and that the inference is, therefore, worthless. The State does not exist in an exclusively monarchic form. Its government may be aristocratic or democratic.[91] Moreover, according to Scripture, the Church is a religious democracy consisting of all believers throughout the world. It is a spiritual body bound together by a common faith and baptism. This spiritual community is not bound to Rome under an ecclesiastical monarch by divine right, and it is no heresy not to be in communion with Rome. It is, in the words of the Creed, the communion of saints. It exists wherever Christians are to be found. Nor does it consist in the outward ecclesiastical organisation developed under Roman auspices,[92] and he draws a sharp distinction between the Church in the spiritual sense, in which its true being consists, and in the ecclesiastical sense, which is merely its outward form.[93] Of this spiritual democracy Christ is the only head. This thesis he develops with no little force of argument and scriptural quotation against the objections which the Romanists urge against it in favour of the papal headship.[94] He makes sport of the ridiculous notion that finds in Aaron and the Jewish high priest a figure of St Peter and the Pope, and which Alveld gravely inflicts on his readers. Though his own exegesis of Old Testament passages is still influenced by the allegoric method, Aaron as a figure of Christ is at least better than Aaron as a figure of the Pope. His opponent boasts that the Papacy is an agelong institution, in spite of the fact that many have contested its claims. Luther meets his boast with the retort that, though the popes have striven so long to maintain their claims, they have signally failed to enslave the whole Church of God. "Therefore I say, though the Roman tyrant has striven against the Gospel to transform the common power into a tyranny, Christ's word, 'The gates of hell shall not prevail against it,' has vindicated

[91] "Werke," vi. 292.
[92] *Ibid.*, vi. 294-295.
[93] *Ibid.*, vi. 296-297.
[94] *Ibid.*, vi. 297 f.

itself. This Roman pretension to power over the whole of Christendom has never been realised."[95] Christ's kingdom is far wider than the Roman Church, and though the Romanists denounce those outside it as heretics, this does not alter the fact that a large part of Christendom refuses to acknowledge the papal pretensions. If the Papacy is a divinely ordained institution and yet half of Christendom does not recognise it, would it have been said of it that the gates of hell shall not prevail against it?[96]

The most sweeping declaration of his defiance of Rome came in his final reply on June 1520 to Prierias, who had asserted against him the papal absolutism in the most uncompromising terms. If Rome deliberately professes this extreme doctrine, then Rome is Babylon and the Pope and the cardinals are the abomination of desolation standing in the holy place (Dan. ix. 27; Matt. xxiv. 15). He will go forth from this Babylon in which faith has become extinct, the Gospel is perverted, and Christ an exile. "Adieu, therefore, unhappy, lost, and blasphemous Rome. The wrath of God is come upon you, as you have at last merited."[97] Rome has exalted itself above all power on earth and leads the enslaved nations to the devil. "Be dumb, O heaven, be horrified, O earth. See, O Christians, what Rome has become."[98] In his wrath against this tyrannic system his language reaches the climax of violence. He calls on the Emperor, kings, and princes, in the ultimate resort, to destroy it root and branch as a criminal against humanity. "To me it appears that, if the madness of the Romanists goes on at this rate, no other remedy remains than that the Emperor, kings, and princes should gird their arms, attack these pests of the earth, and decide the matter not with words, but by force and the sword. If we punish thieves with the gallows, robbers with the sword, heretics with fire, why do we not the more attack with every arm at our command these masters of perdition, these cardinals, these popes, and the whole brood of the Roman Sodom which corrupts the Church of God without end, and wash our hands in their blood, and so liberate ourselves from

[95] "Werke," vi. 310-311.
[96] *Ibid.*, vi. 311.
[97] *Ibid.*, vi. 329.
[98] *Ibid.*, vi. 336.

this common and most dangerous conflagration ?" [99] Wild rhetoric assuredly which even the strain of persecution does not excuse in a Christian theologian. It is, however, questionable whether he meant it to be taken literally, since he had already condemned the use of force in the service of religion, even against the infidel Turk. It would, nevertheless, have been well had he scored out the passage before sending this effusion to the printer. At the same time he is only re-echoing the language of the orthodox zealots throughout the Middle Ages who had proclaimed the crusade of fire and sword against the heretic in behalf of Roman tyranny over soul and conscience and exalted the papal supremacy over the State as well as the Church.

He is already beginning to seek in the State an ally in the cause of a radical reformation of the Church. In the Commentary on Galatians which he had delivered as lectures in 1516-17 and published in revised form in September 1519,[100] with a dedication to Lupinus and Carlstadt, he adumbrates this policy, though in less truculent fashion. "These wicked rascals (Prierias, etc.) make sport of and exhaust the whole of Germany with the lead and wax of the Roman Curia. What other do they show by their mockery of the holy names of the Pope and the Roman Church than that they regard us Germans as mere blockheads and simpletons, barbarians and beasts, whilst they ridicule our gullibility and our incredible patience under this spoilation. . . . I rejoice, therefore, that the German princes in recent Diets (Augsburg) have discriminated between the Roman Church and the Roman Curia, have refused the tenths, twentieths, and fiftieths demanded by

[99] "Werke," vi. 347. The attempts of Protestant writers (Walther, "Für Luther Wider Rom.," 250 f. (1906), and Kalkoff, "Entscheidungsjahre," 120 f.) to explain this passage are not very satisfactory. Köhler thinks that Luther in these words, "wash our hands in their blood," had in mind Ps. lviii. 10-11, in which the judgment of God is about to be fulfilled on the wicked. Luther believed that this judgment was once more about to be exemplified in a divine castigation of the Church, and applies the language of the Psalmist to his own time. "Das Katholische Lutherbild der Gegenwart," 33-34 (1922). This may be correct, but it is hardly a justification for the violence of this outburst.

[100] Enders, ii. 139; *cf.* 156.

the Curia, and have in virtue of this discrimination recognised that Council and Pope may err and have erred. . . . They have at last resolved that the Roman Church and the Gospel are not the same thing as the insatiable pursuit of money by the Roman Curia and its legates. The example of these lay theologians is worthy of the highest commendation. This resistance of the princes and other laymen is proof of greater piety than if they were to take up arms against the Turks." [1]

The appeal to the State to take up the work of reformation appears also in the "Sermon on Good Works." The sermon is really a treatise which he wrote at Spalatin's instigation [2] and published at the end of May 1520 with a dedication to Duke John, the Elector's brother. It had, he informed Spalatin, swelled into a book, and in his opinion it was the best of all that he had hitherto written, though it might not please his critics.[3] Its object, he tells us in the dedication, was to enlighten the laity on the fundamental principle of faith in relation to good works as the indispensable condition of true piety and morality. This principle he had inculcated in his sermons in the parish church at Wittenberg and had touched on in those on the sacraments which he dedicated to the Duchess of Brunswick-Lüneburg and other occasional pieces in the vernacular. Throughout the controversy which had developed over his Ninety-five Theses on Indulgences he had addressed himself mainly to his fellow-theologians, and had at first, at least, sought to keep the discussion within the academic sphere. His opponents had, however, compelled him to explain or defend his views, on occasion, in the vernacular in order to counteract misrepresentation or calumny. They had, in fact, contemptuously referred to him as a mere scribbler of popular sermons and tracts in spite of the goodly number of controversial pieces, fraught with learning and full of audaciously original ideas, which had made his name famous or infamous far beyond the bounds of Germany. In the dedication he retorts that he is well content to spend his life in seeking

[1] "Werke," ii. 447-449. [2] Enders, ii. 331; *cf.* 340.

[3] *Ibid.*, ii. 366, 25th March 1520. Adeo augescit inter scribendum, et si sic processerit erit meo judicio omnium quæ ediderim optimum.

to instruct and improve the ordinary laymen. In this service he will gladly leave to others the honour of producing works of learning after the fashion of the schools.[4] Moreover, he had by this time come to realise the necessity of appealing to the people through the press if his cause was to prevail. Hence this deliberate attempt to enlighten the laity on the fundamental issue of faith *versus* works which had, though gradually and at first unconsciously, led him into opposition to the whole mediæval ecclesiastical system as well as the scholastic theology.

Good works are what God has commanded, just as sin is what He has forbidden. He therefore discusses the subject in relation to the Ten Commandments, viewed in the light of the Gospel. From the Christian point of view the fundamental fact underlying all good works is faith in Christ, as Christ Himself taught in reply to the question of the Jews, "What must we do that we may work the works of God?" "This is the work of God," answers Christ, "that ye may believe in Him whom He hath sent" (John vi. 28-29). It is from this faith that, under the Christian dispensation, all good works spring and derive their goodness. But this faith is no mere belief in Christ. It is distinctively trust, confidence that God accepts our works as pleasing in His sight, and it is this that imparts to us a good conscience towards Him. The fiducial element in faith, which is already discernible in the Commentary on Romans, has become for Luther in the sermon on "Good Works," as well as in the Commentary on Galatians,[5] the

[4] "Werke," vi. 203.

[5] *Ibid.*, ii. 458. Fabulæ ergo sunt opinatorum scholasticorum hominem esse incertum in statu salutis sit nec ne. Cave tu ne aliquando sis incertus, sed certus quod in teipso perditus; laborandum autem ut certus et solidus sis in fide Christi pro peccatis tuis traditi. Quomodo potest fieri ut hanc fidem, si sit in te, non sentias, cum beatus Augustinus asserat eam certissime videri ab eo qui habet? See also Ihmels, "Das Christenthum Luther's in Seiner Eigenart," 16 (1917). Luther's first course on Galatians, delivered in 1516-1517 and elaborated into the Commentary of 1519, has been edited by Von Schubert from a student's notebook, under the title of "Luther's Vorlesung über den Galaterbrief, 1516-1517" (1918). The comments are much briefer than in the elaborated commentary, though his distinctive teaching is there.

distinctive, the essential element.[6] Without this trust, this good conscience towards God, the vital thing in religion is lacking. It begets in us love, peace, joy, hope; whereas the lack of it fills the heart with unrest, doubt, and fear which inevitably result from the mistaken attempt to satisfy God and gain His favour by our own works and merits. For we can never be sure of gaining God's favour by such works and merits in virtue of the element of uncertainty inherent in such an attempt. Without the fundamental principle of fiducial faith, religion can only be, in the words of the Psalmist, "labour and sorrow," as vain as it is burdensome, since without this faith our works cannot be pleasing to God. For not on their own account, but on account of this faith are they good in God's sight. Vain, therefore, the attempt to find peace in running to St James of Compostella, Rome, Jerusalem, and other places of pilgrimage, praying to the saints, fasting, confessing, etc. Still more hopeless to face, without this faith, the trials and sorrows of life, the torment of an accusing conscience. To build on the foundation of our own works and merits, however great, and not on a confiding faith, in absolute dependence on God's merciful acceptance of us, is, he says, to build on sand and water, and those who teach the people otherwise are blind leaders of the blind.[7]

In thus applying the test of fiducial faith to the current religion, Luther was repeating what he had previously said in more technical theological language in his expositions and controversial writings. He has in mind his own earlier experience of seeking and failing to find a gracious God by the system of work righteousness and his long struggle with the problem of sin, righteousness, the law, his long drawn-out effort to attain a good conscience towards God. For him the path to an assured relation to God and a life of joyous confidence in God did not lie in this direction. His modern Roman Catholic critics [8] deny his contention that the mediæval faith was lacking in the fiducial element.

[6] The distinctive terms in which he describes it are "trawn," "vertrawn," "zuversicht." "Werke," vi. 205-206.

[7] "Werke," vi. 207-209.

[8] Denifle, "Luther und Lutherthum," ii. 727.

But, as Brieger has pointed out, the object of this faith was the Church, as the intermediary between God and the soul, rather than God Himself.[9] Characteristic of mediæval piety was the idea of obedience to rather than trust in God.[10] At all events, Luther was proclaiming something new in emphasising absolute dependence on, confidence in God as the distinctive element in faith, in contrast and opposition to the current mediæval conception of religion.

It is this fundamental principle that he applies to the whole life of the Christian in his effort to realise the will of God as contained in the Decalogue. He follows Paul's method of interpreting the law in the light of Christianity, and, as in his case, some of his interpretations are rather forced and far fetched. The sermon, it must be remembered, is not a strictly objective discussion, but a popular homily. He makes the first commandment, for instance, forbid the idolatry of good works without justifying faith, though he by no means condemns the prescribed ecclesiastical ordinances, if observed in the right spirit and with the true insight.[11] At the same time, whilst vigorously denouncing this "idolatry," he protests against the inference of his critics that his teaching is fitted to undermine the moral life as well as the institutions of the Church. "Faith," he says, "must be the master craftsman and director of works."[12] Exercise yourself in faith and you will have enough to do in bringing forth the works of faith. Herein lies the radical difference between his piety and that of the conventional Christian. Faith does voluntarily and gladly what is pleasing to God. The Christian who lives by faith needs no prescription to bind him, though he must take care not to let his liberty degenerate into licence or slothfulness in well-doing. Ecclesiastical ordinances have their religious value in the case of those who are weak or elementary in the faith, and with whose weakness the strong must bear, whilst resisting the blind leaders who mislead them by their slavish doctrine of works.[13] But how is it possible to maintain

[9] "Luther und Wir," 15.

[10] Preuss, "Luther's Frömmigkeit," 12 (1917).

[11] "Werke," vi. 209-212.

[12] *Ibid.*, vi. 213.

[13] *Ibid.*, vi. 213-214.

this confidence towards God in the face of sin, to which all are subject and which makes even the best of our works sinful in the sight of a perfectly righteous God? Luther replies by pointing the sinner to Christ, the great Advocate with the Father and the propitiator of sin, through whom the mercy of God becomes operative in forgiveness, and his trust in God is vindicated in spite of sin.[14]

In the sermon Luther not only gives a popular exposition of good works from the evangelical standpoint, he proposes to reform the Church and Society in accordance with this teaching. The sermon is alike an evangelical homily and an aggressive reform manifesto. It is, in fact, in a considerable degree an anticipation of the Great Reform manifestos that were erelong to follow. From beginning to end he is on the warpath against the evils rampant in the Church and the world. We are, he says, living in the time of the prophets and the apostles over again in their struggle for a new and better order of things.[15] The sermon is, therefore, not merely critical; it is constructive. In the place of the false religion, which he regards as a travesty of true Christianity, he would simplify and spiritualise the worship and the institutions of the Church. His standpoint is that of Christ in His reply to the Samaritan woman, "God is a Spirit and they that worship Him must worship Him in spirit and in truth."[16] He would restore the Mass, which has become an official performance without any real meaning or efficacy for the congregation, to its original institution as a memorial of Christ's covenant with His disciples, in which we are assured of the forgiveness of sins through His death and an occasion of thanksgiving for the benefits of this covenant. He would have bishops and priests preach the Gospel, of which the Mass in its original significance is the essence and of which they are grossly ignorant, instead of the absurd fables which they are wont to foist on the people from the pulpit.[17] He would reduce the number of holy days or even abolish them, since they serve to foster sloth, self-gratification, and a superficial formalism.[18] He

14 "Werke," vi. 215-216.
15 *Ibid.*, vi. 228.
16 *Ibid.*, vi. 233.
17 *Ibid.*, vi. 231-232.
18 *Ibid.*, vi. 229-230.

would to God that only Sunday were left and that people were content to worship our Lady and the saints on this day.[19] He would make of prayer a heartfelt utterance of personal faith, trust in God, instead of the endless repetition of prescribed forms in churches and monasteries without spiritual efficacy or improvement.[20] He would limit fasting to what is necessary to discipline the flesh and strengthen the soul in its struggle with the passions, and would disallow the mistaken excessive asceticism which is injurious to health and of no real spiritual value.[21] He would follow common sense and personal experience in the matter. He would radically reform the ecclesiastical government in order that the hierarchy may devote itself to its spiritual function, instead of concerning itself with material things and worldly power. He would begin by suppressing the whole system of trafficking in ecclesiastical offices, buying and selling benefices and other devices by which Rome not only sucks the wealth of Germany to maintain its corrupt régime, but dishonours God and destroys religion.[22] It is high time to take in hand a thorough reformation of Christendom. Such a reformation is far more clamant than the crusade against the Turk. " When the Turks attack cities, land, and people, we esteem it a great calamity to Christendom. We wring our hands and summon kings and princes to the holy war. But when faith goes under, love grows cold, God's Word is neglected, and all kinds of evil take the upper hand, no one thinks of waging a spiritual warfare for the reformation of these abuses. Yea, popes, bishops, priests, and ecclesiastics who should be the leaders and captains of this spiritual warfare, are themselves the leaders and pioneers of such a Turkish, devilish army as Judas was of the Jews who came to seize Christ." [23]

The sermon seeks to apply the law, evangelically interpreted, in the political, social, and economic sphere as well as in that of the religious life. Good works are not limited to the spiritual side of life. Everything we do, in whatever

[19] "Werke," vi. 243.
[20] *Ibid.*, vi. 233.
[21] *Ibid.*, vi. 246.
[22] *Ibid.*, vi. 256-257.
[23] *Ibid.*, vi. 257-258.

relation we do it, has its religious and moral aspect. It is good or bad according as it is pleasing to God or not.[24] We are to serve God in the family, the State, our ordinary calling as well as in the church or the monastery. He expounds the second Table of the law in its bearing on the relation of parents and children, subject and prince, master and servant, man and his neighbour. In all these relations we are to exercise ourselves in good works done in faith. The family is a divine institution for the Christian education of the young in obedience, the repression of selfwill, the fear of God as well as the honour of father and mother. Unfortunately the reality of family life corresponds very ill with the ideal of the sixth commandment, and the responsibility for the failure to realise it he lays on the Church, which neglects this part of its duty, as well as the parents themselves who lack a true sense of their Christian vocation and whom the clergy mislead by their false teaching and their bad example.[25]

For Luther the State is also a divine institution and fulfils an ethical end. He, indeed, distinguishes sharply between the State and the Church. It has nothing to do with matters of faith, and its function is, in comparison with that of the Church, much less exalted and important. In its own sphere it is entitled to the absolute obedience of the subject, even in case of misgovernment. He defends this questionable principle on the ground that whereas opposition to ecclesiastical misgovernment is imperative in the interest of the faith, it is not admissible in the case of misgovernment by the civil authority, on which the spiritual welfare of the soul does not depend. The subject is, therefore, bound to bear injustice and oppression without complaint or resistance.[26] Only if it seeks to compel him to do what is against God's commandments may he refuse obedience, since such transgression of the divine law looses the bond of obedience. If, for instance, a prince undertakes a war in an unjust cause, his subjects shall not abet and help him, because God has commanded us not to kill

[24] "Werke," vi. 205-206. [25] *Ibid.*, vi. 250 f.
[26] *Ibid.*, vi. 258-260.

our neighbour, or do him an injustice, and we must obey God rather than man.[27] At the same time, he emphasises the duty and the necessity of just and wise government in the interest of the people and warns against the danger of misgovernment. He reminds rulers, too, that there is much in need of reformation in the State as well as the Church, and he would drastically repress such evils as excessive eating and drinking, the growing luxury of the upper classes, the practice of usury, the licensing of prostitution, the extortion of the clergy.[28] Whilst upholding the existing social and economic order, condemning the prevailing popular unrest, and emphasising the duty of subjection and respect on the part of the masses, he recognises the right of the workers to considerate Christian treatment at the hands of their lords and masters and quotes Paul in support of his plea for such treatment.[29]

[27] "Werke," vi. 265.

[28] *Ibid.*, vi. 260-262.

[29] *Ibid.*, vi. 263-264. The original MS. of the sermon on Good Works is printed in "Werke," ix. 229 f., edited by N. Müller.

CHAPTER VII

THE CONDEMNATION OF LUTHER

I. Resumption of the Process

The anxiety of the Pope to counter the candidature of Charles of Spain for the imperial crown on the death of Maximilian had, as we have seen, interrupted the official prosecution against Luther in the spring and early summer of 1519. In a final effort in June of this year to secure the rejection of Charles and persuade the Elector either to support the candidature of the King of France or himself accept the imperial crown, he had included among other inducements the offer of a cardinal's hat for " one of his friends." [1] The " friend " in question was, it seems, no other than Luther himself! [2] Nothing came of this extraordinary proposal which implied, of course, that Luther, as Miltitz had previously represented to Rome, was prepared to be reconciled on its own terms to the Papacy. Well might the astonished Elector ask what the poor monk of Wittenberg would do with such a high dignity? He was assured that the Pope would provide him with an adequate income in the shape of a rich bishopric.[3] In any case Luther, whose real sentiments Miltitz had misreported to Rome, was not the man to enter into such a visionary arrangement to suit the political plans of the Curia. Moreover, the Elector was not disposed to countenance the unconstitutional expedients to secure his election which the unscrupulous papal diplomacy had suggested, though he was prepared to accept election by the legitimate vote of his fellow-electors.[4] The Pope was,

[1] " Reichstagsakten," i. 823-824.

[2] Kalkoff, " Entscheidungsjahre," 111-112. [3] Kalkoff, *ibid.*, 112.

[4] "Reichstagsakten," i. 656-657. Should the majority of the electors not support the papal policy, the Pope was prepared to sanction a minority vote in favour of his own nominee. The proposal was a glaring

therefore, fain at the last moment to acquiesce in the inevitable and inform the electors through Cajetan of his willingness to recognise the election of Charles,[5] who was accordingly elected on the 28th June.

In spite of this rebuff, the Curia did not immediately resume its suit against the Elector's protégé. Cajetan had, indeed, sought to take advantage of the papal proposal to extort from the Elector the repression of the arch-heretic.[6] Frederick was neither to be bribed nor browbeaten in this matter and the impotent legate was made the scapegoat of the papal chagrin over the failure to prevent the election of the King of Spain and Naples. But whilst he fell into disfavour and shortly after took his departure from Germany, Miltitz was at last empowered to hand over the Golden Rose which the Pope had for nearly a year vainly dangled before the Elector's eyes as a bribe for the surrender of Luther, and thus earn for himself the perquisites usual on such an occasion (25th September 1519).[7]

He was, moreover, allowed to continue his informal efforts to mediate Luther's submission to the Holy See. In May 1519 he had invited him to appear at Coblentz

infringement of the Golden Bull of Charles IV., which regulated the imperial election. See the Elector's letters to Cajetan (Walch, xv. 887-889) and Orsini (" Reichstagsakten," i. 766), in which the Elector expresses his determination to act in this matter in accordance with his duty as a Christian prince. See also Kalkoff, " Z.K.G.," xxv. 415-416. He ultimately, according to Kalkoff, did consent to his own election, and on the 27th June 1519 was actually elected by four votes, including his own, as Emperor, and for three hours possessed this dignity in virtue of this vote. The vote was, however, departed from, in view of the imminent risk of civil war on the part of the Habsburg-Spanish party, and Frederick IV. abdicated rather than incur this risk in the face of the odds against his being able to maintain his imperial dignity against the Habsburg-Spanish power. See Kalkoff, "Z.K.G.," xliii. 180-182, and xliv. 416-417. Wolf, Zur Frage des Kaisertums Friedrichs des Weisen, "Z.K.G." (1927), 22 f.) contends against Kalkoff for the usual view that Frederick refused the imperial dignity which three of the Electors (Trier, Palatinate, Brandenburg) were prepared to confer on him and with his own vote would have given him the majority. Kalkoff's contention is at most little more than an inference which the definite testimony of Spalatin as to Frederick's refusal renders very questionable. Kalkoff's view is also contested by Kirn, " Friedrich der Weise und die Kirche," 132 f. (1926).

[5] " R.A.," i. 832-833. [6] Walch, xv. 888-890. [7] *Ibid.*, xv. 894.

before the Archbishop of Trier and Cajetan as arbiters, in accordance with the agreement arrived at at Altenburg in the previous January.[8] Luther flatly declined the invitation. He had not promised to appear personally before the archbishop, but only to submit his writings for his judgment, and with the legate he would have nothing more to do after his experience at Augsburg. Moreover, Miltitz had no real authority from Rome to refer the case to the archbishop and Luther preferred to defend it publicly at Leipzig. He had only too good reason for distrusting the unveracious and unreliable commissary and broadly hinted that it was not safe to trust himself in his hands. Without a safe conduct, of which Miltitz had, significantly enough, made no mention, it would be far too risky to expose himself to the plots of his enemies.[9] In these circumstances, to have gone to Coblentz would have been to walk into the lion's den, and, as he wrote to Spalatin, he was not such a fool as Miltitz imagined him to be in making such a ridiculous proposal.[10]

Four months later, towards the end of September, Miltitz made an attempt to reopen the question of his submission in the belief that the delivery of the Golden Rose would at last induce the Elector to second his efforts.[11] "Doctor Martin is in my hands," he is reported to have boasted at Dresden.[12] The Elector went the length of agreeing to his proposal to interview Luther at Liebenwerda,[13] and the interview took place on the 9th October. Luther reported to Spalatin that they had discussed the subject of the papal power without any definite conclusion and that he had expressed anew his willingness to abide by his promise to submit his case to the Archbishop of Trier.[14] In his version of the interview to the Elector, Miltitz asserted that he had promised to accompany him to Trier to confer

[8] Enders, ii. 18-20.

[9] *Ibid.*, ii. 53-55, 17th May 1519.

[10] *Ibid.*, ii. 46; *cf.* 51. Letter to Lang. Homo suavis simul confitens se nondum ex Urbe (Rome) recepisse mandatum, et sperat me tam crassæ naris esse ut non vocatus nisi sua temeritate veniam. Video ubique, undeque, quocunque modo animam meam quæri.

[11] *Ibid.*, ii. 159.

[12] *Ibid.*, ii. 139.

[13] *Ibid.*, ii. 160-161.

[14] *Ibid.*, ii. 187-188.

with the archbishop.[15] This Luther denied and found in this "fabling" another proof of the unreliability of the pretentious busybody.[16] Miltitz sought to justify his statement in a letter to the Elector, who pointed out the discrepancy between his report and that of Luther,[17] and evidently preferred to accept Luther's version of the incident. At all events he shelved the proposal by informing Miltitz that he had already come to an understanding with the archbishop at the Electoral Diet at Frankfurt to bring Luther to the next Diet for the purpose of submitting his views to the archbishop's judgment.[18]

Meanwhile the Curia had resolved to discard the policy of drift and resume the prosecution of the unconscionable Wittenberg professor. Luther was informed of this change of policy by his old Erfurt fellow-student, Crotus Rubianus, then sojourning in Italy and thus able to speak from personal observation. From this well-informed source he learned in a couple of letters which Crotus addressed to him on the 16th and 31st October 1519 [19] that his name had acquired a very bad odour at Rome, where it was heresy to approve his writings. A friend, Andrew Fuchs, Canon of Bamberg, had sent him his Resolutions on his Ninety-five Theses and his account of the Augsburg Conference (Acta Augustana), which it was only safe to read in secret. Those of the Italian theologians who agreed with him at heart were fain to dissent from his views in public, not so much from fear of the Pope as from dread of the disturbance which the diminution of the papal power would cause in the Church. For this reason the common opinion at Rome was in favour of maintaining the absolute power of the Pope as Vicar of Christ and the infallible organ of the Holy Spirit. To argue to the contrary from Scripture was utterly vain. A hundred Pauls would not induce them to give up their false opinion. At Rome only the judgment of the Holy See, not that of Scripture, carries the victory. Equally

[15] Enders, ii. 189.

[16] Letters to the Elector and Spalatin (Walch, xv. 907-908; Enders, ii. 192-193).

[17] Enders, ii. 190, 198-200.

[18] *Ibid.*, ii. 190.

[19] *Ibid.*, ii. 204 f.

futile to adduce the papal misrule of the Church, the oppression and corruption of the Curia. The Dominicans reply that all this happens by divine providence and it is not permissible to dispute the will of God. Roman impiety has sunk so low that a good Christian and theologian is held in utter contempt.[20] Processions may be seen in the streets of Rome in which the Eucharist is carried amid a crowd of shameless women and prostituted boys. "I was lately at Rome with Hess. I saw the monuments of ancient times; I saw the seat of pestilence. It was useful to have seen it; yet with disgust have I beheld it." [21] Luther's appeal to a General Council has especially roused the wrath of the Medici faction and their creatures (the mercenary relatives of the Pope) who are bent on upholding at all costs the wretched and corrupt exploitation of Germany, under the pretext of the liberties of the Church, and will not listen to the demand for reform. Let him, nevertheless, proceed in his struggle against this corrupt régime and convert Germany to his cause, whilst avoiding these rash public disputations which only serve to display the verbosity of disputants like Eck and tend to recrimination unworthy of a theologian.

Eck, he tells him in the second letter, is celebrated at Rome as the victor of Leipzig and the Curia has decided energetically to espouse his cause against Luther and the Hussites. He has written a letter which the Pope com municated secretly to two of his confidential theologians (one of them, doubtless, Prierias) and the contents of which Crotus has learned through a friend, a physician of the papal court, who furtively overheard the conference. It gave an account of the Leipzig disputation and urged the necessity of making an example of the champion of the Bohemian heresy. If the Pope did not act promptly, Saxony would be lost to the Church and the contagion would spread to other parts of Germany. Eck has suggested the means to be taken to this end and also against the

[20] Enders, ii. 207. Eo enim impietatis progressum est ut qui vocetur bonus Christianus vel theologus is extremo contemptu spretus esse videatur.

[21] *Ibid.*, ii. 207.

humanists, especially against Hutten, whose epigrams against Rome afford convincing evidence of the nefarious effects of the new culture. The Pope should compel the Universities of Paris and Erfurt to pronounce judgment in Eck's favour and appoint a commission to draw up the condemnation of Luther's heresy.

This last recommendation, which resembles Luther's demand for a hearing before a German ecclesiastical tribunal, did not commend itself to the Curia. But the missive was deemed so important that its author was summoned for consultation to Rome [22] (November 1519).

The effect of Eck's communication was erelong apparent in an Instruction despatched to Miltitz to inform the Elector of the Pope's displeasure at the continued delay in suppressing the Lutheran movement, and announcing his determination to take effective measures against the heretic and his protectors. It contained, in fact, a threat to place the electoral dominions under an interdict as well as Luther under the papal ban. With this portentous missive Miltitz was on his way from Torgau to the Elector at Lochau when he was intercepted by Spalatin on the 8th December and taken back to Torgau, whence he forwarded the gist of its contents.[23] In reply Frederick and his councillors drew up a diplomatic exculpation of the attitude hitherto adopted by him on the Lutheran question. He disclaimed all responsibility for the delay in settling the case. He had always acted in this matter as a Christian prince and an obedient son of the Holy See. Miltitz had himself begged him not to banish Luther in view of the danger of thereby affording him an opportunity to continue his activity elsewhere. Luther had not broken the agreement to keep silent, which was conditional on his opponents refraining from further controversy. He had only vindicated his honour in replying to these and taking part in the Leipzig debate. His teaching was regarded by many learned men as well founded and might, therefore, be defended without detriment to the Church. He had agreed to accept the

[22] Kalkoff, "Forschungen," 70; "Z.K.G.," xxv. 436.
[23] Walch, xv. 910-912.

Archbishop of Trier as arbiter, and neither he nor the Elector, but Miltitz himself was to blame for the delay in carrying out the agreement. Moreover, the archbishop had, at the Frankfurt Diet, found it advisable to postpone the consideration of the matter to the next Diet. His case was, therefore, still *sub judice* and the Elector failed to understand what he had done to merit the threat of interdict.[24]

This plausible document is not to be taken at its face value. It mingles fact with diplomatic fiction. Frederick was not so innocent as he professed of responsibility for the evasion and delay in dealing with the question. He had, in fact, all along been exercising his diplomatic ingenuity to frustrate the prosecution of his famous professor. In his negotiations with Cajetan this had been his supreme concern, and this concern also governed his attitude towards the go-between Miltitz. He had himself suggested to the Archbishop of Trier the postponement of the case till the next Diet. He had never seriously contemplated the removal of Luther from Saxony. True, he found it difficult to exercise any real control over Luther, who, in the pursuit and defence of what he believed to be the truth, concerned himself little with mere political calculations and had often enough tried his protector's patience and jeopardised his diplomacy by his fearless and aggressive assertion of his convictions. At the same time, he was in full sympathy with his brave stand against the corrupt and oppressive Roman régime. He seems, too, to have appreciated his evangelical teaching and was by this time not too enthusiastic over the indulgence privileges which Miltitz had brought along with the Golden Rose and did not consider it worth while to be present personally to receive them.[25] He had persistently intervened to shelter him from the tyranny of Rome by diplomatic means. He had only done so at the expense of a good deal of diplomatic finesse. He and his councillors were adepts in the art of diplomatic fencing, with which the politicians of the Curia were, how-

[24] See the documents in Walch, xv. 912-919; also Kalkoff, "Z.K.G.," xxv. 437-441.

[25] Walch, xv. 894-895.

ever, by no means unfamiliar. At Rome, as at Lochau and every other princely residence, to govern was to dissemble, and in this respect the document bears the trace of the diplomatic make-believe of the age. At the same time, the responsibility for the continuance of the controversy did not lie on his shoulders, but on those of the theologians, and not least on those of the ultra-Romanist zealots who would promptly have settled it by burning Luther and interdicting his protector. After all, it was his duty as a ruler to protect his subjects from oppression even if the oppressor was the holy Roman Church, of which he professed to be an obedient son, but which was widely regarded in Germany as the incarnation of corruption and misgovernment and whose interest it was to destroy the brave monk who had dared to arraign it. If Luther was to have a fair hearing it could only be by keeping him in the meantime safe at Wittenberg and countering every device of his Dominican enemies to entrap him and send him to a heretic's doom. Frederick took his own way in the game of checkmate—the way suited to the genius of the wary politician, though it would have been more straightforward, if less politic, to follow Luther's example and tell the plain truth, instead of seeking to hide behind a cloud of diplomatic special pleading. It was not Luther's way, and Luther, at any rate, who was risking reputation and even life for the sake of his convictions, was not consulted in the drafting of this document. And yet, humanly speaking, what would have been his fate had there been no Frederick to exercise his diplomatic ingenuity on his behalf ?

The Pope and his Vice-Chancellor, Giulio de Medici, saw in this evasive missive a proof of the Elector's veiled antagonism to the head of the Church. Hence the unmeasured denunciation of him and his advisers in the public oration delivered in the papal presence on the 11th January 1520 on the occasion of the reception of Cardinal Bibiena on his return from an embassy to the King of France. The impassioned orator went the length of denouncing the Elector by name and his advisers in general as tyrants and enemies of the faith who, under the influence of Luther, were misleading and seducing Germany, and demanding the prosecution and repression of this German "hydra." [26] The Pope did not go the length of citing the Elector himself for trial at Rome as the orator demanded, and contented himself with warning him through Serralonga of the accusation against him as the enemy of religion.[27] On the other hand, he determined to resume the process against Luther as the instigator of the revolt which, as the orator put it, was in dire danger, through his activity, of utterly undoing religion. As a preliminary he nominated on the 1st February 1520 a commission, drawn from the mendicant Orders, under the direction of Cardinals Cajetan and Accolti, to examine his teaching and formulate a list of his heresies. Whilst Cajetan was an erudite theologian and Accolti a distinguished canonist and patron of Reuchlin,[28] the monkish members of the commission were unfitted for such an investigation. They seem to have contented themselves with consulting the condemnation drawn up by the Louvain theologians without taking the trouble to study Luther's writings or evaluate his views, as Cajetan seems to have desired. With the exception of the two cardinals, they were as incompetent as they were eager to pass judgment, and at Cajetan's instigation the Vice-Chancellor had them displaced by a second commission, consisting of trained theologians and including Luther's opponents Prierias and Rhadino (11th February).

Under Cajetan's influence the new commission made an attempt to discuss and appraise Luther's teaching in a more objective spirit and to discriminate between what was deemed heretical and what was merely scandalous or offensive to pious ears (*scandalosa et offensiva*). It proposed, moreover, to try the effect of a policy of moderation, and

[26] The oration was reported by Melchior von Watt, Schulte, "Quellen und Forschungen aus Italienischen Archiven und Bibliotheken," published by the Königlichen Preussischen Hist. Institut in Rom., Bd. vi. Heft i. 174-176; Kalkoff, "Forschungen," 15 f., 36 f., 71. Kalkoff assumes that the speech was composed, if not delivered, by Aleander. *Ibid.*, 175-176; "Entscheidungsjahre," 134.

[27] Kalkoff, "Forschungen," 16 and 40; "Entscheidungsjahre," 136.

[28] Enders, i. 327, 331; Kalkoff, "Z.K.G.," xxv. 99-100. See also Schulte, "Die Römischen Verhandlungen über Luther," 1520. König. Preuss. Hist. Institut, vi. Heft i. 32 f. (1903).

whilst rejecting Luther's views in a new decretal without, however, mentioning their author, to give him another chance to retract them before proceeding to the extreme course of condemnation [29] (15th March). It reflects the influence of Cajetan and the more moderate party among the Roman theologians who, as Crotus Rubianus had informed Luther, wished to forestall an upheaval in the Church. To this end Venetus, the General of the Augustinian Order, was directed to write to Staupitz to use his influence to bring about Luther's submission. Let him take to heart the disrepute into which he has brought his Order by his attack on the Papacy and the institutions of the Church and the continued provocation which he has given the long-suffering Pope, and cease attempting by his writings to undermine the rock on which the Lord has founded the Church. Let him take warning in time. The patience of the magnanimous Leo is not inexhaustible. A Bull against his writings, if not against his person, is being prepared, though the Pope is ready to give him a last chance of "coming to himself." [30]

The Pope was, however, not disposed to implement the conciliatory policy of the commission. Under the influence of Eck, who arrived at Rome shortly after and revealed the far reaching character of Luther's attack on the papal power, which had not been fully grasped at Rome,[31] he empowered a third commission to deal with the case. This commission consisted of the two cardinals, Eck himself, and "a Spanish doctor," [32] and towards the end of April the Pope himself discussed in a long audience the list of forty-one errors in the form of a Bull of condemnation, which it had laboriously drafted and which was to be submitted to the Consistory for discussion and final adjustment.[33] It was based partly on Eck's report of Luther's contentions on the question

[29] Kalkoff, "Entscheidungsjahre," 140; "Z.K.G.," xxv. 101-102.

[30] The letter, dated 15th March 1520, is given by Brieger in "Z.K.G.," ii. 478-480.

[31] Eck's letter of 3rd May in "Opera Latina Var.," iv. 256. Bonum fuit me venisse hoc tempore Romam, quod alii parum pernoverunt errores Lutheranos.

[32] *Ibid.*, iv. 257.

[33] *Ibid.*, iv. 257.

of the power of the Pope, partly on the condemnation of the Louvain and Cologne theologians.[34]

Four meetings of the Consistory were held between the 21st May and the 1st June before the draft was formally passed as it had been presented. The discussion, which was long and sometimes lively, turned not so much on the contents of the articles, though there was some opposition on the question of the power of a General Council, which was voiced particularly by Cardinal Carvajal.[35] It was mainly concerned with the question whether Luther should be condemned forthwith, or be allowed a fixed interval to retract the errors specified ; whether these errors should be condemned *en bloc* or discrimination be made specifically between those which were heretical and those which were scandalous and offensive to pious ears ; whether the articles were in verbal accord with Luther's writings.[36] Ultimately it was decided to grant a specified period for retraction, but not to discriminate, as Cajetan proposed, between the articles, which were all alike condemned as erroneous.[37] On the 15th June the Bull *Exsurge Domine,* as thus completed, was duly signed by the chancery officials and shortly after publicly proclaimed, with the accompaniment of the burning of Luther's works in the Piazza Navona.[38]

II. The Bull Exsurge Domine

The Pope commenced the Bull with the invocation of the Psalmist, " Arise, O Lord, and judge Thine own cause." Hence its distinctive name, *Exsurge Domine.* He further invokes the aid of Peter, Paul, the saints, and the universal

[34] Kalkoff, " Forschungen," 188 ; where the points, taken from these theologians and embodied in the Bull, are given in detail. See also " Z.K.G.," xxv. 104 f.

[35] Kalkoff, " Z.K.G.," xxv. 120.

[36] *Ibid.*, xxv. 112 ; " Entscheidungsjahre," 143 f.

[37] The only attempt to discriminate was the use of the word " respectively " after the list of errors particularised. The adverb did not, however, convey to the reader what particular error was to be deemed heretical or merely offensive and scandalous.

[38] Kalkoff, " Z.K.G.," xxv. 129.

Church in vindication of the faith and the maintenance of the peace and unity of the Church against the lying teachers, misled by the father of lies, who twist the Scriptures to the destruction of the truth. He has lately heard with unspeakable grief that heresies, formerly condemned by his predecessors and by Councils, have been disseminated in the renowned German nation, which had hitherto distinguished itself in the defence of Catholic truth and the liberty of the Church. Witness the condemnation of Wiclif, Hus, Jerome by the Council of Constance, the war against the Hussites and the recent confutation of Hussite (*i.e.*, Lutheran) error by the Universities of Louvain and Cologne. In virtue of the pastoral office entrusted to him by divine grace, the Pope can no longer tolerate the poison of these pestiferous errors, which he proceeds to specify without referring to Luther by name. Here follow the forty-one articles bearing on original sin, concupiscence, the Sacrament of Penance, justifying faith, communion in both kinds, the treasures of the Church, indulgences, excommunication, the papal power, the authority of General Councils, the unjust condemnation of Hus, good works, the burning of heretics, war against the Turks, free will, purgatory, the destruction of the mendicant Orders. No one of sane mind can fail to see how pestiferous, pernicious, scandalous these errors are, how seductive of pious and simple souls, how subversive of love and reverence for the Holy Roman Church, ecclesiastical discipline, and obedience which is the fountain of all virtues. After intensive examination and discussion, and mature deliberation by commission and Consistory, the Pope pronounces them to be contrary to the doctrine and tradition of the Catholic Church and the received interpretation of the Scripture, which Augustine declared he would not have believed but for the authority of the Church. Acceptance of these errors would prove that this self-same Church, which is directed by the Holy Ghost, errs and always has erred, which is contrary to the teaching of Christ and the Fathers and the express canons of Councils and popes, disobedience to which has always been the source and cause of heresies and schisms. With the counsel and consent of the Consistory and the authority of Almighty God and the blessed Apostles Peter and Paul as well as his own, he therefore condemns and rejects these errors and requires all Christians to do likewise under penalty of the greater excommunication, and in addition, in the case of ecclesiastics, deprivation of their benefices; of convents, chapters, universities, their rights and privileges; of laymen, their feudal rights and possessions. All dissenters are further deprived of Christian burial, of legal rights, and incur the infamy and the penalties due by canon law to heretics and traitors, without any further declaration and without possibility of absolution except by the Pope himself or his special deputy. The whole body of the faithful, and particularly the ecclesiastical hierarchy and the civil power, are accordingly debarred from affirming, defending, maintaining publicly or privately the aforesaid heretical teaching, and are enjoined to seize and burn, in the presence of clergy and people, the writings of "a certain Martin Luther," in which it is embodied.

The Bull then concentrates on Luther himself, who had so far not been named. It tells of the long-continued and paternal efforts of the Pope to bring him to renounce his errors, including the invitation to come to Rome, with the offer of a safe conduct and provision of the necessary money for this purpose. These marks of the papal kindness he had contumaciously spurned and had indurately remained for over a year under the censures of the Church. Worse still, he had dared to appeal to a future Council, the authority of which he, nevertheless, refuses to recognise, against the decrees of Pope Pius II. and Julius II., which declared such an appeal to be heresy. On this account the Pope might proceed without further citation or delay to condemn him as notoriously suspect of heresy, yea as truly a heretic.[39] Nevertheless, he prefers to imitate the divine clemency which desireth not the death of the sinner, in spite of the enormity of his offence against him and the Holy See, and give him an opportunity to retract and return like the prodigal to the bosom of the Church. He adjures him and his adherents to desist from disturbing the peace, unity,

[39] Tanquam de fide notorie suspectum, imo vere hæreticum.

and truth of the Church in order that they may thereby experience his paternal affection and clemency. An interval of sixty days after the publication of the Bull in Germany is allowed for this purpose. Failing compliance, they are to be cut off as withered branches and suffer punishment as notorious and pertinacious heretics. Even his writings which contain no heresy are to be delivered to the fire in order that the remembrance of the heretic may be utterly erased from the company of the faithful. The ecclesiastical and civil authorities are required to seize and deliver him and his accomplices to Rome for punishment or banish him from their territories, with the promise of reward for compliance and the denunciation of interdict against all places where they may reside. The clergy are enjoined to publicly proclaim them heretics if they should not retract within the prescribed period and to order the faithful to cease all intercourse with them. Finally, excommunication and anathema are denounced against all of whatever rank and condition who should refuse to comply with the provisions of the Bull.[40]

The Bull thus condemns unconditionally Luther's teaching and his writings, whilst extending to himself the benefit of what was known as the "Evangelical Monition" in cases of heresy, whereby an opportunity of amendment and retraction was given. In this concession the influence of the canonists led by Accolti is discernible as against that of the theologians led by Eck, who had demanded his immediate and unconditional condemnation. The Bull thus does not actually excommunicate the heretic, but makes actual excommunication contingent on his refusal to retract, and fully six months elapsed before this supplementary Bull was promulgated.[41]

[40] The Bull, with Hutten's comments, is given in "Opera Latina Var.," iv. 263 f. German translation in Walch, xv. 1692 f. A copy of it, as printed at Rome, is in the library of the University of Munich and is critically examined by Druffel in "Sitzungsbericht der Münchener Academie der Wissenschaften, Philos. Hist. Klasse," 1880. See also Kalkoff, "Z.K.G.," xxv. 129-130. Spalatin's German translation is given by Kalkoff in "Z.K.G.," xlv. 384 f.

[41] Bull Decet Romanum, 3rd Jan. 1521.

This concession is represented as an evidence of the papal magnanimity and wisdom in the treatment of the heretic, and was apparently intended to create in Germany a favourable impression of the action of the Curia and secure an obedient reception of the Bull. If so, the Pope and his advisers were to be speedily disillusioned. The Bull contained too many problematic, if plausible statements to be received at its face value, and in view of the state of public feeling in Germany it was fitted to intensify rather than remove the widespread revulsion against the Papacy and the Curia. The Pope professes to have been actuated throughout the whole course of the proceedings against Luther by purely religious motives, to have shaped his action solely by such considerations, and to have had in view only the interests of Germany in the exercise of his jurisdiction as head of the Church. The plea was too specious to be taken seriously. Politicians like the Elector knew too much about the political manœuvres of the Curia over the imperial election to be deceived by such idealist professions. Was it, for instance, pure zeal for religion or the interest of Germany that had led the Pope to suggest and back up the election of the King of France to the imperial throne in place of one who, if ruler of Spain, was at least of German descent? Was it zeal for religion that had proposed to make Luther a cardinal? Was it zeal for the salvation of souls and the benefit of the Fatherland which sold German benefices at Rome and conferred them on a crowd of grasping curial officials and Italian clerics, and patronised the mercenary indulgence traffic engineered by the Archbishop of Maintz and the Pope in order to fleece the German people? These were awkward questions which inevitably suggested themselves to politicians like the Elector as well as reformers like Luther, and might occur even to the man in the street whom Luther had been enlightening in the vernacular on the corruption of the modern Babylon. Further, there was not a word in the Bull about the glaring evils against which Luther had forcibly protested, or the clamant necessity of their reform which he had emphasised. Some indication of a sense of these evils and of an intention to remove the cause of heresy would have been more fitted to commend the Bull than the dubious sentimental rhetoric about the papal magnanimity towards the perfidious heretic. Nor was there any attempt to meet his appeal from Scripture or to refute his teaching by giving a statement of the reasons why it was heretical. To adduce the authority of the Church as the guarantee of the true interpretation of Scripture and assume the absolute power of the Pope as the arbiter of the faith was really to beg the question at issue. The Church, as it exists, in spite of its rampant corruption, is assumed to be indefeasible. *Noli me tangere,* is the assumption and spirit of the Bull. No allowance is made for honest difference of opinion, for conscientious convictions on the questions, whether theological or ecclesiastical, in dispute.

To address a manifesto of this kind to a nation that was seething with discontent was, to say the least, very naïve. To demand that a man of Luther's genius and spirit should revoke without reasons given was simply to invite defiance and revolt. Equally futile to assume the tone of the spiritual dictator without the moral force and prestige which could alone lend weight to the papal absolutism. The old conciliar spirit was by no means quiescent, and even in the Consistory there was some opposition to the deliverance that it was heresy to appeal to a General Council.[42] The absolute tone which might influence and impress the age of a Gregory and an Innocent was out of season in the age of the successor of an Alexander VI. and a Julius II. Not only had the widespread degeneration of the Church fostered the spirit of revolt on national and economic as well as religious and ethical grounds. The critical spirit of the Renaissance was at work in evaluating doctrines and institutions in the light of their origins, in testing dogma and tradition by historic inquiry, and credulity and superstition by reason. To condemn Luther and his adherents was to condemn not merely the monk of Wittenberg and his associates of the Wittenberg theological faculty and his Order. It was to condemn the most

[42] Kalkoff, "Z.K.G.," xxv. 119 f.

powerful and resourceful prince of the empire against whom, next to Luther, the Bull was undoubtedly aimed. It was to condemn the more aggressive spirits of the humanist party who were rallying to Luther's side, a large section of the nobility, the middle class, and the people who already saw in him the deliverer from Roman corruption and tyranny.[43] Assuredly the Pope and his advisers overshot the mark in fulminating this dictatorial parchment against one who, if he might from the traditional standpoint be a heretic, was fast becoming a national hero. Only on the assumption that the Church in its secularised form was what the Bull declared it to be—the absolute, unerring, and immaculate organ of truth—was this policy of unconditional and indiscriminate repression explicable. If the degenerate mediæval Papacy and the absolute system of doctrine for which it stood were to continue, it was essential to destroy Luther. But the attempt to destroy Luther, without any attempt to reform either, was to risk the destruction of both. A decadent system or institution that will not change in the face of changing conditions and new forces is doomed. It was assuredly a case of *Quos Deus vult perdere cæcos facit.*

With this fatal document Eck, well supplied with papal ducats, was despatched to Germany on the 18th July for the purpose of notifying the Bull to the ecclesiastical and secular authorities. With him was associated Aleander, who had been professor at Paris and Chancellor of the Bishop of Liege before becoming secretary of the Vice-Chancellor, Giulio de Medici, in 1517.[44] The choice of these agents for such a mission was, to say the least, maladroit. As an Italian and a member of the Curia, Aleander was not likely to conciliate the goodwill of the Germans. More distinguished as a humanist and a diplomatist than a theologian, he was nevertheless the protagonist of the papal absolutism and the traditional orthodoxy. In the case of Eck the choice was still more objectionable. To

[43] Enders, ii. 390. Multos habes, Martine, socios in ea hæresi . . . cognitus quidem mihi es, sed quotidie magis magisque appares; post nubila sentimenti ortus nobis est sol. Crotus to Luther, 28th April 1520; *cf.* ii. 409, in which Hutten assures him of widespread support.

[44] Pastor, "History of the Popes," vii. 404-405.

confide the proclamation of the Bull to one who had distinguished himself by his zeal in the prosecution of Luther might seem good tactics in the eyes of the zealots of the Curia. But it could only serve to deepen the impression in Germany of the injustice and unfairness of the proceedings against the national reformer, and certainly did not tend to procure for the Bull or the papal agents a submissive reception. The sequel of the mission was, in fact, erelong to prove that if the Papacy was inerrant, it was at least singularly short-sighted. In shrewd common-sense political foresight it was no match for the Saxon Elector and his advisers who knew how to turn to account such a tactical blunder.

III. In Prospect of the Bull

Neither the Elector nor his protégé was taken by surprise by the papal thunderbolt. In the preceding March, Pellican had conveyed to Luther from Basle a report that measures were being taken at Rome to excommunicate him and the Elector.[45] Some weeks later (middle of April) another clerical friend (Nicolas Demuth) wrote from Halle to the same effect.[46] There came, too, from Halberstadt the inevitable popular story that a certain physician, who could make himself invisible, had received a mandate to kill Luther![47] Luther did not take these reports tragically,[48] though he communicated them to Spalatin, who consulted the jurists on the attitude which the Elector should eventually adopt.[49] On the 4th June, Hutten, writing from Maintz, prematurely professed to know that Luther was already excommunicated, and that Eck had returned loaded

[45] Enders, ii. 358. Nunc dicitur de excommunicatione in Principem Vestrum et te. Pellican probably derived his information from Melchior Watt.

[46] *Ibid.*, ii. 383; *cf.* Melanchthon to John Hessus ("Corp. Ref.," i. 160, 17th April) and to Lang (*ibid.*, i. 163).

[47] Enders, ii. 383.

[48] Melanchthon to Hessus, "Corp. Ref.," i. 160. Nos omnia ingenti animo expectamus.

[49] Kalkoff, "Z.K.G.," xxv. 448-449.

by the Pope with benefices and gold,[50] whilst Melanchthon four days later mentions a still more misleading report from Rome that the case was at a standstill there.[51] A fortnight later (21st June) Luther himself had heard from Rome that Eck was the moving spirit in the proceedings against him, but does not yet know the outcome of his efforts.[52]

Meanwhile, in the face of these sinister rumours his resolution to brave the worst that Rome can do remains inflexible. "I believe," he writes to Lang on the 21st March, in reference to Eck's journey to Italy, "that even Rome is subject to Christ who, if I am worthy, will undertake for me; if I am unworthy, I do not desire that He will intervene on my behalf."[53] "It is no new thing," he tells Spalatin on the 30th May, in exhorting him to constancy in the Lord, "if the world is troubled on account of the Word of God. Was not Herod disturbed at the news of the birth of Christ? Was not the earth shaken and the sun darkened at the death of Christ? To me it is truly a sign that the doctrine is sound if many, and these the great and the wise, take offence at it."[54] "The miserable Romanists rage against me," he writes to Jonas on the 21st June, "and seek my life. But Christ lives and reigns."[55] His confidence was rooted in his unshakable faith in God. At the same time, he was aware that his teaching was taking a grip of the nation and he found a mainstay in the growing strength of public opinion in his favour. He knew that the humanists, including even the cautious Erasmus, were rallying in his support. Melanchthon's influence was telling in this direction and his own aggressive onslaught on the papal absolutism and its obscurantist champions was winning enthusiastic recruits from the humanist party. Tributes of admiration and appreciation, incitements to hold fast and persevere in the cause of truth and liberty came thick and fast from far and near. Crotus Rubianus, returned from Italy, congratulates him from Bamberg on his spirited defence against the obscurantists of Cologne and Louvain and

[50] Enders, ii. 409.
[51] "Corp. Ref.," i. 201.
[52] Enders, ii. 420; *cf.* 412.
[53] *Ibid.*, ii. 365.
[54] *Ibid.*, ii. 404-405.
[55] *Ibid.*, ii. 420.

assures him that he has many companions in this "heresy"[56] and that powerful magnates like Sickingen are ready to protect him, as Hutten has informed him. From Hutten himself, who two years before had expressed his contempt of the hairsplitting over-indulgences by contentious monks,[57] came an offer of friendship and alliance against the common enemy (4th June 1520). Eck has denounced him as an adherent of Luther. In this he has not spoken falsely, for, he adds not quite correctly, he has always thought alike with him as far as he was able to understand him.[57] It was, however, the national aspect of the movement that really appealed to him. "In me you have a confirmed ally, whatever the issue may be. Henceforth confide to me all your plans. Let us vindicate the common liberty; let us free the Fatherland so long oppressed. We have God on our side, and if God is for us who can be against us."[58] Similar letters came to him from Bucer, Capito, Justus Jonas, Pellican, Caspar Hedio, and many others.[59] He was overwhelmed, he writes to Spalatin, with these epistolary testimonies of goodwill and devotion, and was by no means averse that the Elector should know how widespread was the support of his cause. "Good God, how great is the concourse of men to us, how many the promises of support expressed in this multifarious correspondence."[60] Still more important, letters came from magnates like Silvester von Schaumburg, not only professing adherence to his teaching as grounded on God's Word, but beseeching him not to think of seeking a refuge in Bohemia, and guaranteeing him the protection of a hundred of the Franconian nobility until it has been subjected to the decision of a General Council, or an impartial tribunal.[61] Another offer came (18th June) through Hutten[62] from the redoubtable Sickingen, who had acquired a widespread reputation as a leader of mercenary

[56] Enders, 386 f.

[57] See his letter to Count Hermann of Neuenahr, April 1518. "Opera," i. 167, ed. Böcking.

[58] "Opera," i. 356.

[59] Enders, ii. 397, *passim*.

[60] *Ibid.*, ii. 397-398.

[61] *Ibid.*, ii. 415-416, 11th June 1520.

[62] "Corpus Refor.," i. 201, Melanchthon to Hess.

soldiers.[63] Early in the year Hutten had suggested in letters to Melanchthon that Luther, if it came to the worst, should seek the protection of his powerful friend,[64] and Crotus Rubianus at his instigation had commended the plan to Luther himself by representing that Sickingen's influence had done more to overawe the Dominican opponents of Reuchlin than all the decrees of the Emperor and the Pope. He enforced it by pointing out that the Curia was bending all its energies to the task of alienating the Elector from his cause in the hope of compelling him to seek a refuge in Bohemia and thus discrediting his cause. Hence the advisability of favourably considering this more acceptable alternative.[65] Luther did not definitely reject either offer, though he told Spalatin that he wished to rely on no protector except Christ,[66] and seems to have replied to both in a recognisant spirit.[67] But the reputation of Sickingen as a military adventurer, whom Melanchthon rather indiscriminately describes as "the rare glory of the German nobility,"[68] was not such as to make him a suitable patron of the Gospel, and the turbulent Franconian nobility were also questionable allies in such a cause. Moreover, Luther had too good ground for his confidence in the Elector's fidelity to exchange his tried and resourceful protection for that of such problematic friends. At the same time, he was quick to see the advantage of holding these offers in reserve in the game of checkmating the machinations of his enemies at Rome. He could add these offers to other substantial proofs of the formidable character of the movement which the Curia had determined to crush by fulminating against him and his adherents the terrors of excommunication. Thus supported he could afford to view

[63] Ulmann, "Franz von Sickingen" (1873).

[64] "Corp. Ref.," ii. 132, 138, Jan.-Feb. 1520.

[65] Enders, ii. 392.

[66] *Ibid.*, ii. 402. Quod ut non contemno, ita nolo nisi Christo protectore niti qui forte et hunc ei spiritum dedit. To Spalatin, 13th May, in reference to Schaumburg's offer; *cf.* 444 and 456.

[67] The replies are mentioned in letters to Spalatin, 29th June and 10th July. Enders, ii. 426, 432. But they have not survived. Ulmann, "Franz von Sickingen," i. 172.

[68] "Corp. Ref.," i. 201. Equitum Germaniæ rarum decus,

with equanimity these terrors which in any case his faith in God had determined him to meet without flinching. This support would, moreover, serve as an additional weapon wherewith the Elector could parry the expected fulmination from Rome against the heretic.

Undoubtedly, too, it encouraged him in his determination to resist to the uttermost. "Remember," he wrote to Spalatin on the 17th July, in reference to further reports from Rome, "that it behoves us to suffer for the Word of God. For now that Silvester von Schaumburg and Franz von Sickingen have made me secure from the fear of man, the fury of the demons must needs break forth. It shall be a struggle to a finish with this diabolic power. Such is the will of God."[69] "We fear nothing more" (for the progress of the Gospel), he assures a member of his Order at Magdeburg in communicating to him (3rd August) the offers of Schaumburg and Sickingen.[70]

Such was the situation when on the 6th July letters from Rome reached the Elector from Cardinal Riario and Tetleben, the agent of the Archbishop of Maintz.[71] These letters were evidently inspired by the Curia and were a final attempt, pending the adjustment of the Bull, to detach Frederick from his protégé, and thus ensure his suppression whether he retracted or not. In his epistle the cardinal sees in Luther's attack on the Papacy and the Church merely the spirit of contention, ambition, and vainglory—the motives usually ascribed to heretics—which is inspired by the devil and leads to the devil. Though the man is unknown to him, he has heard that he is highly distinguished by his intellectual gifts, his learning, and knowledge of the Scriptures. The greater the pity that he has devoted these gifts to the common ruin. It is, therefore, the Elector's duty to bring about his revocation. He has the power to do so, if he only will, and the other princes will certainly not neglect to do their duty. This was a broad hint of the

[69] Enders, ii. 443.

[70] *Ibid.*, ii. 456.

[71] That of Riario is dated 3rd April 1520, that of Tetleben 30th May; but they did not reach Lochau before the 6th July. Enders (ii. 430-431) wrongly ascribes the first to Cardinal Petrucci. They are given by Kalkoff in "Z.K.G.," xxv. 587 f.

excommunication and isolation of both in the event of a refusal, and the warning was emphasised by Tetleben, who announced the preparation of the forthcoming Bull and indicated the grave consequences to the Elector and his house that must ensue if he persisted in favouring the heretic and opposing the papal will by diplomatic dissimulation.[72]

The Elector sent these letters to Luther, with a request for suggestions to be embodied in his reply. In a note to Spalatin on the 9th July, Luther appeals to the testimony of his writings to prove that he was not actuated by ambition and vainglory in this matter. He had been compelled to defend himself by the attacks of his opponents.[73] Had he not repeatedly offered to cease further agitation and vainly asked to be instructed? Eck was responsible for the discussion of the papal power, which he had initiated for no other purpose than thereby to bring him into contempt and ruin him and the university. Now that by divine providence he has been worsted, the Romanists insanely accuse him of seeking his own glory, who only desires to be allowed to do his duty unobtrusively and without publicity. Let him who wills have his office and burn his books. At the same time, he will not submit to be deprived of the liberty of discharging his duty in the ministry of the Word. He is burdened with sins enough. But he will not add to their number the unpardonable one of demitting this ministry and rendering himself guilty of so many thousands of souls by an impious silence or abandoning the truth. Let the Elector hold himself, as he has hitherto done, irresponsible for his teaching and let him renew his demand that he be instructed or convinced of his error, seeing that he himself is not qualified to instruct or judge or execute until the case has thus been first tried and conclusively settled. Let him further tell them that it is necessary to obey God before men and that he cannot be urged to act against

[72] "Z.K.G.," xxv. 592. Sub dissimulatione quadam erroris ansam aliquando præstitisse videatur.

[73] Enders, ii. 429. Testes sunt mei editi libelli in quibus totus confiteor et queror me in hanc rem nulla libidine, sed per vim tractum esse.

his conscience, or, by any divine precept, against one whom he does not know to be innocent or not. From Luther himself they may obtain all due obedience, but only if they do not ask him to suppress the truth of the Gospel and if they permit the way of salvation to be free to the Christian. What more worthy could he ask? He is certainly not after a cardinal's hat, or gold, or anything that Rome holds in high esteem. In this matter neither threats nor promises will make him untrue to the convictions for which he suffers. He trusts, in conclusion, that the Elector will not forget to point out how much Germany, by the hidden judgment of God, has been the victim of Italian oppression and trickery.[74]

A second note on the following day (10th July) strikes a far less tractable tone. He has just heard of the publication at Erfurt of the satire in which Eck has been so mercilessly "planed down" (*Eccius Dedolatus*), and he almost wishes that this vaunted and savage Bull against his teaching had arrived from Rome. He sends the letter of Schaumburg and desires the Elector to make known its contents to Cardinal Riario in order that the Romanists may know that they will only make things worse for themselves if they succeed in expelling him from Wittenberg. He need not flee to Bohemia. He can find a refuge in the heart of Germany itself among those who are willing and powerful enough to protect him in spite of all their fulminations. Secure under their protection, he can deal the Romanists more lusty blows than if he remained in his chair at Wittenberg under the Elector's auspices and obliged to reckon with his susceptibilities. "Let them, therefore, realise that what I have hitherto spared them, they owe not to my modesty or to their tyranny or their merits, but to my consideration for the name and authority of the prince as well as the common interest of the students. But for my part the die has now been cast (*jacta mihi alea*). I hold in contempt alike the fury and favour of Rome. I will not be reconciled to them; I will nevermore hold communion with them. Let them condemn and burn my books. I will return the compliment and wherever I can get

[74] Enders, ii. 428-430.

fire, I will condemn and burn the whole papal law, that brood of heresies, and will make an end of the humility so long and vainly exhibited by me, and no longer puff up with this profession of obedience the enemies of the Gospel. They attempt by force to maintain their ignorance, whilst fearing that they may not succeed so easily as in the days of yore. I doubt not that the Lord, who knows that I am a wretched sinner, will accomplish His cause either through me or through another." [75]

This outburst was meant for the benefit of the Elector and his advisers as well as the Romanists. Luther was plainly getting impatient of the diplomatic game which they had been playing so skilfully on his behalf and with which he had had perforce to reckon in the assertion and defence of his convictions. He saw that this sort of thing would not eventually save them and him from the alternative of submission to or defiance of Rome. For his part he had made his choice—*jacta est alea*—and was now in a position to show his electoral patron that he was no longer solely dependent on his favour in the assertion of convictions which had nothing to do with the calculations of the politicians. At the same time, he was sufficiently level-headed to grasp the diplomatic value of Schaumburg's offer in parrying the threatened stroke from Rome. In a more restrained postscript he suggests that the Elector should point out to the Curia that his teaching was so widespread and deeply rooted that unless Rome eschews violent measures and has recourse to persuasion on grounds of reason and Scripture, Germany will become a second Bohemia. The Germans are of such an unruly, independent temperament that it would not be safe for ever so many popes to provoke their antagonism, especially since the new culture is spreading fast, even among the laity.[76]

Thus prompted, the Elector, in his reply to Riario, repeated in his own diplomatic fashion his tantalising assurances of respect and obedience and his innocence of or complicity with Luther's action, and adduced once more Luther's readiness to be tried and instructed by an impartial tribunal and the fact that his case had been referred to

[75] Enders, ii. 432-433. [76] *Ibid.*, ii. 433.

the Archbishop of Trier, before whom he was ready to appear. He adroitly added an expression of sympathy for Riario personally without particularising the ill-treatment to which he had been subjected by his brethren of the Curia whom, inferentially, it ill became to pose as paragons of political virtue. In the missive to Tetleben he incorporated, along with these generalities, the gist of Luther's suggestions, and thus gave the Curia fair warning of the upheaval which the Bull would inevitably provoke in Germany.[77]

The warning was, of course, too late to avert the fatal fulmination. Several weeks before the despatch of these letters, the Bull, which conveyed the fatal ultimatum had been signed and sealed at Rome, and on the 8th July the Pope had indicted a brief to the Elector denouncing Luther as "a monster of Satan," sending him a copy of the Bull and diplomatically expressing in flattering terms his confidence that Frederick will, in case of his refusal of submission, arrest and imprison him pending further instructions.[78] With these documents Eck was already on his way to Germany in the latter part of July. In the beginning of August, Luther and his patron were still ignorant of these facts and Luther mentions a report that Eck had so far achieved nothing at Rome![79] It was only in the middle of August that Spalatin learned, probably from Miltitz, that Eck was on his way to Germany with the Bull, though the report that he had already arrived at Meissen was incorrect.[80] Nothing definite as to the tenor of the Bull had, however, so far transpired, and throughout the month the Elector continued his efforts to influence the Curia in favour of moderation. Though Luther had explicitly declared that for him "the die was cast," he consented at his instigation to draft a letter to Cardinal Carvajal praying

[77] The letter to Riario is given in "Opera Latina Var.," ii. 351-352, but with the wrong date, 5th Aug. 1518. That to Tetleben in v. 7-10, also wrongly dated 1st April 1920. They are also given with the right dates, along with those of Riario and Tetleben to the Elector, by Kalkoff, "Z.K.G.," xxv. 587 f. and 508-509.

[78] "Opera Latina Var.," v. 10-12; Walch, xv. 1667-1670.

[79] Enders, ii. 456, 3rd Aug. Eccius dicitur adhuc nihil expedivisse in Urbe.

[80] *Ibid.*, ii. 460, 14th Aug.; *cf.* Kalkoff, "Z.K.G.," 519-520.

him to use his influence in favour of a settlement by arbitration.[81] To the same end he consented also to issue in both Latin and German an "Offer" (*Erbieten*) to arbitrate and to write a letter to the Emperor Charles. In the "Offer," after it had been drastically edited and toned down by Spalatin,[82] he tells how he has during nearly three years of controversy suffered persecution and calumny for evangelical truth at the hands of his implacable opponents. His sole motive had been, as an obedient son of the Church, to vindicate the truth, not to serve his own ambition or vanity, and in this spirit he had offered repeatedly to be instructed from the Scriptures and submit to the arbitration of a free and impartial tribunal. His only reward had been his bitter and persistent denunciation as a heretic and schismatic. This offer he now renews and he begs forgiveness for the violence of his controversial language, in view of the provocation he had suffered and his single-minded desire to serve the truth.[83]

In the letter to the Emperor, 30th August, he likewise protested that he had sought only to vindicate the truth of the Gospel against the superstitious opinions of human traditions, until he had either been refuted or justified, with adequate reasons given. He has no desire to be protected if he is found to be a wicked heretic. He only asks that he shall not be condemned unheard or unconvinced.[84]

These documents are to be ascribed to the initiative of the Elector and his secretary rather than to Luther himself, and the original draft of the "Offer" is hardly recognisable in the sugared version which finally went to the printer

[81] Enders, ii. 464-465, 23rd Aug. The proposed letter does not seem to have been actually despatched. Kalkoff, "Z.K.G.," xxv. 512-514.

[82] *Ibid.*, ii. 464, 466.

[83] The original draft of the *Erbieten* is couched in much less tractable terms than the version actually published. It is given in "Werke," ix. 303-304, from the original in the ducal library of Gotha. Another version of it along with that actually published is given in "Werke," vi. 476. Also the Latin version, "Doctoris Mart. Lutheri Oblatio sive Protestatio." In "Opera Latina Var." it bears the wrong date, 17th Jan. 1520.

[84] Enders, ii. 468-470; "Opera Latina Var.," v. 2-4, also misdated 15th Jan. 1520; Walch, xv. 1636-1639, also wrongly dated.

from the hands of Spalatin, who also edited the letter to the Emperor.[85] He had not much faith in this diplomatic manœuvring, though he penned the epistle to the Emperor in the belief that he would favour the cause of reform. He repeats in a letter to Lang his conviction that "the Papacy is the seat of the veritable Antichrist, against whose fraud and iniquity it is permissible to make use of every effort for the salvation of souls. For my part I confess that no obedience is due by me to the Pope." [86] In these words he was referring to the publication of his "Address to the German Nobility," which he hurled forth in the middle of August from the press,[87] and the publication of which the cautious and fearful Staupitz vainly attempted to prevent.[88] He believes that in thus taking up the war against Antichrist he is inspired by a higher power than his own will and wish. "Who knows but that the Spirit moves me by His own impulse, since I am certain that I am not borne onwards by the pursuit of glory, or money, or my own satisfaction. Of vengeance I say nothing. Let the Lord forgive. Nor do I undertake this in order to stir up sedition, but in order that I may assert the liberty to have recourse to a General Council." [89] He was already following up this trumpet call to a practical reformation by another manifesto on behalf of the deliverance of the Church from the bondage of the mediæval sacramental system. The "De Captivitate Babylonica Ecclesiæ" was in the hands of the printer at the end of August.[90]

A last and wholly gratuitous attempt by the busybody Miltitz was now utterly futile. After vainly seeking to induce the Elector to stop the publication of the "Address to the Nobility," [91] Miltitz attended the Chapter of the Augustinian Order at Eisleben on the 28th August, at which

[85] Enders, ii. 464.

[86] *Ibid.*, ii. 461. Luther does not use the phrase *nobis omnia licere* in the sense that any expedient, moral or immoral, is allowable against Rome, as some Roman Catholic writers represent, but only that any attempt to counter the evil which Rome incorporates, such as he has just made in his "Address to the German Nobility," is justifiable.

[87] *Ibid.*, ii. 456, 457, 461.

[88] *Ibid.*, ii. 463. [89] *Ibid.*, ii. 463. [90] *Ibid.*, ii. 471.

[91] Letter to the Elector in Walch, xv. 924-927.

Staupitz resigned his office as Vicar-General in favour of Link. He proposed that the Chapter should intervene to restrain their bellicose member. Staupitz, it appeared, was no longer prepared to follow his former disciple whom he had helped so materially to start on his reforming career, and responded all the more readily to a proposal which the General of the Order had already some months previously so earnestly urged. Miltitz still kept up the farce of adducing his commission as Nuncius from the Pope to justify his intervention,[92] and in deference to his request the Chapter decided to send a deputation to Wittenberg to urge Luther to write a submissive letter to the Pope.[93] This decision was conveyed to him by Staupitz and Link, the new Vicar-General, and Luther went the length of agreeing to write to Rome that, throughout the long controversy he had never intended or desired to attack Leo personally. "What," he asked, "can I write more easily and truly?"[94] Though, on hearing that Eck had published the Bull at Meissen on the 21st September and subsequently at Merseburg and Leipzig, he was at first disposed to resile from his promise,[95] he ultimately, in deference to the Elector's behest, met Miltitz at Lichtenburg on the 12th October and agreed to indite the proposed epistle in Latin and German as a preface to his tract on "Christian Liberty."[96]

There certainly was no sign of constraint or surrender on Luther's part in the missive itself. To the dismay of the peacemakers, it proved in fact to be a terrific arraignment of the Papacy, whilst assuming the innocence of the Pope personally of the evils which it denounced so scathingly.

[92] Enders, ii. 467. Locutus sum Fratribus, he wrote to Luther on 29th Aug., ex potestate papæ in Capitulo.

[93] *Ibid.*, ii. 478.

[94] *Ibid.*, ii. 478. To Spalatin, 11th Sept., after the interview; *cf.* Miltitz's letter to the Elector, 2nd Oct., Walch, xv. 929.

[95] *Ibid.*, ii. 486.

[96] *Ibid.*, ii. 494-495. Luther to Spalatin, 12th Oct.; Walch, xv. 949-951. Miltitz to the Elector, 14th Oct. In order that the letter might not appear to have been written under the constraint of the publication of the Bull, it was antedated the 6th Sept., Walch, xv. 950.

Though it served as a preface to one of his least bellicose writings, it was really a public manifesto in defence of his position as a reformer in the guise of an appeal to the Pope, and it is not surprising that it never reached its destination.

Though he has appealed from the Pope to a Council, without respect to the foolish and tyrannical decrees of Popes Pius II. and Julius II., which forbid such an appeal, he has never ceased to pray for God's blessing on him and his See. Whilst fearlessly withstanding those who have sought to terrify him with his name and authority, he has never spoken of him anything that is not honourable and excellent. He has, in fact, sought to vindicate his blameless reputation against the intemperate zeal of men like Prierias, who have done their best to tarnish it by their impious flatteries. Though these encomiums sound rather ironic, Luther had apparently succeeded in retaining his naïve conviction that the pleasure-loving, easy-going and egotistic politician who occupied the chair of Peter was the innocent victim of a set of corrupt cardinals and curial officials. This at all events is the assumption that dominates the epistle and enables him, following the example of the prophets, Christ, and Paul, to lash the brood of evil-doers at Rome who misgovern the Church in his name. The Pope himself cannot deny that Rome is more corrupt than Babylon or Sodom ; and this corruption he feels bound to expose in order to lessen the ruin of souls. "For many years now nothing has overflowed into the world from Rome but the devastation of goods, of bodies, of souls, and the worst examples of all the worst things. This is clearer than daylight, and the Roman Church, formerly the most holy of all, has become the most lawless den of robbers, the most shameless of all brothels, the very kingdom of sin, death, and hell, so that not even Antichrist, if he were to come, could devise any addition to its wickedness." [97] Meanwhile, the hapless, well-intentioned Pope, like Daniel in the midst of the lions, Ezekiel among the scorpions, sits in the midst of wolves and can do nothing in the way of remedy. If he and the few good cardinals were to attempt

[97] "Werke," vii. 44.

a reformation, they would die of poison before effecting anything. "It is all over with the Roman Curia. The wrath of God has come upon it to the uttermost. It hates Councils; it dreads to be reformed; it is helpless to mitigate the madness of its impiety; it fulfils the sentence passed on its mother, of whom it was written, 'We would have healed Babylon, but she is not healed. Let us forsake her.'"[98] The disease is past cure. The Roman Curia is not worthy of Leo, who deserves to have ruled in a better age, but only of Satan, who is in truth more the ruler in this Babylon than he. "Is it not true that under the vast heaven nothing is more corrupt, more pestilential, more hateful than the Roman Curia? It incomparably surpasses the impiety of the Turks, so that in truth it, which was formerly the gate of heaven, is now manifestly a sort of mouth of hell, and such a mouth that the urgent wrath of God cannot be walled up. Only one expedient is left us wretched mortals—to call back and preserve whatever we can from this Roman abyss."[99] He then recounts his controversy with Eck, on whose wiles and vainglorious action in drawing him into the discussion of the papal power, and on Cajetan's imprudent conduct lies the blame for the progress of his quarrel with Rome. He adduces the efforts of the Elector and Miltitz to bring about peace and his own willingness to do his part to this end, which had been frustrated by Eck's folly and vanity. At Miltitz's instigation he makes this last effort to secure the papal restraint of the enemies of peace. Only let there be no mistake about this. He is not going to recant. "I will not submit to the prescribed laws of interpreting God's Word, since God's Word, which teaches liberty, ought not to be bound. Saving this, there is nothing that I am not willing to do and suffer."[100] Let the Pope, therefore, beware of those who seek to make of him a demigod and not a man, who exalt his authority as if he were lord of the world and babble of his power over heaven, hell, and purgatory, who elevate him above Councils and the whole Church, and give him alone the right to interpret Scripture. How unlike Christ such a Vicar in whose heart

[98] "Werke," vii. 44. [99] *Ibid.*, vii. 45. [100] *Ibid.*, vii. 47.

Christ does not dwell ; and of whom these flatterers make an Antichrist and an idol. In writing thus boldly he has only done his duty both as a friend and as a subject. If Leo cannot see this, there is One who sees and judges. As a testimony of his desire for peace he sends him in conclusion this little treatise on "Christian Liberty," wherein he will find a summary of the Christian life in small compass.

The denunciation of Rome must be read in the light of the evil repute which Rome had acquired under the later pre-Reformation Popes, as well as Luther's proneness to vehement generalisation. In Luther the outraged moral sense of Christendom at last makes itself heard in the form of this violent ultimatum to reform itself or take the consequences of revolt and schism. The time has at length brought the man, and against this man Eck and his Bull in defence of the Papacy are but a shield of paper. In laying the blame for this dogmatic quarrel solely on his opponents—Prierias, Eck, Cajetan, etc.—he ignores the part played by his own dogmatic temperament. He had begun the attack and his disclaimer of all responsibility for the development of it is to a certain extent special pleading. But his plea for a clamant reformation in the interest of a purer Christianity, based on the teaching of Christ and the Apostles, and for the freedom of the Gospel, on which he will not give way an inch, is unassailable. The degenerate travesty of this teaching, which his opponents defend in the papal interest and which the Bull seeks to enforce by excommunication and death, had no longer the prestige and the moral force to win or overawe the people. Behind Luther were arrayed the national feeling and the moral force of a large section of Germany.

IV. Luther and the Bull

This fact was already being brought home to Eck in his mission of publishing the Bull of condemnation. In Leipzig, where he arrived at the end of September, he had his first taste of the unpopularity of his mission. He was ridiculed in satiric verses which were sung in the streets, whilst hostile placards were displayed in various quarters of the town. He daily received threatening letters and was fain to confine himself to St Paul's monastery for fear of the violence of the populace and the contingent of Wittenberg students, who made the atmosphere so hot for him that he fled by night to Freyberg[1] (4th October). The university at first refused to publish the Bull and ultimately only did so in February 1521 by direction of Duke George. Even so it was pelted with filth and torn down, as likewise happened at Torgau, Döbeln, Erfurt, and other places.[2] Erfurt and Vienna followed its example, and even at Ingolstadt there was some resistance. Wittenberg, sure of the Elector's support, flatly declined and persisted in its opposition.[3] Many of the bishops—Naumburg, Freising, Augsburg, Passau, Bamberg, even the Archbishop of Salzburg, etc.—declined or procrastinated its publication, and among the secular princes the example of the Elector was followed by the Dukes of Bavaria, who requested the ecclesiastical authorities in their territories to waive proceedings, pending the meeting of the Diet of Worms, on the ground of the popular disturbances which its publication would provoke.[4] The same argument was used by the Elector in justification of his refusal to enforce the Bull at the behest of the papal Nuncios, Aleander and Caraccioli, at Cologne in the beginning of November.[5] The argument was no mere diplomatic evasion, as the widespread hostility to Eck was proving. This hostility was not lessened by the fact that in publishing the Bull at Meissen he had summoned,

[1] Miltitz's letter to the Elector, Walch, xv. 930. Luther to Spalatin, Enders, ii. 487. See also on the opposition at Leipzig, "Akten und Briefe zur Kirchenpolitik Herzog Georgs," i. 143 f.; *cf.* 161.

[2] Enders, ii. 503, 511; iii. 104, 106.

[3] Melanchthon to Hess, "Corp. Ref.," i. 284. Bullam Eceianam apud nos nemo probat præter eos qui ventri suo potius quam Evangelio consultum volent, 20th Feb. 1521. See also the documents relative to the publication of the Bull at Wittenberg and elsewhere, Walch, xv. 1875 f.

[4] Wiedemann, "Eck," 153 f.; Pastor, vii. 408 f.; Schubert, "Sitz. Ber. der Heidelberger Akad. der Wissensch.," 1912, 19 f.; Kalkoff, "Die Entstehung des Wormser Edikts," 7.

[5] "Opera Latina Var.," v. 245; Kalkoff, "Z.K.G.," xxv. 531-532.

besides Luther, half a dozen of his adherents by name—Carlstadt, Pirkheimer, Spengler, Aegranus, Feldkirch, and B. Adelmann—to recant within the prescribed period.[6] He was, indeed, empowered by his commission to mention any name he pleased.[7] But he had the bad taste to select his personal enemies and thus intensified the resentment which the choice of Luther's chief antagonist as papal Nuncio had excited in Germany. Pirkheimer, Spengler, and Adelmann allowed themselves to be overawed and asked for absolution. But Carlstadt stood firm. For him, as for Luther, the die was cast.[8] Luther's books were burned by the zealots at Cologne, Louvain, Liege, Halberstadt, Ingolstadt, and Maintz.[9] But this obscurantist folly only contributed to intensify the zeal of Hutten, whose books had also been condemned and who had been dismissed from the service of the Archbishop of Maintz,[10] and the more militant humanists on his behalf.[11] Even the cautious Erasmus found courage in an interview with the Elector at Cologne to denounce the Bull and abet Luther's plea for a fair and impartial hearing.[12] "Luther's crime," he remarked, "consisted in two things. He had attacked the Pope's crown and the monks' bellies."[13] Luther was the recipient of numerous letters from powerful sympathisers and from less known well-wishers far and near. The publication of the Bull discovered to him the full extent of his hold on the upper classes as well as the people. Whilst Duke George of Saxony[14] took the lead among the princes

[6] See the document in Barge, "Karlstadt," i. 219. See also Eck's letter to the University of Wittenberg, Walch, xv. 1874, and "Opera Latina Var.," iv. 305-306.

[7] The charge of overstepping his commission in so doing brought against him by the Elector, "Opera Latina Var.," v. 245, and repeated by Protestant historians, has been shown by Kalkoff to be groundless. He was entitled to do so by his commission, "Z.K.G.," xxv. 532 f.

[8] Enders, ii. 487. Carlstadius et ipse jacta alea in Pontificem Rom., cornua sumit; *cf.* Barge, i. 221.

[9] *Ibid.*, ii. 532, 534; iii. 2, 21.

[10] "Opera," i. 364.

[11] See letters of Capito, Crotus, Hutten. Enders, iii. 3 f.

[12] "Opera Latina Var.," v. 241-242.

[13] *Ibid.*, v. 239.

[14] Gess, "Akten und Briefe zur Kirchenpolitik Herzog Georgs von Sachsen," i. 143 f.

as the executor of the Bull, Duke John Frederick wrote him to go on preaching and writing and stand firmly by the Gospel in spite of the Bull.[15] From Duke Barnim of Pomerania came an assurance of support,[16] whilst Sickingen renewed his offer of protection [17] in response to his letters.

Luther himself was the least disturbed by the news of the publication of the Bull. "I will laugh their Bull and their bombast to scorn," he wrote on the 28th September to Günther von Bünau, Canon of Merseburg, on hearing of the arrival of Eck "barbed, bulled, and bribed," as he put it.[18] "What will happen," he reflects in a letter to Conrad Saum, a Wittenberg disciple, "I know not, nor am I anxious to know. Certain I am that He who sits in heaven governing all things has foreseen from eternity the beginning, the progress, and the end of this enterprise, which I await. However the lot may fall, it will not move me, because it will not fall except in accordance with the best will. Be not anxious, therefore; your Father knows what things you have need of even before you ask Him." [19] Danger only steeled his bellicose spirit. "The more the adversaries, the better I am pleased," we read in a letter to another friend. "I am never more defiant and audacious than when I hear that I am displeasing the enemy. Be they doctors, bishops, princes, what then? If the Word of God were not impugned by them, it would not be the Word of God. The kings of the earth have set themselves and the rulers take counsel together against the Lord and His Christ. I should greatly grieve if these should praise me." [20] Whilst humouring the Elector and Spalatin so far as to talk with Miltitz about the letter to the Pope (and what a letter!), he tells Spalatin that it is to be a fight to a finish against the Bull.[21]

Hence the two philippics directed against it in the course of October under the titles, "Eck's New Bulls and Lies"

[15] Enders, iii. 22-23, 20th Dec. 1520.
[16] *Ibid.*, ii. 500-501.
[17] *Ibid.*, ii. 506, 3rd Nov.
[18] *Ibid.*, ii. 482.
[19] *Ibid.*, ii. 484, 1st Oct.
[20] *Ibid.*, ii. 497-498.
[21] *Ibid.*, ii. 490-491. Venit tandem Bulla ista Romana per Eccium allata. . . . Ego tum contemno et jam invado tanquam impiam et mendacem omnibusque modis Eccianam.

and "Against the Execrable Bull of Antichrist." In these fulminations Luther professes to believe that it was a mere lying concoction of his chief antagonist, although, as he wrote to Spalatin, he was convinced of its authenticity.[22] In the former [23] he bases his incredulity on the twofold fact of his appellation to a Council and the reference of his case to the arbitration of the Archbishop of Trier, which has, he holds, invalidated such an attempt to silence him by force. Moreover, it is impossible to believe that the Pope can have made his chief adversary judge in his cause and the executor of this *ex parte* judgment. Let Eck produce the original for his inspection and not merely copies of this fraudulent document.[24] This profession of incredulity, in view of his communication to Spalatin, was a mere device to discredit the Bull in the eyes of the people, and it would have been more straightforward to discard this fiction and frankly acknowledge its authenticity. More effective for his purpose was the exposure of its misrepresentation of his teaching which he ascribes to Eck, whom he lashes with a satire and a wealth of vituperation which leaves him without a shred of reputation for veracity or learning. With this vituperation he mingles a spirited defence of Hus against the Council of Constance, of which Eck had in the beginning of October published a vindication at Leipzig. The Council, he now boldly asserts, in condemning Hus, had condemned Christ over again, and Paul and Augustine to boot. If he had read Hus's works before the disputation at Leipzig, he would have spoken very differently on the subject. Let the tyrannical persecutors of the truth take warning. Their tyranny will avail no longer against its champions. "The Truth is asserting itself and will burst all the bladders of the papists. The very stones cry out against the murderers of Hus. The papists have striven for 100 years against the truth, and the more they have striven the more it has become evident that it will and shall not remain hidden." [25]

[22] Enders, ii. 491. Agam tamen adhuc presso nomine papæ tanquam in effictam et mentitam Bullam, quamquam credo veram et propriam esse eorum.

[23] Von dem neuen Eckischen Bullen und Lügen, "Werke," vi. 579 f.

[24] "Werke," vi. 592-593.

[25] *Ibid.*, vi. 590.

In the second effusion [26] he still professes scepticism about the Bull. But if it is authentic, he proclaims his defiance of the Roman Antichrist: "You Leo X. and you Lord Cardinals of Rome and whomsoever is of any importance at Rome, I upbraid and say freely to your faces: If the Bull has gone forth in your name and with your knowledge and you recognise it as yours, I shall make use of my power in virtue of my baptism, by which I became a child of God and a co-heir with Christ, and exhort and admonish you in the Lord that you take to heart your diabolic blasphemies and put an end to your audacious blasphemies, and this without delay. Unless you do this, know that I, with all who worship Christ, will esteem your seat possessed and oppressed by Satan, the damned seat of Antichrist, to which we will not render obedience or be subject, or be united, but will detest and execrate as the chief and supreme enemy of Christ. We are prepared in behalf of this conviction not only to bear your censures, but even to ask that you may never absolve us and may fulfil your cruel tyranny. For the sake of this conviction we offer ourselves to death and by these writings we proclaim that, if you persist in your fury, we condemn and deliver you, along with your Bull and all your Satanic decretals, to the destruction of the flesh in order that your spirit may be delivered with us in the day of the Lord." [27] He would not be surprised, he adds in the German version, if the princes, nobility, and people knocked the Pope, bishops, parsons, and monks on the head and chased them out of the land, though he disclaims any desire to incite the laity to violence against the clergy, and would have them pray for them that God may avert His wrath and deliver them from the evil spirit which possesses them.[28]

The Antichrist whom Luther thus defiantly indicts is not the shadowy figure of Biblical eschatology, though the name is borrowed from this source. It is the corrupt system which the Papacy actually represents and which has practically become a travesty of Christianity. Luther has his own way of describing this travesty and the description may sound

[26] Adversus Execrabilem Antichristi Bullam, "Werke," vi. 597 f.
[27] "Werke," vi. 604. [28] *Ibid.*, vi. 621.

arrogant and extreme in modern ears. In reality it was substantially justified by the gross degeneration of the Papacy and the Church under the auspices of Leo X. and his more immediate predecessors. " For over a century," says Pastor, " a cry for the reform of both the head and members of the Church had resounded from all parts of Europe. . . . Many pious, enlightened, and wise men, religious as well as laymen, rose up in response to the call and tried to apply a remedy to the evils of the day. Many hands were laid to the difficult task, though no decisive results were obtained ; for even the best-intentioned efforts made but slight impression on the general deterioration of ecclesiastical discipline. The task was made the more difficult by the bad example of those belonging to the Roman Curia, which worked against the reformers. With the dawn of the new century the cry for reform sounded louder and louder from both sides of the Alps, taking the shape of treatises, letters, poems, satires, and predictions, the theme of which was the corruption of the clergy, and especially the worldliness of the Roman Curia. To many the ancient Church seemed to be as rotten as the Holy Roman-Teutonic Empire, and many foretold the downfall of both these buttresses of the mediæval system. The signs of the times became more and more threatening. To observant spectators it seemed as if, with the advent to power of the Medici, a heavy storm must break over the Church. . . . With unprecedented optimism Leo X. looked into the future without anxiety, and frivolously deluded himself as to the importance of the times. He never gave a thought to reform on the grand scale which had become necessary. . . . He did not co-operate in the half measures taken, nor in the superficial attempts made to carry out the salutary decrees of the Lateran Council. Therefore the Roman Curia, which had for a long time been held in contempt and made the object of the bitterest satires, remained as worldly as ever." [29]

On the 17th November, Luther renewed his appeal to a General Council and declared his readiness to appear

[29] " History of the Popes," vii. 4-5.

and present his cause for judgment. He, therefore, begs the Emperor, Electors, princes, nobility, and other secular authorities of the empire to support his appellation in resistance to the madness and tyranny of the Pope, or at least refrain from enforcing the Bull until his case has been considered and decided by equitable judges in the light of Scripture and other credible evidence.[30] At the same time he issued a German version in less legal form for the information of the people.[31]

On the 10th December he proceeded to the extreme step of publicly burning the Bull at Wittenberg, in retaliation for the burning of his books by Aleander at Louvain, Cologne, and Maintz. A public announcement, composed by Melanchthon, summoned the students and others to assemble at 9 o'clock at the chapel of the Holy Cross outside the walls for the cremation of certain obnoxious writings in accordance with the apostolic example.[32] At the appointed hour one of the Masters of Arts in the presence of the assembled doctors, masters, students, and populace lighted the pile into which Luther solemnly threw the Decretum of Gratian, the papal decretals, the Summa of Clavisio on the Sacrament of Penance, the writings of Eck, Emser and others of his opponents, and finally the Bull itself, with the apostrophe, "As thou hast confounded the truth of God, so may He this day consume thee in the fire."[33] Luther's action was intended as a public demonstration to the whole of Germany that he had foresworn Antichrist and all his works. He performed the ceremony, as he later informed Staupitz, "trembling and praying."[34] The students took the matter less tragically and after singing the Te Deum and the De Profundis around the burning pile dispersed to give vent to their anti-papal zeal in a frolic-

[30] "Werke," vii. 80-81. [31] *Ibid.*, vii. 85 f. [32] *Ibid.*, vii. 183.

[33] Enders, iii. 18. Luther to Spalatin, 10th Dec. See the account of an eye-witness in "Werke," vii. 184 f. The words used by Luther are given in a recently discovered account of the incident, which differs from that of the former, and published by Perlbach and J. Luther in the "Bericht der Preuss. Acad. der Wissenschaft," 1907; Grisar, "Luther," ii. 51.

[34] Enders, iii. 70.

some procession. Before commencing his lecture next day Luther impressed on them the gravity of the situation and admonished them that the mere burning of the papal Bull was not sufficient. They must destroy the papal system itself. "Unless you discard with your whole heart the papal kingdom, you cannot attain the salvation of your souls."[35] Apparently he was unconscious that in such an utterance he was really professing the intolerant papal principle that makes salvation depend on one's ecclesiastical opinions. This extreme proposition he endeavoured to substantiate in a manifesto in Latin and German, giving his reasons why he had burned the Bull. It consists largely of quotations from the canon law with comments thereon tending to prove the enormity of the papal claims and their contradiction of the teaching of the Scriptures.[36] In the beginning of January 1521 he added, at the Elector's request, a more detailed defence of the articles condemned in the Bull than he had been able to give in the previous two fulminations against it.[37]

[35] "Werke," vii. 186.

[36] Warumb des papst's und seiner jungernn bucher von Doctor Martin Luther vorbrant seynn, "Werke," vii. 161 f.

[37] Assertio omnium Articulorum M. Lutheri per Bullam Leonis X. novissimam damnatorum, "Werke," vii. 94 f.

CHAPTER VIII

THE REFORMATION MANIFESTOS OF 1520

I. The Appeal to the Nation

Early in June 1520 Luther intimated to Spalatin his intention of publishing a manifesto to the Emperor and the nobility of Germany against the tyranny and wickedness of the Roman Curia.[1] From the same communication we learn that the impulse to this resolution was furnished by the Epitome of Prierias and the vernacular work of Alveld in defence of the papal power which had just come into his hands.[2] Prierias's exaltation of the papal power, in particular, provoked the violent ultimatum to Rome contained in the preface and conclusion with which, as we have seen, he reprinted the Epitome. Though he treated the effusion thus summarily, the extreme claim on behalf of the absolute, infallible power of even a wicked Pope filled him with amazement and anger. "I believe," he exclaimed in the note to Spalatin, "they have all become unmitigated madmen and fools at Rome. Now we see what we are to expect from Rome which allows this infernal effusion to go forth to the Church. Truly these portents overwhelm me with the enormity of their stupidity."[3] Hence the resolution to arraign the Curia at the bar of German public opinion in the Address to the Emperor and the nobility.

Despite the oft-repeated assertion which ascribes the

[1] Enders, ii. 414. Est animus publicam schedam edere ad Carolum et totius Germaniæ nobilitatem adversus Romanæ Curiæ tyrannidem et nequitiam.

[2] Köhler overlooks this fact when he ascribes the impulse to the composition of the work to the prompting of Hutten and Crotus Rubianus. "Luther's Schrift an den Christlichen Adel," 283, 287 (1895).

[3] Enders, ii. 414; *cf.* 412.

genesis of this famous appeal to Hutten and Schaumburg,[4] it is evident that, in the first instance at least, it had nothing to do with the offer of alliance and protection made by Hutten and other representatives of the lesser nobility. Luther, as we have noted, received Schaumburg's original offer in the middle of May rather doubtingly,[5] and the motive which prompted him to begin the writing of the Address was concern, not for his own safety, but for the commonweal of Germany against what he had come to regard as the antichristian régime of Rome.[6]

Its composition occupied him intermittently throughout June and July and into the month of August, and in accordance with his custom it was sent in portions to the printer as the writing progressed.[7] On the 18th August he was able to announce to Lang the fact of its publication, with a dedication to his colleague, Nicolas von Amsdorff, and the immediate sale of the whole edition of 4,000 copies. He had only one copy left which he sent to his friend.[8]

The intermittent character of its composition appears, indeed, from the work itself. It is by no means an organic whole. Luther was not as a rule a systematic thinker or writer. He wrote too much and too rapidly, and in the rush of his thoughts he was apt to dash down his ideas without much concern for their arrangement or for symmetry of workmanship. In the case of the Address, in particular, he had apparently not thought out clearly the plan of the

[4] Köhler, for instance ("Luther's Schrift an den Christlichen Adel," 283 f.), who follows Maurenbrecher, "Studien und Skizzen zur Geschichte der Reformationszeit" (1874), and Kampfschulte, "Die Universität Erfurt" (1860), who are controverted by Knaake in his introduction to the Address. "Werke," vi. 381 f. See also Kohlmeyer, "Die Entstehung der Schrift Luther's an den Christlichen Adel," 34 f. (1922).

[5] Enders, ii. 402.

[6] *Ibid.*, ii. 414. Sic postulat argumenti necessitas, prodenda tandem sunt Antichristi mysteria. Ita enim se ipsa urgent et latere amplius nolunt.

[7] *Ibid.*, ii. 444. Editur noster libellus in Papam de reformanda ecclesia vernaculus, 20th July; ii. 456, Jam edo librum vulgarem contra Papam de statu ecclesiæ emendando, 3rd Aug.; ii. 457, Classicum meum, etc.

[8] *Ibid.*, ii. 461.

work from the outset, or if he had done so in general, he did not exactly adhere to it in the writing of it. As finally issued from the press, it professedly consists of three parts: (1) a refutation on theological grounds of the extreme claims of the Papacy [9]; (2) an exposure of the abuses of the curial régime [10]; (3) a series of proposals for the reformation of the abuses rampant in both the Church and the nation.[11] But the second part not only exposes certain abuses. It also suggests reforms, and a large part of it forms a digression from the professed purpose of exposing abuses in order particularly to show how the Curia, in countenancing such abuses, acts in contradiction of its own (the canon) law.[12] Similarly the third part not only presents a large scheme of reforms, but exposes a large number of abuses which he had not specified in the second part. He thus mixes up in both parts the matters which he proposes to treat distinctively in each, and is clearly guilty of a certain inconsistency in the execution of the professed plan of the work.

The probable explanation of this lack of symmetry is that he wrote the work not consecutively, but intermittently. Parts I. and II. appear to form a unity, though the greater portion of Part II. is a digression from his professed theme, *i.e.*, the exposure of abuses. Between Parts II. and III. there was evidently a pause, and in taking up the subject anew, he both exposes a large number of abuses which he had not mentioned in Part II. and intensifies the attack on the Pope and the Curia in the sweeping charges made against them and the formidable series of reforms demanded. The challenge to both becomes more comprehensive and uncompromising and begets the impression that something had happened to widen and intensify both his denunciation and his defiance. This "something" was evidently the intimation conveyed in the letters from Riario and Tetleben, which the Elector received on the 6th July, that the Pope had resolved to issue the Bull of condemnation against Luther. Moreover, he had by this time, as he informs

[9] "Werke," vi. 404-415.
[10] *Ibid.*, vi. 415-427.
[11] *Ibid.*, vi. 427-469.
[12] *Ibid.*, vi. 418-427.

Spalatin on the 10th July,[13] received another letter from Schaumburg offering him the alliance and protection of the lesser nobility.[14] Encouraged by this offer, he tells Spalatin that for him the die is cast. Let them condemn and burn his works. He in turn will publicly condemn and burn the whole papal law, that brood of heresies, and will make an end of the humility which he has hitherto exhibited in vain and with which he will no longer inflate the enemies of the Gospel.[15] He tells him further a week later that Schaumburg and Sickingen have delivered him from the fear of men.[16] This offer had secured him against the possibility of succumbing defencelessly to the expected papal attack even if, in order to ward off the threatened interdict against the Elector's territories, he should be forced to seek a refuge elsewhere. This refuge was now assured him, and to the extent of encouraging him to hurl defiance against the Pope and leading him to intensify and widen the attack on Rome, which he had begun in the first two parts of the Address, the influence of Schaumburg and Sickingen is certainly traceable in the highly bellicose third part of it.[17]

That the Address was originally inspired or materially influenced from this source is, however, an untenable assumption. The main incentive to its composition was, in the first place, the recent works of Alveld and Prierias, and, in the second place, the threatened fulmination of Rome against him and his writings. The fact that the manifesto was addressed to the nobility is no proof that he had joined the party of Hutten and the lesser nobles and made himself

[13] Enders, ii. 432.

[14] *Ibid.*, ii. 415-416, dated the 11th June.

[15] *Ibid.*, ii. 432-433.

[16] *Ibid.*, ii. 443; *cf.* 456.

[17] Kohlmeyer ("Die Entstehung der Schrift Luther's an den Christlichen Adel" (1922)) argues forcibly in favour of this view of the third part of the Address. He also adduces strong grounds for the conclusion that it was not written consecutively and that there was an interval between the conclusion of Part II. on p. 427 and the writing of Part III. under the influence of the news from Rome and also the communication from Schaumburg. Köhler, on the other hand ("Zeitschrift für Rechtsgeschichte," xliv., "Kan. Abt.," vi. 1 f.), controverts this view and contends that the work was written consecutively. His arguments do not seem to me conclusive. In his reply ("Z.K.G.," 1925, 582 f.) Kohlmeyer substantially maintains his position, whilst slightly modifying it.

the mouthpiece of the ideas and aims of this class in this "trumpet call"[18] to reform. It was not even addressed to this class, for the term "nobility,"[19] or *Adel*, means the princes and the higher nobility as well as the lower. As a matter of fact, it is directed to the ruling classes of the empire—to the *Obrigkeit*, consisting of Emperor, princes, nobles, knights, and the imperial cities—in a word, the estates of the empire represented in the imperial Diet. In certain passages the appeal is addressed to every corporate local authority (*gemeinde*) whether actually represented in the Diet or not. He had already in the dedication of his Commentary on Galatians,[20] in his sermons on Usury and on Good Works,[21] summoned the various estates to begin the work of reform either by their own initiative or through a General Council, and in the Address he has in view the interest of the nation as a whole, not that of any particular class within it. Such an assumption, too often made by partisan Roman Catholic writers and others, needs no refutation, if only in view of the sorry rôle played in the State by the lesser nobility, many of whom lived by oppression and robbery, and were more concerned with getting hold of Church lands for themselves and their families than reforming the abuses from which they were only too eager to profit. That he should have taken his inspiration from this class or have made himself the mere mouthpiece of its interest, a mere glance at the spirit and aim of the work is sufficient to disprove.

It is a different question whether and how far he was influenced by the writings of Hutten who belonged to this class. Whilst concerned for the interests of his Order, Hutten had conceived the idea of a national reform on anti-Romanist lines.[22] He was an ardent member of the

[18] Classicum, as Lang called it. Enders, ii. 461.

[19] Enders, ii. 414. Ad totius Germaniæ nobilitatem; *cf.* ii. 444, ad universam nobilitatem Germaniæ. See Kohlmeyer, "Entstehung," 35 f. [20] "Werke," ii. 449. [21] *Ibid.*, vi. 45; *cf.* 52, 258.

[22] Ch. Meyer, "Ul. v. Hutten und Franz von Sickingen," 19 f. (1890). Strauss's "Life of Hutten" (English translation by Mrs Sturge, 1874) is too indiscriminating and one-sided. See the chapter on "Die Entwickelung der Legende von Hutten und Sickingen," in Kalkoff's "Ulrich von Hutten's Vagantenzeit und Untergang," 31 f. (1925).

radical humanist party in the struggle against the old culture and its obscurantist defenders who waged war on Reuchlin as well as Luther, and he had latterly been attracted to the Lutheran movement as a promising adjunct of this cause, not by the moral and religious aspect of this movement which he was ill fitted to appreciate. With this radical humanism he combined the aspiration for a reform on national grounds. It was this combination that made him the militant foe of the ecclesiastical system which oppressed and exploited Germany for the benefit of a corrupt alien régime as well as strove to suppress the radical humanist party. Rome had determined to proscribe Hutten and his freethinking associates along with Luther, and in this respect both were now allies in the same cause of antagonism to the Roman oppressor. With Hutten, however, the main motive of this antagonism was the humanist and nationalist one; with Luther the religious and moral one. In his own sphere Luther had nothing to learn from, but much to teach him. He had, moreover, started on his career as a reformer independently of Hutten and the humanists. The secret of his reforming mission lay in his religious experience which had gradually led him to attack ecclesiastical and even social abuses as well as what he deemed theological error. From 1515 onwards he had, even in the thick of theological controversy, incidentally at least, sounded the call to a reformation of these practical abuses, and it would be possible to construct out of his lectures, sermons, and controversial writings from 1515 to the summer of 1520 the main outlines of the reform programme which he presented in the Address to the Nobility. At the same time, the pronouncedly national note of the Address evidently owed something to Hutten's "Vadiscus" or "Trias Romana" and his "Inspicientes" (Observers) which appeared in April 1520 and which Luther had read soon after their publication.[23] But this influence was not very

[23] See Kohlmeyer who gives instances of this influence on the Address ("Entstehung," 47 f.), which Knaake in his introduction to it ("Werke," vi. 388-389) had denied too categorically. See especially the passages of the Vadiscus, "Hutteni Opera," iv. 163-165 and 255-257. Kohlmeyer thinks that there are traces of this influence even in the

far-reaching and by no means warrants the assertion that the Address is merely an echo of the "Vadiscus" and the "Inspicientes." Kalkoff believes that, whilst Luther glanced through these satires, they exercised practically no influence on the Address.[24] This judgment is, however, too extreme and there is more force in Kohlmeyer's conclusion that the "Vadiscus" quickened Luther's sense of the evils of the Roman régime from the national point of view, and that it lent a wider scope and an added force to the appeal for reform on national as well as religious grounds. He rightly, I think, sees in the spirited defence of the imperial crown and the purely national interest against the claims of the Papacy and in the idea of a national Church, for instance, "new notes" in Luther's polemic—"the echo of the national humanism" of Hutten.[25]

It is difficult to determine exactly what were the specific sources of the Address.[26] In addition to the Scriptures —his grand authority in this as in his other controversial writings—he evidently drew on some of the Fathers, the decrees of the Council of Nicæa, the papal Decretals and the Canon Law, the decrees of the reforming Councils of the fifteenth century, especially that of Basle. He does seem to have drawn directly from the works of the early fourteenth-century publicists, John of Paris, John of Jandun, Marsiglio of Padua, and Occam, the defenders of the independence of the State against the papal claims, and the right of the secular power to take steps to reform the Church. This independence and this right they based on the doctrine of the sovereignty of the people, and with

sermon on Good Works and in "Von dem Papstthum Zu Rom." "Entstehung," 50 f. See also Köhler, 307-314, and Reindell, "Luther, Crotus, und Hutten," 57 f. (1890).

24 "Entscheidungsjahre," 171; *cf.* "Ul. v. Hutten's Vagantenzeit und Untergang," 68 f.

25 "Entstehung," 60-61; *cf.* Kolde, "Luther's Stellung zu Concil und Kirche," 71-72 (1876).

26 In his work, "Luther's Schrift an den Christlichen Adel," Köhler has subjected the Address to a minute examination with a view to finding evidence of its sources. The result is, on the whole, rather inconclusive in regard to many of the possible sources adduced and discussed.

this doctrine Luther does not seem to have been familiar. At all events, if he was, it does not seem to have appealed to him. He develops no political philosophy and vindicates the claims he makes for the State on religious rather than on political grounds. It is more probable that he owed something to the works of the fifteenth-century leaders of the conciliar party, D'Ailly, Gerson, and Nicolas de Tudesco, leader of the Council of Basle and Archbishop of Palermo, to those of Dietrich von Nieheim,[27] and to Valla's exposure of the so-called Donation of Constantine. We can with more confidence assert or assume his acquaintance with the reforming publicism of his own time. He had, for instance, almost certainly in his mind the traditional *gravamina* or statement of grievances presented afresh to the Augsburg Diet in 1518.[28] The grievances thus summarised were the common stock of the publicists of the period who indicted or satirised the abuses rampant in the Church. They form the commonplaces of this satirical literature and Luther was undoubtedly acquainted with it. In November 1517 he mentions one of these satires in a letter to Spalatin, whilst deprecating the levity with which it treats so grave a subject.[29] On the other hand, he enjoyed the "Dialogue between Julius II. and Peter"[30] and pays a tribute to the skill of the author in exposing the régime of the worldly, bellicose Pope. It must, he judges, bear good fruit if seriously read, and he is sorry that it is not better known at Rome. For him it contains nothing new, though it tends to confirm the general impression of the tyranny and wicked audacity of Rome with which the world is ringing.[31] The "Encomium Moriæ" (Praise of Folly) of Erasmus, which Luther had undoubtedly read,[32] had in fact powerfully contributed to set the current of public

[27] Köhler, 39-41, 111 f.

[28] He expressly refers to this document in the dedication of his Commentary on Galatians in 1519. "Werke," ii. 448.

[29] Enders, i. 121.

[30] Dialogus Julii et Petri.

[31] Enders, i. 433, 20th Feb. 1519. The Dialogue was attributed to Erasmus, who disclaimed its authorship. It was probably written by Faustus Andrelinus.

[32] See the dedication of the Address to Amsdorff.

opinion against the evils of the papal régime. He was, too, probably acquainted with Wimpheling's more serious indictment [33] of the ecclesiastical abuses from which Germany in particular was suffering. His correspondence with Crotus and Hess, both of whom had recently visited Rome, and his intercourse with Dr van Wick, who had returned thence in the summer of 1520 and paid him a visit at Wittenberg, supplied him with some details of the conditions prevailing there.[34]

At the same time, the Address is very far from being a mere compilation from such sources. It is characteristically Lutheran in conception, spirit, style, and contents. On the face of it is the stamp of his genius and personality as a national reformer. Only Luther could have written it. Only he could have imparted to it the moral and religious conviction, the drastic style, the uncompromising defiance which sweeps onwards like a hurricane over a doomed world. In this hurricane the lightning of his wrath darts forth again and again and we can almost hear the crash of these lightning strokes which prostrate the rotten system of the Roman régime to the ground. So vivid, so elemental, so shattering is the impact.

At the outset of the Address, Luther announces his determination to appeal from the clergy to the laity for a reform of the Church. The oppression and misery of Christendom, and especially of Germany, under the papal régime have compelled him to make this appeal. General Councils have hitherto utterly failed to provide a remedy. The German emperors relying on their own strength, the force of arms, in their struggles with the Papacy, have been equally impotent. The accession of the young Emperor Charles has, however, awakened fresh hope of an effective

[33] "Remedium contra Gravamina Germaniæ Nationis" (1519). Also his "Responsa et Replicæ ad Aeneam Silvium" (1515). See Knaake, "Werke," vi. 394. Wimpheling's Gutachten, or report on the same subject submitted to the Emperor Maximilian in 1510 seems to have been unknown to Luther at the time when he began to write the Address, since it was published only at the end of May 1520.

[34] Enders, ii. 432, 443. See also Kohlmeyer, 82 f. In a passage of the "Table Talk," Feb. 1538, he acknowledges his indebtedness to Wick. "Tischreden," iii. 567.

reformation and in this spirit of optimism Luther summons him and the Estates to take steps to this end in reliance not on themselves, but on the divine assistance.[35]

The Romanists have hitherto persistently frustrated the reform of the Church. They have entrenched themselves behind three walls in defence of their anti-reform policy. In the first place, they assert that the temporal power has no jurisdiction over the spiritual, whilst claiming for the spiritual power jurisdiction over the temporal. In the second place, if they are faced with the evidence of Scripture to the contrary, they contend that the Pope alone is entitled to interpret Scripture. In the third place, if they are threatened with a General Council, they claim that the Pope alone can summon a Council. By these pretexts they have frustrated a reformation, and he, therefore, sets himself in the first or preliminary part of the work to invalidate them.

He demolishes the first wall by denying that there is any essential distinction between the spiritual and the temporal estate. He treats the subject from the theological, not the political standpoint, and seeks the proof of his contention in the Bible which appears to be for him a text-book of political science. In virtue of the spiritual priesthood of all believers, all Christians, as possessing a common baptism, a common faith and Gospel, belong to the spiritual estate. The only distinction between Christians is one of office or function (*Amt*), not of estate (*Stand*). The clergy differ from the laity only in being chosen by their fellow-Christians to perform a certain function—that of ministering the Word and the sacraments. They have no specific, indelible character in virtue of their ordination, differentiating them from their fellow-Christians.[36] From the spiritual priesthood of all believers, it follows that the temporal power, which consists of baptized believers, is also part of the Christian body. It is, moreover, ordained by God for the maintenance of law and morality, and is thus divinely endowed with an ethical function. To it all are subject

[35] "Werke," vi. 404-406. "Ausgewählte Werke," ii. 5-6, edited by Kalkoff (1914).

[36] "Werke," vi. 407-408.

according to the explicit testimony of Scripture. It is, therefore, entitled, nay bound, to exercise its function towards all its subjects without restraint or restriction whatsoever. Any claim to immunity from its jurisdiction on the pretext of ecclesiastical law is inadmissible. This claim is merely an invention of Roman arrogance. If the Pope and the clergy are guilty of grave dereliction of duty, of scandalous evils to the danger of souls and the detriment of the common weal, it may and shall punish and reform them without respect to their threats and excommunications,[37] although apparently it shall not otherwise interfere in the performance of their specific function in their own sphere. "Now I conclude the first paper will is overthrown, inasmuch as the temporal power has become a member of the Christian body, and although its work is of a bodily nature, yet it belongs to the spiritual estate. Therefore it must perform its work without let or hindrance towards all the members of the whole body, to punish and ordain wherever guilt deserves or necessity demands, without respect of Pope, bishop, or priest, let them threaten or excommunicate as much as they will." [38]

The pretension of the Pope to be the exclusive and infallible interpreter of Scripture and the arbiter of the faith is a lying assumption. It merely means that the Pope is at liberty to decree what he chooses, however ignorant or wicked he may be, and that the unlearned gentlemen at Rome possess *ex officio* a monopoly of the Holy Spirit, who, however, can only dwell in pure hearts. This pretension is contrary to Scripture which every pious Christian, in whom is the mind of Christ, is able to understand and judge for himself. Let no one, therefore, allow himself to be deprived of this inherent right as a Christian by such an usurped authority.[39]

Equally unscriptural and baseless is the claim that it belongs to the Pope alone to summon a Council. Scripture confers on each member of the Christian community the care of the welfare of all its members and with it the right to call the community together for this purpose. There is

[37] "Werke," vi. 409-410.
[38] *Ibid.*, vi. 409-410.
[39] *Ibid.*, vi. 411-412.

not a word in Scripture to justify this arrogant claim which rests only on the papal decrees, and these decrees are binding only in as far as they are not injurious to Christendom and the laws of God. The first Council was not convened by Peter, but by all the Apostles, and the most famous of all, the Council of Nicæa, by the Emperor Constantine, not by the Roman bishop. So in the case of many others which were nevertheless regarded as Christian assemblies. This they could not have been if the power of convening them had resided only in the Pope. Therefore, when necessity demands and the Pope is a cause of offence to Christendom, every individual Christian is to strive to bring about the meeting of a free Council. By none can this be so effectively done as by the temporal power which, in its capacity as Christian, is amply entitled to do so. In view of the anti-christian Roman régime its duty in this matter needs no proof. To adduce the authority of the Pope in such a case is mere empty talk. " No one in Christendom has power to do harm or forbid any one to prevent harm. There is no power in the Church except for the reformation of what is amiss." [40] If, therefore, the Pope uses his power to prevent the convention of a free Council for this purpose, we are to pay no heed to him and his authority, and if he threatens and excommunicates, we are to pay him back in his own coin. To exercise his power to prevent reformation is to do the work of the devil and of Antichrist.[41]

He proceeds in the second part to review the abuses that should be reformed by a Council, or in case of its failure, by the temporal power, though, as we have noted, he does not, in this part, do so systematically and exhaustively, and mingles demands for reform with the exposure of abuses. He adduces, in particular, the infinite detriment accruing from the Roman misgovernment of the Church to both the material and the religious welfare of Germany. On both economic and religious grounds a reformation is urgently necessary. The Curia has become an organisation for the financial exploitation of Germany by means of a variety of mercenary devices, by which German wealth is drained to Rome for the support of a host

[40] "Werke," vi. 414. [41] *Ibid.*, vi. 413-414.

of cardinals, curial officials, and papal parasites who live in luxury and vice at Germany's expense. In virtue of these devices—provision of aliens to rich German benefices, annats or first fruits, appropriation of livings by the Pope under various pretexts, pallium money, commendams, reservations, compositions, indulgences, dispensations, etc., which he describes in detail, Germany is impoverished and threatened with ruin.[42] It is the victim of Roman avarice, fraud, knavery, robbery. The Turk himself could not have more completely devastated the nation. Germany, he calculates, pays more to the Pope every year than it formerly paid its emperors. Is it surprising that all classes—princes, nobles, burgesses, clergy, and people—grow poorer? The wonder is that they have anything left to eat. And this to maintain a swarm of vermin at Rome, these ravenous wolves in sheep's clothing![43] The annats, for instance, supposed to be used for the defence of Christendom against the Turk, are a mere pretext for filling the bottomless sack at Rome. They imagine that the mad, drunken Germans, as they call them, are such infinite, inveterate fools that they will go on for ever pouring their money into this sack.

His denunciation culminates in the vehement description of the traffic in sacred things as manipulated by the *Datarius* (the official who issues and registers certain documents) at Rome and the Fugger, the papal bankers at Augsburg.[44] In this section the moral sense of Christendom utters itself in Luther in a vehement protest, in scornful condemnation of the corruption and spoliation of the Roman Curia. It is couched in the language of the prophet rather than the judge—of the prophet invoking doom on the modern Babylon, Sodom, Gomorrah, as he alternatively terms Rome. The Address is a manifesto to the nation against the overflowing iniquity of the curial régime, not an objective indictment in a law court. At Rome there is such a state of things that baffles description. There is a buying, selling, exchanging, cheating, roaring, lying, deceiving, robbing, stealing, luxury, debauchery, villany, and every sort of contempt of God that Antichrist himself could not possibly

[42] "Werke," vi. 415 f. [43] *Ibid.*, vi. 417-419.
[44] On the Fugger, see Schulte, "Die Fugger in Rom" (1904).

rule more abominably. Venice, Antwerp, Cairo are nothing compared to this fair and market at Rome, except that things are done there with some reason and justice, whilst here they are done as the devil himself wills. And out of this ocean flows a like virtue into the whole world. Is it not natural that such people should dread a reformation and a free Council and rather set all kings and princes by the ears than that, by their unity, they should bring about a Council? Which of them would like to have such villany exposed? Finally, the Pope has constructed a special shop for this fine traffic, that is, the house of the *Datarius* at Rome. Hither all must come who bargain in this way for prebends and benefices, etc. . . . If you bring money to this house, you can get all the things that I have mentioned, and not only these, but any sort of usury is here made legitimate for money. What has been stolen, robbed is here legalised. Here vows are annulled. Here the monk may buy freedom to quit his Order. Here the clergy can purchase the marriage state, the children of harlots obtain legitimacy, dishonour and shame be made respectable, evil repute and crime be knighted and ennobled. Here marriage is allowed that is within the forbidden degree, or is otherwise defective. Oh what oppressing and plunder rule here! So that it seems as if the whole canon law were only established in order to snare as much money as possible, from which every one who would be a Christian must deliver himself. Here the devil becomes a saint and a god to boot. What heaven and earth may not do, this house can do. They speak of compositions. Compositions, forsooth! Much rather confusions. Oh what a poor treasure is the Toll on the Rhine compared with this holy house! Let no one think that I say too much. It is all notorious so that even at Rome they are fain to confess that it is more terrible, worse than words can describe. I have not touched, nor do I wish to touch on the infernal dregs of private vices. I speak only of well-known public evils, and yet I cannot find words strong enough to characterise them. I have, however, still a last greeting which I must also deliver. Since this unspeakable greed is not satisfied with the treasures that would be sufficient for three powerful kings, they have added to this traffic by selling to the Fugger of Augsburg the right to traffic in bishoprics and benefices, and thus this fine bargaining in ecclesiastical property has got into the right hands and spiritual and temporal things have become a common business. . . . Since this devilish régime is not only a public robbery, deceit, and tyranny of the gates of hell, but also the destruction of Christendom in soul and body, it is our bounden duty to ward off this misery and desolation of the Christian commonwealth. If we desire to wage war against the Turks, let us begin here, where they are worst of all. If we justly hang thieves and behead robbers, why should we allow Roman greed to go free, which is the greatest thief and robber that has appeared or can appear on earth, and this in Christ's and St Peter's holy name! Who can at long last suffer this or maintain silence about it?" [45] We must make allowance for a certain tendency to overcolouring in Luther's style. Nevertheless this vehement arraignment of the evils rampant in the Roman Curia can be paralleled from official Roman sources. For instance, in the indictment by Pope Hadrian VI. himself a couple of years later and in the report of the commission, appointed by Pope Paul III. seventeen years later, and presided over by Contarini, to suggest a scheme of reform.[46]

He proceeds in the third part to treat of the reform of such abuses which the temporal power or a General Council shall undertake. In the course of this lengthy scheme the Council is, however, largely ignored and the work is mainly to be done by the secular authority. Moreover, as we have seen, he introduces many abuses which he had not particularised in the second part, and under the influence of the imminent fulmination against him from Rome, violently attacks the Pope personally as well as the Curia. In order to get a conjunct view of these reforms we shall here include those which he had already suggested in the second part.

This iniquitous and oppressive exploitation of Germany

[45] "Werke," vi. 425-427.

[46] "Consilium de emendanda Ecclesia," 1537. Luther's translation of it is given in "Werke," l. 288 f.

the temporal power shall forthwith redress by a series of drastic enactments, whether by the Reichstag for the whole empire, or by the territorial authorities within their respective spheres.[47] Moreover, the temporal power shall not only take drastic measures to put an end to the economic evils arising from this exploitation. It shall take in hand the thorough reformation of the Church itself. For the Address contains a detailed scheme of ecclesiastical reform on the ground that these and other evils are ruinous to the service of God. Luther would begin the reform by a radical diminution of the power of the Pope. He would deprive him of his triple crown and the pomp and luxury unbefitting the chief pastor of Christendom. He should leave these things to Antichrist and remember that Christ's kingdom is not of this world and fashion his life after His example who on earth took upon Himself the form of a servant. He would drastically reduce or even abolish the cardinalate and the swarm of curial officials who batten on German benefices like wolves lying in wait for the sheep.[48] One per cent. of this corrupt officialdom would suffice. Whilst disposed in the second part to excuse the Pope personally as the victim rather than the cause of a bad system,[49] he regards him in the third part as "the common enemy and destroyer of Christendom and the salvation of souls."[50] He would utterly destroy the papal legatine system and expel from Germany all papal legates who sell faculties legalising all kinds of iniquities. As he thinks of the gross immorality of this system his indignation impels him to challenge and disown the papal power in the person of the Pope himself. "Hearest thou, O Pope, not the most holy, but the most sinful? Would that God would hurl thy chair headlong from heaven and cast it down into the abyss of hell! Who has given thee the power to exalt thyself above thy God, to break and to loose what He has commanded, to teach Christians, especially the German nation, who are of a noble nature and are praised in all the histories for their uprightness and faithfulness, to be unreliable, breakers of their oaths, traitors,

[47] "Werke," vi. 419-420, 427 f.
[48] *Ibid.*, vi. 415-418.
[49] *Ibid.*, vi. 419.
[50] *Ibid.*, vi. 428.

villains, and lacking in faith? God has commanded us to keep oaths and troth even with enemies and thou takest it upon thee to cancel such a command, setting forth in thy heretical, antichristian decrees that thou hast such power, and through thy mouth and pen Satan lies as he never lied before, and thou dost twist and pervert the Scriptures according to thine own arbitrary will." [51]

He would deprive him of the right of confirming bishops and archbishops and restore the canon of the Council of Nicæa which conferred this right on neighbouring bishops, or the metropolitan of the province, and of the right of exempting abbots and other prelates from their jurisdiction to the detriment of the episcopal government. He would at most only allow appeal to him in cases in which primates and archbishops are unable to agree. Otherwise he would restrict his office to the spiritual oversight of Christendom. In no case should temporal matters be submitted to Rome, but should be dealt with by the temporal authorities, to whose province they belong, and who should disallow all excommunications on this ground and only recognise those relative to faith and morals, which rightly belong to the sphere of the spiritual authority. He would, however, allow questions relative to ecclesiastical benefices to be settled by the bishops concerned under the Primate of Germany in a national ecclesiastical assembly for the government of the national Church, and thereby emancipate Germany from the wretched tyranny and misrule of Rome.[52] He would, in addition, deprive the Pope of the investiture of the bishops of the national Church and abolish the oath of fealty to him, as in France and other countries, and thus rid the national episcopate of this servility to the papal tyranny.[53] He would even restore to the local Church (*gemeinde*) the right to elect its minister or bishop (these

[51] "Werke" vi. 453.

[52] *Ibid.*, vi. 429-431. In his ultimate estrangement from Rome over the question of the papal infallibility, Döllinger's conception of a national German Church under a German Primate and a national ecclesiastical assembly and provincial synods was a revival of that of Luther. See Wendt, Ignaz von Döllinger, "Z.K.G.," xxiv. 292 f.

[53] *Ibid.*, vi. 433.

functionaries being synonymous in the New Testament), whom the members should support and who should have as assistants several priests or deacons in the preaching of the Word and the administration of the sacraments.[54] He would sweep away root and branch the papal claim to feudal superiority over the German Emperor and thus vindicate the rights of the empire as a sovereign State as well as of the national Church. The Pope may anoint and crown the Emperor as a bishop crowns a king, but he would disallow all the servile acts by which the Emperor does homage to the Pope as his superior. These claims are the inventions of the devil, the true work of the Antichrist who exalts himself above God. Except in the spiritual sphere the Pope is not superior, but subject to the temporal power. He is not the vicar of the ruling Christ in heaven, who needs no vicar, but only of Christ as He lived on earth in lowly subjection, in working, teaching, suffering, and dying. Otherwise he is the very counter or Antichrist who, by his usurpation of an authority that does not belong to him, hinders and destroys the will of Christ. The so-called Donation of Constantine conferring such authority is an unspeakable lie. How can the rule of this world consort with the mission entrusted by Christ to the Apostles, which consisted in preaching, prayer, study, the care of the poor? This is the invention of the knaves who would fain become lords of the world and rule it in the Pope's name, and thus perpetuate the old Roman empire. He would deprive him even of his pretended feudal superiority over Naples and Sicily, of the possessions in Italy which he has seized by force and fraud, would, in fact, strip him of all temporal government whatever and relegate him to his purely spiritual function. In a word, the Pope's flatterers must cease to make an idol and a god of him. His pretensions and his powers must be swept away as absolutely incompatible with the teaching and example of Christ.[55]

He would not only thus radically reform the constitution

[54] "Werke," vi. 440.

[55] *Ibid.*, vi. 433-436; *cf.* the long digression on the subject of the empire and the Papacy, 462-465. He enlarged the section dealing with this subject in the 2nd edition. Enders, ii. 464.

of the Church. He would drastically apply the pruning knife to its usages. He would abolish or materially limit pilgrimages to Rome where people learn only contempt of God and His commandments. Hence the proverb, "The nearer to Rome, the worse a Christian." Hence also the saying, "The first time one goes to Rome one goes to seek a rascal; the second time he finds him; the third time he brings him home with him." Nowadays people have become so skilful that they can do these three journeys in one, and have brought with them the further saying, "It would be better never to have seen or known Rome." [56] Such a pilgrimage is, moreover, economically bad. It is a waste of money which would be better devoted by the pilgrim to the care of his neglected wife and children and service of his neighbour instead of spending it to pamper Roman greed and usurped authority. He would, in fact, abolish all pilgrimages, which serve only to foster begging, vagabondage, the false delusion of human merits, and other evils. He would repress or drastically reduce the mendicant Orders without respect to the ordinances of St Francis or St Dominic, or even the reputed founder of his own Order, St Augustine, especially as he suspects that the Pope supports the crowd of begging friars as a bulwark of his power against the secular clergy. He would further make the monasteries free schools of Christian instruction, as he thinks they originally were, and would suppress the perpetual obligation of monastic vows. Monasticism is nothing but a tyrannic human institution. He would at the same time abolish the obligation of celibacy in the case of the priesthood and thus do away with the scandal of clerical concubinage. Enforced celibacy is an unwarrantable interference with Christian liberty and an oppression of the Christian conscience by tyrannical laws which are contrary to the ordinances of God and Scripture. Similarly he would abolish or drastically diminish ecclesiastical festivals, processions, masses for the dead, interdict, excommunication, except as far as Scripture enjoins it; ecclesiastical censures in various degree, which, he thinks, should be buried ten fathoms deep in the earth; saints'

[56] "Werke," vi. 437.

days, which foster only idleness, gluttony, drinking, loss of income, mendicity, for which he would substitute a strictly controlled system of local poor relief; fraternities which nourish only drunkenness and gluttony, etc.[57]

Lastly, in connection with the Hussite question, he would make a radical breach with the system of force and treachery in the treatment of heretics and would have the Reichstag recognise the Bohemian national Church, whether the Pope agrees or not. "If the Bohemians do not wish to submit to the Roman ecclesiastical law, we should not force them to do so; but in the first place be content to see that they live aright in accordance with faith and Scripture. For the Christian faith and estate may very well exist without the Pope's intolerable laws, yea, they cannot exist well until there are less or even none of these laws. We became free at our baptism and subject to God's Word alone. Why, then, should a mere man seek to make us the captives of his word. As St Paul says, 'Stand fast, therefore, in the liberty wherewith Christ has made you free and be not again entangled with the yoke of bondage.'"[58] In matters of belief he even proclaims the Christian principle of toleration against the mad principle of an enforced submission to authority. He boldly denounces the martyrdom of Hus and the abominable principle that faith is not to be kept with heretics. "God has commanded to observe a safe conduct and this command we must obey even if the world perish, so much the more even when it is a question of liberating a heretic. We should seek to overcome heretics with arguments, not with fire, as the Fathers of old did. If skill consists in overcoming heretics with fire, the hangman would be the most learned doctor on earth. There would be no need for study, but every one that could lay hands on another would be entitled to burn him."[59]

Finally, he submits a sketch of educational, legal, and social reform which the Estates are to undertake in addition to the reformation of the Church. He would thoroughly remodel the course of study in the Faculties of Arts and Theology and extend to all the universities the reforms already in operation at Wittenberg. In his revulsion from

[57] "Werke," vi. 437 f. [58] *Ibid.*, vi. 456. [59] *Ibid.*, vi. 455.

the scholastic theology and philosophy he allows his aversion for Aristotle, who dominated the schools, to carry him too far in denunciation of "the blind heathen teacher," whom he regards as the perverter of the true theology. He would banish his physics, metaphysics, ethics, and his treatise on the soul from the curriculum, and whilst retaining his logic, rhetoric, and poetics as practically serviceable, he would exclude the notes and commentaries on these texts. The present system of using them merely for disputation is a weariness of the flesh and educationally valueless. His violent criticism is, he claims, not due to ignorance or arrogance, since he has read him with more understanding than Aquinas or Scotus. For this dreary and pernicious scholasticism he would substitute the study of Latin, Greek and Hebrew, mathematics and history. As an educationist, if not altogether as a theologian, he has definitely adopted the humanist spirit and standpoint. In the Faculty of Theology he would make the Bible the supreme study instead of wasting time and imbibing error on that of the Sentences. A man may be a doctor of the Sentences and yet be profoundly ignorant of the Gospel, which lies dusty and unheeded beneath the benches. Popes, emperors, universities may make doctors of arts, medicine, law, the Sentences, but a true doctor of Holy Scripture can be made by no one but the Holy Spirit, who does not consider whether a man is a priest, monk, or layman, nay, who once spoke by an ass against the prophet who rode on it. Would God we were worthy to have such doctors! He would make the Bible also the chief vehicle of religious instruction in the elementary and in the high schools, to which only the apter pupils should be sent, and he presses this reform on both princes and magistrates of cities.[60] Of the canon law he speaks in terms of the utmost contempt, especially as it has become practically equivalent to what is contained in the *Scrinium* or shrine of the Pope's breast (*Scrinium pectoris*), and is therefore what he chooses to make it. He has a higher opinion of the civil law. But what a wilderness it has become! There is far too much of it, and he much prefers the common law and usage of the land and would have

[60] "Werke," vi. 457-462.

every nation governed by its own simple laws, instead of by the elaborate and burdensome code of ancient Rome.[61]

He touches, in conclusion, on the evils in the State itself which clamantly need reform. He would have the Reichstag pass sumptuary legislation against the prevailing luxury and extravagance which are impoverishing both nobles and people. He would have all classes be content in the matter of clothing with the simple resources of the country in flax, fur, and wool, and discourage commerce in the expensive stuffs and articles of luxury from foreign lands. The dealers in these things are bidding fair to abet the Pope in ruining the country. This commerce only thrives on usury (interest) and he cannot see the justice of amassing wealth in this way, as the Fugger and similar banking and commercial companies do, though he does not profess to be an expert in these matters. There is also far too much excess in eating and drinking, with their attendant vices, in which Germany has acquired an evil reputation in foreign lands, and which the temporal authorities should exert themselves to repress. On one glaring social evil he has no hesitation in speaking with certain voice. He would forthwith suppress the public brothels maintained in the large towns as a disgrace to a Christian nation. For this scandal those in authority assuredly have a grave responsibility, and it is their duty to amend it for the good of their subjects. Honourable wedlock ought to be held up as the ideal before the young, and the vicious results of sowing their wild oats, which will certainly bear a crop of wild oats, impressed upon them. But these necessary reforms are only too sadly neglected by the temporal as well as the spiritual authorities. "O what a rare sight will, for such reasons, a lord and a ruler be in heaven, although he has built a hundred churches and raised all the dead." [62]

The Address challenges criticism when read in the calm of the historian's study. It bears ample trace of Luther's tendency to extreme, unqualified generalisation. It is hardly a historically-minded statement. It is the speech of the counsel for the prosecution and sentence of the criminal at the bar, and its tone is very violent and

[61] "Werke," vi. 459-460. [62] *Ibid.*, vi. 465 f.

uncompromising. It contains exaggerations of fact and misstatement of motive. Luther, we feel, is fairly on the warpath, in the mind to swear at large. At the same time, he has undoubtedly a very strong case, so strong that one is disposed to conclude that he might well have stated it more moderately without any loss to its strength. Its vehemence, in fact, rather tends to weaken its force for the modern reader. Apart from this weakness, however, we cannot but appreciate the skill, the moral force, the impassioned eloquence with which the counsel for the prosecution handles the overwhelming evidence against the criminal at the bar, though he inclines to ramble at large at times. One feels that the hour of Nemesis has at last struck for Roman corruption and misgovernment. Rome had for generations been steadily heading for this crisis, and in the monk of Wittenberg the hour has brought the man of elemental force that fits him to be the agent of Nemesis. This force consists in the combination of profound moral and religious conviction with a marvellous gift of thought and telling expression, and in Luther it perforce functions in its own way like the lightning or the whirlwind. If the combination has its weakness as well as its strength, it must be remembered that Luther, as the agent of Nemesis, is there not to examine the case historically and judicially, but to utter the judgment of God on the gross corruption and misgovernment of the Church which must at long last be mended or ended, and for which he rightly holds Rome responsible. In this sense Rome has in verity become the Antichrist, and the Reformation can only begin by sounding the knell of doom, the trumpet of the last judgment on this Antichrist. This preliminary function Luther performs in the Address with elemental power and for the effective performance of this function it needed just the qualities which constitute this elemental force—the religious genius, the moral strength, the dogmatic, albeit one-sided conviction, the courage, the audacity, the tremendous power of utterance which the Address reveals.

Luther is thus the man for the hour. But for the work of construction as well as destruction, which an effective Reformation demands, organised effort is indispensable, and for this organised effort Luther turns not to the Church but to the State. His expedient is, indeed, a Council summoned and abetted by the State. In practice, however, it is by the State—the Reichstag, or in a subordinate capacity the individual estates—that the contemplated Reformation is operated. A General, or even a National Council, without the Pope, summoned for this purpose, would in the circumstances have proved an impossible expedient, for the clergy were under canonical obedience to the head of the Church and could not constitutionally assemble without the papal sanction. Practically, therefore, Luther is fain to rely on the Reichstag for the realisation of his scheme of reform, and he vindicates the right of the State to reform the Church on the ground, generally, of its divine institution, and particularly his principle of the priesthood of all believers. In the third part it is virtually through the temporal power that the Reformation is to be effected. He distinguishes, indeed, between the spheres of Church and State and upholds the right of the Church within its own sphere. In reality the Reformation is carried out by the temporal authority which, in virtue of necessity, is empowered to undertake the task. The contention of Karl Müller [63] and Holl [64] that in the Address Luther restricts the activity of the State to the removal of abuses of an economic and political character and assigns to the Council that of the more purely ecclesiastical evils is, as Kohlmeyer [65] has shown, not conclusive. The State is the only available power by which that of the Papacy can be countered, and Luther, whilst maintaining in theory the distinction between the two spheres and the autonomy of the Church in the spiritual sphere, has perforce to resort to this power in the actual work of reformation. In this respect he shows a rather naïve tendency to idealise the State which strikingly contrasts with the tendency to see only evil in the actual Papacy. He is strongly influenced by his respect for the integrity of his own sovereign, the Elector, and by the

[63] "Kirche, Gemeinde und Obrigkeit nach Luther," 17 f. (1910).

[64] "Gesammelte Aufsätze," i. 280 f. (1921). See on the other side Kohlmeyer, "Z.K.G.," 1925, 589 f.

[65] "Entstehung," 17 f.

ational optimism which saw in the accession of the young Emperor the promise of a regenerated empire, of a new era of national reform, of which the Reichstag, under his auspices, would be the active instrument for the general welfare.

Equally naïve the assumption that the Estates, under such auspices, would bring to bear on the task of reforming the Church purely religious considerations. Many of the princes and the nobility were only too likely to view this task from the angle of their own aims and interests. The princes and other territorial magnates had been only too ready to profit from the traffic in benefices, for instance, for the benefit of their relatives, and from other abuses which they were now asked to remedy solely for the glory of God and the religious good of their subjects. There was a real danger of substituting for the papal tyranny and exploitation the interested and bureaucratic régime of the territorial prince over the territorial Church, of transforming the Church into a department of State under princely auspices. In christianising the State in virtue of his doctrine of the priesthood of believers, Luther did not sufficiently realise the danger lurking in this device for the autonomy of the Church and the Christian liberty which he defends in theory, but which under the plea of necessity he unwittingly surrenders.

Similarly his conception of a national reformed Church which might still recognise a reformed Papacy was an ideal which was hardly feasible. The only feasible alternative was to disestablish the Papacy within the borders of the empire and substitute for the papal régime an independent national Church. This alternative he was personally prepared to adopt, though he shows a conservative reluctance to face this extreme step. If Rome will not renounce Antichrist, Germany will renounce Rome. This is his alternative to the unreformed Papacy. But he still assumes that the mediæval Papacy may be brought to reform itself, or allow itself to be reformed to the extent of renouncing all the claims and pretensions and oppressions which had made it an intolerable burden to the nation, and confine itself to the purely spiritual oversight of Christendom. It was a pious imagination that contemplated the possibility that the

Papacy would thus forswear itself. A Papacy existing merely on sufferance, a Papacy divesting itself of all its developed canonical rights and powers and perpetuating itself merely as a nominal relic of the past, was a chimera. Luther's contemplated constitution of a national Church and a national assembly under a German primate, with the Pope as its nominal head, was merely a paper constitution. The Reformation had to do without the Pope, if only because the Pope would in no case have consented to lay aside his triple crown at the behest of the monk of Wittenberg or even the Reichstag. John Calvin or John Knox would hardly have suggested such a paper constitution. Having, like Luther, rejected both the divine and human right of the Papacy and denounced the Pope as the representative of Antichrist, they would have logically denied to the Bishop of Rome any function whatsoever within the national Church.

Finally, as an educational and social reformer Luther is more practical. He has turned his back for ever on scholasticism and is now marching in the van of the progressive educational movement of his time, though his denunciation of the pagan knave Aristotle is lacking in discrimination and enlightenment. His demand for the reformation of national life is admirable and deserves to have succeeded. In his zeal for religious reform he is not blind to the evils that are festering in the body politic, and he can trounce a prince, a lord, a financial magnate on occasion as well as the Pope. But his political economy is rather primitive, as he himself acknowledges, and whilst seeking to better the condition of the people economically as well as morally, his programme of social reform is silent on the grave question of serfdom which was agitating the masses and was verging towards a reform of larger scope than he was capable of grasping.

II. The Attack on the Sacraments

In "The Babylonic Captivity of the Church"[66] he reappears as the theological reformer. Its genesis is to be found in the "Sermons on Penance, Baptism, and the

[66] "De Captivitate Babylonica Ecclesiæ."

Eucharist," published in the autumn of 1519, in the passage relative to the Mass in the "Sermon on Good Works,"[67] and in the "Sermon on the Mass" which appeared in revised and enlarged form in August 1520,[68] and in which he anticipates to some extent what he was to say at length on the subject in "The Babylonic Captivity." In a letter to Spalatin on the 18th December 1519 he had mentioned his growing scepticism about the remaining four sacraments and his intention to discuss the subject in a future work.[69] The promised work gradually took shape in his mind as the result of frequent and intensive discussions with Melanchthon on the priestly office and the sacramental system. It was in the course of these discussions that, as we learn from this letter, he grasped his characteristic conception of the priesthood of all believers and of the priestly office as a ministry of the Word and sacraments for the benefit of the Christian community. This ministry is something very different from the official priesthood which is the creation of human ordinances, which the Roman Curia has imposed on the Christian community, and by which it holds the Church in bondage. It was this fundamental change in his view of the priesthood and the sacraments that he worked out in the course of the discussions with Melanchthon and now developed in "The Babylonic Captivity of the Church."[70] The idea of a Babylonic bondage of the Church under the papal régime had already

[67] "Werke," vi. 230-231. Luther refers to this passage in a letter to John Hess, 27th April 1520. Enders, ii. 385. Institutionem sacerdotalem . . . quantum vero ad spiritum fidei nonnihil confert sermo germanicus.

[68] Enders, ii. 455; *cf.* 385. Ein Sermon von dem neuen Testament, das ist von der heiligen messe. "Werke," vi. 353 f.

[69] Enders, ii. 279.

[70] Enders, ii. 279. Officia sacerdotis, he wrote to Spalatin, quæ ex me quæris ignoro, cum quanto magis cogito, non inveniam quod scribam nisi çeremonialia; deinde valde me urget Petrus Apostolus, 1 Peter ii., dicens nos omnes esse sacerdotales; idem Johannes in Apocalypsi, ut hoc genus sacerdotii, in quo nos sumus, prorsus non differre videatur a laicis, nisi ministerio quo sacramenta et verbum ministrantur. Cætera omnia sunt æqualia, si ceremonias et humana statuta demas, et satis miramur unde ordo nomen sacramenti invenerit. Mira hæc tibi nonne? Sed præsens plura una cum Philippo (Melanch-

occurred to him in connection with the exclusive claim of the Pope to interpret the Scriptures.[71] In the "De Captivitate" he uses the phrase specifically of the bondage to which the mediæval priestly and sacramental system has reduced the Church. As in the case of the Address to the Nobility, the actual impulse to its composition came in part at least from Alveld, who in July had controverted his doctrine of communion in both kinds,[72] though without mentioning him by name. To this effusion of "the Leipzig ass," as he contemptuously termed Alveld, he did not deign to reply directly. But, as he informed Spalatin, it prompted him to set to work on the "De Captivitate."[73] In the preface to the work itself he, in fact, ironically includes the Leipzig Franciscan among the teachers—Prierias, Eck, Emser—to whom he owes his progress in the knowledge of the Gospel. As Prierias had led him utterly to reject indulgences as an imposture of Rome and Eck had helped him to deny to the Papacy even a human right, so Alveld had greatly contributed to clarify his ideas on the subject of the Lord's Supper. He profusely thanks the Leipzig lecturer on the Bible for the service he has thus unwittingly rendered him and, along with him, a certain friar of Cremona, who has also contributed, in the philippic he has penned against him, to his enlightenment.[74]

thon), quoniam has res et sæpe et acute tractavimus. Proinde officium tuum a communibus laicorum officiis nihil differet exceptis oneribus, quæ Romana Curia sine delectu omnibus sacerdotibus imposuit.

[71] In the course of his preliminary studies for the Leipzig disputation, see Resolutio Lutheriana, "Werke," ii. 214-215. Absit, absit ista plus quam Babylonica Captivitas. It recurs in the work against that of Alveld on the Apostolic See written under his direction by his secretary, Lonicer, and published in the beginning of June 1520. Tota hodiernæ ecclesiæ lerna sub Romano pontifice captivitatem plus quam Babylonicam servientis. "Werke," vi. 485.

[72] Alveld entitled his work "Tractatus de communione sub utraque specie." See the reference to it in Luther's letter to Spalatin, 22nd July 1520, Enders, ii. 446.

[73] Enders, ii. 457. Alveldio non respondebitur, sed occasione ejus dabitur in lucem quo magis viperæ irretentur.

[74] He refers to the "Revocatio Mart. Lutheri ad Sanctam Sedem," which Enders (ii. 527) misdates Nov. 1520, and which Luther mentions in a letter to Voigt, 3rd Aug., ii. 455-456. "Werke," vi. 497-499.

The work, which was dedicated to his colleague Hermann Tulich, was the fulfilment of the threat contained in the conclusion of the Address to sing another song for the benefit of the Romanists. Unlike the Address, however, it was intended for the enlightenment of his fellow-theologians and the cultured class, not of the people, who were quite unfitted to understand the theological issues which it raised. It was accordingly written in Latin and was aimed straight at the heart of the mediæval sacerdotal system. In the history of the development of Luther's doctrinal teaching it deserves to take rank alongside the Commentary on Romans, of which, in fact, it was the logical outcome. Like the Commentary, it is both critical and constructive. Luther here combats the mediæval notion of the sacraments as the media of God's grace, on which the priestly power was based and by which the religious life was conditioned and controlled, and he pits against this notion the necessity of individual faith and individual contact with God as the essential thing for the reception and experience of His grace. In thus stressing individual faith he was sounding the death knell of mediæval sacerdotalism. He not only reduces the number of the sacraments to three at the most; he deprives them of their magical significance and efficacy and the priest of his vicarial power as the mediator of sacramental grace. He remorselessly strips off the sacerdotalism which had encrusted their original simplicity in the course of the development of the papal and priestly power. He does not profess to exhaust the subject. His work is only a prelude (*prœludium*) or introduction. It reflects, too, the haste with which it was actually written, though the subject had been simmering for some time in his mind. He began it after the publication of the Address in the middle of August. At the end of the month he writes rather impatiently that the printer is not able to keep pace with the composition of the manuscript.[75] Both printer and author were evidently working their hardest during September, for in the beginning of October he announces to Spalatin that its publication will take place on the 6th of that month.[76] Moreover, it

[75] Enders, ii. 471. [76] *Ibid.*, ii. 487.

reflects the influence of the Nominalist theology in which he had been trained, and from which he had not been able to shake himself free. At the same time, it marks a truly marvellous emancipation from mediævalism in religion, and was to his age the stunning revelation of the originality and independence of the audacious prophet of Wittenberg. It was credited by some to Erasmus, an assumption which hardly needed his disclaimer to refute. With all his gifts Erasmus could not have penned such an indictment of mediæval sacerdotalism. His courage would have oozed in the attempt.

The thesis of the Babylonic Captivity is that there are only three sacraments, or better expressed, one sacrament and three sacramental signs, and that the Roman Curia has reduced these to a miserable bondage and thereby spoiled the Church of its liberty. In other words, through its doctrine of the sacraments Rome has imposed on the Church an intolerable bondage to its sacerdotalism.[77] From this bondage he will deliver it by controverting the mediæval conception of the sacraments and setting forth the scriptural teaching on the subject, which Rome has wrested and perverted in its sacramental system, though one is bound to admit that his own magisterial interpretation of Scripture is not always infallible.[78]

He has no difficulty in proving, in the case of the Sacrament of the Lord's Supper, that communion of the laity in both kinds is the scriptural doctrine. The attempt to restrict the cup to the priests is, in the face of the evidence, pure sophistry.[79] With this evidence he boldly challenges the mediæval practice. "I conclude, therefore, that to deny both kinds to the laity is wicked and tyrannical, nor is it in the power of any angel, much less of any Pope or Council. Nor do I care for the deliverance of the Council of Constance, for, if its authority is valid, why should not that of Basle be equally valid, which, on the contrary, decreed that the Bohemians should be allowed to receive in both kinds."[80]

[77] "Werke," vi. 501.

[78] *Ibid.*, vi. 502. He maintains, for instance, that the Eucharistic discourse in John vi. has nothing to do with the sacrament.

[79] *Ibid.*, vi. 502-506.

[80] *Ibid.*, vi. 506-507.

He does not go the length of maintaining that communion in one kind is sinful, nor that communion in both kinds should be forcibly insisted on by the laity. He contents himself, rather tamely, with asserting that the right and liberty of the individual Christian to use both should be proclaimed and with condemning the priesthood for denying this right and liberty. He would have them restored by a General Council which should take up the question and formally vindicate communion in both kinds against the tyranny of Rome.[81]

The second form of bondage with which Rome has invested this sacrament is the doctrine of transubstantiation, which it has unwarrantably made an article of faith. He tells us that already as a student of the scholastic theology he was led to doubt this doctrine by a passage in D'Ailly's "Commentary on the Sentences," in which he asserts that it would be far more reasonable to believe that real bread and wine and not merely their accidents remained after consecration by the priest, if the Church had not decreed otherwise. It was this that first led him to question the teaching of Aquinas on the subject and to adopt that of Wiclif, viz., that the substance of the bread and wine is not transmuted by priestly consecration into the body and blood of Christ, so that only the accidents, *i.e.*, form, colour, etc., remain, but that the actual bread and wine remain and Christ is bodily present in them in virtue of this consecration. This, he holds, is what the New Testament teaches, and he cares not if it is denounced as Wiclifite or Hussite heresy. The New Testament knows nothing of the subtle distinction between substance and accident falsely foisted by Aquinas and the schoolmen on this teaching. Nor did the Church, he rather rashly adds, know anything of this dogma of theirs for 1,200 years.[82] Discarding their subtle reasoning

[81] "Werke," vi. 507.

[82] Both the idea and the term were in vogue earlier. Transubstantiation was made a dogma of the Church by the fourth Lateran Council under Innocent III. in 1215, and the theory was known to Albertus Magnus, Alexander of Hales, William of Paris, the predecessors of Aquinas. Hildebert of Tours first used the term (1134) to define the doctrine; though it had been applied in the previous century by Peter Damian.

in its support, he prefers to take the words of institution, "This is my body, this is my blood," in their literal significance and to believe not in transubstantiation, but in consubstantiation, *i.e.*, the real or bodily presence of Christ in the elements in virtue of their consecration. It does not occur to him that the literal sense is not necessarily the true sense and that the symbolic sense is alone in accordance with the historic meaning. He realises the difficulty of taking the words literally and assuming the actual eating and drinking of Christ's body and blood. He tries to get over the difficulty by merely saying that faith is above reason.[83] "What if philosophy cannot understand these things? The Holy Spirit is greater than Aristotle."[84] But surely there is another alternative interpretation which is not only the obvious one, but far more likely to be in accord with the mind of the Spirit than the crass notion which he declares to be the true one. In this matter he has still one foot in the Middle Ages. He is still under the influence of the material as against the spiritual view of the Supper and has recourse to the Nominalist tendency to exalt faith above reason in order to maintain this material view, though he also, in the "De Captivitate," accepts reason as a source of the knowledge of God. Another instance in which his interpretation of Scripture is by no means above question. At the same time, he leaves others at liberty to believe in transubstantiation as long as they grant him the liberty to believe in consubstantiation. Evidently, however, he would not tolerate those who believe in neither.

The third form of bondage is the conception of this sacrament as a meritorious or good work (*opus operatum*) and a sacrifice. In this conception Rome has departed still further from the primitive institution, and in order to show this he explains at length that Christ in instituting the Supper entered into a new covenant or testament with the believer, that the distinctive feature of this covenant is the promise of forgiveness of sins through His

[83] "Werke," vi. 508-511.

[84] *Ibid.*, vi. 511. Major est Spiritus Sanctus quam Aristoteles.

death,[85] and that the essential thing for the realisation of the promise is faith, by which God's free and undeserved mercy in Christ becomes available to the believer. He thus interprets the sacrament in the light of his doctrine of justification by faith, by which the remission of sin is attained. This is what the Mass, as instituted by Christ, reflects, and this, its simple significance, has been obscured and perverted by means of superstitious ceremonies, from which the priesthood derives its authority and no little pecuniary profit. It is the visible sign of God's forgiving love in Christ to those who have faith in His promise. The word or promise and the sign which faith makes effective—just as the rainbow was the sign to those who believed in the promise that the deluge would cease—these are the simple essentials of the Mass. We must, therefore, eliminate from it the superstition which regards it as a good work, *i.e.*, in itself an efficacious thing as performed by the priest, an *opus operatum*, and assigns to its mere performance by the priest a magical efficacy and a merit apart from the faith of the recipient. Audacious as it may appear to reject the sacramental doctrine and overthrow the institutions of centuries—masses for the dead, anniversaries, etc., which are so profitable for the priesthood—he will not be restrained by the number or the magnitude of these errors and traditional practices from proclaiming the truth. "Truth is stronger than all these. . . . Unheard of and astounding statements, you exclaim. But if you examine the real nature of the Mass, you will acknowledge that I have only spoken the truth." [86]

Still more erroneous is the notion that in the Mass the priest offers Christ as a sacrifice to God, as the words of the canon of the Mass, "oblation," "sacrifice," "offering," seem to imply. In the Mass we receive a gift; we offer nothing to God except our prayers. Christ in the Supper did not offer Himself to God. He only announced His testament or promise and instituted the sign and seal of its fulfilment. The nearer the Mass approaches to this first

[85] In his reasoning on the covenant or testament and the promise contained in it, he is influenced especially by Heb. ix. 15-17.

[86] "Werke," vi. 522. Fortior omnium est veritas, etc.

simple Mass, the more Christian it is. It had no display of vestments, gestures, incantations, or other ceremonies. It was simplicity itself. He does not absolutely condemn the elaborate ceremonial that has gradually grown up around it. But we should not be deceived by its outward accidents and should remember that in primitive times when the believers met to celebrate the Supper, they brought gifts of food and drink called "collects," from which were taken the bread and wine to be consecrated for the sacrament. They were consecrated by word and prayer in accordance with the Hebrew rite of elevating them, and this custom of elevation, he explains rather hazardously, prevailed after the primitive usage of bringing the gifts had died out and the "collects" came to signify the prayers. But this offering and elevation of the host by the priest are not to be understood as a sacrifice. It is only the relic of an old rite which had quite a different significance. In this matter the priest must follow the Gospel and not later superstitious observances. He is simply there as the minister of the people to offer prayers for himself and them and should not communicate alone. In the matter of the Mass all are equal, priests and laymen.[87]

The Sacrament of Baptism also involves a promise of the forgiveness of sin, appropriated by faith, of which it is the sign. It is well that this sacrament is reserved for childhood, since thereby the complete dependence of the helpless soul on God for salvation is unequivocally expressed. But this has been obscured by the scholastic idea that, while baptism takes away original sin, in the case of sins committed after baptism we must seek to assure their remission by works of penance—"the second plank of salvation," as Jerome called them—instead of relying on the promise of forgiveness appropriated by faith at our baptism. Hence, in the case of this sacrament also, the vicious accretion of works and tyrannical human opinions and traditions which do wrong to the truth of God and to faith.[88]

For Luther baptism, as embodying the promise of forgive-

[87] "Werke," vi. 512-526. [88] *Ibid.*, vi. 527.

ness appropriated by faith, is essential to salvation. Unlike Calvin, who denied its absolute necessity for salvation,[89] he ascribes to it a cardinal importance as the medium of the remission of sin (baptismal regeneration). He retains the traditional doctrine that God's grace in the remission of sin is mediated through it and effects the regeneration of the soul. He speaks of it as the first of the sacraments and the foundation of them all, without which we possess none of the others.[90] "He that believeth and *is baptized* shall be saved." But whilst baptism is a condition of the remission of sin, he rejects the traditional notion of its magical efficacy in itself. Faith in the promise is the essential requisite of its efficacy, and without faith it has no justifying effect. "Unless this faith exists and is applied, baptism profiteth us nothing." [91] When, therefore, we are conscious of sin we must eschew alike all thought of the magical efficacy of the rite in working the grace of remission and all attempts to secure it by penitential works and fall back simply on the promise appropriated by faith in our baptism. Here again, as in the case of the Sacrament of the Altar, he views baptism in the light of his doctrine of justification by faith and lays stress on faith as the sole means of remission. "Thus baptism justifies no one and profits no one, but faith in the word of promise, to which baptism is added. It is this that justifies and fulfils that which baptism signifies. . . . Thus it cannot be true that there inheres in this sacrament an efficacious power of justification or that it is an efficacious sign of grace. For all these things are said to the complete detriment of faith in ignorance of the divine promise, unless they are said to be efficacious in the sense that, if unhesitating faith is present, the sacraments do confer grace most assuredly and efficaciously." [92] If it is objected that infants cannot have faith, he answers by saying either that the faith of the parents avails for their children, or that God, through the prayers of the Church, miraculously infuses faith into the heart of the infant.[93]

As a sign, Luther holds with Paul that baptism specifically

[89] Hunter, "The Teaching of Calvin," 150.
[90] "Werke," vi. 528, 538.
[91] *Ibid.*, vi. 527.
[92] *Ibid.*, vi. 532-533.
[93] *Ibid.*, vi. 538.

signifies death to sin and resurrection to new life, the immersion of the old man and the emersion of the new.[94] From this point of view he would prefer immersion to sprinkling, though it is not absolutely necessary to change the traditional practice. This dying and rising to new life is, however, not a single act, but a lifelong process only complete with life itself. Spiritually we need to be baptized continually in this sense by faith [95] in the process of the mortifying of the flesh and the vivifying of the spirit.

All this has been miserably obscured by the bondage to human works, for which he holds the Pope responsible. Instead of being the guardian of Christian liberty, he has become its oppressor by his decrees and laws which ensnare to his tyrannical power. He denies his right thus to enslave the Church and defiantly asks who has given him this power? In reply he pens one of his finest pleas for the liberty of the individual Christian. "I say, then, that neither Pope, nor bishop, nor any man has the right of constituting a single regulation over the Christian man unless it is done by his own consent. Whatever is done otherwise is done in a tyrannical spirit. Therefore prayers, fasts, contributions, and whatever of this kind the Pope statutes and exacts in his decrees—as numerous as they are iniquitous—he statutes and exacts by no right, and he sins against the liberty of the Church as often as he has attempted anything of this kind. Hence it has come to pass that the clergy of to-day are indeed the strenuous guardians of ecclesiastical liberty, *i.e.*, of stones, logs, lands, and money (for thus to-day things ecclesiastical are regarded as the same as spiritual things). By these fictitious words they not only take captive the true liberty of the Church, but utterly destroy it even more than the Turk, contrary to the word of the Apostle who says: 'Be ye not the slaves of men.' For this is truly to be the slaves of men to be subjected to their statutes and tyrannical laws." [96] "I admit, indeed, that this accursed tyranny is to be borne

[94] "Werke," vi. 533-534.

[95] *Ibid.*, vi. 535. Semper baptisandus fide, semper moriendum, semperque vivendum.

[96] *Ibid.*, vi. 536.

by Christians, like any other violence of this world, in accordance with the Word of Christ, 'Whosoever smiteth thee on thy right cheek, turn to him the other also.' But of this I complain that the impious popes boast that they have the right to do this, and that they presume that they are providing for the interests of the Christian cause under the guise of this, their Babylon, and seek to persuade all to this opinion of theirs. . . . In behalf of this liberty and conscientious right I call aloud, and I faithfully proclaim that no law can be imposed by any right on Christians, whether by men or by angels, unless in as far as they will; for we are free from all (*liberi enim sumus ab omnibus*). If they are imposed, they are so to be borne that the consciousness of liberty may be reserved, which knows and with certainty affirms that injury is done to it. . . . I at least will set free my mind and vindicate my conscience, upbraiding the Pope and all papists and declaring that unless they abandon their laws and traditions and restore their due liberty to the churches of Christ and cause this liberty to be taught, they are guilty of all souls that perish by reason of this miserable captivity, and the Papacy is truly nothing more than the kingdom of Babylon and the very Antichrist." [97]

The worst form of tyranny is that exercised through the Sacrament of Penance, to which, in the conclusion of the work, he denies the attribute of a sacrament. In practice, at all events, it has become a mere device for completing the tyranny of Pope and priest in virtue of the words "Whatsoever thou shalt bind" (Matthew xvi. 19; xviii. 18; John xx. 23). Christ established not a priestly domination through the sacraments, but a ministry in the Church. In that of penance, which consists of three parts—contrition, confession, and satisfaction—they have substituted for this ministry a priestly domination and have put the copestone on their tyranny. Of contrition they have made a merit instead of the result of faith in God's promise and threats, producing both repentance and consolation, and have invented the lower

[97] "Werke," vi. 536-537.

form of attrition for the benefit of the wicked and unbelieving, which in their case they have made the equivalent of real contrition. Confession is a scriptural and salutary practice. But it ought to be free and be made to any brother, not necessarily to the priest, who has no monopoly of absolution. This reservation of confession to the priest is merely a means of tyranny and extortion, an unwarranted usurpation by a venal priesthood in order to enslave the Christian freeman. Satisfaction, which is a change of life, they have made into a burdensome pursuit of merits by means of external works, to the torture of conscience by all sorts of scruples and the gratification of priestly greed and avarice.[98] "In the first place they have so taught it that the people have never understood true satisfaction, which consists in newness of life. In the second place they so insist and render it so necessary that they leave no room for faith in Christ, miserably tormenting consciences with scruples that one runs to Rome, another here, another there, to some convent or other place, another scourging himself with rods, another injuring his body with watchings and fastings, and all crying out with equal zeal 'Behold here or here is Christ and the kingdom of God,' which nevertheless is within us, thinking that it cometh with observation. All these enormities we owe to thee, O Roman See, and to thy homicidal laws and rites, by which thou hast so ruined the whole world that people imagine they can satisfy God for sins through works, who can only be satisfied solely by the faith of a contrite heart. This faith thou hast not only put to silence, but hast oppressed in order only that thou, like an insatiable leech, mayst have some to whom to say, 'Bring, Bring,' and thus make a traffic in sins." [99]

Repentance is a very different thing from penance, and conditions the whole life in the process of mortifying the flesh. From this point of view the granting of absolution before satisfaction is utterly reprehensible.

For the remaining four sacraments—confirmation, matrimony, orders, and extreme unction—he can find no warrant

[98] "Werke," vi. 543-549.
[99] *Ibid.*, vi. 548.

in Scripture and therefore rejects them. Without such warrant the Church cannot institute a sacrament or impose such an institution as an article of faith. Here again, however, he would make no violent or radical alteration, but submit to recognise these institutions, whilst claiming the right as a Christian to individual liberty and refusing to yield perforce to what he regards as error and tyranny.[100] The Word of God is incomparably above the Church, which is the creature, not the lord of the Word, and whose part it is to be guided and regulated by its directions. This power only it possesses, and even in exercising it, it is liable to error, and has in fact often erred. He emphasises anew in treating of orders his conception of the priesthood as a ministry, which only exercises its function with the consent of the Christian community, and strongly reasserts the principle of the priesthood of all believers who entrust the office of serving the community to one of its members specially set apart for this purpose. This office is specifically the ministry of the Word—to preach the Gospel and dispense the Sacraments of Baptism and the Supper—and all attempts to prove from the New Testament an indelible distinction between clergy and laity and to erect this ministry into an ecclesiastical caste, on which the bondage and the questionable institution of celibacy is imposed, are vain. The so-called Sacrament of Orders, of which the mystic Dionysius in his "Celestial Hierarchy" makes so much, is nothing more than a rite by which men are called to minister in the Church, chosen as preachers of the Gospel, and the fact that so many of the clergy neglect this essential of their function is a lamentable proof of the evil of the present pernicious system.[1]

The realisation of these ideas would necessitate a profound modification of the mediæval Church and its institutions. The "Captivity" is from beginning to end a plea for spiritual religion and the liberty of the individual Christian as against mediæval sacerdotalism and the mediæval priestly caste.

100 "Werke," vi. 549, 560-561.

1 *Ibid.*, vi. 560 f. He takes occasion in speaking of Dionysius to declare his revulsion from mystic theology of this kind, and has evidently largely outlived the mystic phase of his religious development.

It reminds one of Paul's controversy with the Judaisers in his attempt to emancipate Christianity and the individual Christian from Judaism. Luther wages a similar controversy against the vast accretion of tradition and practice which had accumulated throughout the Middle Ages and which, he holds, has entangled and enthralled religion in a network of usages and ideas incompatible with primitive Christianity and Christian liberty. For the mediæval Church he would substitute the Church of the New Testament, as emancipated by Paul, and of the first two centuries, in which the priestly conception of religion was little, if at all, developed. The work reveals the independence and daring of an extraordinarily original mind, though it is confessedly not exhaustive. It is for the most part a complete revulsion from, a thorough-going confutation of the sacerdotal teaching of the schoolmen, to whom he ascribes the development of the sacerdotal doctrine of the Church.[2] Though he arraigns the Pope as the main defaulter, he says that most of the popes of the previous 1,000 years were intellectual mediocrities and incapable of serious theological thought. They have merely borrowed from the schoolmen the rationale of ecclesiastical ideas and practices.

We are struck on the one hand by the boldness of the attack, and on the other by the self-restraint with which it is developed. In this respect it is an extraordinary combination of courage and prudence. He starts section by section to prove his case, and having proved it he invariably hesitates to draw the inevitable practical conclusion. He prefers to tolerate and compromise. It is sufficient to vindicate liberty in principle, and if you recognise the principle he is ready to leave the practice as it is. It is all very generous and tolerant. But one cannot help wondering at the same time at the logic or the problematic morality of the conclusion. One begins to doubt whether Luther, whilst undoubtedly an original thinker, has also the gift of initiating and organising the reform movement which he has called into being. His plan of campaign in the "Captivity" seems to be to point out

[2] "Werke," vi. 571.

error and abuse in doctrine and practice and leave God to remedy them by means of the Word acting on public opinion. He has not yet seriously faced the problem of the practical remedy. He was indefinitely conscious of being carried onwards by a power above himself, whither he knew not. He is not in control and has evidently no organising outlook. He is a strange combination of the progressive and the conservative mind—capable in a marvellous degree of striking great transforming ideas from the anvil of his heart and intellect; incapable of marshalling them in a definite plan of action. There is to be a revolutionary change without a revolution. He proclaims his principles in a militant enough tone, but when it comes to the question of their realisation he is apt to play the quietist, and decline to play the man of action. This half-hearted policy will hardly prove feasible in the long run. He will be obliged to modify or abandon it under the stress of events and the influence of more logical and practical minds.

Meanwhile it must be acknowledged that the enunciation of these startling revolutionary ideas was in itself a surpassingly daring enterprise and may explain the hesitation to go further in the meantime. *Festina lente* is in the circumstances as much as we can expect, though it was not in this way that Paul fought and won the battle of the emancipation of Christianity from Judaism. As it was, the "Captivity" cost him the adhesion of some of his supporters in the more advanced humanist party. Erasmus, for instance, wondered and wavered. To a number of reforming churchmen, who were at first sympathetic towards the movement, it became a stumbling-block. On the other hand, the German translation of Thomas Murner, revised and published by the Strassburg printer, Johann Prüss, carried its startling message beyond the limited circle of the learned and thus contributed to diffuse a knowledge of it among the people.[3]

[3] Luther was not too pleased with the translation, as he did not consider the subject a fit one for the unlearned class, and, besides, complained with some reason that Murner had not correctly rendered the Latin text into German. He concluded that Murner had falsified the text in order to injure his reputation. He had certainly taken liberties with the Latin text. But he does not seem to have originally falsified

III. The Liberty of a Christian Man

The " Babylonic Captivity " is a polemic from beginning to end. In this respect it contrasts strikingly with the third of the triad of reform manifestos which he wrote in October and published in November. It owed its genesis to the conference with Miltitz at Lichtenburg on the 12th October, at which he undertook to write a conciliatory letter to the Pope. In order not to appear before his holiness empty-handed, he had composed this modest treatise, which, however, contains a *summa* or compendium of the Christian life as he had learned to conceive it. From it the Pope may learn with what he would have preferred to occupy his mind had his impious flatterers not diverted him from his proper pursuit by their persistent attacks.[4] He offers it as an irenicon (on the understanding, of course, that the Pope accepts its teaching), and the reduction of the controversial element to a minimum bears out his profession. The title, " The Freedom of a Christian Man," aptly conveys the scope of its contents. It sets forth his cardinal doctrine of justification by faith as alike an emancipation, through faith, of the individual Christian from the bondage of external works, and a limitation of this freedom in virtue of the obligation of individual self-discipline and service for others. It reminds us that the fierce controversialist could also be the saint and that the influence he wielded was due to the saint as well as the controversialist. It is indeed the reflection of evangelical piety at its best. It was written in Latin for the purpose of presentation to the Pope, and he made a free translation for the benefit of the people,

it with intent, though he later took credit for having rendered a service to the Church in translating it. In any case, the object of the Strassburg publisher, who acquired the manuscript and revised it before publication, was not to damage but to further Luther's cause. See Kalkoff, " Luther's Ausgewählte Werke," ii. 273 f. There is an English translation by Wace and Buchheim (1896).

[4] See the conclusion of the Latin version of the letter. " Werke," vii. 48-49.

with a dedication to Hermann Mühlpfort, Stadtvogt of Zwickau.[5]

In "The Liberty of a Christian Man" he discusses faith experimentally. He writes with his experience of the quest for a gracious God in his mind, of the futility of his attempt to render God gracious by his own works, and the necessity of trusting for salvation to God's mercy in Christ. The little book is a simple exposition in the vernacular of his doctrine of justification by faith for the instruction of the people, though it was originally written in Latin for submission to the Pope.[6] It is entirely divested of the scholastic terminology in which, as expounded in the Commentary on Romans, this doctrine was originally entangled. The language is that of religion rather than of theology. It expresses concisely and maturely the certainty of salvation as due, as far as man is concerned, to simple faith alone in dependence solely on God.

He treats the subject from the double standpoint of the freedom and the subjection of the believer, in virtue of his faith. It takes us out of the atmosphere of controversy into that of personal piety, the fountain of which Luther finds in faith manifesting itself in love.[7] He starts with the double proposition that the Christian man is the most free lord of all and subject to no one, and that he is the most dutiful servant of all and subject to every one. He derives it from Paul, "Though I be free from all men, yet have I made myself the servant of all" (1 Cor. ix. 19). "Owe no man anything but to love one another" (Rom. xiii. 8).

From the religious point of view the believer is independent of all external things—from works in the ecclesiastical and even the ethical sense. He is dependent only on the Word of God, the Gospel,[8] received in faith.

[5] Not Hieronymus, as Luther calls him.

[6] "Tractatus de Libertate Christiana," "Werke," vii. 49 f. Luther's free translation in more concise form, vii. 20 f. English translation by Wace and Buchheim (1896).

[7] "Werke," vii. 49, (Fides) fons enim vivus est, saliens in vitam æternam.

[8] *Ibid.*, vii. 50-51. Verbum Dei or evangelium Dei.

It is faith that makes the Gospel operative for salvation which is due not to works, not even to works conjoined with faith, but to faith alone.[9] By its very nature faith is an inward thing and its primary function is that it begets the sense of sin, unworthiness, absolute dependence on, need of God in Christ, reliance not on human merit, but on the merit of Christ alone.[10] This is proved by numerous quotations from the New Testament, with one thrown in from Isaiah (x. 22-23), which, however, does not really prove his point and only serves to show his tendency to force his doctrine of justification into Old Testament passages which have really nothing to do with the subject.[11]

But how is this compatible with the moral precepts of the Old Testament? The Old Testament, the law, he answers with Paul, shows us what we ought to do, but does not give us the power to do it. The law teaches us our moral impotence and leads us to turn in our impotence from the precepts to the promises, from the Old Testament to the New, from the law to the Gospel. "God alone commands; God alone also fulfils."[12] This is the second function of faith, to lead us from precept to promise, from works to the Gospel. The result is that "to the Christian man his faith suffices for everything and that he has no need of works. But if he has no need of works, neither has he need of the law. If he has no need of the law, he is certainly free from the law and it is true that 'the law is not made for the righteous man' (1 Tim. i. 9). This is that Christian liberty, our faith which demands not that we be careless or live a bad life, but that no one should need the law or works for justification and salvation."[13]

In thus trusting in God solely for salvation, faith, in the third place, honours God by acknowledging Him to be true

[9] "Werke," vii. 51. Sola fide.

[10] *Ibid.*, vii. 51. Hace fides non nisi in homine interiore regnare possit. . . . Ideo dum credere incipis simul discis omnia quæ in te sunt esse prorsus culpabilia, peccata damnanda . . . in eum credens alius homo hac fide fieres, donatis omnibus peccatis tuis et justificato te alienis meritis, nempe Christi solius.

[11] *Ibid.*, vii. 52.

[12] *Ibid.*, vii. 53. Ipse solus præcipit, solus quoque implet.

[13] *Ibid.*, vii. 53.

and righteous, worthy of our confidence, and thus makes His promises effective. In return God honours us by imputing to us truth and righteousness. It is here that the doctrine of imputation comes in, by which faith is imputed for righteousness, as Paul teaches and as he had developed in detail in his Commentaries on Romans and Galatians. He does not here expatiate on the Pauline idea, which is rather for the theologian than the simple Christian. He simply glances at it as an experience of faith which gives to us the sense of righteousness in the sight of God.[14]

It is, further, a function of faith that it unites the soul to Christ who is mystically represented as the husband of the spiritual marriage of the soul, which thereby becomes possessed of all that Christ possesses, exchanges its sin, death, and condemnation for the grace, life, and salvation attainable through Him.[15] It participates in all that Christ is as king and priest. As king He is lord of the spiritual world. As priest He intercedes with God for us. So the Christian, through this spiritual union, becomes possessed of all that He possesses in this twofold capacity. He, too, is king as well as priest, king of a spiritual empire, lord over sin and death, lord of all things in a spiritual though not in a material sense. He becomes a participator in his priestly power which enables him to appear in God's presence and intercede for others. In this connection he once more rejects the distinction between clergy and laity and insists anew that the only distinction is that of the specific function of the ministry of the Word for the promotion of faith.[16] Luther's piety is thus steeped in the mysticism of the Pauline epistles and the epistle to the Hebrews, which he ascribes to him. He had in his formative period been strongly attracted and, to a certain extent, influenced by the mediæval mystics—Tauler and the author of "The German Theology"—whom, as we have seen, he regarded without sufficient discrimination as the pioneers of his evangelical teaching. In the "De Libertate Christiana" he has left the mediæval mystics behind him. There can be no doubt as to the source of the mystical element which

[14] "Werke," vii. 54. [15] *Ibid.*, vii. 54-56. [16] *Ibid.*, vii. 56, 59.

he thus imparts to his doctrine of justification in this beautiful little treatise. It is drawn directly from the New Testament, which has become the sole source of his teaching on the subject. His mysticism consists not in the absorption of self in God, mere *Gott Leiden*, but in personal faith in God in Christ, emancipating the soul from the burden and bondage of sin and endowing it with a spiritual power, a lordship over both sin and death.

This spiritual power appears in active operation in the second part of the little treatise in which he treats of works, the Christian life as the external expression of personal faith. "The Christian man is the most dutiful servant of all and subject to every one." In discussing this part of the subject Luther is at his very best as a religious teacher. The discussion is perhaps the finest thing he ever wrote, the gem of Reformation literature. If faith alone justifies, why concern ourselves with works? If, he replies, man were a purely spiritual being works would, indeed, be superfluous. He would forthwith attain by faith to the fullness of the inner, spiritual life. But he is a being of flesh and blood, not of pure spirit, and can only advance in the spiritual life by the practice of self-discipline and service for others. Hence the limitation of his spiritual freedom in the development of Christian character and in the life of active well doing. "Although, as I have said, man is inwardly, according to the spirit, amply justified by faith, having everything that he ought to have except that it behoves him to increase this self-same faith and riches from day to day until the life to come, nevertheless he remains in this mortal life on earth in which it is necessary to rule his own body and have converse with other men. Here, then, works begin. Here he must not take his ease. Here he must assuredly take care to exercise the body with fastings, watchings, labours, and other regulated disciplines, and subdue it to the spirit that it may become obedient and conform to the inward man and to faith; and that it may not rebel and become a hindrance, as its disposition is, if it is not restrained. For the inward man, being made conform to God and created in the image of God, through faith rejoices and is made glad on account of Christ, in whom so many benefits are conferred on him. Whence he places only this object before him, that he may serve God with joy and without reward in free charity." [17]

He considers the subject from the point of the individual and from that of the individual in relation to others. Individual self-discipline is an essential of the Christian life. But here, too, the motive principle must be faith which creates the aspiration and lends the inspiration to do what is pleasing to God. Works of this kind are to be done solely in this spirit and with this object, not with a view to justification and not as merits to this end. Luther has in view, in particular, the monastic life and its ideal of work-righteousness, which he has completely outlived, though he is still a monk by profession. He evidently speaks from his own experience when he refers to those who, in their quest for self-righteousness, "injure their brain and extinguish nature, or at least render it useless" by their ascetic excesses. "This is an immense folly and ignorance of the Christian life and of faith, to wish to be justified and saved by works without faith." [18] Such works, he roundly declares, "are nothing but impious and damnable sins." [19] In this matter everything depends on the person, the inner disposition, as he had demonstrated at length in the Commentary on Romans. "Good works do not make a good man," and conversely, "evil works do not make an evil man." The person must be good or bad before the works can be either. From the religious point of view goodness or badness depends on the condition of the soul. "A work is good if done in faith, bad if done without faith." [20] It is the principle and the motive that matter. In the sphere of religion egoism is necessarily bad, however good it may outwardly seem, however devoted even to higher things. In self-discipline the principle, the motive of works must be to do all freely and solely with the object of pleasing God. This granted, good works are an essential of the individual Christian life. "We do not, therefore, reject good works. Nay, we embrace them and teach them

[17] "Werke," vii. 59-60.

[18] *Ibid.*, vii. 60.

[19] Impia et damnabilia peccata.

[20] *Ibid.*, vii. 62. Bonum si in fide, malum si in infidelitate.

in the highest degree. Not on their own account do we condemn them, but on account of the impious addition and perverse seeking of justification by them." [21] "Therefore, although it is good to preach and write concerning penitence, confession, and satisfaction, nevertheless if we stop there and do not go on to teach faith, such teaching is without doubt deceptive and devilish." [22]

In discussing the subject from the point of view of the relation of the individual to others, he gives expression to a splendid Christian altruism. It would, indeed, be difficult to find a finer expression of it. Faith works by love and of this love service for the common benefit is an instinctive, inherent element, though here again he warns against the tendency to do this service in a wrong spirit and for a wrong object. "Lastly we shall speak of those works which we are to exercise towards our neighbour. For man lives not for himself alone in the works which he does in this mortal life, but for all men on earth, yea he lives only for others and not for himself. For to this end he subjects his body in order that he may be able the more freely and wholeheartedly to serve others, as Paul says in Romans xiv.: 'For none of us liveth to himself and none dieth to himself For whether we live, we live unto the Lord, or whether we die, we die unto the Lord.' It is not possible, therefore, to take his ease in this life and abstain from works towards his neighbour. For, as has been said, he must perforce live and have converse with men, as Christ, made in the likeness of men and found in fashion as a man, lived among and had intercourse with men. . . . To this end the Christian must have a care for his own body and strive to maintain it in health and fitness in order to be able to minister to the help of those who are in need, so that the strong may serve the weak and we may be sons of God, caring and labouring the one for the other, mutually bearing each others' burdens and so fulfilling the law of Christ. Behold this is the truly Christian life—this is truly faith working by love—which with joy and love makes itself profitable in the freest service, serving freely and willingly, providing abundantly out of the fullness and riches of its faith." [23]

[21] "Werke," vii. 63. [22] *Ibid.*, vii. 63. [23] *Ibid.*, vii. 64.

He appeals to the altruistic ethic of Paul and to the example of Christ as the model of the Christian life. He would have every Christian live this example over again, freely and spontaneously taking His yoke upon him; limiting his liberty by the obligation of Christian duty, as citizen and individual, whatever his station or calling, for the sake of others. He would even submit to the usages and regulations of the mediæval Church in the spirit of Christian expediency, which he here again characteristically inculcates, provided his cardinal principle of faith is recognised. In this connection he warns against allowing liberty to degenerate into licence. "It is not from works, but from the belief in works that we are set free by the faith of Christ."[24] The Christian is to walk in the middle path between the extreme ceremonialists and the extreme anti-ceremonialists. At the same time, in using his liberty in this way, he must be careful not to give offence to a weak brother who is unable to dispense with use and wont, or apprehend the full liberty of faith.

This magnificent delineation of Christianity regarded as service for the common benefit differs strikingly from the egoistic, materialist form of it embodied in the degenerate, oppressive, corrupt system in which he had been reared and the reformation of which was inherent in his doctrine of justification by faith. Even the economic side of the life of faith is not lost sight of, though for Luther the religious aspect of it is the main one. He finds room to stress the obligation of assiduity, faithfulness in the common work of life for the common benefit. He gives us a new ideal of the ordinary life in the world in opposition to the mediæval, monastic view of separation from the world in the quest for individual salvation. The true sphere of the Christian is in the world, not apart from it. The economic bearing of this religious principle was to find its expression in the marked industrial activity of the lands which adopted and exemplified his teaching in this respect. If this was due also to the Calvinist doctrine of the sovereignty of God, it owed not a little to Luther's conception of the consecrated individual life, not in the cloister, but in the arena of the world.

24 "Werke," vii. 70.

CHAPTER IX

THE DIET OF WORMS

I. THE EMPEROR AND LUTHER

THE advent of the young Emperor-elect in Germany in the autumn of 1520 was an event of critical import for the Lutheran movement. On the 23rd October he was crowned King at Aachen and took the oath to maintain the faith, defend the Church, and render due subjection to the Pope and the Roman See.[1] Three days later he was empowered by papal Bull to assume the title of " elected Roman Emperor " pending his coronation as Emperor by the Pope himself.[2] The young King-Emperor thus bound himself to maintain the *status quo* in religion in Germany. He had already, in fact, given proof of his orthodox zeal by issuing an edict ordering Luther's books to be burned in his hereditary dominions of Burgundy and the Netherlands.[3] The papal Nuncio, Aleander, at whose instigation the edict was published, assured the Pope that Charles was a staunch supporter of the Church,[4] whilst Erasmus augured the worst for Luther and his cause from this preliminary act of repression. The imperial court, he wrote, was full of mendicant monks and the hope that he would favour a Reformation in the Lutheran sense was vain.[5]

Charles was, indeed, favourable to a practical reformation, such as Ximenes had effected in the Spanish Church under

[1] " Reichstagsakten," ii. 96.

[2] *Ibid.*, ii. 101.

[3] *Ibid.*, ii. 455-456.

[4] *Ibid.*, ii. 461, Constantissime a nobis stat; Kalkoff, " Depeschen des Aleander," 33 (1897). Kalkoff has translated the dispatches of Aleander to the papal Vice-Chancellor, and these dispatches are of the highest importance for the history of the Diet of Worms. The originals are given by Brieger, " Aleander und Luther," 1521 (1884).

[5] Enders, ii. 491; *cf.* iii. 90.

the auspices of his grandparents, Ferdinand and Isabella, and his former Dutch tutor, Cardinal Hadrian, advocated in the Church at large. He had, too, inherited from Ferdinand and Isabella the policy of curbing the papal power in the interest of that of the Spanish crown But he was very devout and staunchly orthodox, whilst not too strict in his morals, and was not disposed to countenance any deviation from the traditional faith. He might welcome the reform of the abuses in the German Church and was not disposed to defend the Papacy and the hierarchy as far as they were responsible for them. His confessor, Glapion, even credits him with a certain sympathy with the Lutheran movement, previous to the appearance of the "Babylonic Captivity."[6] If so, it certainly did not extend to his doctrinal teaching.[7] That an individual monk should challenge the sacramental system of the Church could only appear in his eyes an act of apostasy, all the more reprehensible inasmuch as rebellion in the Church was, he was led to believe, fitted to lead to rebellion in the State. This construction was sedulously emphasised by Aleander and his fellow-Nuncio Caraccioli, and his apprehension on this score was intensified by the revolt of his Spanish subjects against the autocratic government inaugurated by Ferdinand and Isabella, which had broken out in the rising of the Communeros after his departure from Spain in May 1520[8] to assume the imperial crown. Moreover, the unity of the Church seemed to him an indispensable adjunct of the unity of the State, especially as he was not only the head of an empire which was merely a loose federation, but the ruler of vast dominions both widely scattered and devoid of any real political cohesion. He not only wielded the imperial sceptre. He was King of Spain, Sicily, and Naples,

[6] "Reichstagsakten," ii. 479. Dan seine kei. Mt. hette vorhin eher die Babylonica ausgangen seins schreibeus etzlicher mass auchgefallen gehabt.

[7] The assertion occurs in a discussion of the confessor, who was an expert in diplomacy as well as a reformer on Erasmian lines, with the Saxon Chancellor, Brück, at the Diet of Worms, and was actuated by diplomatic motives. See Kalkoff, "Der Wormser Reichstag," 243 f. (1922).

[8] See MacKinnon, "History of Modern Liberty," ii. 217 f.

Duke of Burgundy, Lord of the Netherlands, and the vast Spanish dominions in the new world. To the ruler of this widespread and heterogeneous inheritance the maintenance of ecclesiastical unity might well seem, from the political point of view alone, an axiom of statesmanship. Apart from his undoubted interest in practical reform, he was, moreover, ill fitted to respond even to the national element in the German reform movement. He was a Netherlander by birth and could not even speak the German language.[9] At Aachen he responded in Latin, not in German, to the questions put to him on the occasion of his coronation.[10] The political centre of gravity lay for him in Spain rather than in Germany, and the widespread national antagonism to Rome could hardly appeal to one who, though his German descent had contributed to his election, was practically a foreigner and had more of a political than a national interest in his imperial office.

On the other hand, there were considerations of a political nature which made it necessary to walk warily in dealing with the religious question in Germany. The tide of public opinion was setting strongly in favour of Luther. Aleander was the object of widespread hostility, which found expression in satiric effusions at his expense, and was fain to confess that some of the princes, most of the nobility and people, and even a large section of the clergy were hostile to Rome.[11] He might urge the Emperor to repeat in Germany the edict against Luther and his books which he had promulgated in the Netherlands. But in the face of the widespread popular hostility Charles hesitated to adopt such an autocratic policy and was obliged to reckon with the will of the Estates, especially of the Elector of Saxony, in considering the measures to be taken to carry out the Bull against the arch-heretic of Wittenberg. He was, moreover, bound by his coronation oath to maintain

[9] Ranke, "Deutsche Geschichte im Zeitalter der Reformation," i. 470.

[10] "Reichstagsakten," ii. 96. Sed tantum majestas sua Latine et loquitur et intelligit.

[11] *Ibid.*, ii. 460-461. Kalkoff, "Die Depeschen des Aleander," 26-28; *cf.* 44.

the old concordats, which permitted an appeal to a General Council, and not to place any of his subjects under the imperial ban unheard.[12] He and his advisers declined, therefore, to issue at Aachen a mandate against Luther without consultation with the Estates.[13] As the result of a conference at Cologne on the 1st November 1520 with the Elector,[14] who, with the support of Erasmus, proposed anew that Luther's case should be referred to the judgment of a competent and impartial commission, Charles gave the answer that "the monk would be dealt with in accordance with the laws of the empire and should not be condemned unheard." [15] Ultimately, on the 27th November, he invited him [16] to bring the monk with him for this purpose to the Diet which he had summoned to meet at Worms on the 6th January 1521. He only stipulated that meanwhile Luther should refrain from writing or printing anything against the Pope and the Holy See.[17]

Aleander and his fellow-Nuncio Caraccioli, on the other hand, in an interview with the Elector at Cologne on the 4th November, urged him to execute the Bull and forthwith arrest and surrender Luther to the Pope. The wary diplomatist evaded a direct reply and on the 6th professed once more, through his councillors, his innocence of complicity in his professor's doings, adduced the fact that his case was still under reference to the Archbishop of Trier as a sufficient reason for delaying the execution of the Bull, and parried the demand for his surrender with the counter-demand for an impartial hearing in Germany. Aleander retorted that the commission to the archbishop had lapsed with the transference of the case to Rome and that the judgment of the Pope, formally given in the Bull, was decisive

12 "Reichstagsakten," i. 871, 873.

13 "Depeschen," 33; Kalkoff, "Entscheidungsjahre," 187 f.

14 Owing to illness the Elector was not present at the coronation at Aachen.

15 Kalkoff, "Entscheidungsjahre," 192, and "Erasmus, Luther und Friedrich der Weise," 86 f. (1919).

16 The letter was written from Oppenheim whilst the Emperor was on his way to Worms. Another to the same effect came from his ministers, Chièvres and Count Henry of Nassau. Walch, xv. 2018-2022.

17 "Reichstagsakten," ii. 466-468.

and admitted of no further evasion.[18] Whilst this reasoning might appear conclusive from the point of view of canon law, which recognised the Pope as the supreme judge in matters of faith, it was not so cogent from that of the law of the empire which recognised the right of appeal to a General Council. Aleander, nevertheless, persisted in acting on the old adage, *Roma locuta causa finita,* and this assumption he strove to impress on the imperial ministers, Chièvres and Gattinara.[19] He so far succeeded that on the 17th December, as the result of his arguments at a sitting of the Imperial Council on the 14th, the Emperor revoked the invitation to the Elector to bring Luther to Worms. The reason adduced for this change of attitude was that, as Luther had not recanted within the period prescribed by the Bull, he was now under the imperial ban. Only if he submitted to the Pope should the Elector bring him, not to Worms, but to Frankfurt, or other place, there to await further instructions. Should, however, he refuse submission, he was to remain at Wittenberg pending personal consultation with the Elector in the matter.[20] The fact that the Pope had definitely agreed to take the side of the Emperor in the impending conflict with his rival, Francis I., materially contributed to this change of attitude on the Lutheran question.[21] The Emperor even went the length of entrusting Aleander with the task of drafting a mandate or edict in execution of the Bull against Luther, as the subverter of political and social order as well as the papal power, in virtue of the imperial authority and without reference to the will of the Diet.[22]

Meanwhile the Elector had himself decided to abandon his intention of bringing Luther to Worms and, in justification of his decision, had adduced the burning of Luther's books at Cologne, Maintz, and elsewhere. Such violence was, he protested, incompatible with the understanding that he should receive a hearing by impartial judges, before whom

[18] "Reichstagsakten," ii. 462-466.
[19] "Depeschen," 33 f.; *cf.* 51.
[20] "Reichstagsakten," ii. 468-470.
[21] Kalkoff, "Entscheidungsjahre," 202.
[22] *Ibid.*, 202 f.

he had publicly offered to appear if granted a safe conduct, and to whose decision he was prepared to submit, if he should be proved from Scripture to have erred.[23] He repeated the demand for an impartial hearing in an audience with the Emperor after his arrival at Worms on the 5th January 1521, and once more succeeded in extracting the promise that his protégé should not be condemned unheard. This promise he communicated to Luther, with the request that he should forward for presentation to the Emperor a copy of his *Erbieten*, or offer to appear before an impartial tribunal subject to the grant of a safe conduct. With this request Luther gladly complied on the 25th January 1521 and assured the Elector of his readiness to come to Worms in accordance with the terms of this document.[24] His confidence in the imperial goodwill proved, however, too sanguine. Aleander was doing his utmost to frustrate the Elector's policy and secure the issue of a summary edict against the arch-heretic in spite of the opposition of his supporters in the Diet,[25] which began its actual session on the 27th January.[26] "The Emperor," he wrote on the 8th February, "holds firmly to the good cause."[27] Two days before (6th February) Charles gave a signal demonstration of his real attitude towards the heretic when Stein, the court marshal of Duke John of Saxony, handed him Luther's *Erbieten* with the request that he would see justice done to the petitioner. In the presence of his courtiers he tore the document in pieces and threw it on the floor—"a clear indication to the whole Diet," adds Aleander, "of what the Emperor thinks of Luther."[28]

The Elector and his supporters were, however, not overawed by this exhibition of the imperial animus against

[23] "Reichstagsakten," ii. 470-475. The Elector's letters to the Emperor, 20th and 28th Dec. The Elector refers to Luther's Oblatio or Erbieten of 30th Aug.

[24] *Ibid.*, ii. 476-477; Luther's "Werke," 53, 56, No. 24 (Erlangen edition); Kalkoff, "Entscheidungsjahre," 208-209.

[25] "Depeschen," 72-73.

[26] "Reichstagsakten," ii. 157-159.

[27] "Depeschen," 78; Brieger, 55, el qual pero sempre e constante al bene.

[28] "Depeschen," 78-79; Brieger, 55.

the arch-rebel of Wittenberg. They persisted in their determination that he should have a hearing before the Reichstag under the imperial safe conduct. Hence the long duel between Aleander on the one hand, and the Elector and his supporters on the other, over this crucial issue which lasted till the beginning of March. Though the Nuncio could rely on the personal goodwill of the Emperor in his demand for the summary execution of the Bull in virtue of his imperial authority, the imperial ministers were very dubious about the feasibility of such an autocratic policy in the face of the active sympathy of the nation for Luther and its embittered feeling against Rome. Even Aleander was fain to admit in his reports that Luther was the leader, not of a mere sect, but of the nation in his attack on the Roman régime. "The whole of Germany," wrote he on the 8th February, "is in open revolt. Nine-tenths of it shouts for Luther and the other tenth, if it cares not for the Reformer, cries 'Death to the Roman Curia.' All are united in the demand for a Council to be held in Germany." [29] The only expedient he can think of for countering the danger is to send him money to bribe influential officials, though even with the aid of this expedient it is difficult to effect anything. If the Curia hesitates longer, it is to be feared that the Lutherans will obtain the upper hand and the Imperial Council will not have the courage to launch the desired edict against them. The Germans have lost all respect for and openly ridicule papal excommunications. The clergy will not, or dare not, preach against Luther. It rains Lutheran books daily, German or Latin, and in Worms itself the printing press and the booksellers are busy diffusing this pro-Lutheran literature. Without money he is at his wits' end to deal with this menacing situation.[30] Erasmus has thrown the weight of his influence on Luther's side, and the word of Erasmus, who has written worse things against the faith than even Luther, excites far more confidence than his own. To the reader the fact is not surprising, for, on his own naïve confession, he was driven on occasion to have recourse to downright lying in the interest of the

[29] "Depeschen," 69-70; Brieger, 48.
[30] "Depeschen," 70-73; Brieger, 49 f.

faith and his mission.[31] When he appears in the streets people lay their hands on their swords, gnash their teeth, and hurl threats and oaths at him. His life is not safe and he is in constant apprehension of being murdered.[32] If the good Emperor should show the slightest tendency to give way, the whole of Germany would be lost to the Roman See.[33]

Aleander's plea for a summary edict against Luther was strengthened by the Bull of Excommunication which the Pope, on the 3rd January, had launched against him and his adherents as obstinate heretics.[34] The Bull reached the Nuncio on the 10th February along with a papal missive to the Emperor enjoining its immediate execution. In response Charles, whose ministers still emphasised the necessity of securing the co-operation of the Diet in carrying out the papal demand, requested him to address the Estates on the subject on the 13th. In an oration which took three hours to deliver,[35] Aleander accordingly sought to impress his audience with the gravity of the Lutheran movement on political as well as ecclesiastical grounds. He adroitly reminded the Estates that the Hussite movement had led to the subversion of the existing political and social order in Bohemia A like fate must befall Germany as the result of Luther's teaching. He enlarged from the papal point of view on the efforts made to reclaim the heretic, who had not only persisted in his heresy, but had aggravated it by attacking the sacraments and the ritual of the Church and by preaching his doctrine of universal priesthood, as he showed by reading extracts from his recent works on the "Babylonic Captivity of the Church" and on "Christian Liberty," and from his "Assertio." He had even dared openly to espouse the opinions of Wiclif and Hus and to asperse the Council of Constance as heretical for condemning them. He further quoted from the Bull of the Council of Florence in 1439, which he professed to have discovered in the archives at Worms, to disprove his

[31] "Depeschen," 75-76; *cf.* 84, 108.
[32] *Ibid.*, 90-91.
[33] *Ibid.*, 81.
[34] The Bull Decet Romanum, German translation in Walch, xv. 2030 f.
[35] "Depeschen," 85. In a letter to Eck he says two hours,

assertion that the Greeks had never recognised the papal headship of the whole Church. He repelled his assumption that the Bull, "Exsurge Domine," was a fabrication of his enemies and his assertion that his books had been burned without the Emperor's knowledge and will in his defence of the burning of the Bull. Luther, in short, was a dangerous anarchist, a subverter of Church and State, a perverter of Scripture, though like the devil he could quote Scripture for his own pernicious purposes. How falsely, therefore, his defenders aver that he teaches only the evangelical truth, and claim that he is a pious man of unblemished life. His life may outwardly be correct. But heretics have always been hypocrites. Inwardly they are ravening wolves, and if Luther were a pious Christian, he would not presume to know better than the Holy Fathers and Mother Church of Christendom. As to the plea that he should be heard before being condemned, if only because of the danger of a popular insurrection in his behalf, what could be the use of hearing one who has spurned the Pope and the authority of Councils and has declared that he will not change his opinion even if an angel from heaven should teach otherwise. Moreover, in matters of faith it belongs to the Pope alone to judge. From him the Emperor and the princes derived their imperial rights, since the empire was conferred on Charlemagne and his successors by the Pope, and to refuse to recognise the papal power would be to forfeit these rights. It behoved the Emperor and the Estates, therefore, to take measures for the suppression of his pestilential heresy and forthwith to issue an edict directing the burning of his books and forbidding the printing and sale of them in future.[36]

The speech was a skilful *ex parte* appeal on behalf of the

[36] "Reichstagsakten," ii. 495 f. A summary of the speech made by the Saxon Chancellor Brück from notes taken by the Elector's secretaries. *Cf.* Aleander's shorter account of his speech, "Depeschen," 85-87; Brieger, 61-62. The speech was largely a recapitulation of an instruction drawn up, at the end of Dec. 1520, by Aleander, which was to form the subject of an imperial communication to the Elector of Saxony with the object of detaching him from Luther and preventing him from bringing Luther's case before the Diet. See Kalkoff, "Der Wormser Reichstag," 217 f,

existing system in Church and State against the daring religious innovator, with intent to excite the self-interest as well as the religious passion of the audience. The orator studiously ignored the abuses of the papal régime and represented the reform movement as an attack on constituted authority by an opinionated and dangerous anarchist. It seems to have made an impression on the assembled Estates, though Aleander noted in the course of its delivery the scowls on the faces of the Lutheran members,[37] and was erelong to discover that the Diet was not disposed to gloss over its grievances on the score of the papal misgovernment of the Church. Its effect on the Emperor and his ministers is observable in the resolution to submit the draft of an edict against Luther, on which a commission had been at work for some weeks, to the Diet on the 15th February. Though the Nuncio opposed its reference to the Estates and urged its immediate issue in virtue of the imperial authority alone,[38] he had no reason to quarrel with the draft itself, which was in fact largely his own composition.[39] It decreed the burning of Luther's books and his arrest and imprisonment pending further proceedings against him, and declared his adherents and abettors of whatever condition guilty of high treason if they should persist in their disobedience.[40] As Aleander had feared, it met with the bitter opposition of the Lutheran members.[41] In the chamber of the Electors the deliberation gave rise to a violent altercation between Joachim of Brandenburg, the leader of the anti-Lutherans, and the Elector of Saxony, in the course of which both grasped their sword hilt and would have come to blows had not the others thrown themselves between them.[42] The Elector of

37 "Depeschen," 87; *cf.* 117.

38 *Ibid.*, 91-92.

39 *Ibid.*, 72.

40 "Reichstagsakten," ii. 509-513.

41 On the attitude of the members of the various Estates towards the Lutheran movement see Kalkoff, "Der Wormser Reichstag," 277 f.

42 "Depeschen," 93. According to Aleander, the Archbishop of Salzburg was one of those who thus intervened. The archbishop, however, could not have taken part in the sitting of the Electors. Lehmann thinks that the incident is not historic, "Historische Aufsätze und Reden," 22 (1911). Kalkoff adduces strong reasons in favour of its historicity. "Z.K.G.," xliii. 194-195.

the Palatinate, usually so taciturn, "bellowed like a steer"[43] in support of his Saxon colleague. Ultimately, on the 19th, the Estates, whilst acknowledging the Christian zeal of the Emperor, adduced in a common statement the grave danger of a popular outbreak if Luther were condemned unheard. They accordingly proposed that he should be examined, under a safe conduct, by a commission on the question of the authorship of the books ascribed to him, though he should not be allowed to dispute on their contents. If he agreed to recant his errors against the faith, he should then be heard on the other points bearing on the reform of the Church. If not, they were prepared to abet his majesty in vindicating the faith of their fathers. At the same time, they pointedly reminded the Emperor of the ecclesiastical abuses and grievances from which the empire was suffering in consequence of the misgovernment of the Church and urged their effective reformation.[44] Aleander had thus not succeeded in his attempt either to prevent the reference of the edict to the Estates, or to blink the urgent question of a reformation, which, though it did not extend to Luther's characteristic theological doctrines, evidently did include his views on the papal power and its abuse.[45]

In response the Emperor on the 2nd March announced his readiness to summon Luther under safe conduct for examination on the authorship of his books, but without the right of disputation thereon, and submitted for the opinion of the Estates a fresh draft of an edict. At the same time, he requested them to draw up a statement of grievances against the papal régime and promised to consider any representation they might make on the subject.[46] This second draft, whilst granting Luther a hearing on the conditions thus intimated by the Emperor, ignored the demand of the Estates that he should be allowed, in case of retraction, to discuss the reform of abuses, denounced his heretical enormities in very severe language, and

[43] "Depeschen," 97. Ludwig V. does not, however, seem to have been a Lutheran by conviction. Kalkoff, "Wormser Reichstag," 13, 277.

[44] "Reichstagsakten," ii. 515-517.

[45] Kalkoff, "Wormser Reichstag," 308-309.

[46] "Reichstagsakten," 519-520.

directed that his books should meanwhile be destroyed.[47] It accordingly provoked once more lengthy and heated debate and failed to secure the approbation of the Estates (5th March). On the following day, Charles and his ministers were fain, for political reasons, to waive any further attempt to reach an agreement on the draft and to put an end to the deadlock by citing Luther to Worms in accordance with the demand of the Estates.[48] The citation, in striking contrast to the proposed edict, was courteously worded. In agreement with the Estates the Emperor summoned him to appear for the purpose of being examined on his teaching and writings. To this end he is granted a safe conduct for the journey to Worms and back and assured of the imperial protection, and is required to appear within twenty-one days after receiving the citation.[49] On the 11th March the Elector, after some hesitation, added his own safe conduct.[50]

To Aleander the imperial decision seemed a dangerous truckling to a condemned heretic, against whom it was the duty of the Emperor and the Estates to execute forthwith the papal sentence. He was greatly perturbed at the prospect of Luther's appearance before the Diet. "If Luther comes, the worst is to be feared." [51] His fears were shared by the Elector of Brandenburg,[52] and in co-operation with him and other anti-Lutherans he strove to counter the danger by pressing the publication of the edict against his writings, even without the approbation of the Estates, in the hope that its publication would scare Luther from

[47] "Reichstagsakten," ii. 521-526.

[48] For the details of this protracted negotiation see Kalkoff, "Wormser Reichstag," 302 f.

[49] "Reichstagsakten," ii. 526-527.

[50] *Ibid.*, ii. 532. The delay in doing so was due to negotiations with the Emperor who had suggested that the Elector should himself cite Luther. This responsibility the Elector declined to take upon himself and insisted that the Emperor should do so ("Reichstagsakten," ii. 528). In virtue of the agreement with the Diet, the imperial safe conduct would have the guarantee of the Estates behind it, which a summons by an individual member would not have.

[51] "Depeschen," 99; *cf.* 118 f.

[52] *Ibid.*, 104.

obeying the citation. He eventually succeeded in securing its promulgation in a modified form at Worms on the 27th March in the name of the Emperor.[53] But the hope of thereby frightening Luther from facing the Diet was foiled by the indomitable resolution of the brave monk to dare the worst in behalf of his convictions.

II. Before the Summons

During these months of intrigue and debate at Worms, Luther had inflexibly continued the crusade against Antichrist and his abettors in Germany. He paid as little heed to the Bull of Excommunication as to the Bull of Condemnation, and was not disposed to take his orders even from the Emperor in this matter. Charles's request to the Elector in November 1520 to put a stop to his writing against the Pope[54] shows a singular ignorance of the character of the man who, by sheer strength of conviction, had raised a storm which was to shake the Papacy to its foundations and to eventuate in the disruption of the mediæval Church. He was undoubtedly the strong man and also the great man of the age. All the other actors on the stage of this world upheaval are mediocre figures compared with this Colossus whose genius and potent personality are laboriously shaping a new world out of the old. Though the Emperor wields a vast power, he is merely the embodiment of the old order in Church and State. He has neither insight into nor sympathy with the religious and moral forces which, concentrated in the personality of this monk, are bursting the old order like new wine in old wine skins. His ministers, Gattinara and Chièvres, are merely clever politicians, adepts in the art of diplomatic make-believe, by which, like their master, they imagine that they can counter the force of ideas as well as out-manœuvre

[53] "Depeschen," 140-142; "Reichstagsakten," ii. 529-538; the correspondence of Spalatin with the Elector, Waitz, Epistolæ Reformatorum, "Z.K.G.," ii. 120 f.; Kalkoff, "Wormser Reichstag," 311 f.; and "Die Entstehung des Wormser Edikts," 156 f. (1913).

[54] "Reichstagsakten," ii. 468.

their opponents in the diplomatic game. Pope Leo is a worldling whose main concern is the extension of his temporal dominion and the preservation of the corrupt ecclesiastical system of which he is the unworthy creation and figurehead. His representative Aleander is an able ecclesiastic of the conventional type, professionally devoted to the system which affords him position and livelihood and busily employed in bribing benefice hunters to co-operate in bringing the reformer to the stake. The Elector and his advisers are very astute diplomatists of the ordinary type who would have been little known to history except for the fact that they have some understanding of the issues, religious and national, involved in this theological conflict and creditably make use of their shrewdness and sense of justice to prevent Dr Martin from sharing the fate of Hus and Savonarola. Erasmus, who figures in Aleander's dispatches as a damnable patron of Luther and the treacherous mentor of the Elector, is the greatest scholar of the age and a reformer, even an aggressive one, up to a point. But Erasmus is lacking in intensity of religious conviction and in the moral courage that would have made him the compeer of the monk of Wittenberg in a fight to a finish against the power and corruption of Rome. As he himself said, "if it came to a crisis he would play the part of Simon Peter over again." Though Hutten had more of the fighting spirit, he was not fitted in character and religious conviction to be the lieutenant of the protagonist of justification by faith, whilst the enterprising Sickingen did not essentially rise above the level of the filibuster leader of his time. Luther, too, had his limitations if weighed in the balance of historic criticism. But in no one else in this age were the qualities of the maker of history in the religious and moral sphere so combined as in this prophet of a faith which, while positing complete self-effacement, vitalises at the same time the force of a powerful intellect, an inflexible will, a compelling devotion to the truth as he apprehends it. The most convincing proof of this is the fact that, as the supreme crisis of his fate approaches, he shows himself equal to it.

The attacks of his opponents during the winter months

of 1521 only steeled his polemic temper and led him to formulate his antagonism to the Pope even more aggressively, as well as to give full play to his rough humour and mordant sarcasm at their expense. Whilst the mutual recrimination of this press warfare is not edifying to the modern reader, the resourcefulness and the reckless courage of the writer, with his back to the wall against a world of enemies, are truly astounding. In addition to Emser new assailants appeared in the Strassburg monk Murner, the Italian Dominican Ambrose Catharinus,[55] Marlianus,[56] Bishop of Tuy, Latomus of Louvain,[57] and others. After a skirmish in a couple of pamphlets with Emser,[58] whom he regarded as the virulent mouthpiece of Duke George of Saxony and who had ventured to controvert his "Address to the Nobility," [59] "the Leipzig Bock," as he dubbed him, received due castigation in his most satiric style in a philippic [60] in which he also dealt faithfully with the short-comings of Murner. Against Catharinus he demonstrated at length from Scripture in his own exegetical fashion that the Pope was the Antichrist of Daniel.[61] To the people he addressed an "Instruction," in which he denied the right of the priests to refuse their penitents absolution unless they surrendered his books. He advised the people to do without absolution thus arbitrarily refused, and even to abstain from the Sacrament of the Altar rather than act against their conscience and the Word of God, which the Pope had condemned in the Bull. The Word is indispensable to

[55] On this controversialist see Lauchert, "Die Italienischen Literarischen Gegner Luther's," 30 f. (1912).

[56] See Kalkoff, "Wormser Reichstag," 152 f.

[57] Enders, iii. 98; "Depeschen," 38-39.

[58] An den Bock zu Leipzig, Jan. 1521, "Werke," vii. 262 f.; and Auf den Bock zu Leipzig Antwort, *ibid.*, vii. 271 f., in answer to Emser's An den Stier zu Wittenberg, given by Enders, "Luther und Emser," ii. 3 f.

[59] Enders, iii. 84, 87, and "Luther und Emser," i. 3 f.

[60] Auf das Buch Bock's Emser's in Leipzig Antwort, "Werke," vii. 621 f., and Enders, "Luther und Emser," ii. 47 f.

[61] Ad Librum Eximii Magistri Amb. Catharini Responsio, "Werke," vii. 705 f., and "Opera Latina Var.," v. 289 f. It was finished by the end of March, but not published till June.

salvation. Absolution, sacraments, priest, and Church are not, and Christ Himself, the true bishop, could spiritually feed them without the sacrament.[62] For the popular edification he also translated and amplified his "Assertio" of the articles condemned in the papal Bull and sent it forth from the press in the beginning of March.[63] He reiterated and vindicated the views on the sacraments, the priestly office, the ritual of the Church, which Aleander had summarised from the "Babylonic Captivity" and the "Assertio" and had denounced as heretical in his speech to the Estates in the middle of February.[64]

To the strain of this incessant polemic was added the burden of his daily official duty of lecturing and preaching and the preparation for the press of his revised course on the Psalms, an exposition of selected portions of the Gospels and Epistles,[65] and of the Magnificat in German.[66] "I am oppressed by many troubles; my life is a cross to me," he complains in a letter to Pellican at the end of February, in which he recounts the harassing and wearing experience of these months.[67] The nervous strain accounts in part for the violence of his polemic, though there is no sign of lack of intellectual vigour as the result of bodily exhaustion and mental perturbation. His mind is, in fact, incredibly fecund under the probing of his many assailants, "the gnats," as he contemptuously calls them.[68] It is in a continuous turmoil which, he confesses, he is powerless to control. "You rightly admonish me to

[62] Ein Unterricht der Beichtkinder über die Verpotten Bücher, Feb. 1521. "Werke," vii. 290 f.; Enders, iii. 81, 87.

[63] Grund und Ursach aller Artikel D. Mart. Luther's so durch Römische Bulle unrechtlich verdammt sind. "Werke," vii. 308 f.; Enders, iii. 98.

[64] Responsio Extemporaria ad Articulos quos Magistri nostri ex Babylonica et Assertionibus ejus excerpserunt. "Werke," vii. 608 f.; Enders, iii. 113, March 1521.

[65] Enarrationes epistolarum et evangeliorum quas postillas vocant. "Werke," vii. 463 f., March 1521.

[66] "Werke," vii. 544 f. Though it was being printed in March, it was not completed and did not appear till the end of August or the beginning of September.

[67] Enders, iii. 93.

[68] *Ibid.*, iii. 98.

observe moderation," he writes to Pellican. "I myself feel the need of it. But I am not master of myself (*sed compos mei non sum*). I am gripped by I know not what spirit, though I am conscious of wishing ill to no one. But these men urge me on most furiously, so that I am not sufficiently on my guard against Satan. Pray the Lord for me that I may think and speak and write what becomes both Him and me, though not them." [69]

At the same time, he is absolutely convinced that he is on the right path and will not move an inch from what he deems the truth, whatever befall. When Spalatin communicates to him in December 1520 the Emperor's suggestion that the Elector should bring him to Worms for a hearing, he replies that, well or sick, he will comply and dare the consequences for the sake of the Gospel. The Lord lives and reigns who preserved the three youths in the furnace of the king of Babylon. Even if he perish, what is that to the fate of Christ Himself who died for the Gospel? Spalatin may rest assured that he will do all that is required of him except consult his own safety and deny the Gospel.[70] He reminds the weakly Staupitz, who had shrunk before the storm and submitted at Salzburg, that he has not forgotten his encouraging assurance that he had begun this enterprise in the name of Christ. The hand of God, not of man, is still patently in it, and to this faith he will cling in spite of the raging tumult and the floods with which he is battling and which are sweeping him along.[71] He grieves over Staupitz's weakly surrender to Antichrist who, in condemning him, has condemned Christ This is surely not the time, when Christ is suffering anew, for fearing, for hesitating between the Pope and Christ, for giving way, but for speaking out. Staupitz has exhorted him to humility and warned him against arrogance. But if he has shown too much arrogance, Staupitz has shown too much humility. "If Christ gave Himself for us, shall we not fight and give our life for Him? More is at stake in this issue than many believe. The Gospel itself is involved. 'Whosoever shall confess me before men, him will I confess

[69] Enders, iii. 93. [70] *Ibid.*, iii. 24-25. [71] *Ibid.*, iii. 70-71.

before my Father.' They may accuse me of every sort of vice—arrogance, self-seeking, adultery, murder, anti-popery. But may I never be convicted of an impious silence when the Lord Himself is being crucified afresh. The Word of Christ is not the word of peace, but the word of the sword. . . . If you will not follow me, permit me at least to go on and to be carried away. By the grace of Christ I will not keep silent about the monstrous evils of this monster Antichrist." Nor is he without powerful supporters. Hutten and many others, he adds, are mightily advocating his cause, and poems daily appear which are anything but delectable to that Babylon. The Elector is exerting himself prudently and firmly in his behalf, whilst he himself is keeping three printing presses busy against Antichrist.[72] The people are on his side, as the opposition to the burning of his books at Maintz has shown.[73]

Hutten has, in fact, proposed to oppose force with force and to decide the issue by an appeal to arms.[74] Luther decisively rejects the proposal of an armed revolution on behalf of the Gospel, though he had in a couple of passages in his notes on Prierias's "Epitoma" and in his "Address to the Nobility" seemed to incite to a violent overthrow of Antichrist.[75] "You see what Hutten wants," he wrote in forwarding his letter to Spalatin on the 16th January 1521. "I do not wish to contend for the Gospel with force and slaughter, and I have written to tell him so. By the Word the world was conquered and the Church has been preserved, and by it the Church will be reformed. For as Antichrist established himself without arms, so will he be overthrown by the Word without armed force."[76] A war against the clergy would only be a war against women and children.[77]

[72] Enders, iii. 83-85, 9th Feb. 1521.

[73] *Ibid.*, iii. 71.

[74] *Ibid.*, iii. 15-16. Hutten's letter to Luther, 9th Dec. 1520.

[75] In his reply to Emser he explains that he did not mean this passage to be taken literally. He does not believe in the use of force in matters of religion. But if the Pope will insist on burning heretics, he thereby gives the right to use force against him in self-defence, though personally he is opposed to such violent methods. "Werke," vii. 645-646.

[76] Enders, iii. 73.

[77] *Ibid.*, iii. 90.

In defence of the Word as the supreme rule of faith he was, however, determined to defy the Emperor as well as the Pope. He had learned with regret in the middle of January of the imperial decision to resile from the invitation to Worms.[78] Two months elapsed before he heard that he was to be asked to recant the articles which Aleander had culled from the " Babylonic Captivity " and the " Assertio," and which Spalatin sent him. The Emperor, he replied, might save himself the trouble of summoning him to Worms for such a purpose. " You need be in no doubt that I will revoke nothing, since I see that they adduce no other argument than that I have written against the rites and usages of the Church such as they imagine it. I will, therefore, assure the Emperor, if summoned only for the purpose of recanting, that, if it were only a question of recanting, I could do this here at Wittenberg equally well. But if he means to summon me for the purpose of killing me and shall hold me for an enemy of the empire as the result of my answers to his questions, I shall offer to come. With the help of Christ I will not flee, nor will I prove unfaithful to the Word in the battle. Certain I am that these bloody men will not rest till they have sent me to the stake and I should wish that if possible only the papists were guilty of my blood. . . . The will of the Lord be done. Meanwhile persuade whoever you can not to take part in this wicked Council of the Malignants." [79] " At Worms," he wrote to an unknown correspondent on the 24th March, " they are exerting themselves to get me to recant a large number of articles, but my revocation will be as follows : Formerly I have said that the Pope is the Vicar of Christ. This I now revoke and say, the Pope is the enemy of Christ and the apostle of the devil." [80]

Two days later, the 26th March, the herald arrived at Wittenberg with the imperial citation and safe conduct.

[78] Enders, iii. 73.
[79] *Ibid.*, iii. 113. Letter to Spalatin, 19th March.
[80] *Ibid.*, iii. 117.

III. LUTHER AND THE DIET

The citation made mention only of an investigation, not of a revocation, and on the 2nd April, Luther accordingly set out on his momentous journey to Worms. He was accompanied by his colleague Amsdorf, his fellow-monk Petzensteiner, and a student Swaven, besides the friendly herald Sturm. At Leipzig his arrival excited little interest, though the Town Council sent him a present of wine.[81]

The interest increased as he proceeded and in the Thuringian towns the people came out to meet his waggon and see the daring heretic "who had thrown down the gauntlet to the Emperor and all the world." "Some," relates Myconius, "comforted him very badly by saying that at Worms, where so many cardinals and bishops were assembled, he would be burned to ashes as Hus had been at Constance." "If," retorted Luther, "they make a fire that would fill the sky between Wittenberg and Worms, he would go on in the name of the Lord, since they had summoned him, and would walk into the jaws of Behemoth and confess Christ between his teeth."[82] At Weimar or Erfurt he read the imperial edict against his books, which had practically condemned him beforehand. He turned pale for a moment, and the herald asked him whether he would proceed farther—"I will enter Worms if all the devils were in it," was the reply.[83] He at once divined that the object of this decree was to scare him from continuing his journey, and wrote to Spalatin from Frankfurt that he would enter Worms in spite of the powers of hell and the principalities of the air.[84] At Weimar, Gotha, and Erfurt he preached to large congregations. So great was the throng at Erfurt that the gallery of the church began to crack and a panic was only prevented by the self-possession of the preacher, who called out to the people to keep quiet.

[81] Warbeck to Duke John of Saxony, "Reichstagsakten," ii. 851.
[82] "Geschichte der Reformation," 34, ed. Clemen.
[83] "Tischreden," iii. 284-285.
[84] Enders, iii. 121.

The devil was only trying to create a false alarm.[85] At Weimar he was joined by Justus Jonas, canon at Erfurt and his future colleague at Wittenberg, and outside his old university city he was welcomed by a goodly array of sympathisers, on the 6th April, at the head of which rode his old friends Crotus Rubianus, now Rector of the University, and Eobanus Hessus, and feasted in honour of the Word of God. The evangelical sermon which he preached on the following day is extant in the notes of a hearer[86] and consists of an aggressive exposition of the doctrine of justification by faith, not by works, as the scholastic doctors and the preachers erroneously proclaim, and thereby pervert the Gospel. "I will and must proclaim the truth. For this purpose I stand here." The truth consists in the acceptance of the Gospel in confiding faith in Christ the Saviour, not in the work-righteousness prescribed by the Church and proclaimed in the fables of the perverse and ignorant preachers of human superstition and penitential performances. The sermon is a battle cry against the conventional religion and clearly portends what may be expected of him at Worms. At Eisenach he had a sudden attack of illness, evidently the result of the fatigue and excitement of the Erfurt reception. The attack passed off after some blood-letting and a sound sleep, induced by drinking some strong wine with which the Justice of the Peace, John Oswald, presented him.[87] But it left him very languid and the languor continued all the way to Frankfurt, which he reached on the 14th April.[88]

At Offenheim, Bucer brought him an invitation to seek a refuge in the Ebernburg. On the publication of the edict against his books Hutten had indited a series of violent letters to the Emperor, the papal Nuncios, the Archbishop of Maintz, and the bishops.[89] Scared by the threat of a religious war, with Hutten as its prophet and Sickingen as its leader, the imperial ministers sought to silence the

[85] Report of an eyewitness, Greser, quoted in "Werke," vii. 803.
[86] "Werke," vii. 808 f.
[87] Myconius, "Geschichte," 34.
[88] Enders, iii. 120-121.
[89] "Opera," ii. 12 f.; "Depeschen," 146 f.; Brieger, 122-123.

dangerous firebrand by sending the imperial chamberlain, Armsdorf, and the confessor Glapion, to offer him a pension of 400 gulden and suggest the invitation to Luther to confer with the confessor at the Ebernburg. Their object was to prevent Luther from continuing his journey to Worms. As the result of the interview with Glapion, Hutten accepted the imperial bounty, and both he and Sickingen, whilst insisting on a drastic practical reformation of the Church, whose wealth they coveted, allowed themselves to be persuaded, for the time being at least, that Luther had gone too far in his attack on its teaching.[90] Hence the invitation to Luther which would simply have meant that the prescribed period for his appearance at Worms would have lapsed and with it the imperial safe conduct. This was what the Nuncios and the imperial ministers were eager to achieve. But unlike the volatile and shifty Hutten, Luther was not to be thus easily entrapped. He declined to be wheedled by such a wild-goose project from his purpose of testifying to the truth before the Emperor and the Diet. He sent word to Glapion that, if he wished, he might speak with him at Worms.[91] He repeated in a letter to Spalatin from Offenheim his declaration to the herald that he would enter Worms even if there were as many devils in it as tiles on the roofs of the houses.[92] "And so I went on in mere simplicity of heart."[93]

On the morning of the 16th he entered Worms in the

[90] Such is the version of the interview given by Aleander, "Depeschen," 157-158, and it receives some confirmation from Hutten's letter to Spalatin, "Z.K.G.," ii. 126-127; "Reichstagsakten," ii. 538-540. See also Kalkoff, Ulrich von Hutten und die Reformation, "Quellen und Forschungen zur Reformationsgeschichte," iv. 287 f. and 358 f. (1920).

[91] "Tischreden," iii. 282, 285; v. 69; Walch, xv. 2172.

[92] The letter is not extant, but Spalatin records the saying in his "Annals," ed. by Cyprian, 38. In his "Table Talk" he says distinctly that he did use these words in the letter to Spalatin from Offenheim, "Tischreden," v. 65. See also Walch, xv. 2174. In a previous letter from Luther to Spalatin, written from Frankfurt, 14th April, he says that he will enter Worms in spite of the gates of hell and the powers of the air. Enders, iii. 121.

[93] "Tischreden," iii. 285. Ego vero ex mera simplicitate processi. There seems to be no ground for the assumption that it was at Offenheim that he wrote his famous hymn, "Ein feste Burg ist unser Gott." See the discussion of the question by Lucke, "Werke," xxxv. 203 f.

waggon in which he had travelled from Wittenberg, a blast of the trumpet of the watchman from the cathedral tower signalling his arrival. In front of the waggon rode the herald, behind Justus Jonas, who had preceded him to Worms, and a number of noblemen who had ridden out to meet him. A crowd of several thousand citizens convoyed him through the streets to his lodging in the Hospital of the Knights of St John.[94] On alighting he was embraced by a priest and, adds Aleander viciously, "looking around him with his demonic eyes, exclaimed 'God will be with me.'"[95] The Elector had taken good care to secure him a lodging to which his councillors could have free access to him and decide the tactics to be followed in the audience before the Diet, to which he was formally summoned by the Marshal von Pappenheim at four o'clock on the next day, the 17th April. If asked to recant he was to request time for deliberation and avoid a definite avowal. This non-committal attitude was prescribed by the Elector's advisers[96] and by Hieronymus Schurf, who acted as his legal assessor, in order to frustrate the tactics of Aleander, who had drawn up the questions to be put to the arch-heretic[97] for the purpose of securing a partial if not a complete recantation, which would at least tend to discredit him from the outset in the eyes of the Diet and the nation.[98] Though this

[94] Warbeck, an eyewitness of the scene, to Duke John of Saxony, "Reichstagsakten," ii. 850-851; "Tischreden," v. 69.

[95] "Depeschen," 167.

[96] This is indeed only an inference. But it is highly probable that the Elector's advisers discussed with Luther the tactics to be followed before the Diet. See the arguments of Miss Wagner against this probability, "Z.K.G.," xlii. 373 f., and Kalkoff's reply, *ibid.*, xliii. 205. In writing to Spalatin from the Wartburg in September, Luther reminds him that, but for his advice and that of other friends, he would have spoken more aggressively at Worms. Enders, iii. 230.

[97] "Depeschen," 169.

[98] Kalkoff, "Der Wormser Reichstag," 338 f. Aleander ("Depeschen," 168-170) says nothing in his dispatch to Rome about a partial retraction, and represents that, in accordance with the Bull, he asked for a complete retraction. The fact is, however, that he had arranged with the official of Trier so to put the question in order that Luther might be induced to retract partially and thus discredit himself and his cause. It was this manœuvre that Schurf sought to disconcert.

prudent tactic was probably not in accordance with Luther's inclination, he allowed himself to be guided in the matter of procedure by the astute Schurf, and its adoption certainly does not imply any wavering on his part in his determination not to surrender his convictions to expediency.

At four o'clock on the 17th he was brought by the marshal and the herald by a bypath to the episcopal palace, in which the Estates were assembled, in order to avoid the crowded streets.[99] At the entrance to the palace voices were heard exhorting him to play the man and not to fear those who could only kill the body, but not the soul.[100] Even inside

[99] Acta et Gestæ D. Mart. Luth. in Comitiis Principum Vuormaciæ, "Reichstagsakten," ii. 547. The Acta are also given in "Werke," vii. 825 f., and "Opera Latina Var.," vi. 5 f.

There are several main original sources for Luther's appearances before the Diet:—

1. The Acta et Gestæ. These incorporate the notes of Luther's speech on the 18th April, made by himself, and were apparently composed under his direction by an adherent whose identity is uncertain. They have been ascribed by Köstlin and others to Spalatin on somewhat questionable grounds. Knaake concludes in favour of Bucer. Kalkoff decides in favour of Justus Jonas ("Wormser Reichstag," 330 f.). The question of their authorship is, however, still an open one.

2. A German translation of Luther's speeches on the 18th ("Reichstagsakten," ii. 575 f.; "Werke," vii. 867 f.). This has been attributed by Kalkoff ("Wormser Reichstag," 334-335) and others to Spalatin. The authorship is, however, dubious.

3. An account emanating from Johann von Ecken, the official of Trier, and worked up by Aleander ("Reichstagsakten," ii. 588 f.; "Werke," vii. 825 f.).

4. Report by a Spaniard who was present, evidently in attendance on the Emperor (*ibid.*, ii. 632 f.).

5. Reports by the representatives of Frankfurt, Augsburg, Nürnberg, and others (*ibid.*, ii. 862 f.).

6. Aleander's dispatches edited in the original Italian by Brieger, under the title, "Aleander und Luther," 1521. Well informed, if one-sided, though he himself refrained from attending the sittings out of respect for the papal Bull.

7. Luther's letters and his reminiscences or references in his later works and in the "Tischreden," iii. and v.

[100] The story that Frundsberg accosted him with the words, "Little monk, you are treading a difficult way," etc., is not historic.

the assembly words of encouragement reached his ear [1] as he followed the marshal to his appointed place opposite the official of the Archbishop of Trier, Dr John von der Ecken, who acted as interrogator. He retained his self-composure in the presence of the Emperor and the august assembly of magnates, secular and ecclesiastical, including the ambassadors of foreign nations,[2] who surrounded him. He greeted Peutinger, who was present, with the exclamation, "Dr Peutinger, are you also here!" [3] So little was he overawed in the presence of the august assembly that the marshal was fain to remind him, in reference to these communications, not to speak unless asked to do so.[4] "The fool," reports Aleander, "entered with a smile upon his face and moved his head constantly from side to side in the Emperor's presence." [5] Charles, it would appear, shared the Nuncio's prepossession which could only, as a matter of course, see in the heretic a depraved specimen of humanity to whom the orthodox scandalmonger was already attributing every vice. To Aleander the man with the pinched features and the piercing eyes, whom the incessant overstrain of years of toil and conflict had reduced to a skeleton, is a libertine and a drunkard! The youthful Emperor, sitting in state before him, could hardly be expected to be favourably impressed by the unconventional ease of manner which presumed to inspect the situation with lively curiosity and showed no sign of being unnerved in the face of the assembled majesty and might of the empire. "This man," he exclaimed, according to Aleander, as Luther entered, "will never make a heretic of me." [6] Luther at all events was no less determined that the Emperor should not make of him a recreant to his conscience and the Word of God.

He was asked by the official whether he acknowledged

[1] "Reichstagsakten," ii. 549. Inter eundum ad audiendum *Cæsaris* mandatum et cum jam esset in ipso principum consessu ab aliis alia voce commonebatur.

[2] "Reichstagsakten," ii. 632. Spanish report.

[3] *Ibid.*, ii. 862.

[4] *Ibid.*, ii. 547. Ne quid loqueretur nisi qæsitus.

[5] "Depeschen," 171.

[6] *Ibid.*, 196.

the authorship of the books on the table before him and whether he was prepared to recant any part of them? "Let the titles of the books be read," called out Schurf who stood beside him. Aleander had taken pains to make a fairly complete collection since his arrival in Germany, and after a secretary [7] had recited the titles, Luther answered the first question in the affirmative, whilst adding that the list was not exhaustive. To the second he replied by asking time for consideration on the ground of the supreme importance of the issue involved. "Since it is a question of faith and the salvation of souls, and concerns the Word of God, than which nothing is greater in heaven or earth and which it behoves us all duly to revere, it would be rash and dangerous for me to proffer anything without due reflection. Moreover, since, without due premeditation I might say less than the matter demands, or more than the truth admits, and thereby incur the judgment of Christ who said, 'Whoever shall deny Me before men, him will I deny before My Father in heaven,' I therefore supplicate your imperial majesty to grant me time for deliberation in order that I may answer without detriment to the Word of God and danger to my salvation." [8]

Following the example of the official, he spoke in Latin and repeated what he had said in German for the benefit of those who were not familiar with Latin. The Emperor and the Estates thereupon retired for deliberation, and on reassembling the official expatiated on the enormity and danger of his heresy and expressed surprise that he was not prepared with a definite answer, in view of the fact that he knew the purpose for which he had been cited, viz., to acknowledge his books and recant their contents. He concluded his harangue, which, according to Aleander, was inspired by the Emperor rather than the Estates, by intimating that, as the result of the deliberation, his majesty, in order to avoid any semblance of acting precipitately, had resolved to grant him an interval of twenty-four hours for consideration. Luther might fairly have disputed the

[7] According to the Spanish report, "Reichstagsakten," ii. 633.

[8] "Reichstagsakten," ii. 548-549.

official's version of the citation, which made no mention of a recantation, but only of an examination of his books and teaching. But he was precluded from replying, and according to the Nuncio did not appear as cheerful on retiring as on entering. He was, in fact, acting a prescribed part in thus declining definitely to answer the second question. Even so, he had made it sufficiently clear that for him the Word of God was the supreme standard and arbiter in this controversy and that his answer would be conditioned by this imperative consideration. The inference that in thus evading an explicit answer he had lost his nerve in the presence of the Emperor and the Estates is not supported by the reports of the sitting, with a couple of exceptions. That of the official himself bears that he spoke in a somewhat subdued, but nevertheless intelligible tone.[9] Aleander, as we have noted, explicitly remarks on the self-confident attitude in which he faced the assembly. Peutinger, whom he greeted on his entrance, avers, in his report to the senate of Augsburg on the 19th April, that he had never found or seen him otherwise than in good spirits from beginning to end of the hearing before the Diet.[10] Fürstenberg, the Frankfurt representative, reports, indeed, that he spoke in a low voice as if terrified and horror-stricken,[11] and the Spanish reporter says that he did so "with much terror and little calm."[12] But Fürstenberg admits the inexactitude of his report[13] and the Spanish scribe betrays a marked tendency to represent Luther in an unfavourable light. Certain it is that in the brief account which he wrote on the same evening to a humanist well-wisher, John Cuspinian of Vienna, there is no trace of the slightest hesitation on the subject. "Assuredly, with Christ's help, I shall not recant one jot."[14]

[9] "Reichstagsakten," ii. 589. Summissive aliquanto, sed tamen intelligibili voce dixit.

[10] *Ibid.*, ii. 862. Ich haben in nit anderst gefunden und gesohen dan das er güter ding ist.

[11] *Ibid.*, ii. 862. That he spoke in a low voice at the first hearing is explicable from the fact that it took place in a small chamber before the Estates only.

[12] *Ibid.*, ii. 634. Con mucha Ansia y poco Sosiego.

[13] *Ibid.*, ii. 865.

[14] Enders, iii. 123.

On his arrival at the episcopal palace at four o'clock on the following day (the 18th), he was kept waiting for two hours while the Emperor and the Estates were deliberating in an upper chamber on other business.[15] It was nearly six o'clock before the hearing, which took place in a larger hall than on the previous day,[16] began in the presence of a crowded audience of spectators as well as members. The official, speaking in Latin and German,[17] opened the proceedings with a speech in which he extolled once more the imperial clemency in granting him a respite for reflection, though every Christian and especially a learned professor should have no hesitation in giving forthwith a reason for his faith. He concluded by demanding whether he was prepared to defend all the books which he had recognised as his, or to retract anything?[18] The assembly, note the reporters, awaited the answer with bated breath. Luther, who by all accounts spoke on this occasion in a clear and animated voice, did not answer with a direct refusal, but proceeded to show why he should not be requested straightway to recant. He began by asking his august audience to excuse him if he should not observe the mode of address usual in courts with which he was not familiar. As a simple monk he was accustomed to speak and write in simplicity of heart and with a view to the glory of God and the truth. He acknowledged anew the authorship of his books which, he pointed out, were of various content. One section dealt with practical religion and morals, and even his opponents were fain to confess that he had treated these subjects in so simple and evangelical a fashion that they were without reproach and worthy to be read by all Christians. Even the papal Bull, whilst condemning his books with cruel

[15] "Reichstagsakten," ii. 549; "Depeschen," 173. The former says that he arrived at five o'clock; the latter at four o'clock, which is the more probable hour, and is confirmed by the Spanish report.

[16] *Ibid.*, ii. 634. See Kalkoff, "Wormser Reichstag," 335-338.

[17] It did not escape notice that the German version was couched in less virulent terms (*virulentius*) than the Latin one, which was given mainly for the benefit of the clerical members. "Reichstagsakten," ii. 510.

[18] *Ibid.*, ii. 550. Visne libros tuos agnitos omnes tueri. An vero quicquam retractare?

and monstrous injustice, had described some as harmless. Should he retract these, would he not be condemning what friends and foes alike regarded as the truth? Another category was directed against the Papacy and the Curia which have devastated Christendom, both body and soul, by their doctrines and their corruptions. Who could doubt or deny, in the face of the universal experience and complaints of the papal régime, that the consciences of the faithful were miserably ensnared, oppressed, and tormented by the laws and human doctrines of the Pope. The substance of the German nation was being devoured by this intolerable tyranny which was condemned by the canon law itself, from which he quoted. If he should revoke these, would he not, therefore, be strengthening this tyranny and opening not merely the windows but the doors more widely to further oppression of the people? Nay, would he not thereby make himself the tool of the oppressor, who could then adduce the authority of the Emperor and the empire in support of his tyranny? The speaker knew that he could count on the sympathy of his audience in thus arraigning the papal misgovernment, and gave free rein to his invective until he was checked by the Emperor who, according to Aleander, commanded him to forbear further reference to the Pope, whilst allowing him to continue his speech.[19] A third category dealt with the writings of individuals who had defended the Roman tyranny and had striven to overthrow his conclusions. Whilst he admitted that he had written more sharply than befitted his profession, he had defended the teaching of Christ, not his own opinions, and his revocation of these writings would also only conduce to aggravate the evils from which the Church was suffering. At the same time, since he was a man, and not God, he was ready to say with Christ, "If I have spoken evil, bear witness of the evil." Unlike Christ he was liable to err and was ready, as he ought, to hear such "witness." He, therefore, besought his majesty, the Estates, or anyone else,

[19] "Depeschen," 175. Charles had little knowledge of Latin and did not understand German, and Kalkoff supposes that his confessor directed his attention to the violence of Luther's language. "Entscheidungsjahre," 238.

high or low, to bear witness and convince him of his errors from the Scriptures. If thus convinced, he would most readily revoke and be the first to throw his books into the fire.

As to the reproach directed against him by the official at the previous sitting that his teaching tended to excite strife and tumult, the Word of God must inevitably give rise to strife and tumult, in accordance with the saying of Christ, "I came not to send peace but a sword." Let them not forget that God is wonderful and terrible in His counsels, and beware of making an inauspicious beginning of the reign of the young Emperor by condemning the Word of God. "I speak thus, not because I imagine that this august assembly stands in need of instruction or admonition from me, but because I may not deny to Germany the service which I owe to her. And thus I commend myself to your majesty and lordships, humbly asking that you may not suffer me without cause to be calumniated by the machinations of my adversaries." [20]

The Emperor and his advisers who, on the strength of his apparent hesitation on the previous day, had reckoned on at least a partial recantation, thereupon retired for consultation. As the result of this consultation the official was instructed to demand a definite reply and to hold out the lure that, if he recanted his errors against the faith, the Emperor was prepared to intercede with the Pope on his behalf and would not insist on the indiscriminate burning of his books. The orator, who had also been well primed by Aleander before the sitting,[21] again adopted a hectoring tone. In a long harangue he strove to invalidate Luther's plea for a judicial examination of his books on the assumption that the received faith in its mediæval form was not open to question. To discriminate between his writings was merely to evade the issue. Had he not, after his condemnation by the Pope, put forth far more execrable writings than even before? Had he not asserted the heresies of John Hus to be true and thus utterly destroyed the authority of a General Council? All heretics have

[20] "Reichstagsakten," ii. 551-554.

[21] "Depeschen," 172-173.

mingled the false with the true and thus made their books only the more dangerous. All have appealed to Scripture in defence of their own notions. Luther has adduced nothing new, but merely repeated the contentions of the Beguines, the Waldensians, Wiclif, and Hus, and other condemned heretics. What the Catholic Church has judicially determined and our fathers have held as the true faith Luther would presumptuously reject on the assumption that he alone has discovered the true faith, and thus make Christianity a laughing-stock to Jew and Turk. What audacity to arrogate to himself alone a knowledge of the Scriptures against all the doctors of the Church and to be wise above all others! Let him, therefore, abandon all thought of disputing what he was bound to believe with firm and unquestioning faith, and give a definite and straightforward answer [22] to the question whether he will revoke and retract the errors contained in his works.[23]

Luther had at last come to the parting of the ways in the face of the issue thus stated between a faith based on tradition and corporate authority and a faith based on individual conviction. The hour of destiny had come and with it the man. He uttered only a single, though very involved sentence. But this utterance was to prove the most fateful in modern religious history. It involved not merely a reformation, but a revolution of the mediæval Church. "Since, therefore, your majesty and your lordships desire a simple answer, I will give you one straight to the point and without (intentional) offence.[24] Unless I am convinced by the testimony of Scripture, or by an evident

[22] Non ambigue, non cornute respondeas.

[23] "Reichstagsakten," ii. 591-594.

[24] Responsum neque cornutum neque dentatum—"with neither horns nor teeth." The phrase literally translated is rather unintelligible. The *non cornutum* refers to the assumed evasion by Luther of the official's question. The *non dentatum* to the desire of Luther not to give an offensive answer and evidently refers to the previous rebuke of the Emperor, who had interrupted him in his attack on the Papacy and commanded him to refrain from what he deemed offensive language. For the most recent and at the same time illuminating discussion of the phrase, see Kalkoff, "Wormser Reichstag," 347 f. See also Meissner, "Archiv für Reformationsgeschichte," iii. 321 f.

reason (*ratione evidente*)—for I confide neither in the Pope nor a Council alone, since it is certain that they have often erred and contradicted themselves—I am held fast by the Scriptures adduced by me, and my conscience is taken captive by God's Word, and I neither can nor will revoke anything, seeing that it is not safe or right to act against conscience. God help me. Amen." [25]

This deliberate declaration decisively frustrated the attempt to extract from him even a partial retraction. It created a profound sensation. "There was a great noise," remarks Peutinger,[26] as the excited and exhausted members began to leave the hall. Amid this hubbub the official made a final effort to secure a recantation. "Your conscience, Martin, is in error and you may safely let it alone and recant. Conscience is no valid plea against a General Council, which cannot err and which you cannot possibly prove to have erred in matters of faith, though it may possibly have erred in matters of morals." [27] To which Luther retorted that General Councils had erred and he was prepared to prove it. Whereupon the Emperor impatiently rose from his seat, exclaiming that he had had enough of this argumentation against Councils, and retired in angry mood from the excited assembly.[28] As Luther made his way out accompanied by two guards, the Spanish courtiers broke into hisses and jeers.[29] In the excitement and confusion his friends concluded that he was being led away to prison and protested loudly until Luther reassured them.[30] Outside he was greeted by the Spanish guards

[25] "Reichstagsakten," ii. 555; *cf.* Luther's brief recapitulation in his letter to the Emperor, 28th April, Enders, iii. 131. The usual version of the final words, "Here I stand, I can do no other," are found in an account printed shortly afterwards at Wittenberg. They are evidently an amplification of the words actually uttered by Luther. The German translation of the Latin version of the speech also contains only the words, "God help me. Amen." "Reichstagsakten," ii. 582; "Werke," vii. 877. Luther, who had so far spoken in both Latin and German, delivered this fateful declaration only in Latin.

[26] *Ibid.*, ii. 862.

[27] *Ibid.*, ii. 594.

[28] "Depeschen," 176.

[29] "Reichstagsakten," ii. 558.

[30] So Luther himself related long afterwards. "Werke," 64, 370 f. (Erlangen edition); *cf.* "Tischreden," v. 71.

with the cry, "To the fire with him!"[31] Luther and his adherents, on the other hand, appeared in exalted mood and passed on with uplifted hands after the old German fashion of celebrating a victory.[32] "I am through, I am through,"[33] he cried joyfully on reaching his lodging and receiving the congratulations of his friends. Had he a hundred heads he would gladly lose them all rather than belie the truth.

He had no little reason for jubilation. His heroic declaration had evoked the admiration of not a few of the members of the Diet who might not understand or share his theological views. The Elector was emphatic in his approbation: "Right well has Dr Martin spoken in Latin and German before the Emperor, the princes, and all the Estates. He is much too bold for me."[34] He sent his chaplain to let him know that he could count on his continued support, and the approval of the wary strategist was a guarantee that his enemies would not be allowed to crush him. Duke Eric of Brunswick, though a good Catholic, showed his goodwill by sending him a goblet of beer to cool himself after the exertion and excitement of the day's ordeal, whilst the young Landgrave Philip of Hesse paid him a visit and parted with the words, "Dear Doctor, if you are in the right, may God sustain you."[35]

These encouraging omens doubtless contributed to the exaltation with which he emerged from the ordeal of these two days. The real secret of it was, however, the consciousness that he had achieved a moral victory, whatever the Emperor and the Diet might devise against him. This victory did not consist merely in the fact that he had faced unflinchingly the majesty and might of the empire. Its significance lies rather in the fact that he had dared to challenge an even greater power to which a large part of Christendom as well as the empire owned allegiance, to pit individual conviction against the principle of corporate

[31] "Reichstagsakten," ii. 636. Spanish report.
[32] *Ibid.*, ii. 636; "Depeschen," 176.
[33] *Ibid.*, ii. 852. Ich bin hindurch, ich bin hindurch.
[34] Spalatin, "Annales," 49 f.; *cf.* "Tischreden," v. 71.
[35] "Tischreden," iii. 285; v. 81.

infallibility which the Roman Church embodied and had implacably maintained against both sect and individual. To challenge this principle had hitherto been equivalent to challenging Christianity itself. And this was the audacious thing that Luther had ventured to do. If the conscience and reason of the individual are to decide, what becomes of the truth, or, what might seem even more ominous to the ecclesiastical mind, what becomes of the Church? Would this challenge not lead to universal anarchy in the State as well as universal error in the Church? What a convulsion had it not led to in the case of the Hussites 100 years earlier, and what dire results must not be apprehended from this revival of Hussite heresy? If a General Council can err in matters of faith, what of the faith and where to find the truth? The truth, retorted Luther, resides in the conscience and reason of the individual, enlightened and guided by Scripture. It was indescribably daring, superlatively heroic. This Augustinian monk was by no means the first thus to challenge the principle of corporate infallibility in things religious. A long line of confessors and martyrs had dared and died for conscience sake throughout the centuries. Hus had spoken as unflinchingly at Constance as Luther spoke at Worms, and Hus was, if possible, the more heroic of the two, inasmuch as the circumstances of the age in the early fifteenth century were more hopeless for the speaker than in the early sixteenth. Nevertheless, even Luther, with the Elector to protect him and the national feeling of Germany largely arraying itself behind him, and with a more conscientious Emperor than Sigismund to observe his pledged word, in spite of the prompting of an Aleander to break it, must have felt that, in adducing the plea of the individual conscience against the authority of the Church, he was still attempting the impossible thing.

Happily for his cause, the world had made some advance, under humanist influence, in enlightenment since Hus's day, though it had burned Savonarola less than a quarter of a century ago, whereas the Papacy and the Church had continued to lose in moral, if not material strength. Moreover, the anti-papal feeling in the Diet was too strong and too well justified by the grievances (*gravamina*), which a committee was engaged in formulating,[36] for the Emperor and his ministers to succeed in enlisting forthwith the condemnation of the heretic. When, therefore, on the following day (19th) Charles summoned the Electors and a number of the princes to deliberate on his fate, they asked time to consider the question. "Good," returned the Emperor; "but I will tell you beforehand my own conclusion on the subject." [37] He was, he said, resolved to abide by the faith of his ancestors. It was preposterous that a single monk should be right in his opinion and the whole of Christendom in error for 1,000 years and more. It would be a disgrace to the German empire, which had been constituted the guardian of the Catholic faith, to tolerate even the suspicion of heresy. In view of the stubbornness shown by Luther on the previous day, he regretted that he had delayed so long in proceeding against him and his false doctrine. He had resolved not to give him a further hearing, but to take the necessary measures for the suppression of his heresy, whilst observing meanwhile the safe conduct granted to him.[38]

The majority of the Diet was not to be thus intimidated. In the electoral chamber, indeed, Joachim of Brandenburg carried a motion to aid and abet the Emperor, against the Electors of Saxony and the Palatinate.[39] But his brother, the Archbishop of Maintz, took fright at the placards which appeared overnight on the walls of the Rathhaus and other buildings, threatening a popular rising in defence of Luther and bearing the ominous words *Bundschuh* (the war cry of the peasants) thrice repeated.[40] In his alarm the archbishop

[36] "Reichstagsakten," ii. 661 f.

[37] "Depeschen," 177.

[38] "Reichstagsakten," ii. 595. The emphatic declaration was read in both French and German. Many of the princes, notes Aleander, in his jubilant dispatch to Rome, turned deadly pale during the reading of it.

[39] *Ibid.*, ii. 596-598. Aleander erroneously says ("Depeschen," 178) that the decision was unanimous, but corrects himself on p. 183.

[40] "Depeschen," 182. At the same time a placard containing a denunciation of Luther and his heresy appeared for the purpose of discrediting him and his cause. Kalkoff, "Wormser Reichstag," 352-355.

urgently represented to the Emperor the danger of provoking a civil war.[41] Charles laughed at his fears. The placard was but the dodge of some would-be Minutius Scævola, and in reality these threats were merely the fireworks of one of Luther's humanist friends, Hermann von dem Busche. But he could not afford to ignore the will of the Estates who, under the influence of the astute Elector,[42] united in representing the desirability of affording the heretic a further hearing with a view to his recantation. Having regard to his request to be shown his errors and in order that the people might not be led to believe that he had been condemned unrefuted, they proposed that a commission of three or four men learned in the Scriptures should be nominated to discuss with him the main points, doctrinal and institutional, for the purpose of bringing about a reconciliation. They strengthened their proposal by reminding his majesty that God willeth not the death of a sinner, but that he should repent and live. They ignored the papal Bull of Condemnation and left the arbiters free to examine Luther's writings afresh and draw up a set of articles which he was to be asked to revoke, with reasons given for this demand. This procedure, they pointed out, would tend to forestall the evils which were otherwise to be apprehended. If Luther should nevertheless persist in his opinions, they would then support the Emperor in taking measures against him as an incorrigible heretic, subject to the due observance of the safe conduct granted him.[43] To this request the Emperor reluctantly acceded on the 22nd April, and granted an interval of three days for the proposed conference. If the Estates succeeded in thereby bringing about the submission of the heretic, he was prepared to intercede with the Pope for him. But he emphatically refused to take part in the conference, or allow his ministers to do so.[44]

[41] "Depeschen," 182-183.

[42] *Ibid.*, 184.

[43] "Reichstagsakten," ii. 598-599. In this answer the Estates used the French language in which the Emperor's communication had been written. Charles understood only Spanish and French.

[44] *Ibid.*, ii. 601; "Depeschen," 184.

IV. The Edict of Worms

On the 24th April, Luther accordingly appeared before a representative commission of the Estates consisting of the Archbishop of Trier, who presided, the Elector of Brandenburg, Duke George of Saxony, the Bishops of Brandenburg and Augsburg, the Master of the Teutonic Order, Dr Peutinger of Augsburg, and the representative of Strassburg, with Dr Vehus, Chancellor of the Margrave of Baden, as orator instead of the official of Trier. On this occasion he was accompanied by Schurf, Amsdorf, and Justus Jonas. The commission was certainly not distinguished by its theological learning, for both Peutinger and Vehus were jurists and the prelates were ecclesiastics rather than theologians, and were no match for the Wittenberg professor in either intellectual ability or erudition. Dr Vehus, who opened the conference with a long speech, disclaimed in fact any pretension to speak as a theological expert,[45] and in this confession his fellow-members might well have joined. He adopted a very different tone, however, from that of the hectoring official, and sought to persuade Luther in a brotherly spirit to reconsider his refusal to retract. He enlarged on the duty of submission to the decisions of General Councils as the authoritative organ of the Holy Spirit. Councils might have decreed diverse but not *contrary* opinions (*diversa*, but not *contraria*), and by this scholastic distinction he sought to disprove Luther's assertion that they had contradicted themselves. With equal plausibility he sought to overthrow the appeal to conscience by reminding him that distrust of self, humility, and the avoidance of offence and strife were also enjoined in the Gospel, and by pointing out the grave danger involved in his principle to civil government and social order and the risk of frustrating, by his obstinate adherence to his own opinions, the growth of the good seed which he had undoubtedly sown in some of his

[45] "Reichstagsakten," ii. 612 and 618. Report of Vehus on the conference.

books. Let him, therefore, desist from his opinionated opposition to authority and submit his writings and his teaching to the judgment of the Emperor and the Estates.[46]

In reply, Luther cordially acknowledged the moderate and kindly spirit which had dictated this admonition. He had no intention of bringing the authority of Councils into contempt. But the Council of Constance, in condemning the doctrine of Hus that the Church consists in the whole body of the predestined, had condemned the Word of God and the article of the creed, " I believe in the Holy Catholic Church." He would submissively accept sentence of death at the Emperor's hands, but he refused to be compelled to revoke the plain Word of God, in the defence of which it was incumbent to obey God rather than man. It was not possible to avoid offence in matters of faith and morals. Christ Himself was the great stumbling block. He had always taught obedience to governments and magistrates, even to bad ones. But he refused to be compelled to deny God's Word against his conscience.

Would he, then, agree to submit his writings to the judgment of the Emperor and the Diet ? He expressed his readiness to do so. Nay, he would accept the humblest Christian as judge, provided the judgment rested on the authority of the divine word. He quoted Paul and Augustine in support of this principle. " Do I understand you to say," asked the Elector of Brandenburg, " that you will not submit unless convinced by Holy Scripture ? " " Yes, most gracious lord," replied Luther, " or by clear and evident reasons." [47]

Thus the matter ended as far as the commission of the Estates was concerned, and a final effort made by the Archbishop of Trier on his own responsibility was equally unsuccessful. He invited Luther, Schurf, and Amsdorf to dine with him along with the Frankfurt theologian, Cochlæus, a former humanist sympathiser whom the " Babylonic Captivity " had alienated and who was on the outlook to advance his own interests. The official, supported by Cochlæus, argued afresh that heretics like

[46] " Reichstagsakten," ii. 612-618. [47] *Ibid.*, ii. 561-563.

Arius had based their heresy on Scripture in order to prove that such heretical appeals to Scripture had no validity against the decrees of a General Council.[48] After dinner Cochlæus continued the discussion with him and his friends in Luther's lodging and suggested the expedient of a public disputation, if Luther would waive his safe conduct, which he, of course, refused to do, whilst carrying on the discussion in an amicable and even jovial mood.[49] As the three days respite granted by the Emperor (22nd to 24th April) extended only to the evening of the 24th, the archbishop begged and received an extension of two days. He accordingly notified Luther to meet Vehus and Peutinger in further conference on the morrow, the 25th. Vehus again pressed on him the proposal to submit his writings to the judgment of the Emperor and the Estates. Luther objected that the Emperor had burned his books before the meeting of the Diet and had issued a mandate against him whilst proceeding under safe conduct to Worms. He nevertheless asked an interval for consideration, and on resuming the conference in the afternoon he once more insisted on the cardinal condition that his writings should be judged only in accordance with the testimony of Scripture. Vehus then suggested that he should agree to submit them to the judgment of a future Council. This he was willing to do provided that it was convened without delay, that the articles to be submitted should be specified to him beforehand, and that he should be free to write and preach in accordance with the Word of God on all matters not contained in these articles.[50]

This agreement Vehus communicated to the archbishop who thereupon summoned Luther to a private conference with himself, to which Spalatin was later admitted.

[48] "Reichstagsakten," ii. 563-564, and the report of Cochlæus. *Ibid.*, ii. 625-627.

[49] *Ibid.*, ii. 627-631.

[50] *Ibid.*, ii. 619-623. Luther, in his letter to the Emperor and the Estates after his departure from Worms, says that he assumed that the articles were to be considered in the light of the evidence of the Word. Enders, iii. 131, 138. "Hic," he says, "fuit controversiæ totius cardo."

"What," asked the archbishop, "if the articles to be referred to the future Council included matters condemned by the Council of Constance?" "In that case," was the reply, "I cannot and will not undertake to remain silent. Certain I am that in these decrees the Council condemned God's Word, and I will rather lose my head than prove false to the clear Word of God."[51] According to Aleander the archbishop also attempted to persuade him to retract by offering him a rich priory in his diocese and undertaking to protect him if, in consequence of his retraction, his followers should threaten to kill him. Luther indignantly rejected the offer and also refused to make even a partial retraction, the effect of which would have been, as Aleander remarks, to discredit him and his cause in the eyes of the people, and which the archbishop proposed with this intent.[52]

The negotiations of these laborious days thus ended in failure. The baffled archbishop notified the fact to the Emperor, who forthwith sent Luther a mandate to leave Worms on the morrow, the 26th, to return to Wittenberg within twenty-one days, and to refrain from preaching or writing during his journey thither. The failure was inevitable in view of Luther's determination to oppose to the demand for a recantation the appeal to Scripture. To demand that his opponents should accept the Scriptures as the only arbiter of the question at issue was in reality to ask them to renounce many of the doctrines and institutions of the Church in its mediæval form. To make them the only test of doctrine and practice was to cut at the root of the papal and priestly power and the mediæval sacramental system and to ask his opponents to commit ecclesiastical suicide. On the other hand, to convince him of the truth of the mediæval doctrines and practice to which he objected was equally impossible for the simple reason that Scripture, historically interpreted, could not be made to sanction what was the product of a gradual and lengthy evolution. To his opponents his insistence on the exclusive authority of

51 "Reichstagsakten," ii. 567.

52 "Depeschen," 190-192. The proposal was in keeping with the policy of Aleander and the Romanists from the outset to entrap Luther into a partial retraction.

Scripture appeared as mere stubbornness and diabolic perversity. He certainly was dogmatic enough in maintaining this principle. There is doubtless also something of the doctrinaire in his contention that his interpretation of Scripture is the only permissible one, though he professes his willingness to accept a better one and, in theory at least, observes the attitude of the open mind. He stands, too, for persuasion and toleration against the brutal principle of suppressing conscience by threats and violence and denying freedom of thought in things religious. He does so on religious rather than on broad human grounds. His contention on behalf of the liberty of the individual springs from religious conviction rather than from the objective search for truth as an indefeasible right of the individual reason. It might be difficult to argue on the merits of the case with one whose convictions are based on faith rather than reason. Nor does he make due allowance for the fact that the interpretation even of Scripture cannot, in the nature of the case, be a thing of mathematical certainty and necessarily tends to difference of opinion. For Luther the evidence of Scripture is simple, clear, and convincing, though he admits that it is not all on the same level of absolute credibility. The Epistle of James, for instance, compared with those of Paul, is of limited authority.

At the same time, from the historical point of view, the appeal to the sources of Christianity as the true norm of what its founders taught and ordained is a very strong one. If the object of the controversy was to establish whether the doctrines and institutions of the mediæval Church were in accord with original Christianity, Luther was amply justified in his contention that the issue could only be settled in the light of the New Testament evidence. To adduce the decisions of later Councils as of equal authority and obligation with the dicta of Christ and the Apostles, on the assumption that Councils cannot err and the Pope is the infallible judge of the faith, was historically inadmissible. This assumption was open to the gravest objection if only in view of the dissensions of which these Councils were the arena, the limited knowledge of their members, the difficulty of arriving at a true judgment in matters historical, the difference of time and circumstance, the subtle influence of the tendency to read the present into the past, the play of human passion and prejudice from which no assembly, even of ecclesiastics, is exempt. It was, indeed, a questionable inference that what such an assembly decreed was *ipso facto* infallibly true and binding on the individual reason and conscience. This could at most be only a matter of belief. It was not capable of proof. However much Luther might emphasise faith, he had lost all confidence in this species of it. Moreover, he had no confidence in the unconditional reference of his case to such a Council. The proposal was in reality but a device to evade the real issue he had raised and disarm him in the meantime. The Council could not possibly have treated the issue as an open question. It could not overthrow the decision of the Council of Constance without virtually justifying both Luther and Hus and without profoundly modifying, if not revolutionising, the mediæval Church.

Luther received the imperial mandate on the evening of the 25th with complete equanimity, though he refused to be bound by the imperial prohibition not to preach on the return journey, and in the sequel did not observe it. "As it has seemed good to the Lord, so let it be. Blessed be the name of the Lord." He expressed his gratitude to the Emperor and the Estates for according him a hearing and for the honourable observance of the safe conduct. "I have sought nothing but a reformation of the Church in accordance with Holy Scripture. I would suffer death and infamy, surrender life and reputation for his imperial majesty and the empire. I would reserve nothing but the liberty to confess and bear witness to the Word of God alone." [53] Apart from this irrefragable faith, he had substantial reason for his equanimity in the knowledge that the Elector had taken measures to protect him from the ultimate consequences of his heroic refusal to retract. At ten o'clock on the 26th he set out on the return journey, ostensibly to Wittenberg. His real destination was the Wartburg, though the secret was known only to the Elector's

[53] "Reichstagsakten," ii. 568.

advisers, to himself, the Warden of the Wartburg, Hans von Verlepsch, and the trusty Knight of Altenstein, Burkhard von Wenkheim, to whom was entrusted the duty of intercepting him in the Thuringian Forest.[54] On the 4th May he had reached Altenstein. Here in the gathering darkness he was seized by a party of horsemen under the command of the Knight and the Warden and hurried away by a roundabout route to the Wartburg overlooking Eisenach,[55] where, as Ritter George, he was to spend nearly a year in safe obscurity. From Friedberg he had sent back the herald Sturm with letters to the Emperor and the Estates, reiterating his readiness to render due obedience in temporal things, but claiming and maintaining the right and duty of obeying God, not man, in things pertaining to the salvation of the soul. He had shown his obedience as a subject by appearing at Worms, in spite of the fact that his safe conduct had been violated by the mandate against his books. As his opponents had not refuted his teaching from Scripture, the only norm of Christian truth, he begged his majesty and the Estates not to resort to violence to coerce his conscience, and renewed his offer to submit to the judgment of an impartial tribunal, on condition that its judgment was based on God's Word alone.[56]

This appeal was addressed to deaf ears as far as the Emperor at least was concerned,[57] though a month elapsed before he, on the 26th May, signed the Edict placing Luther and his adherents under the ban of the empire. On the 30th April he communicated to the Estates his intention to proceed against the Lutheran heresy and asked their advice. The Estates in reply requested that the proposed Edict should be submitted to them for consideration and

[54] The Elector himself, whilst arranging the plan with his advisers ("Tischreden," v. 82), did not prescribe the place and left this to Feilitzsch and Thun in order to be free to profess his ignorance on the subject. See "Depeschen," 235, and the Elector's "Briefwechsel mit Herzog Johann," 15 f., ed. by Förstemann.

[55] See his own account in "Tischreden," v. 82.

[56] Enders, iii. 130 f., 28th April.

[57] The Elector in fact could find no one courageous enough to present it to the Emperor, so that it did not come into his hands. Kalkoff, "Wormser Reichstag," 379.

report.[58] In professing to be guided by "the advice and foreknowledge" of the Estates, the Emperor was only acting in accordance with the constitution of the empire, which required him to secure their agreement in a matter of this kind affecting the national interest as well as the fate of Luther. In all important national affairs he was in fact limited by the co-operation and consent of the Diet and was not entitled to issue an Edict of such importance on his own responsibility.[59] The reply of the Estates clearly assumes this constitutional principle on which the action of the Emperor in intimating his intention for their consideration was based. He was, moreover, obliged to avoid precipitate measures in view of the necessity of securing their sanction of a large force in the impending war with France. The task of drawing up the proposed Edict was, however, committed, not to the German commission which, under the presidency of the Archbishop of Salzburg,[60] had previously dealt with the subject, but to Aleander,[61] who by working all night presented the Latin draft to the Chancellor Gattinara on the morning of the following day (1st May).[62] To his chagrin, instead of accepting it as it stood, the chancellor submitted it to the Emperor's German Privy Council, whom the Nuncio suspected of partiality for Luther.[63] The revision did not materially modify the

[58] "Reichstagsakten," ii. 893. Report of Schwarzenberg to the Dukes of Bavaria. Wurde beslossen das kei. mt., wie die irer mt. fur guet ansehen, stellen lassen, die si, die stände, in underthänigkeit ersehen und auf ir mt. begern ir guetbedunken auch darin anzaigen wollten; *cf.* the report of Spengler to Nürnberg, *ibid.*, ii. 898.

[59] See on this subject the arguments of Kalkoff, "Wormser Reichstag," 358 f., against Paulus, who maintains the legality of the Edict as finally issued by the Emperor. "Zur Geschichte des Wormser Reichstags," Hist. Jahrbuch, 269 f. (1919); *cf.* Paquier, "Aleandre," 270 (1900).

[60] The archbishop, who was out of favour with the court, had withdrawn from Worms, and his withdrawal provided the Emperor and his ministers with the opportunity of transferring the task to Aleander. Kalkoff, "Entstehung des Wormser Edikts," 195 (1913).

[61] "Reichstagsakten," ii. 638; "Depeschen," 206.

[62] "Depeschen," 206-207; "Entstehung," 196-197.

[63] "Depeschen," 207-208; "Entstehung," 235. Aleander's suspicion was unfounded.

contents, however, and as thus revised it was translated into German, and on the 8th May presented by Aleander to be forthwith printed and published.[64] The printing was already being proceeded with and on the 12th May Aleander handed the Emperor the Latin original and the German translation, written on parchment, for signature. To his astonishment Charles declined to sign on the ground that he deemed it necessary to submit it for the consideration of the Estates.[65] He had not yet secured their co-operation in the war against France and hesitated to affix his signature to a document which outlawed many of his German subjects, as well as the heretic himself,[66] and was fitted on this account to endanger the negotiations for the grant of 4,000 horse and 20,000 foot for the war.[67] Moreover, Sickingen and Hutten were assuming a threatening attitude in defence of Luther. At the same time he assured the Nuncio that the proposed reference would be merely formal.[68] Though the Estates on the same day agreed to grant this force on certain conditions, it was not till the 23rd that they formally declared their intention to support him against the enemy.[69] He had, too, by this time concluded a formal alliance with the Pope which bound him to use all his strength for the suppression of the Lutheran heresy.

There was, therefore, now no reason for further reserve in the matter of the Edict, and two days later (25th May) he closed the Reichstag, whose ranks had been thinned by the departure of the Electors of Saxony and the Palatinate and many others, without having submitted it for its

[64] "Reichstagsakten," ii. 639; "Depeschen," 214-215.

[65] "Depeschen," 230.

[66] The dubiety of the Archbishop of Maintz and others on this head appears from Aleander's letter to the archbishop. "Reichstagsakten," ii. 640; *cf.* "Depeschen," 243; Balan, "Monumenta Reformationis Lutheranæ," 263 (1884).

[67] "Depeschen," 232-233. The negotiations were also concerned with the establishment of the Reichs regiment or the government of the empire in the Emperor's absence from Germany, and the Reichskammer or imperial court of justice.

[68] *Ibid.*, 231.

[69] "Reichstagsakten," ii. 931.

consideration and approval.[70] In order to give it at least the semblance of the sanction of the Estates, he convened on the evening of the same day the four remaining Electors and a few of the bishops and the princes at the episcopal palace. Here Aleander handed him a papal brief, thanking him for his zeal for the faith, which was read by the Chancellor Gattinara amid the applause of the Spanish and Italian courtiers, who were present in large numbers. Aleander also distributed briefs of a similar tenor to the Electors and the princes. Whereupon, after the withdrawal of the papal representatives, the Emperor called for the Edict, which was produced by Dr Ziegler, the Vice-Chancellor. "This," said Charles, speaking in French, "is the Edict which I propose to execute in the affair of Luther." It was apparently the German version of it which was read by Dr Spiegel amid the tense attention of the magnates present, and which had been further revised for the purpose of toning down and compressing the virulent rhetoric of the original Latin version, without substantially altering its sense.[71] At the conclusion of the recital the Elector of Brandenburg acted his part in this prearranged performance by declaring the approval and consent of the Estates, who would not desire to alter a single jot of the Edict, and requested its execution against the heretic and his adherents. On the following day, the 26th, the Emperor put his signature to the parchment copies of the Latin original and the German version, publicly and ostentatiously presented to him by Aleander at the conclusion of High Mass in the cathedral,[72] and issued a proclamation announcing that it had been enacted "with the consent and will of the Estates" and commanding its execution throughout the empire.[73]

[70] "Reichstagsakten," ii. 937 f.; "Depeschen," 245-246. The closing sitting was held in the Rathhaus, where the Diet usually sat.

[71] Kalkoff, "Entstehung," 251 f.; "Entscheidungsjahre," 266.

[72] "Depeschen," 249-250. See also "Reichstagsakten," ii. 947. Report of the Venetian Contarini.

[73] "Reichstagsakten," ii. 659-661. Wir haben aus merklichen, beweglichen ursachen, mit rat und willen unser und des heiligen reichs churfürsten, fürsten und stände, hie bei uns versamelt, ein edict und gebotsbrief Martin Luther und ein Gesetz die druckerei berurend ausgeen lassen.

The professed consent of the Estates was, to say the least, misleading. The Diet had been formally closed and this surreptitious meeting of a few magnates, devised by the plotters behind the scenes, was evidently a ruse to invest the Edict with what was really a fictitious sanction.[74] The proclamation conveys the impression that it was voted at an ordinary sitting of the Reichstag. In reality it was only approved by a rump manipulated for this purpose. This underhand tactic certainly suggests the conclusion that the Emperor and his advisers were afraid to put the Edict to the test of a regular discussion and vote and were fain to evade, in this surreptitious fashion, the request of the Estates on the 30th April that it should be submitted for their consideration and approval. It had been the striving of Aleander all along to prevent or evade such discussion and vote, and in unison with the Emperor and Gattinara, he had succeeded in his purpose. Even so, as his dispatches show, a good deal of bribery in money or promises was required to secure this questionable declaration in vindication of the faith against a heretic who was also the mouthpiece of a national revulsion from Rome. As it was, Aleander was so anxious about the final issue, in view of the undoubted sympathy of the people for Luther and the possibility of vacillation on the part of the anti-Lutherans at the last moment, that, even after the declaration of the evening of the 25th, he spent a sleepless night and was only relieved from his anxiety when the Emperor at last put his signature to the fateful document and directed the issue of the proclamation for its execution on the following day.[75] Even the date of the document, the 8th May, was apt to be misleading, though in retaining the date of the draft on which it had been submitted to and practically approved by the Emperor, instead of inserting that of the actual acceptance of the so-called enactment, the Emperor and his advisers were not necessarily guilty of an act of bad faith.

[74] Armstrong (" Emperor Charles V.," i. 79) says that " the Diet on its last day unanimously approved the Edict of Worms." He does not seem to have grasped the situation.

[75] " Depeschen," 248-249.

The Edict recites the efforts made by the Pope to bring Luther to recant, the condemnation of his teaching, and the steps taken by the Emperor, in obedience to the papal will, to execute the Bull of Condemnation. Instead of repenting of his perversity and seeking absolution, Luther had persisted like a madman in his heresies and blasphemies, and had aggravated his offence by continuing and widening his attack on the doctrines and institutions of the Church. Details are given of the revolutionary and calumnious contentions contained in his books against the papal and priestly power, the sacraments, the authority of the Fathers and Doctors recognised by the Church. His teaching is subversive of government as well as religion and morality, and tends to excite nothing but rebellion, strife, war, murder, plunder, and conflagration. It is both anarchic and antinomian inasmuch as he advocates freedom from all law, ecclesiastical and civil, and has in fact written worse things against the temporal than against the ecclesiastical power. He has aspersed with his dirty mouth the Council of Constance as "a synagogue of Satan," and denounced the Emperor Sigismund and the princes of the empire, who carried out the burning of Hus, as apostles of Antichrist and murderers. He has boasted that if Hus was a heretic, he was tenfold more a heretic. He is the very devil himself in the form of a man in monk's cowl, who has collected all the forgotten heresies of former times in one stinking puddle, with some new abominations of his own, especially his doctrine of justification by faith, under the pretence of proclaiming the Gospel. The Emperor, in duty bound to protect and support the Holy See, and to stand fast in the faith of his ancestors, then details the steps taken in conjunction with the Estates to secure the retraction of the notorious and obdurate heretic. In consequence of the failure of these efforts and his obstinate refusal to retract, he has decreed, in virtue of his imperial authority and "with the unanimous consent and will" of the Estates, to execute the Bulls issued by the Pope, the competent judge in the case, against the said Martin Luther as an excommunicated heretic. He accordingly places him under the imperial ban, prohibits all his subjects under pain of high treason from holding intercourse with or affording him assistance of any kind, and commands them to seize him wherever found and notify the fact to the authorities. Similarly, they are empowered to arrest his adherents and protectors and take possession of their property, unless they can show that they have received the papal absolution. Further, no one may read, possess, buy or sell or print his books, even those which otherwise contain good teaching, since a single drop of the poison of heresy is fitted to ruin the soul, and all are bound to burn them under the aforesaid penalties. In consequence of the abuse and danger of the freedom of the press, no book may henceforth be written or printed tending to discredit the faith, the Pope, the Church, the clergy, and the scholastic theology, and all such writings shall also be burned, their authors and publishers seized and put to death, and their property confiscated for the benefit of those arresting them. The prohibition and the penalty were extended even to pictures and engravings. For the future the censorship of books treating of the faith is entrusted to the bishops and their representatives, with the co-operation of the University Faculties of Theology. Even the publication of all books, whatever their subject, is likewise made dependent on the episcopal approval. The Edict concludes by denouncing the sentence of outlawry against all who shall contravene its provisions.[76]

The narrative part is manifestly an *ex parte* and hopelessly biased statement of the Lutheran movement. It ignores the grave evils which had called Luther into the arena against the corruption and misgovernment of Rome and the manifold abuses in the Church. It represents him as solely actuated by a diabolic perversity and grossly misrepresents his teaching. It reeks of the bitter animus of its author, the Italian Aleander, his most persistent and also his most unscrupulous antagonist. If Luther taught anarchy, as the Edict falsely asserted, Aleander certainly did his best to outdo him in inciting in this fanatic deliverance to confiscation and violence on behalf of the faith. The purely enacting part displays clearly enough the

[76] "Reichstagsakten," ii. 643 f.

tyrannic régime which Luther dared to challenge in the name of individual liberty of thought and conscience, as he understood this liberty. It was not only an attempt on the part of Aleander and those for whom he spoke to erect a bulwark around the traditional faith and ecclesiastical authority against their redoubtable antagonist. It was an attempt to stifle the progressive forces at work in the Renaissance in the interest of obscurantist bigots and corrupt ecclesiastics, to gag all criticism of the scholastic system and the oppressive mediæval régime in Church and State. It was in fact directed as much against Erasmus and the new learning, against Dürer and the new art, as against the heretic of Wittenberg. It is not surprising that Erasmus thought it time to exchange Louvain for Basle as a residence,[77] and Dürer, who was then at Antwerp, made tracks for Nürnberg.[78]

[77] So at least his enemies represented the motive of his departure, which he himself denied. See Emerton, "Desiderius Erasmus," 347 f. (1899).

[78] Dürer gives expression to his distress on learning the news of Luther's disappearance. See his Diary of a Journey in the Netherlands in Dürer's "Briefe, Tagebücher, und Reime," ed. by Thausing, 119 f. (1888). He left Brussels on the 12th July 1521.

CHAPTER X

CONCLUSION

I. Infatuation of the Papacy

THE breach with Rome was complete. Rome had cast out Luther from its communion and the Emperor, in obedience to the papal decree, had outlawed him. Rome had no place in its system of unquestioning obedience to the absolute will of the Pope in matters of faith for one who persisted in adducing the plea of individual conviction and the individual conscience as a reason for refusing such obedience. It had only one way of dealing with this refusal—excommunication by the ecclesiastical power and death at the hands of the secular power as the executor of its sentence. Heresy was not only an offence against the faith. It was a crime which the temporal power was bound to punish. In casting the heretic out of the Church and requiring the State to proceed against him, the Pope was acting in accordance with ecclesiastical law and usage which did not admit the validity of any plea based on the individual reason and conscience. From the point of view of canon law Luther, having been found guilty of heresy, had unchurched himself. The papal action in instituting an examination of his writings in response to the accusation of his opponents and, on the ground of this examination, finding him guilty of heresy, was legally correct. If a retraction were not forthcoming, excommunication and the extreme penalty attaching to heresy were inevitable. In recognising the prerogative of the Pope to act as he had done for the preservation of the faith and adducing the obligation of the temporal authority to execute the papal will,[1] the Edict of Worms was in accordance with ecclesiastical

[1] "Reichstagsakten," ii. 644 and 654.

law and practice. If by the law of the empire the heretic was entitled to be tried by a national tribunal,[2] the Emperor had, formally at least, given him a hearing before the Diet and professedly issued the Edict in the name of the Estates as well as by his own authority. The hearing, as it turned out, might merely be for the purpose of giving him a last chance to recant, and the profession of issuing it with the consent and authority of the Estates might be but a pretence. But, from the point of view of Rome, such an objection did not count, since the proceedings at Worms, after the Pope had authoritatively declared Luther a heretic, were inadmissible and invalid. Its representatives at Worms had accordingly done their utmost to frustrate his citation and had taken no part directly in these proceedings, whilst indirectly exerting themselves to the utmost to secure his outlawry in obedience to the papal will. In the end they had succeeded in their efforts, and on the 26th May 1521 Luther, who was already under the ban of the Pope, was placed under that of the empire. In so doing they had at the same time succeeded in disrupting the Western Church, though they little recked that this would prove the result of their triumph. They seem, indeed, to have expected a popular convulsion which might eventuate even in a religious war. But the bloodshed and havoc would only ruin Germany and in the end the papal supremacy would emerge triumphant amid the slaughter and the extermination of the heretics.[3] Doubtless a truly Christian consummation for the zealots who strove to maintain an unreformed Papacy and Church to contemplate!

There can be no doubt at any rate of the infatuated folly of the whole business from the point of view even of the interest of Rome, not to speak of that of the Church and religion. The real interest of both lay not in proscribing Luther as a heretic, but in responding betimes to his urgent

[2] "Reichstagsakten," i. 871-873. Arts. 18 and 24 which ordain that no member of any Estate was to be put under the ban without regular process.

[3] Enders, iii. 80. Paulus questions the menacing language attributed to Aleander ("Hist. Jahrbuch," xxxix. 273 f., 1919). Kalkoff adduces weighty reasons for accepting its authenticity. "Hutten und die Reformation," 583-584.

demand for a drastic reformation of both the Roman Curia and the Church. Legally Luther might have earned and even provoked excommunication and outlawry. His developing attack might seem at last to allow of no other alternative if the Pope was to continue in the enjoyment of his claims and powers as the absolute head of Christendom, and if the misgovernment and corruption for which the Papacy actually stood were to subsist for the benefit of the crowd of ecclesiastical hirelings at Rome and throughout the Church. But to adopt this alternative in the interest of an unreformed Papacy and Church was nothing short of madness. To assume that merely to destroy Luther was to save the Papacy and the Church, and yet refuse or neglect to reform either was to court disaster with open eyes. For Luther's thesis that Rome was the seat of Antichrist was no mere declaration of an apocalyptic visionary. It was only a Biblical phrase for expressing the outraged conscience of at least the serious-minded section of his compatriots and the indignation, on at least material grounds, of a widespread public opinion in Germany. In casting out Luther and insisting on his outlawry Rome, with incredible blindness, overlooked the fact that it left him, too, no other alternative than to appeal to public opinion which, on moral or material grounds, was widely alienated from the Roman régime, and which, as it turned out, was to render the Edict of Worms largely a dead letter. Mere legality was not a very forcible pretext to adduce in these circumstances. The corruption, oppression, hypocrisy, and worldliness which Luther had denounced were far more concrete and convincing arguments in favour of espousing the side of the heretic against the degenerate papal absolutism that reigned at Rome, and nevertheless presumed to dictate in matters of faith and morals. Moreover, Luther's appeal to a General Council as the supreme arbiter of both might well seem, even from the constitutional point of view, of greater weight than the papal appeal to canon law. The old conciliar party still had its adherents in Germany as well as in the Universities of Paris and Louvain, in spite of the fact that the recent Council of the Lateran had condemned and disallowed such an appeal. Even his appeal to the

Scriptures as the only norm of the truth found a ready response in the increasing number of his adherents who were prepared, if need be, to support him against the Pope and even a Council. And though the Pope had acted in accordance with canon law in arraigning, condemning, and excommunicating him, there was no little point in Luther's contention that his case had not been fairly and impartially considered. The Curia had too readily espoused the side of his opponents in the indulgence controversy without subjecting the outcry of his Dominican accusers to anything like judicial criticism. It had joined with them in blinking the fact of the scandal and evil of the system which he had dared to call in question and which it suited its financial interest to maintain. It acted on the principle that his attack on the system was in itself a proof of disloyalty and defiance, and evaded the arguments on moral and religious grounds adduced against it. It held fast to both the theory and the practice and refused to admit Luther's claim to criticise either, and his demand for an adequate discussion of even debatable points. It simply reaffirmed the traditional doctrine and practice and ignored both abuse and difference of opinion. Here again it showed a fateful opaqueness of view. For the time had gone past when either the accusations of the zealots for the old order, who raised the cry of heresy, or even the fiat of the Pope could overawe and silence the voice of criticism. The attempt thus to shirk the issue only in fact led Luther to challenge the dogmatic dicta of his opponents and the fiat of the Pope and rallied public opinion to his side. The responsibility for the development of the conflict, with all its fateful consequences for an unreformed Papacy and Church, is thus traceable to the intransigent and infatuated tactics of his opponents and their patrons in the Curia. It was not without reason that Luther ironically described them as his instructors, his masters in heresy. From the outset, by their intransigent attitude in the matter of reform, they left him no alternative but to challenge, and ultimately to disown and defy, the papal absolutism and materially contributed to justify the widening scope of the attack in the eyes of the people. They made him, in fact, the hero of the nation in his struggle with a corrupt and oppressive alien régime which he at last proclaimed to be the very Antichrist.

Throughout this developing attack Luther nevertheless had no intention of separating from the Church and fomenting schism, though the attack was gradually tending towards this climax. He had an inborn reverence for authority even if there was in him the making of a rebel and even a revolutionist. In the disputation of Leipzig he had emphasised the unity of the Church (*nostra unitas*) as the supreme obligation in reference to the Hussite schism. He was prepared to remain within the Church in spite of the rampant abuses which disfigured and defamed it. Separation, as he said in his Instruction to the people, would not make things better. He persistently distinguished between the Catholic Church and the Papacy and was prepared, even up to the final breach at Worms, to recognise a reformed Papacy within a reformed Church. In spite of the most violent diatribes against Antichrist, the most revolutionary innovations in both doctrine and usages, he was prepared to tolerate and compromise if he were permitted individual freedom to maintain his convictions. His attitude might be illogical and inconsistent and ultimately proved impracticable. But the fact remains that if the Curia had adopted a more considerate and impartial attitude and refrained from slamming the door against even a practical reformation; had it been wise enough to moderate or abandon the old policy of compulsion in matters of faith and conscience, it would have found in his innate reverence for authority, his ingrained conservatism, the elements of a possible *modus vivendi*. At all events Luther later asserted that if the Pope and his advisers had adopted a less tyrannical attitude and shown more skill and insight, they would have obtained a very different response on his part. He was, in truth, a strange blend of the fighter and the pacifist, and in his later years of failing strength doubted whether he would have the courage to play the part he had acted at Worms over again.[4] But, he adds, the Papacy had to fall, if only in virtue of its own corruption, since

[4] "Tischreden," v. 69.

Rome was no longer the fountain of justice, but a house of harlots [5] and the rule of the devil. The Curia had, indeed, appeared at times to recede from the policy of violence and unconditional submission in deference to political expediency, and during one of these intervals of enforced moderation Luther, in the negotiation with Miltitz, had gone the length of agreeing to cease from further controversy. But moderation based on mere political expediency was a poor substitute for the higher statesmanship which such an emergency demanded, and the recourse to such expediency only attests the incapacity of the Curia to cope with the situation. Regarded even from the point of view of its own supposed interest, such political scheming only eased the situation for Luther without securing any real advantage for Rome. Regarded from the higher point of view, it was utterly fatuous to assume that it could avail in dealing with a man of Luther's calibre, who was not only actuated by profound religious conviction, but had behind him the force of an awakening public opinion. The method of manœuvring and finessing on such an urgent question as the reformation of the Church in deference to expediency was out of place in the age of the Renaissance, in which the critical, independent spirit was so powerfully at work in the search for truth and the prestige of the Papacy had been so widely sapped. The age of the Renaissance was indeed also the age of Machiavelli in ecclesiastical as well as secular statecraft. But it was also the age of a Luther to whom conscience and the Gospel were imperative realities, which would neither be manœuvred nor compelled into abeyance to suit the ecclesiastical politicians at Rome.

II. Luther's Development as a Reformer

What strikes one most in surveying those four years of conflict between 1517 and 1521 is the rapid progress of Luther's development as a Reformer. How far has he moved from his earlier standpoint as a zealous monk when

[5] "Tischreden," iii. 212, ed. Förstemann; *cf.* Weimer edition, v. 72-73.

the Papacy was to him the very keystone of true religion and rebellion against it the most nefarious of heresies! He had shared to the full Augustine's view of heretics as breakers of the unity of the Church and the reprobate champions of human opinions against its divine teaching. Again and again in his early writings he had aspersed the heretical sects as the enemies of the truth. Long afterwards on looking back on his early years as a monk and a theological teacher, he declared that he was so fervid a papalist that he would have been the first to lay hands on and burn the heretic. Even after the discovery of his cardinal doctrine of justification by faith and his first tentative efforts as a reformer, he had continued to cherish and maintain the conventional view of heresy. In his attack on the scholastic theology he was convinced that he was vindicating the faith and the true teaching of the Church against its perverters, and in challenging abuses like the indulgence system nothing was farther from his mind than the thought that he was guilty of heresy, as his opponents contended. In the course of the ensuing conflict with the ecclesiastical authorities he rebutted the charge and sought to prove that it applied to his opponents, not to him. Even in the face of the papal Bull he maintained that not Martin Luther but the Pope was the arch-heretic, yea the Antichrist, and his final and fixed conviction was that the mediæval papal Church was, in essential points, a heretical divergence from the early Church, which it was his mission to vindicate in the interest of the true faith. He was the renovator, not the innovator of the faith. He was doubtless sincere in his contention that the mediæval Church had perverted the faith and had departed from that of the Apostles and the Fathers in dogma, constitution, and usage. At the same time, he could only maintain this contention at the expense of admitting that he himself had departed from what he formerly held to be the true faith and had diverged into what he formerly abhorred as heresy. Judged by his own former standard, which was that of the mediæval Church, he had become by 1520 in essential respects what the Bull declared him to be, a renegade from the faith in its mediæval form. All attempts to invalidate this charge could only be of the nature of special pleading. The only valid plea was that he had, on cogent grounds, come to renounce what he had formerly fervently believed, that the grounds he adduced were so compelling that he had no other alternative, and that in adopting this alternative he was restoring, not subverting, the faith of the Apostles and the Fathers. Apart from a tendency in his dialectic encounters with his opponents to blink the fact at times that he was at variance with the received dogmas, this was the plea that he maintained with such resource of argument and such passionate earnestness.

The outstanding feature of this development is the rapidity with which, under the stress of the controversy with his opponents, he worked out the ideas which brought him, one might say almost in spite of himself, into irreconcilable antagonism to the mediæval Church. It says much for the receptivity of his mind that this development was practically completed within the years 1518-20. When in December 1520 he hurled the papal Bull into the fire, the process which had positively begun but three years before was finished, though it might be said that its preconditions came into being with the discovery of the specific meaning of Romans i. 17 nearly seven years earlier. Its root lies in his cardinal doctrine of justification by faith, which had materially changed his spiritual outlook as the result of this discovery in his cell at Wittenberg shortly before the summer of 1513. This doctrine was the offspring of his religious experience during the protracted spiritual conflict in the monastery in the quest for a gracious God, rather than of reflection or theological research. It is an experienced truth, not a mere dogma, though it is expressed in very dogmatic terms. It was burned into his soul in the furnace of the long spiritual trial begotten by the thought of an absolutely righteous God and the obsession of sin that haunted him for years on end. It became to him the lodestar alike of theology and the religious life. In this experienced verity lies the secret of the impassioned intensity, the daring self-assertion, the uncompromising determination, the intolerance, one might say, with which he took up the struggle with the scholastic theologians and the indulgence preachers, which led him gradually to extend the attack to the papal power and the dogmas and institutions of the Church. The genesis of the Lutheran Reformation is undoubtedly to be sought in the sphere of religious experience rather than in that of theological speculation, though the controversy over faith and works, the law and the Gospel, grace and free will, etc., out of which the Reformation eventuated, savours strongly enough of the scholastic theology. Even when the debate enters on the more concrete sphere of the papal power, the canon law, and ecclesiastical usages the decisive factor is, directly or indirectly, the question how these stand in relation to this fundamental doctrine and the implications involved in it. The genius and temperament of the man himself count indeed for much in shaping this development. But it was his specific experience of this central truth that called into activity the powers of the man and produced the Reformation as a religious movement. It was this that made of the theologian the man with a message and a mission for his time. One cannot read the record of the struggle which eventuated in the breach with Rome—as this record is unfolded in his own works—without being impressed again and again by the surpassing intellectual and moral force that was at work in this daring monk in demolishing the dominant system in religion and fashioning the new order in place of the old. And the mainspring of it all is the one overmastering conception of the gospel of faith as he has apprehended and experienced it. It is in very deed an astounding example of the power of an idea, working through the genius of the solitary seeker for truth in the monk's cell, in moulding and making history in the face of the might and the terror of the dominant system.

This development starts from the conviction that the personal faith of the believer is the bedrock of true religion. This conviction had already appeared in his first course on the Psalms (1513-14). It was developed more fully and independently in those on Romans (1515-16), Galatians (1516-17), and Hebrews (1517-18), the last of which shows a distinct advance in the definiteness of his ideas on the subject (particularly in regard to fiducial faith and the assurance of salvation).[6] This personal faith brings the soul into the right and only feasible relation to God from the religious point of view. It presupposes the recognition of God's absolute righteousness and the impossibility of attaining the good, as measured by this high standard, and the assurance of salvation except in unreserved dependence on, personal trust in God's mercy in Christ. It excludes the system of work-righteousness embodied in the Sacrament of Penance, for instance, and based on the principle of meriting salvation by penitential works, instead of accepting it purely as God's gift and eschewing the false confidence in the efficacy, the merit of such works. It involves the personal apprehension of the gospel of God's grace or mercy, as revealed in His Word or promise, on which faith lays hold in humble but unhesitating trust and in which God's saving plan and purpose are made known to the believer. Hence the supreme importance of the Word as the only reliable and decisive witness and arbiter in all things pertaining to the salvation of the soul. Hence, too, the principle that not the Pope or the hierarchy is the channel of the Holy Spirit, the guardian of the true tradition, and the infallible judge of the true tradition, but the believing soul enlightened and guided by the Spirit acting through the Word. Hence, again, the inference that the believer is entitled to exercise his own judgment in matters of faith and may not be compelled by the Pope, or even the corporate authority of a General Council, to accept doctrines or institutions in violation of his own conviction or conscience, as instructed by the Spirit through the Word. Luther might appeal from the Pope to a General Council, but ultimately even the acceptance of the dictum of a General Council is conditioned by the conformity of this dictum to the Word. The appeal to a General Council, as thus ultimately conditioned, would not, therefore, have prevented the breach with Rome, since a Council could hardly have reversed his excommunication by the Pope as a heretic, though it might have gone a considerable length in yielding his demand for a drastic practical reformation, supposing,

[6] See Ficker, "Luther" (1918).

of course, that it acted independently of the corrupt curial influence. In any case, the Word becomes for Luther the only compelling force over the individual reason and conscience. All recourse to external force in religion on the part of either Pope or Council is inadmissible. The right of freedom of thought, inquiry, and discussion in interpreting the Word, in proving all things and holding fast to that which is good, is insistently demanded. The principle is, indeed, of far-reaching bearing, for it is capable of application in the sphere of science and philosophy as well as religion, though for Luther the main concern is the religious one and there is undoubtedly in his impassioned dogmatism a lurking danger for freedom of thought. It is questionable whether he had grasped the full meaning of the emancipation which he championed. His outlook was limited compared to ours. But he must be judged in the light of his own age rather than that of ours. It is rather what he stood for than how he stood for it that is all-important. Freedom of thought and toleration in the sphere of religion is an essential of his conception of the fundamental importance of personal faith in the Word and promise of God. It made Luther the great freethinker of his time in the sphere of religion. It involves, too, a far-reaching emancipation from human ordinance and regulation as applied to the religious life. The Reformation necessarily becomes an emancipation movement. Its watchword is "Liberty." Liberty not only of thought and inquiry, but liberty from the bondage of monastic and penitential works, by which the mediæval Church has trammelled the individual soul and which, in the case of the Sacrament of Penance in particular, tends, on the one hand, to induce a false confidence in such works and, on the other, to torture the conscience with recurring doubt and despair as to their efficacy in meriting salvation. Liberty in this wider sense is thus the keynote of the Reformation. *Liberi enim sumus ab omnibus* [7] might be taken as the motto of the movement, and the echo of this call in behalf of liberty in the "Babylonic Captivity of the Church" resounds

[7] De Captivitate Babylonica Ecclesiæ, "Werke," vi. 537.

through the other Reformation manifestos. Faith is freedom, limited only by a compelling submission to the Word, the Gospel. It is freedom in the sense that Paul proclaimed that Christ has made the believer free from the law, from the bondage of works which can in no sense make him acceptable in the sight of God. It does not mean freedom to sin, but only freedom from sin, and demands the life of service, of self-denial in the conflict with the flesh, the world, and the devil, in accordance with the teaching and example of Christ and in reliance solely on God's grace.

The insistence on personal faith in God's Word and promise as the essential thing in religion results farther in a profound modification of the conception of the Church. Salvation does not necessarily depend on the Church, with its sacramental system and its priestly hierarchy, as the indispensable media of God's grace, but on the acceptance of the Gospel in reliance on the Word and work of God Himself in Christ. The Church does not consist of this priestly order under its absolute papal head, but of all believers, who are equal in God's sight in virtue of a common faith and baptism. There is no essential distinction between clergy and laity, no exclusive monopoly of God's grace in a priestly caste through which this grace operates. For Luther the great reality is God and the soul rather than God and the Church. All believing souls are priests inasmuch as they are by their faith brought into immediate personal relation to God and are thereby entitled to intercede for themselves and others. All are, through the operation of God's Spirit in believing hearts, in direct union and communion with Him. The doctrine of the priesthood of believers nullifies the development of the mediæval priestly caste and the practice of official priestcraft in the Church, and reduces the distinction between priest and layman to one of function, not of order. The historic development of a priestly order is confronted with the primitive institution of the spiritual priesthood of the New Testament which includes all believers. The official priesthood resolves itself into a ministry as commissioned by Christ Himself, the one and eternal High Priest of the Word and the sacraments, which are limited to baptism and the Lord's

Supper, from which the crass notion of transubstantiation is eliminated, though that of the real presence is retained in the form of consubstantiation or impanation. Hence the transformation of the Church into a religious democracy or brotherhood consisting of the whole body of believers governed by the Holy Spirit operating through the Word and involving a far-reaching modification and adaptation of the hierarchy, in accordance with this spiritually democratic conception, though here, too, Luther would not make any radical change in the Church order if his principle were allowed recognition. Even so, the mediæval Papacy as antichristian must be radically transformed. On Scriptural and historic grounds its claim to an absolute rule over the Church is decisively rejected as an usurped tyranny, incompatible with the freedom of the individual believer and the sole headship of Christ. The papal office is, therefore, reduced to that of a general supervision of Christendom, if indeed it is to be retained at all in the national Reformed Church which emerges as a practically autonomous body. The papal claim to secular power and its pretension to supremacy over the State is also decisively rejected, and the State as well as the Church is emancipated from the papal absolutism. With the rejection of the mediæval Papacy goes the whole canon law, for which there is no room in the new spiritual democracy and which Luther consigned to the flames along with the Bull of the mediæval Antichrist.

Such, in brief, is the gist of this astounding development which made the breach of 1521 inevitable. Its revolutionary character is patent, though this climax was not contemplated by Luther from the outset, and his conservative instinct persistently shows itself in the disposition to be content with the enunciation of principles, without insisting on their general application in practice in the form of a radical and imperative revolution of existing institutions. He was, in truth, as he repeatedly confessed, driven onwards by a force which he did not comprehend and could not control, but in which he recognised the compelling influence of a higher power. Faith, on which he laid such stress, is no mere theological conception, but a living force in his daily life of toil and struggle. The thought of God's nearness to him and his need of God is the compass that guides him in the storm-swept sea he is ploughing. At the same time, in reading the record of this stressful conflict with his theological opponents and ultimately with the corporate authority of the Church, as wielded by the Pope and supported by the Emperor, it is the power of his own personality, inspired by impassioned religious conviction, that strikes one as the arresting thing. He stands out as the seeker for truth, resolute to find, by intense meditation, laborious study, what he seeks, driven step by step in the course of this conflict to test doctrines and institutions in the light of Scripture and history, determined with a splendid courage not to swerve from this search even if it seems to be leading him farther than he would naturally care to go, breaking loose from tradition, defying all the power and prestige of constituted authority, and ready to face death rather than yield to fear or prudence. The motive of all this devotion and daring is religious rather than scientific, though he is undoubtedly influenced by the critical, scientific spirit born of the Renaissance. In this pursuit a profoundly religious nature, a powerful intellect, a dominating will, a capacity to look at things in a new light amounting to genius find striking expression. Such a man is perforce a dogmatist and his impassioned dogmatism has its questionable side. He does not always carry us along with him. His interpretation of Scripture, for instance, is not always convincing. His doctrinaire emphasis on the total depravity of human nature is one-sided. Reason and soul are not always well balanced and he allows the tendency to irrationality too much scope. He sometimes shows a lack of ability to see the force of counter-arguments and is liable, with that facile power of language which distinguishes him, to trounce opponents instead of answering them, to substitute vehemence for argument. It is impossible always to agree with his contentions and conclusions. Nevertheless one feels, and is fain to admit, that even this weakness was also a source of strength in one who had to fight every inch of the way to a Reformation in the face of tremendous odds. In seeking to effect what many before him had tried and failed to do, Luther's dogmatic temperament was an asset with which he could hardly afford to dispense. The man of impassioned conviction was an indispensable prerequisite if the Reformation was to have a chance of prevailing in the face of the evils and the influences against which he had to struggle. As we follow the course of this struggle the reflection is borne in upon us that this is the man, and the only man, sufficient for these things. It is this impression that his reforming writings of this period convey to us, as those of his reforming predecessors do not do to anything like the same extent. The personality of Wiclif and Hus is, compared with that of Luther, lacking in the element of the strong man who overmasters his age, though it must not be forgotten that they were far less fortunate in their age than he. Occam and Marsiglio, the conciliar reformers of the early fifteenth century, Savonarola and Erasmus do not touch him in this respect. He is not a replica of any predecessor unless we go as far back as Paul. Nor is he a mere reproduction of these predecessors rolled into one. He does not merely inherit; he creates. He is the unique Reformer in the qualities and powers he brings to bear on his Herculean task—the prophet of a new age in religion, when religion, as represented by a corrupt Curia and a degenerate Church, had declined so far towards the nadir of degeneration, and the revival of which could only come from one who could create as well as destroy.

This is the surpassing climax that is shaping itself in the recess of Luther's genius and personality during these stressful years, and towards which he advances amid a storm of antagonism and menace with a sublime courage and persistence—self-imposed, self-commissioned, single-handed, *contra mundum.* To this creative genius and dynamic personality is due the inception of that movement which not only brought into existence the Reformed Church on the ancient model, but was to contribute, in far-reaching fashion, to shape modern history in the assertion and vindication of principles which had a wider bearing than the purely religious one. Without the creative mind of Luther, the intensity of faith, the daring courage, the unyielding and, at times, the overweening dogmatism of this monk of Wittenberg, the Reformation in this far-reaching sense would have been impossible. There would and must have come sooner or later a reckoning for the Papacy and the Church in virtue of the forces, political, intellectual, and economic, that were undermining the old mediæval order in religion. An unreformed Papacy and Church could not have afforded for long to ignore or brave these forces unscathed and unchanged. But the Reformation would not have been the formative force which his genius and dynamic personality imparted to it. Both its scope and effects would have been more limited. It would have been, for the individual as well as the nation, far more a matter of accommodation with, than an emancipation from, the absolutist papal and ecclesiastical régime that presumed to lord it over reason and conscience, with all that this emancipation implied for the development of modern liberty in those lands in which it was to find its most logical and active vindication.

III. Luther and His Predecessors

Luther's originality in initiating this movement is evident to anyone who reads through the works which the struggle of these fateful years inspired and coloured. In them we witness the birth throes of a new force in religion. The question of his originality is, indeed, occasionally still being debated in Germany not merely by theologians of the Evangelical and Roman Catholic Churches, but by non-confessional historians like Haller and Ritter, for instance. Haller, in a memorial discourse on "The Causes of the Reformation," [8] maintains that "the greater part, yea all, of what Luther uttered and demanded had already been uttered and demanded before him." This is certainly too sweeping, and in his reply to Ritter's criticism [9] he denies that he had intended to rob Luther of a certain originality.[10]

[8] "Die Ursachen der Reformation" (1917).

[9] In a note to his article, "Die Geschichtliche Bedeutung des deutschen Humanismus," "Hist. Zeitschrift," cxxvii. 433 (1923).

[10] "Z.K.G.," xlii. 328 f. (1923).

There is, nevertheless, force in his critic's contention that such sweeping generalisations leave little enough room for originality.[11] Ritter himself, however, seeks to minimise his originality in the sphere where it appears most distinctively—his doctrine of justification by faith—and would seek it rather in the racial sphere. For him the Reformation is distinctively the result of the operation of "certain mysterious forces of our national being." This in turn is one of those generalisations which, while portentous, do not in reality make us much wiser. To seek to explain a movement like the Reformation on merely national or racial grounds is at most to try to explain the whole by a part. It is an altogether inadequate substitute for the religious experience and intuition which are not distinctively racial, but human. It is a case in which the man and the movement must, in the first place, be viewed *sub specie æternitatis*, and if this point of view is placed in the background the explanation will perforce be partial and inadequate. Luther stands on common ground with Paul and Augustine. Racial psychology counts for little in relation to such spiritual phenomena which transcend the limits of race and time and must be envisaged from the religious and the human angle. The Reformation is not merely a reflection of the German soul, but of the revival of the Pauline type of religious thought and experience operating through the genius and the personality of his great modern disciple.

On the other hand, while the Reformation as a religious movement is essentially the work of Luther, his work is not wholly new. It had its antecedents in the aspirations of preceding reformers, in ideas bequeathed by them, and in forces which were working towards this end. A. Ritschl and his school deny to the Reform Movement of the fourteenth and fifteenth centuries the title of a Reformation in the later sense and practically contend that Luther had no predecessor in the ranks of the earlier reformers.[12] As a historian of dogma Ritschl views the position too exclusively

[11] "Z.K.G.," xliii. 169 f. (1924).

[12] Ritschl, "Die Christliche Lehre von der Rechtfertigung," i. 105 f.; 2te Auflage (1882).

from the dogmatic standpoint. The kernel of the Reformation is, indeed, the doctrine of justification as Luther rediscovered and developed it. There is, however, a danger of overestimating and exaggerating his originality by unduly restricting the view of the movement to the dogmatic standpoint and concentrating exclusively on the doctrine of justification to the neglect of other features of it. His doctrine of justification was undoubtedly the fruit of his own religious experience and intuition. It is certain, too, that as a Reformer he was no mere reproduction of any of his reforming predecessors. But it is also true that he was to a certain extent anticipated and even influenced by those whom Ullmann described as " Reformers Before the Reformation " (the title of his well-known book), but who, to Ritschl, are only " so-called reformers." These so-called reformers represent a reform of varying kind and degree. They include exclusively practical reformers who limited their demands to the abolition of the more glaring abuses ; constitutional reformers like Marsiglio and Occam in the fourteenth century ; D'Ailly, Gerson, and other leaders of the later conciliar party in the early fifteenth ; spiritual reformers like Tauler and the mystics ; doctrinal reformers like Wiclif, Hus, Wessel Gansfort. It is the case that this varied reform movement of the previous two centuries failed to eventuate on such a far-reaching Reformation as that which Luther brought to fruition, and that it was more or less dominated by the mediæval outlook on the doctrine and institutions of the Church. In none of these older reformers do we observe the genius, the creative force that made him the epoch maker in modern religion. At the same time, each class of reformer had some affinity with him and in its own sphere anticipated some phase of his reforming activity. To a certain extent this activity was the culmination of theirs, the result of forces already operating in them. The practical reformers, if they kept strictly within the traditional and orthodox limit in regard to doctrine and institutions, anticipated him in their outspoken antagonism to current abuses. It is narrow and one-sided to contend that mere antagonism to abuse is no reformation at all. As his Lectures on Romans show,

Luther, too, began as a reformer of abuses, the removal of which would have gone far to keep him, with his conservative tendency to find a *modus vivendi*, within the Church. The constitutional reformers, if they refrained from attacking doctrine, went a long way towards his position in their attempt to limit the papal absolutism by contending for the superiority of a General Council as the supreme legislative authority in the Church. Their master, William of Occam, was, in truth, in the domain of ecclesiastical polity as daringly original as Luther, and from the conciliar party, if not from Occam [13] himself, he undoubtedly derived inspiration in developing his attack on the Papacy. With the teaching of the spiritual reformers, of Tauler and the mystics, he was familiar before he began his attack on indulgences. If he outgrew the mystic standpoint, he was strongly influenced by the mystic stress on the inwardness of religion, the union of the individual soul with God, and the striving to spiritualise and vitalise the conventional religion. To doctrinal reformers like Wiclif, Hus, and Wessel Gansfort he owed nothing directly in his formative period as a reformer. With Wiclif's works he does not seem to have been acquainted at all, and those of Hus and Wessel only came into his hands after he had already outdistanced both in his reforming ideas. He ascribed without sufficient discrimination an identity of ideas which did not really exist, though both of them had within limits anticipated some of his contentions. This anticipation is still more apparent in the case of Wiclif, of whom Hus was the disciple. For if even Wiclif had not grasped the Pauline doctrine of justification, he had emphatically asserted the supreme authority of Scripture and denied the doctrine of transubstantiation in favour of that of consubstantiation as well as renounced in principle the secularised mediæval Papacy as antichristian.

Moreover, while creating a distinctive reform movement out of his own religious thought and experience, he owed

[13] He does not seem to have studied Occam's writings on the Church and the papal power as von Below assumes ("Die Ursachen der Reformation," 80), and only in as far as the conciliar party reflected Occam's teaching on this subject did the Occamist influence operate.

something to the forces and the spirit of the age which were already making for a new order of things in both Church and State, preparing the way for his message and his mission. He was, in truth, the fortunate heir of a great inheritance. Humanism was working for his advent in its application of the critical spirit in the sphere of religion as well as science, philosophy, and education. Erasmus, in particular, was his predecessor in this respect, and Erasmus went a considerable way in supporting him in the critical years that culminated in the breach with Rome. Lang, Link, Spalatin, Scheurl, Melanchthon, Jonas, Capito, Bucer, Oecolampadius, Hutten, Crotus, and others were, so far, fellow-workers whose support was an inspiration and an encouragement to the daring rebel of Wittenberg in his unequal struggle with his Dominican opponents and persecutors. The people, with social grievances to redress, were ready to welcome a gospel which proclaimed the spiritual brotherhood of believers and vindicated, in things religious at least, the rights of the individual against a corrupt hierarchy, which was identified with feudal privilege and oppression and was growingly obnoxious to the masses on this account. On national grounds he could count on the support of the higher classes, as well as the people, in his attack on a corrupt alien ecclesiastical régime which exploited the empire for the material benefit of Rome. It is, indeed, significant that the Diet, which was supposed to have joined in his condemnation, presented a detailed statement of grievances against this régime.[14]

IV. Luther and the Elector Frederick

And in the Elector of Saxony, whose subject he was, he had the good fortune to find a protector resourceful enough to foil the attempts of his enemies to crush him, and staunch in his resolution to see fair play done even to the heretic. The part played indirectly by the Elector in bringing to fruition the Reformation was second only to that

[14] "Reichstagsakten," ii. 661 f.

of the Reformer himself. His activity on his behalf has recently been the subject of controversy, which is hardly surprising in view of his enigmatic personality and his predilection for indirect action and diplomatic manœuvre. He seems to have shown a strange lack of interest in Luther personally, in as far as he did not enter into direct intercourse with him, but employed the sympathetic and helpful Spalatin as go-between. This may have been due in part to an ingrained habit of reserve and an exaggerated sense of his princely dignity in accordance with the overweening meticulous formality of the time. Probably the more potent reason was the necessity of avoiding, in his capacity as ruler, anything in his relations with the daring rebel of Wittenberg that would tend to compromise him with the Pope and the Curia. A cautious attitude was imposed on him in the circumstances, alike by etiquette and diplomatic necessity, and it must not be forgotten that an open and declared avowal of Luther's cause would have exposed him and his subjects to excommunication and interdict. This was a contingency not to be lightly risked, and the undoubted difficulty and danger of the situation go far to explain the aloofness and extreme wariness of his attitude. Behind it was, evidently from the outset, the determination to shield Luther from his enemies and secure him a fair hearing. This determination he persistently maintained in his relations with the Curia and its representatives, though at the expense of a good deal of diplomatic fencing and finesse.

The driving force of the movement was, of course, Luther himself, and the Elector's part was that of acting as a buffer against his enemies. But this part was essential for the development of the movement, and in this sense his protection was an indispensable adjunct of Luther's genius. "Without Frederick the Wise," judges Troeltsch, "Luther's activity would not have been possible."[15] Luther, indeed, ultimately gained the support of a section of the nobility. But this support could not have been an effective substitute for that of the Elector, whose influence, as the most powerful magnate of the empire, was a factor to be reckoned with by

[15] "Historische Zeitschrift," cxxiv. 112.

both the Pope and the Emperor in their efforts to crush the Reformer. The service thus rendered by him to the incipient Reformation is indisputable. The only question is as to its extent and its motive, and on this question opinion is divided. Max Lehmann and his pupil, Elizabeth Wagner, contend that the Elector was mainly actuated by political expediency and little, if at all, by religious conviction, and are disposed to minimise his influence on the march of events and magnify the initiative and independent action of Luther himself.[16] Miss Wagner, in fact, traverses the evidence, adduced by Kalkoff, of deep religious conviction and far-seeing statesmanship and finds in his attitude "lack of energetic initiative," "hesitating prudence," "apathy," and "timidity." Hausrath[17] and, more in detail, Kalkoff, on the other hand, maintain that the Elector was actuated not by mere political expediency, but by a keen and growing interest in Luther's teaching and that the persistent skill and resource with which he championed his cause were mainly due to religious conviction.[18] According to Kalkoff, he had from 1518 adopted Luther's teaching on justification, the sole authority of Scripture, and the antichristian character of the Papacy. His profession of neutrality in demanding an impartial hearing was merely diplomatic tactics, which his papal and imperial opponents did not take seriously. Aleander certainly regards him as a confirmed Lutheran and antagonist of the Papacy,[19] and Miss Wagner does not succeed in invalidating his testimony. If he showed at times hesitation and apprehension over the growing boldness of Luther's attacks on doctrines and institutions and rebuked his rashness, it was not because he actively disapproved of his views, but in order to make his diplomacy more effective in outmanœuv-

[16] Lehmann, "Historische Aufsätze und Reden," 35, 175 (1911); Eliz. Wagner, "Luther und Friedrick der Weise," "Z.K.G.," xlii. 331 f. (1923).

[17] "Aleander und Luther," 31; "Luther's Leben," i. 425, 427.

[18] "Wormser Reichstag," 411 f.; "Z.K.G.," xliii. 199 f. (1924), in reply to Miss Wagner.

[19] "Depeschen," 211. Miss Wagner seeks to invalidate this explicit testimony by minimising the value of Aleander's dispatches as an index of the Elector's position. She is, I think, unduly sceptical.

ring the designs of the Curia. He took ample advantage of the political necessity of the Pope not merely for his own ends, but to vindicate freedom of thought and conscience against the obscurantists who, in destroying Luther, would have blighted the growth of the good seed which Luther and his colleagues were sowing in his University of Wittenberg. He chose and made use of advisers, like the Chancellor Brück, von Feilitzsch, and von Thun, favourable to the new theology. He took the risk not only of resisting the Pope and the Curia, but of incurring the enmity of the Emperor. He compelled him to abandon the attempt summarily to execute the papal Bull in Germany, and to summon Luther to Worms and thus afford him an opportunity to vindicate his teaching at the bar of the Estates of the empire. He not only ensured his safety behind the walls of the Wartburg, but refused to countenance or execute the imperial ban. The evidence thus adduced by Kalkoff against the contention of his critics tends in the main to substantiate his thesis, if he at times seems to press his inferences too far.[20] Even if throughout it all the diplomatist is, outwardly at least, more in evidence than the man of religious conviction, it betokens no small courage persistently to pursue this policy of befriending the daring rebel of Wittenberg in the face of the menace of papal excommunication and the imperial enmity. Mere political expediency, apart from strong conviction, can hardly account for such persistence. Luther at all events, not without substantial reason, regarded him as a patron of the Gospel as well as his active protector,[21] and long afterwards, in the preface to the 1545 edition of his Latin

[20] Kalkoff's position is strongly supported by Anni Koch, "Die Kontroverse über die Stellung Friedrichs des Weisen zur Reformation," Archiv. für Ref. Geschichte (1926), 213 f. Kirn, on the other hand, is of opinion that Kalkoff has rather overdone his thesis and takes a too sanguine view at times, "Friedrich der Weise und die Kirche" (1926). See also the review of these works by O. Clemen in "Z.K.G.," xlv. 615-617 (1927). It seems to me that Frederick's subsequent attitude towards the evangelical movement in the early part of 1522 is hardly that of an active protagonist of the Gospel, apart altogether from political and personal considerations.

[21] See "Werke," vi. 105.

works, gratefully remembered how much it owed in these critical years to his personal interest.[22]

Moreover, it is not the least of his merits that, in founding and fostering the University of Wittenberg, he provided Luther with the sphere in which he could develop and promote " the new theology," which was rising like another star in the east on the horizon of the academic youth. He had a keen interest and a justifiable pride in the institution which was reflecting such renown on his principality, and to which an increasing number of students[23] was being attracted by Luther's rising fame and that of his colleagues, Carlstadt, Amsdorf, and Melanchthon. Wittenberg became the focus of the new movement in theology and the higher education. Its reputation was already dwarfing that of the other German schools of learning, and by multiplying Luther's disciples materially contributed to diffuse his teaching and his reforming influence.

[22] Et procedebat feliciter evangelium sub umbra istius Principis et late propagabatur.

[23] Enders, i. 227; ii. 57, and other passages of the letters.

INDEX

A

B

F

G

H

M